JANUA LINGUARUM

STUDIA MEMORIAE
NICOLAI VAN WIJK DEDICATA

edenda curat
C. H. VAN SCHOONEVELD
Indiana University

Series Maior, 63

SOME ASPECTS
OF TEXT GRAMMARS

A Study in Theoretical Linguistics and Poetics

by

TEUN A. VAN DIJK

1972

MOUTON

THE HAGUE · PARIS

Printed in The Netherlands by Zuid-Nederlandsche Drukkerij N.V., Printers, 's-Hertogenbosch

PREFACE

*The progress of a science does not depend merely upon the amassing of
individual insights, but above all upon the formulation of new relationships
and the posing of new questions.*

Manfred Bierwisch, "Linguistics and Poetics"

The aim of this book is to present a provisional framework for the theoretical description of discourse. The formal device needed for such a description will be called
a 'Text Grammar', as distinguished from the current type of generative-transformational 'Sentence Grammars'. It is argued that the only valid 'natural domain' of a
theory of language is an 'infinite set of discourses'. Text grammars must enumerate
formally the abstract objects, called 'texts', underlying these discourses, and assign
structural descriptions to the texts they generate. Moreover, it will be shown that
text grammar is the only adequate framework for the description of sentence structure.
It does not constitute, therefore, a simple extension of current grammar. Many
phenomena which remain problematic in present-day linguistics can in principle be
solved or better formulated if described in terms of intersentential relations in a
coherent text: (in)definite articles, pronouns, relative clauses, tense, sentential adverbs,
conjunctions, topic and comment, presupposition and entailment, etc. Besides these
phenomena characteristic of sequences of sentences, a text grammar is required to
describe the global, over-all structure of a text, which will be called its 'macro-
structure'. Without such a hypothetical construct it is not possible to account for
numerous properties of language and language use in a sufficiently consistent and
simple way.

The development of formal text grammars may contribute to the establishment of
a more relevant basis for interdisciplinary research, e.g. in psycholinguistics and
sociolinguistics. Especially the role of linguistics in literary scholarship (poetics) is
crucially linked with an explicit insight into the structure of texts. Our second aim,
then, is to sketch the foundations of theoretical poetics, to clarify the methodological
relations between linguistics and poetics and to develop a tentative grammar for
literary texts.

In order to provide a sound theoretical basis for the empirical claims of a generative text grammar, it was necessary – as a third main task of this book – to develop briefly some notions of pragmatics. It is argued that a pragmatic theory must be related to, or even included in, the grammar in order to be able to account formally for the ability of native speakers to 'use' their discourses appropriately in given ideal situations. The relevance of (text) grammar for sociolinguistics, sociology, anthropology and content analysis depends on an explicit pragmatic theory. Moreover, pragmatics must specify the constraints upon the so-called 'performative' elements at the syntactic and semantic levels of description.

The interest for the structure of discourse has been rapidly growing in the last few years, especially in European (and above all German) linguistics. We will touch only briefly upon the 'historical' development of such a textual linguistics, with which are associated the names of Harris, Pike, Hartmann, Harweg, Schmidt, Isenberg, Dressler, Bellert and several others. It was not possible to integrate in this book the full implications of recent work done in generative text grammar, e.g. by Ihwe, Rieser, Petöfi, Kummer, and some others. Although we discuss in some detail the textual aspects of pronouns and reference, it was not possible to take fully into account here the recent work of such linguists as Lakoff, Postal, Karttunen, Palek and others about the same subject.

We have based ourselves in general upon the form of generative-transformational grammar known as 'generative semantics', developed e.g. by McCawley and Lakoff, but for the description of semantic structures we borrowed some elements from case grammars, as have been proposed by Fillmore, Chafe and others.

Finally, it has become obvious that a formal characterization of intersentential relations in texts will need models from modern logic, e.g. a predicate calculus for the representation of semantic structures and relations between sentences (presupposition, entailment) as presented for example by Keenan. Different systems of modal logic will be necessary to give a more satisfactory description of these semantic structures of natural language and to represent the relations between textual structures and their interpretations (worlds, models) (cf. e.g. the work of Geach, Scott, Hintikka, van Fraassen, Lewis and many others).

In this framework a tense logic is indispensable for the explication of time consecution in coherent texts, an aspect which we will touch upon only briefly in this book (cf. especially the work of Prior, Rescher, Kamp and Wunderlich). Finally, different types of logical (Montague) and philosophical (Searle) pragmatics will be needed to relate textual structures with structures of communication, of action and event (von Wright, Harrah, Kummer), models which may also be used to represent the semantic coherence of the text. All these models and descriptive devices are only mentioned in this book and will be integrated in later research in text grammar; we have focussed our attention upon the properly linguistic description of textual structures. The same is true for the use of mathematical models for the description of linear coherence in texts, as may be used (cf. the book by Palek) to formalize anaphorical relations. It is clear, however, that such formal models will have their full relevance only when the linguistic categories and relations of sentential and textual structures have been adequately identified.

The present version of this book was submitted as a Ph.D. thesis to the Faculty of Letters of the University of Amsterdam. It originated, as is still obvious in Part II, from an unpublished M.A. thesis in theoretical poetics about linguistic structures in modern (French) poetry. Only in a later stage was it understood that a sound literary theory requires a formal insight into the general structures of texts. Since, three years ago, only very little explicit work had been done in this field, we felt obliged to sketch first a linguistic text grammar, which, actually, turned out to be an autonomous task within theoretical linguistics itself. Hence the somewhat dualistic character of this book: it is intended as contribution both to linguistics and to poetics. Nevertheless, we hope that, thus, on the one hand the literary theorist will become convinced of the relevance of (textual) linguistics and its problems, and that on the other hand the linguist may grow interested in some of the issues raised in the description of literature.

Both within the linguistic and the literary perspective our investigation has been closely paralleled and prefigured by the recent dissertation by Jens Ihwe, who was among the first – together with Hartmann, Schmidt and Petöfi – who recognized the relevance of text grammar for a theory of literature. His extensive historical account permitted us to omit a survey of the development both of modern poetics and of textual linguistics, and allowed us to concentrate upon their systematic construction.

Finally, I would like to thank those with whom I discussed my earlier work on problems touched upon in this book and those who read and commented on its earlier versions and this final version: Harry Brinkman, A. J. Greimas, Peter Hartmann, Jens Ihwe, Willem de Jong, Jan G. Kooij, Werner Kummer, Jan Kamerbeek, Jr., Solomon Marcus, János S. Petöfi, Cees J. van Rees, Hannes Rieser, Siegfried J. Schmidt, Frans de Valk and Paul Zumthor. I further would like to thank Marjolein Olnon for typing the manuscript and Diane Williams for carefully correcting my English. I am particularly indebted to Simon C. Dik who, together with Jens Ihwe, accepted the direction of this thesis and who carefully corrected its worst errors. Clearly, those remaining are mine and can only partially be excused as the results of the inevitable risks which a theorist of literature must run when thus engaging in the construction of a grammar and the establishment of the linguistic foundations of interdisciplinary studies.

Amsterdam, December 1971   T.A. v. D.

CONTENTS

PART II: ASPECTS OF LITERARY TEXT GRAMMARS

PART I

GENERAL PROPERTIES OF TEXT GRAMMARS

TOWARDS A THEORY OF TEXT GRAMMARS

1. SOME ARGUMENTS FOR TEXT GRAMMARS

1.1. *Introduction*

1.1.1. Throughout this book it will be argued that many relevant and systematic phenomena of natural language are properties of 'discourse', and that these properties cannot be adequately described in the existing types of grammar. It is our aim to present decisive formal and empirical arguments in favour of such a view and to elaborate a global framework for a more adequate theory of language. That is, we will have to make explicit within a grammar the abstract notion of TEXT, underlying what is intuitively known as 'connected discourse'.

1.1.2. Such a grammar, accounting for the formal structure of texts, will be called TEXT GRAMMAR, abbreviated as T-grammar. The existing types of structural and generative-transformational grammars are, at least in practice, limited to the formal enumeration and structural description of the sentences of a language and therefore will be called SENTENCE GRAMMARS or S-grammars.

Text grammars are expected to provide a more adequate framework for the description of many problematic phenomena dealt with in modern linguistics. Moreover, they have to provide an explicit basis for the study of all types of texts as they manifest themselves in processes of verbal communication. The second part of this book, for example, will pay detailed attention to a particular type of text: literature. Our claim, then, will be that an adequate study of literature is inconceivable without an explicit insight into the general properties of text structure as it is provided by T-grammars.

1.1.3. T-grammars, however, do not yet exist, and only recently have some attempts been made to gain explicit insight into structures 'beyond the sentence' (Hendricks [1967]). The first part of this book will discuss the general linguistic properties of textual structures. Some important problems of current generative grammar will be reformulated in terms of T-grammar and it will be shown that only in such a frame-work can these problems be expected to get satisfactory, i.e. sufficiently general and consistent, solutions. Moreover, T-grammar enables us to treat very important aspects of systems of natural language which have hitherto been considered to lie outside the scope of grammar.

Before we are able to give an outline of the different aspects of T-grammars, we must first, in this chapter, consider their general properties, tasks, and aims. Clearly, in this stage of research such a theory of T-grammars is still formulated in very informal terms.

1.2. *Empirical arguments*

1.2.1. A first set of arguments in favour of text grammar has an empirical character. That is, T-grammar gives a more adequate account of the systematic phenomena of natural language by describing and explaining 'more facts' and providing more relevant generalizations than existing S-grammars. By 'systematic phenomena of natural language' we refer both to properties of linguistic objects, i.e. structures underlying utterances, and to aspects of linguistic communication, e.g. psychological and psycho-social settings of systems and manifestations of natural language.

1.2.2. Thus, to begin with, one of the basic claims of the theory of transformational generative grammar is that such a grammar is a formal model for the idealized linguistic knowledge of native speakers, the so-called 'competence'. Parallel to the langue-parole or system-use distinctions, competence is conceived as an abstraction and distinguished from concrete verbal behaviour of individuals in processes of communication, so-called 'performance'.[1] This internal, implicit knowledge enables the speaker of a language to produce and interpret all the grammatical sentences of his language, to assign interpretations to semi-grammatical sentences, distinguish grammatical sentences from less or non-grammatical ones, detect deep-structure relations between superficially different sentences, and conversely to distinguish be-tween superficially similar sentences, to provide paraphrases for given sentences, and so on.

---

[1] For discussion of the competence-performance distinction cf. Chomsky (1965) chap. 1, §1, §2 (1968 4, 23, 62, Miller and Chomsky (1963) 419 ff.), Seuren (1969) 5f and Botha (1968) 22, 69 ff. The distinction, however, is not without problems as recent work in psycholinguistics suggests; cf. e.g. Fodor and Garrett (1966) and Campbell and Wales (1970). Especially questioned is the precise psychological status of competence as to its relations with an abstract system of a language. Further-more it will be necessary to determine the role of rules that enable the speaker to use his utterances adequately in appropriate situations, the so-called 'communicative competence' (see below and especially chapter 9 for further discussion and relevant references). We will assume here that a (theory of) grammar has two separate tasks which, however, must be related in order to arrive at empirically interesting explanations of verbal behaviour: the specification of an abstract language SYSTEM on the one hand (cf. Lieb [1970]) and the elaboration of formal MODELS of idealized psycho-logical abilities and of idealized psycho-social conventions.

Notice however that SENTENCES, strictly speaking, are formal constructs of a grammar and not empirical entities (cf. Lyons [1968] 170 ff. and especially Bar-Hillel [1969]). In performance speakers are dealing with UTTERANCES. However, there are no a priori or empirical reasons for maintaining that the formal linguistic unit underlying such utterances should necessarily be the sentence, as has been a hitherto rarely-questioned assumption of most linguistic theories.[2] As a matter of fact we know that most utterances 'consist of' more than one uttered sentence, viz. a sequence of sentences. Such sequences are often referred to as 'discourse' or 'pieces of discourse'. The problem at issue, then, is the following: is it observationally and descriptively adequate to consider utterances/discourse, being the empirical 'units' of verbal behaviour, merely in terms of underlying sentences? Can we describe sequences of sentences simply as concatenations of sentences, and if such is the case, does an S-grammar formulate the necessary and sufficient conditions for grammatical concatenations?

In our opinion, such sentence-based descriptions of the structures underlying utterances are inadequate. Sentences, just as clauses or syntagms, have less significant empirical, e.g. psychological, reality than texts. Only in some cases a sentence may correspond to the empirical unit of the utterance. We therefore introduce the concept of TEXT as the basic linguistic unit manifesting itself, as DISCOURSE, in verbal utterances. Such a text may, of course, consist of n sentences (where $n \geqslant 1$), but will not be described in terms of independent sentence-structures alone. The formal concept of text, then, must account for the important empirical notion of COHERENCE: a native speaker is able to produce and interpret an utterance 'as a whole', that is as 'a piece of CONNECTED discourse', and not merely as a linearly ordered set of discrete grammatical sentences (cf. e.g. Bellert [1970]).

If native speakers, indeed, have the ability to distinguish between (linguistically) coherent and less coherent discourses, their competence should contain a device for distinguishing between grammatical and less grammatical texts. In that case, a grammar will have to formulate ıules for the derivational description of textual structures. Only then may it serve as an adequate formal model for a postulated, idealized psychical system of linguistic knowledge like competence. Our competence, then, is not sentential, but textual. We will see in chapter 9 that there are even decisive arguments in favour of yet a further extension of grammar and competence, viz. with a 'communicative' or 'pragmatic' component. Although theories, and especially grammars, do not 'directly' describe empirical phenomena, but only formally re-

---

[2] Some linguists, however, have advocated that the basic theoretical (or at least empirical) unit of linguistic description should be the 'text' or the 'discourse'. Some of them will be mentioned at the end of this chapter, e.g. Hjelmslev, Harris, Pike, Hartmann. Others recognize explicitly that text or discourse is a legitimate object of a grammar, without, however, providing the relevant descriptional framework, e.g. Dik (1968a), Lieb (1970), Bierwisch (1966). For surveys of earlier attempts towards textually based grammars, cf. Hendricks (1967), Dressler (1970a), Ihwe (1972a), Brinker (1971) and Gülich and Raible (1972). For critical remarks about 'formal' (i.e. morpho-syntactic) discourse analysis as practised by Harris and others, cf. Pak (1971).

construct the entities, relations and systems 'underlying' these phenomena, it is necessary to postulate entities or regularities which are as close as possible to these phenomena, without losing their general character. With respect to the empirical concept of utterance, consisting of discourse, the postulated concept 'text' serves as such an entity providing a more direct link with phenomena of performance. It has to account for the fact that speakers of a language can produce and interpret a virtually infinite set of discourses (utterances, tokens of texts). Similarly, as we said earlier, we must explain how they are able to distinguish between grammatical and ungrammatical texts, to recognize similarities between superficially very different texts (and conversely), to paraphrase texts with the aid of other texts, and so on (Isenberg, [1970]). Actually, all these abilities are applied in any process of verbal communication. This, certainly, is trivial, but as recent psychological research has demonstrated, such abilities cannot be explained in a satisfactory manner by postulating a sentential competence (cf. Johnson-Laird [1970] and chapter 9).

Moreover, if the grammar should also include a pragmatic component, this integration can be operated more easily in the case of a text grammar: among the formal units of the structures underlying verbal communication processes we are dealing with tokens of texts, i.e. discourses, rather than with tokens of sentences (cf. chapter 9 and Schmidt [1971e]).

1.2.3. Another aspect of textual behaviour is the ability of native speakers to disambiguate AMBIGUOUS SENTENCES. Formally speaking, many sentences used in discourse are semantically ambiguous. The process of disambiguation, in current grammatical theory, is simply localized in performance, as a factor determined by 'verbal context' or 'situation'.[3] It is obvious, however, that, within a discourse, the majority of ambiguous sentences are automatically disambiguated by the semantic representation of preceding and/or following sentences. That is, the semantic description of a sentence S_i has to be coherent with that of the sequences $\langle S_1, S_2, ..., S_{i-1} \rangle$ and $\langle S_{i+1}, S_{i+2}, ..., S_n \rangle$. Notice that, again, one linguistic aspect which is traditionally rejected as a property of unsystematic or unknown performance is now in principle modeled within the grammar itself.

To be sure, when textual structure does not disambiguate a sentence, we still have to leave some aspects of the decision procedure to the different components of the communication process ('situation', 'deictic relations', 'reference', etc.), although a pragmatic component might also systematize part of these parameters. The same is true for the ambiguity of a whole discourse, although, again, further study may show that a set of discourses may disambiguate individual discourses of the set.

---

[3] This is essentially the position of traditional but also of modern semantics, e.g. of Katz and Fodor (1963) excluding verbal 'setting' from their theory with the argument that an S-grammar has to provide all the possible meanings of a sentence from which a 'selection' is made in actual discourse. Kooij (1971) rejects this view, but does not himself provide the (con-)textual rules or conditions for disambiguating sentences.

1.2.4. A related and equally important aspect of textual competence of native speakers is their ability to assign well-formed semantic representations (i.e. grammatical interpretations) to semi-grammatical sentences in a discourse. It is well-known that, in oral communication especially, a great part of the uttered sentences are formally semi-grammatical. First of all, this semi-grammaticalness of sentences may be perfectly regular in a text/discourse. The deletion of noun phrases and verb phrases in a given sentence may be a grammatical, rule-governed operation. Secondly, if this is not the case, the semantic representation – and its morphophonological and syntactic manifestation – of preceding and following sentences will often provide the elements necessary for a possible interpretation of otherwise uninterpretable or semi-interpretable sentences. A text grammar must provide the rules determining such an ability, e.g. by establishing formal criteria for degrees of interpretability of sentences-in-text. The empirical relevance of such rules is obvious: as with the other aspects of textual competence mentioned in this section, such rules bring us closer to a study of the (degrees of) ACCEPTABILITY of utterances. By extending our grammar in the proposed way, we have more (formal) criteria for the linguistic foundation of an explanation of this important notion of performance.

It should be stressed again that, even then, the process of interpretation is of course further determined by the systematic (pragmatic, referential) and unsystematic *(ad hoc)* or extralinguistic (psychological, social, historical) factors of the communication process.

1.2.5. The rather general empirical argument outlined in the previous paragraph has some important corollaries. Besides the ability of native speakers to process the great number of formal aspects characterizing coherent discourse (pronouns, conjunctions, etc., see section 1.3. below), a T-grammar models the ability of assigning properties to discourse as a whole, independently of its individual sentences. For instance, we would like to explain how speakers are able to produce/interpret different TYPES of discourses: e.g. daily conversation, literary texts, advertisements, public addresses, propaganda, commands, questions (questionnaires), etc. The ability to differentiate between such different types or subtypes is crucial in the psycho-social systems of interaction in which natural language is used. A text grammar must explain such a differentiation by specifying the formal properties determining a TYPOLOGY OF TEXTS. Since these properties are not merely characteristic of the structure of individual sentences, a sentence grammar cannot provide such a typology, the linguistic relevance of which can certainly not be denied (van Dijk [1971d]).

1.2.6. We assumed above that the recognition of different types of discourse is based on the ability to process texts as 'wholes'. We undoubtedly touch here upon a crucial aspect of communication by means of discourses. One of the main specific tasks of a T-grammar consists in accounting explicitly for such a vague holistic concept as 'text as a whole'. That is, we intuitively know that we do not produce, perceive and interpret texts as an unstructured heap of sentences, nor even merely as a linearly ordered sequence of sentences, but as one global, coherent structure. Such a global textual structure will be called a MACRO-STRUCTURE,[4] as distinguished from the more 'local', sentential structures, which form what may be called the MICRO-STRUCTURE of a text. We shall see in the next section what might be the grammatical status of these structures, e.g. conceived of as the 'deep structure' and 'surface structure' of the text respectively.

A textual competence, then, enables a speaker not only to concatenate sentences into grammatical pairs, triples, …, n-tuples, this ability is further conditioned by the rules underlying macro-structures in texts. It has been demonstrated (Johnson-Laird [1970]) that in the production/perception process of discourse, not only the surface structures but also the underlying semantic structures of previous sentences cannot be (exactly) memorized. Although these individual semantic representations of sentences cannot be stored in our memory, we are able to interpret the whole text as grammatically (in)coherent. Obviously, in this process there must be rules forming more abstract, more global structures underlying the sequence of sentences. It is with respect to such memorizable macro-structures we can 'measure' the coherence of the individual sentences. We will treat such structures in more detail in chapter 3, where it will be shown that linguistic macro-structures have a psychological reality in the form of PLANS.[5] Without such plans, it is impossible for humans to produce and interpret longer discourses. The 'execution' or the (re-)production of individual sentences is 'guided' by such a plan. This very interesting psychological hypothesis, which has its correlates in other cognitive domains, can be explained only in a grammar specifying macro-structures. Text grammar will have as one of its main tasks that of formulating the rules for such macro-structures, and the rules relating them to the structures of the individual sentences.

It is also within such a framework that we may formally explain the ability to give a SUMMARY of a text, i.e. to make an ABSTRACT which is somehow equivalent to the semantic macro-structure, or 'global content' of a text. Together with the operations of PARAPHRASING, TRANSLATING (Dressler [1972]) etc. this operation of abstracting is one of the major 'meta-linguistic' activities in human communication, for which a notion such as macro-structure is indispensable. We will show in the next chapters which properties of texts should be defined in terms of such macro-structures (cf. Hendricks [1969b]).

---

[4] The notion of 'macro-structure' is practically unknown in linguistic theory, but has been used, in different terms, in poetics and other social sciences. Bierwisch (1965) used the term in order to describe some aspects, e.g. narrative structure, of literary texts. Harris ([1968]; see below) also used such terms as 'global' or 'overall' structures. For further reference, cf. chapter 3. Kummer (1972b) adopts the distinction in his description of processes of argumentation.

[5] The concept of 'plan' first received explicit treatment in Miller, Galanter and Pribram (1960) and has received theoretical elaboration in Miller & Chomsky (1963), Neisser (1967). Cf. chapters 3 and 9. It can be traced back to the work of Bartlett (1932) which very early investigated the memorization of discourse.

Finally it should be noted that we explicitly claim that macro-structures (and rules) have a strictly linguistic status. They are not merely aspects of performance, e.g. as non-linguistic cognitive strategies. The generation of textually well-formed (coherent) sentences is possible only when underlying macro-structures are postulated. Their empirical relevance, it should again be stressed, is beyond doubt: (verbal) learning, reasoning, memorizing and thinking must be based on macro-structures, without which such notions as 'coherence', 'consistency' (e.g. of formal and informal proofs, arguments, etc.), 'continuity', 'progression', etc. cannot be properly explained. In this respect the notion of macro-structure widely exceeds the strict linguistic domain, although its grammatical and/or logical foundation is basic in such explanations.

1.2.7. The empirical phenomena, mentioned above, for which a formal linguistic description and explanation is necessary are each decisive arguments in favour of the elaboration of T-grammars. As long as S-grammars cannot provide satisfactory, general and consistent, descriptions of the structures underlying discourses, by formulating the rules which must be mastered by native speakers to be able to perform the different tasks, we have to consider them empirically inadequate.

In the next sections and chapters we will observe in which respect S-grammars cannot in PRINCIPLE account for the relevant structures. As was remarked earlier, the different phenomena are not outside the scope of a linguistic grammar. Discourses are the only justifiable 'natural domain' of an empirically adequate theory of language (cf. Sanders [1969]), since all aspects of sentences are accounted for in T-grammars, which in addition specify other relevant structures. With Sanders (1969) we claim that sentences, no more than morphemes, cannot constitute the natural domain of a theory of language, and that S-grammars are reducible to T-grammars. We will go into some detail about these notions of 'natural domain' and 'reducibility' in section 2.4.

1.3. *Grammatical arguments*

1.3.1. A second set of arguments pertain to the form of the grammar itself and are therefore of more direct interest to the linguist. Even if we might try to account for the empirical phenomena mentioned above with traditional S-grammars together with a specific theory of 'discourse-performance', it is inadequate to ignore the systematic linguistic properties characterizing sentences in a sequence of a text. We will give here a brief enumeration of the different linguistic phenomena for which a textual, or at least a 'sequential' approach is required. Some of them will then be treated in more detail in the next two chapters.

We shall focus especially here on those properties of sentences which seem to be a function of sequences, i.e. on textual 'surface structure', and not on macro-structures, which form a hitherto ignored domain of grammar. The present-day linguist will be convinced of the relevance of T-grammar only if it provides a satisfactory framework for the solution of his main grammatical puzzles. He will be unwilling to extend

his empirical scope to textual structures without at least the hope of a possible treatment of the problems met in the description of sentence structures. He might argue
further that even if the problems formulated by a theory of T-grammar are relevant
for linguistics, they must be considered, at present, to be highly premature and their
solution to be beyond the limits of feasibility. Such an argument, however, is rather
weak and has been adduced, until not too long ago, against the formal treatment of
semantics within the grammar. Surely, text grammars will meet extremely intricate
problems of linguistic relations, dependencies and structures, but it is reasonable to
expect that they can at least partially solve these problems. This is not the case for
S-grammars, where the different issues can not be treated in principle.

1.3.2. Thus, beginning at the level of PHONOLOGICAL surface structures, we must
account for the formal criteria of intonation and STRESS assignment in sentences. This
assignment, as we intuitively know, may also be determined by underlying aspects
of focus, topic and comment, contrast, etc. We will see below that such terms can be
made explicit only on the basis of intersentential relations. A similar case applies
for the study of initial and final intonation patterns, which differ according to the
place of the sentence in a text.

At the MORPHOLOGICAL level some languages have specific morphemes marking the
beginning and/or the end of a text. At a deeper level, such markers may consist of
idioms or phraseological expressions. Such 'boundary markers' presumably have a
psychological relevance: they signal to the listener that a discourse is finished, in such
a way that he may already prepare a possible answer.

1.3.3. Although there are some properties of morpho-phonological structure which
represent intersentential relations, it must be stressed that such relations mainly
characterize the deeper levels: SYNTAX and especially SEMANTICS. It will be argued
that the surface phenomena of intersentential relations are to a large extent
predictable in terms of deep structure. If this hypothesis is true we will have to reject
the recent suggestions from the extended standard model of generative-transformational syntax (Chomsky [1970], [1971]) which states that 'surface structure' may
contribute to the meaning of the sentence. Typically, these suggestions were founded
precisely on phenomena such as focus, contrast, irregular stress, topic and comment,
which are described in terms of relations between sentences in sequences.

At the level of SYNTAX we will have to account for the precise rules determining
article selection and related phenomena i.e. the rules for DEFINITIVIZATION of noun
phrases. There are heavy constraints upon the use of (in)definite articles in sentences
(and their clauses), determined by the syntactic and semantic structure of the previous
sentences in the sequence. The whole problem of DEFINITE DESCRIPTION in linguistic
theory hinges upon such relations with 'antecedent sentences'. The 'contextual'
conditions for definitivization, normally left over to performance, are thus explicitly
brought within the scope of the grammar. We are thus in a better position to recognize

which referential and pragmatical factors determine such definite descriptions in texts.

Closely related, and partially determined by the same rules, are the different processes of PRONOMINALIZATION for which T-grammars have to provide a satisfactory description. It is clear that pronominalization cannot be adequately studied in terms of isolated sentences. We therefore have to investigate the set of conditions determining pronominalization in sequences of sentences. Actually, we will try to show that these conditions are similar for complex sentences, and that a significant generalization can be arrived at by describing such complex sentences also in terms of underlying linearly ordered sequences of 'sentences' (*S*'s). In the frequent current discussions on pronouns, this textual character of the process is given only occasional and still very informal attention.

Another important surface manifestation of intersentential relations are the TENSES, MODES, and ASPECTS of the verb (or the 'predicate'). These can be predicted automatically in terms of the underlying semantic representations of the sentences in the sequence. A sentential description of tense forms can only be *ad hoc*, and cannot arrive at relevant generalizations. This hypothesis, however, will not be confirmed in detail in this book, because it requires a thorough treatment of the status of temporal elements in underlying structures, e.g. in terms of a tense logic. Results in this domain are still very meagre as far as linguistics is concerned. The same is true for sentential modalities, although it is obvious that the 'mode' of a sentence depends on those of its 'surrounding' sentences in a text.

Finally, intersentential relations determine the SYNTACTIC STRUCTURE of sentences, especially those structures known as TOPIC and COMMENT. It will be shown that the identification of a topic (and thus of a comment) in a sentence is regulated by rules analogous to those determining definite description, pronominalization and presupposition (see below), which are all functions of certain identity-, equivalence- and other semantic relations with previous sentences. Transformations (e.g. topicalization, passivization) are often necessary to assign irregular topic/comment functions to the syntactic categories of the sentence. As we have remarked above, such transformations may also result in irregular stress assignment in phonological representations. At the same level we will try to make explicit the structure of COMPLEX and COMPOUND SENTENCES and demonstrate that complex sentences can be transformationally derived, as in early generative grammar, from underlying sequences of 'sentences' (*S*'s). In this process the linear ordering of sentences is crucial and enables us to study also all the other relevant, e.g. semantic, relations between the 'clauses' of a sentence. The present conditions for relativization, for example, are restricted to identity relations between noun phrases. This is a necessary but not sufficient condition for well-formed complex sentences. A textual 'reduction' of complex sentences will further provide the necessary basis for determining relations of SYNONYMY between complex sentences and equivalent sequences.

1.3.4. It will be one of our hypotheses that the textual phenomena mentioned above

are surface manifestations of underlying relations between the SEMANTIC REPRESENTA-
TIONS (or 'propositions') of the subsequent 'sentences' of the text. At this level we
have to reconstruct all the 'transition'- and 'coherence'-relations defining a sequence
of sentences as grammatical, i.e. as a well-formed text. Whereas the rules of the
morphophonological level, and – to a lesser degree – those of syntax can operate
rather independently within the sentence, the semantic rules and the process of
lexicalization are practically wholly dependent on the structures of preceding semantic representations. Intuitive terms like 'continuity', 'progression', etc. have to be
defined in such a perspective. At the strict intersentential (micro-structural) level this
lexico-semantic aspect of text-formation is especially clear in the set of sentential
connectives, i.e. CONJUNCTIONS and the SENTENTIAL ADVERBS. The very fact that their
description in modern grammar has so far been neglected seems to confirm the
assumption that it is to be based on an explicit knowledge of the relations between
sentences in a textual sequence.

At the boundary of formal linguistic semantics and logic we finally have to deal
in T-grammar with another relevant pair of theoretical terms: PRESUPPOSITION and
ENTAILMENT. It will be argued that the presuppositions of a given sentence can at
least be partially identified with (subtrees of) previous sentences. That is, we formally
introduce as grammatical structure of texts the set of propositions forming the presuppositions of a sentence, and are thus able to describe within the grammar their
relations of coherence and consistency. It is clear that only a textual grammar is
formally equipped for an explicit description of such (linguistic) relations between
propositions. The existing treatments of presupposition in S-grammar therefore had
to remain vague about the linguistic or semantic status of presuppositions.

At this abstract level we may establish an analogy with PROOFS in formal languages,
although it is not very common in metamathematics and metalogic to consider
proofs as texts (or discourses). Cf. however the following remark by Keenan (1970)
2: "... (standard logic) characterizes both syntactically and semantically, discourses,
called proofs, which are formed from the sentences in a given mathematical language.
The definition of proof, the deductive system, can be naturally formulated as a grammar which generates texts of sentences. Further, in every proof, every sentence
occurring in it is semantically as well as syntactically related to the rest of the proof
in a specified way". We will not elaborate, in this book, this interesting analogy,
but it will be suggested, indeed, that the formal criteria for textual coherence are
similar to those of deductive (and inductive) derivations, where preceding sentences
(presuppositions) can be considered as the premises of a given sentence as a conclusion (cf. Corcoran [1969] for the mathematical implications of these relations
between (text) grammars and deductive systems).

1.3.5. Lastly, observe that semantic representations and lexicalizations are not only
determined linearly, i.e. by immediately preceding sentences. The notions of coherence
and continuity are ultimately based on underlying MACRO-STRUCTURES, which are the

global constraints upon the semantic formation rules of the sentences of the text. Moreover, these macro-structures may further specify other aspects typical of whole sequences of sentences like PERFORMATIVE CATEGORIES and MODALITIES. When considered as part of macro-structure, such categories dominate the whole surface derivation, which leads to important generalization and simplification in our description of sequences of sentences.

1.3.6. After this brief enumeration of linguistic structures for which a textual treatment seems indispensable, we can formulate the TASKS OF AN ADEQUATE T-GRAMMAR as follows:

(i)   a T-grammar formally enumerates all and only grammatical texts of a language;
(ii) a T-grammar assigns structural descriptions to each of the generated texts, and to a set of semi-grammatical texts not generated by the grammar;
(iii) more specifically, a T-grammar formulates the rules and conditions, at all levels of grammatical description, for the well-formed concatenation of pairs, triples, ..., n-tuples of sentences in a linearly ordered sequence; that is, it will make explicit those properties of sentences which are function of intersentential relations;
(iv) a T-grammar must especially formulate the rules describing macro-structures of texts, and the rules relating such macro-structures with sentential (sequential) structures of the text;
(v)   the global task of a T-grammar is thus the formulation of the rules forming and relating semantic structures with phonological structures of all the well-formed texts of a language.

Note that a T-grammar also has to specify surface structures, i.e. all the possible sentences of a language, although its description of sentences differs from that of existing S-grammars. This implies that the S-component of a T-grammar is at least weakly equivalent to traditional S-grammar, but superior in strong generative capacity, because a T-grammar can arrive at more satisfactory structural descriptions of sentences. T-grammar as a whole is superior in weak and strong generative capacity with respect to S-grammar because the language it specifies, *viz.* an infinite set of texts, properly includes the infinite set of sentences. Moreover it provides structural descriptions of well-formed sequences of sentences, i.e. of texts. Both tasks cannot be performed by S-grammars.

Of course, extensive grammatical and empirical arguments have to be adduced to substantiate these claims. Formal proof, however, would be premature at this moment and would require appropriate and comparable formalization of the two types of grammar. An adequate theory of grammar, however, will have to provide such an explicit comparison as soon as a T-grammar has been worked out in detail. So far, we have had to content ourselves with sketching a framework for the treatment of the relevant linguistic phenomena enumerated above. The formulation of more simple and/or more general rules and constraints, then, is a first step towards such a comparison.

Before attempting a formulation of textual rules, or rather before trying to systematize some informal observations, we must first compare, in somewhat more explicit terms, S-grammars with T-grammars in general.

2. S-GRAMMARS AND T-GRAMMARS

2.1. *S-grammars and linear recursion*

2.1.1. One of the essential characteristics of generative grammars is undoubtedly their fundamental RECURSIVE CAPACITY. A simple typology distinguishes between left-recursive, right-recursive and self-embedding elements. The general rule representing recursion might be formulated as follows: $A \Rightarrow \varphi A \psi$, where φ and ψ are non-null strings in the case of self-embedding and where '$\Rightarrow$' abbreviates a sequence of rewrite rules. The introduction of recursive rules in the base component of a generative grammar is restricted by a set of specific conditions, which will not be discussed here.[6] Relevant for our discussion is the fact that among the possible recursive elements the standard model (Chomsky [1965]) admits the initial symbol S itself. S figures in that case often as an element optionally modifying a noun in a noun phrase, or replacing a whole noun phrase. Such a base rule determines the generation of complex sentences by introducing subject-clauses, object-clauses and other types of clauses. Note that the original model (Chomsky [1957]) defined sentential recursion in the transformational component as a process whereby constituent sentences could be embedded by 'generalized transformations' into a matrix sentence. We shall see in the next chapter that there are some arguments in favour of this 'traditional' way of deriving complex sentences.

2.1.2. Recent suggestions have led further to the introduction of rules which would be able to generate non-hierarchical conjuncts of identical elements, for instance of S. Such rules would account, for example, for phenomena of coordination, and normally take the form of RULE SCHEMATA.[7] These may be represented as follows:

---

[6] For recursion and its specific conditions in generative grammars, cf. e.g. Chomsky and Miller (1963) 290 ff., Chomsky (1963) 394 ff. and the references cited therein.

[7] The discussion on rule-schemata is recent and has shown important shortcomings in the traditional models of transformational grammar, for example in the description of phrasal conjunctions. It was shown that linear conjunction could not be produced by transformational reduction, for example. Since rule-schemata are abbreviations of (infinite) sequences of rules, the grammar ceases to be finite in the strict sense, although we may say that a grammar has a finite set of rules and a finite set of rule-schemata. Cf. Chomsky (1965) 99, 224 f., Lakoff and Peters (1969), Dik (1968a) 98 ff., Brainerd (1971) 245 f., Brettschneider (1971) and Rohrer (1971) 122 ff., 134. There are several ways to represent rule schemata for sentence conjunction; cf. Dik (1968a) 98 ff, Miko (1970) 32, Dougherty (1970a), Drubig (1967).

$A \to A(\& A)^n$ or $A \to (\& A)^n$ ($n \geqslant 1$), where & represents a connective element. Since A may also be S, this rule schema permits the derivation of strings of coordinated S's. A simple recursive rule of the type $S \to S(\&S)$ would only yield a hierarchically structured sequence of sentences and is therefore inadequate for the specification of linear (right hand) recursive structures like coordinate clauses in compound sentences.

Thus, the actual state of generative grammar provides the means for the derivation of strings of linearly ordered 'sentences'. We need therefore to see whether such strings are formally equivalent to the notion of 'text' which we hypothetically introduced earlier. Can we find decisive arguments against such an identification?

2.2. *Sentences and sequences*

2.2.1. A first set of problems we meet here concerns the role of sentential BOUNDARY MARKERS. The rules (rule schemata) embedding or coordinating S-symbols are followed by obligatory transformations deleting the boundary symbols of the embedded (coordinated) sentences, and only the leftmost and rightmost boundary markers of the matrix sentence are not deleted. However, when we assume that a text has the following surface structure: $\#S_1\#$, $\#S_2\#$, ..., $\#S_n\#$, the traditional rules would not account for such structures. That is, they cannot describe strings of sentences separated by phonological (or graphological) boundary markers. Modification of the transformational rules would be necessary here in order to derive the desired string. Observe that intrasentential deletion of boundary markers in coordinative strings is accompanied by the insertion of lexical connectives such as *and*, *but*, etc., whereas intersentential boundary markers are accompanied either by zero-elements or by a partially different set of connectives (*moreover*, initial *however*, etc.). This observation points to the fact that there must be a formal difference between intra-sentential and inter-sentential coordination of S's.

2.2.2. The problem of boundary markers and connectives hinges on the status of the INITIAL SYMBOL, S, itself. Little theoretical work has been done on the theoretical and methodological status of initial symbols. Although we have to consider an initial symbol to be an abstract, arbitrary symbol, element of the non-terminal vocabulary of the grammar, the strings derived from it have the idealized but empirical nature of being 'sentences' of a language. Now, a rule-schema like $S \to S(\& S)^n$, for example, always results in a structure in which one S dominates all others. Even if we would modify the transformational rules and the lexico-semantic rules for the insertion of sentential connectives, in order to derive a surface structure like $\# \& S_1\#$, $\# \& S_2\#$, ..., $\# \& S_n\#$, such a structure would always be called a (one) 'sentence'.[8] This, how-

---

[8] This is however the traditional approach in generative grammar. Katz and Fodor (1963), for example, consider discourse to be one long sentence, generated by repeated conjunction with the aid of *and*, *but*, etc. (Katz and Fodor, 1964). No conditions are specified which would restrict this type of sentential conjunction. Cf. also Jacobs and Rosenbaum (1968) 253ff. for analogous simplifications.

ever, runs counter to our intuitive conception of sentences. We do not call 'sentence' a sequence of structurally independent sentences separated by full stops and (optionally) introduced by connectives which may be restricted to the initial position in the sentence. The theoretical status of the initial, dominating, symbol S in such sequences therefore becomes unclear, whereas its empirical relevance is lost if it may represent formally both a sentence and a string of (structurally independent) sentences, that is a 'sequence'. There are a great number of theoretical and empirical arguments against an identical treatment, in terms of S-dominated structures, of (compound) sentences and sequences. Besides differences in sentential connectives, it would for instance be impossible, in such a traditional account of a sequence, to describe strings consisting of pragmatically different sentences, such as assertion, question, e.g. with the aid of one 'hyper-sentence' which is always attached to, or identical with, the highest S-node (Ross [1970], Sadock [1970] cf. chapter 9 for details about the status of pragmatical elements).

Such arguments will be adduced in the next chapter for each level of grammatical description. At the phonological level stress and intonation patterns are different for (compound) sentences and for sequences of sentences. At the level of syntax we notice differences e.g. in the formation of pronouns, whereas at the semantic level compound sentences necessarily have connective relations between the clauses, which is not always the case in subsequent sentences. Although many of the differences are rather superficial, a treatment of sequences in terms of (compound) sentences would obscure relevant grammatical distinctions. It is obvious that the same is true *a fortiori* for the differences between complex sentences and linear sequences.

One argument in favour of a treatment of sequences in terms of compound or complex sentences would be the 'reducibility' of a sequence to one surface sentence structure. However, many ordered pairs, triples, ... n-tuples of 'sentences' (S's) cannot possibly be transformed into one sentence as we shall see.

2.2.3. These arguments must not obscure the important fact that, besides the superficial differences, there are also many similarities between complex or compound sentences and sequences of sentences. One of the main tasks of an adequate text grammar, indeed, consists precisely of demonstrating that different surface structures may cover synonymous deep-structures. The very notion of paraphrase is based on this deep structure equivalence of semantic representations. Our claim, in fact, is that the semantic deep structures of complex (compound) sentences and of sequences of sentences must be described in the same way in order to account for these and resulting similarities. This, however, cannot be achieved when we maintain one initial (dominant) S-symbol, because the operations, e.g. transformations, defined for S-

---

We here meet one of the most serious drawbacks of existing S-grammars, where no rules, conditions or relations are formulated to determine grammatical embedding, coordination, etc. of sentential structures, except for relations of equivalence between NP's.

dominated strings or trees are specific, and often differ from those operating on sequences. We may therefore hypothetically introduce another theoretical symbol Sq for the derivation of sequences. We shall see later in which respect we must define its relation to the symbol S and to a symbol T for texts. Derivations of sequences starting with Sq would in this case have the following tentative initial rule schema:

(2) $\# Sq \# \rightarrow \# S \# \ (\# \& \ S \#)^n \qquad n \geqslant 0$

where '$\#$' is the boundary symbol for sequences, '$\&$' an abstract symbol for sentential connection, and where n may take any value equal to and greater than zero. When this value is zero we derive a single sentence. In the next chapter we try to find some evidence for considering the proposed base rule at the basis of both sequence and complex or compound sentence formation, thus localizing their differences in the transformational component. In order that these transformations be applied we should perhaps introduce a similar S-dominated rule-schema into the base as a second step:

(3) $\# S \# \rightarrow \# S \# \ (\# \& \ S \#)^m \qquad m \geqslant 0$

We then have to see also whether self-embedding structures are transformationally derivable from this linear recursive structure or whether self-embedding must be considered to be a property of the base. That is, is it possible to reduce conditions formulated in terms of hierarchical relations (e.g. some types of pronominalization, relativization) to conditions based on linear deep structure well-formedness? If this should turn out to be the case we have arrived at an important generalization because the derivation of self-embedding complex sentences, of right or left recursive compound sentences and of sequences of sentences would be determined by the same base constraints.

2.2.4. One task of an adequate T-grammar, then, consists in formulating the conditions determining the combination of sentences in a well-formed sequence. Not any member of the infinite set of possible sentence combinations belongs to the language: the concatenation of two arbitrary sentences, even less than for words, seldom produces a grammatical product. This is trivial, but traditional generative grammars did not specify such conditions, not even for complex and compound sentences. The only condition was framed in syntactic terms in order to describe processes of relativization and ensuing pronominalization: the 'identity' of (syntactic) subtrees. Other, for example semantic, conditions until recently hardly played a role. We further have to make explicit in which respect the syntactic conditions are based on underlying semantic properties of connected sentences. A precise definition of 'identity' or 'equivalence' will be necessary in such a description of relations between sentences.

It is clear that we must not reject S-grammars as inadequate for the description of intersentential relation on the ground of their hitherto rather restricted attention to such problems. We should first be sure that an S-grammar cannot IN PRINCIPLE account for such relations. It might be the case that the conditions determining the well-formedness of complex and compound sentences are similar, if not identical, to those which should be formulated for sequences. The problem, then, can be briefly rephrased as follows: are sequences specific forms of compound 'sentences', or are complex and compound sentences specific forms of sequences? The decision on this matter is determined both by the empirical adequacy of the proposed descriptions and by theoretical criteria such as generality, simplicity and consistency.

Before a tentative answer can be provided, we must first have to sketch the framework of the postulated T-grammar, in terms of which our alternative approach has to be formulated. That is, we must know how a T-grammar is organized, which types of rules it admits and which other derivational constraints distinguish it from S-grammars.

2.3. *The form of T-grammars*

2.3.1. In the first section of this chapter we have listed some tasks of a text grammar at the level of description and explanation. We now have to design a global form for such a grammar, and distribute the specific tasks over its different components.

In the first place we will follow the general theory of grammar and consider a T-grammar as a formal device relating 'form' to 'meaning', i.e. a phonological surface structure with a semantic representation. This general definition of a grammar, however, is not necessarily adequate. In fact we would expect a theory of (a) language not to be restricted to phonological, semantic and intermediate syntactic and morphological rules. It is well-known, though ignored in most current generative writings, that a theoretical description of a natural or formal language, like any semiotic theory, has a syntax, a semantics and a pragmatics. Modern linguistics, strictly speaking, is interested only in the formal syntax of which linguistic semantics, morphophonology and syntax are subcomponents. Formal semantics, or the 'theory of reference' (or 'theory of truth', or 'model theory') is normally not considered part of the grammar. Nor is pragmatics concerned with the structures underlying 'well-formed' (or 'happy', or 'adequate', or 'appropriate') acts of verbal communication by users of the language. Although semantics and pragmatics (in this formal sense), after their development in modern logic, have received recent interest in linguistics, they are not usually considered as components of the grammar. We must therefore either consider a grammar, in the actual linguistic sense, as a partial theory of language, corresponding with its 'logical' syntax, or we must reorganize the grammar such that its actual components are associated within the grammatical framework with a theory of reference and a pragmatical theory. We will in principle adopt this last position, although it is not yet clear how these components should be integrated into the grammar. In the final chapter we will make some observations about the possible tasks, forms, rules and elements of a pragmatic component and about its possible relationship with the traditional concept of grammar. We will, here, restrict ourselves provisionally to the current 'narrow' conception of a grammar, because its components are best known in grammatical theory, especially linguistic syntax and phonology. Our point is only that we must not exclude *a priori* from the grammar those components which are undoubtedly relevant for the derivation of well-formed sentences or texts.

2.3.2. A first distinction in a T-grammar, then, can be made between a MACRO-COMPONENT and a MICRO-COMPONENT. The former formulates the rules for the derivation of textual macro-structures, whereas the latter describes the individual sentential structures of a text and their immediate interrelations within a sequence. A set of TRANSFORMATIONS will relate macro-structures with micro-structures. The macro-structure is considered to be the abstract underlying structure or 'logical form' of a text and will be identified with the DEEP STRUCTURE OF THE TEXT. It consists of global semantic representations defining the meaning of a text 'as a whole'.

Correspondingly, micro-structure is considered to be the SURFACE STRUCTURE OF THE TEXT, which consists of an ordered *n*-tuple of subsequent sentences. Textual surface structure is not identical with the morphonological/syntactic surface structure of its sentences. These have their own levels of deep and surface structure, which for the sake of clarity will be called, respectively, SENTENTIAL DEEP AND SURFACE STRUCTURE. Textual deep structures (macro-structures), as we saw, have an abstract semantic character and will be specified by (macro-)semantic rules. At this level of abstraction these rules obviously cannot be simple PS-rules, since texts as a whole do not have immediate constituents of the well-known type. This is true, in fact, for all semantic descriptions, within the sentence as well. We therefore assume that semantic rules define abstract RELATIONS between underlying macro-categories.

Textual surface structures, i.e. sequences of sentences, are described with the usual components of a generative-transformational grammar. A semantic component formulates the rules generating underlying semantic representations of the sentences of a sequence. A syntactic component provides the rules for describing the syntactic surface structures of the underlying representations, whereas finally the morphological and phonological components assign a surface form to these abstract semantico-syntactic structures. The rules mapping semantic representations onto syntactic structures are probably transformation rules, but are not yet well-known. We will provisionally limit ourselves to 'independent' descriptions of these two levels. This form of the grammar is essentially the one proposed in recent models of GENERATIVE SEMANTICS.[9] Although explicit rules in these 'generative' models are still lacking, we

---

[9] We will not extensively discuss here advantages and drawbacks of generative semantics as it is outlined e.g. in McCawley (1968a), (1968b), (1971), Lakoff (1970b), (1971a), Brekle (1969), Rohrer (1971). For a survey see Abraham & Binnick (1969). Critical remarks in Chomsky (1970), (1971) and Katz (1970), (1971) seem to reduce the suggestions of generative semantics to mere notational variants, although there are a certain number of problems, especially semantic ones, for which a

do not believe that an 'interpretive' ('interpretative') semantics, at least not in any
form which has been proposed up till now, provides an adequate insight into the
structure of semantic representations. The major reason for us to reject a (possibly
more explicit) interpretive approach, is the fact that in that approach semantic
structures are directly modeled by (underlying) syntactic structures, i.e. by PS-rules.
It is well-known, however, that constraints and conditions upon semantic well-
formedness (e.g. as regulated by the structure of the lexicon, projection rules, and
selection restrictions) do not follow the habitual IC-categorizations, as expressed e.g.
in an initial rule 'dividing' *S* in *NP* and *VP* (or *NP* and *Pred P*). The often assumed
formal equivalence of generative and interpretive semantics, reducing them to
'notational variants', to be sure, applies indeed to many proposals made by generative
semanticists, maintaining the usual syntactic category symbols for semantic descriptions. Further, it is clear that this equivalence also holds true for an interpretive
semantic component which maps syntactic structures onto semantic interpretations
having their own rules and categories of formation. However, the model of the
(extended) standard grammar does not contain such a pseudo-interpretive component.

Besides possible empirical reasons, adduced mainly from the side of psycholinguistics, a semantically based (inter-)sentential sub-grammar of our T-grammar is
necessary for the simplicity and coherence of the description of the rules which relate
macro-structures with the deep-structure of the sentences of textual micro-structure
(textual surface structure). It would be highly circumstantial, if not impossible, to
map (macro-) semantic structure onto (micro-)syntactic structures and these again
onto (micro-)semantic representations (interpretations). Furthermore, a semantically
based surface (sentential) component of a T-grammar is more easily representable in
models of an (extended) predicate logic. We thus need rules to relate the logical form
of a text with the logical forms of its subsequent sentences. Although some remarks
about such rules will be made, tentatively, in chapter 3, their precise nature remains
obscure at the moment. The same is true, as we said, for the precise rules relating
sentential semantic representations to their syntactic surface structures.

The surface component of a T-grammar not only specifies sentential structures but
also intersentential, i.e. sequential structures or relations. That is, it has to provide
the 'transitional' constraints upon the following ordered pairs, triples, ... *n*-tuples:
$\langle S_1, S_2 \rangle$, $\langle S_1, S_2, S_3 \rangle$, ..., $\langle S_1, S_2, S_3, ..., S_{n-1}, S_n \rangle$.

We may consider this surface component to be an EXTENDED S-GRAMMAR or a

---

interpretive treatment in the classical sense is highly complicated, if not impossible. Cf. e.g. Postal
(1971) for difficulties in interpreting anaphora. The same holds for the description of paraphrases.
Notice that the semantic base we propose is different from the still very 'syntactic' base components
suggested by e.g. McCawley, Gruber (1967) and Lakoff (1971a) because we make use of specific
semantic categories, e.g. inspired by Fillmore's Case Grammar (Fillmore [1968], [1969a], [1969b],
[1970]), and semantic rules. We thus give priority to the elaboration of an adequate component
specifying semantic representations instead of formulating directly mapping rules or interpretive
rules relating, prematurely, semantic and syntactic structures without having an explicit knowledge
of the structures of semantic representations.

SEQUENTIAL GRAMMAR. This grammar generates sentences under the 'contextual', i.e. sequential, restrictions of preceding and following sequences of sentences. This implies that the extant S-grammar is not as such included in a T-grammar. Both macro-structure and sequential structures impose additional constraints upon the well-formedness of individual sentences. Strictly speaking, then, we want to derive well-formed sequences, of which sentences are major constituents.

Following our hypothesis an extended S-grammar or sequential grammar is not equivalent with a T-grammar, although most recent suggestions on 'T-grammars' limit themselves to surface structures such as sequences. We claim, then, that such types of 'T-grammars', i.e. grammars which do not specify textual deep or macro-structures, are descriptively inadequate. We will see in chapter 3 that a sequential approach is not able to define, for instance, a notion like 'global coherence' in a sufficiently simple way, so that it fails to provide an adequate model of linguistic competence. We will have to substantiate this still rather speculative claim in the following chapters.

2.3.3. Having thus outlined roughly the organization of a T-grammar, we must now turn briefly to its possible categories and the forms of its rules. The grammar itself, firstly, can be defined in general as a quadruple $\langle V_N, V_T, T, R \rangle$, where V_N is a vocabulary of non-terminal or theoretical symbols, V_T a vocabulary of terminal symbols or lexicon, T a distinguished symbol, called 'initial symbol', element of V_N and standing for 'Text', and R a set of rules. We will assume that V_T of a T-grammar is identical with V_T of an S-grammar. The vocabulary of non-terminal symbols, however, will contain presumably, besides T, a set of symbols representing categories unknown in S-grammars, for instance Sq, representing the notion of 'sequence', and probably distinguished boundary markers for sequences and for texts. It was suggested above that V_N will also have distinguished subsets of symbols for the description of semantic representations. Their generality and abstractness will lead to the important hypothesis that the semantic representations of texts and of sentences are isomorphous. V_{Nsem} will contain such symbols as *Pred, Arg, A, Agt, Pat, Obj, Instr.* representing categories like Predicate, Argument, Actant, Agent, Patient, Object and Instrument. Others will probably have to be introduced.

The set of rules has five main subsets, operating in this order:

(R_1) semantic formation rules for macro-structures.

(R_2) transformation rules of macro-structures (so called macro-transformations) having macro-structures as input and transformed macro-structures as output.

(R_3) transformation rules mapping transformed macro-structures onto sequences of underlying semantic representations of sentences.

(R_4) transformation rules mapping semantic representations of sequences onto syntactic representations; this set includes a set of lexicalization rules.

(R_5) rules pairing lexico-syntactic surface structures with morphophonological representations.

The precise properties of these rules are not yet fully known. Even set R_4 is not well-defined as yet in the theory of generative semantics. The standard theory has, instead of R_4, a set of syntactic formation rules of the rewrite type, and instead of R_5, sets of phonological and semantic interpretation rules. It is possible that we should postulate also a set R_3' containing (semantic) formation rules for sentences and sequences of sentences. We will provisionally adopt such a set, as long as we ignore the nature of the rules of R_3. We will thus derive sentential deep structures in a semi-independent way, that is by semantic formation rules. These are possibly analogous to those of R_1, to which supplementary constraints are added.

Both macro- and micro-semantic formation rules may be modelled by the formation rules of a (higher) predicate calculus of relations. Their general form may be represented as follows:

(4) $\varphi \rightarrow \psi(\alpha_{i_1}, \alpha_{i_2}, ..., \alpha_{i_n})$

where φ is a non-terminal category, ψ a terminal or non-terminal category, and $\alpha_{i_1}, \alpha_{i_2}, ..., \alpha_{i_n}$ a set of n variables ($n \geqslant 1$), representing different individual variables or constants, predicate variables (or constants), event variables (or constants), propositional variables (or constants) and sentential variables (or constants). The nature of these variables (or constants) characterizes the type (degree, level, order) of ψ e.g. as n^{th}-order predicate, operator, quantifier or connective element. This relational notation is more general than the usual PS-rewriting-rules. These, however, may also be represented as relations. Instead of using the rule $S \rightarrow NP\ VP$, we might consider S as a relation, that is as the set of ordered couples $\{\langle NP, VP \rangle\}$, and we may thus write: $NP\ S\ VP$ or $S(NP, VP)$. Similarly, we may represent the arguments, which are also relations, by functionals, e.g. as follows:

$S((NP(Art, N)), VP)$, and similarly
$S((NP(Art, N)), (VP(V, NP)))$ and
$S((NP(Art, N)), (VP(V, (NP(Art, N)))))$, etc.

The resulting string is equivalent to the labelled bracketing representing PS-rules. We assume, however, that semantic rules defining relations between categories are independent of linear ordering of immediate constituents in PS-rules. The order of notation of the symbols between angles merely reflects their abstract order in the relation. Thus the ordered pair $\langle Pred, Arg \rangle$ can be considered to be an element of the relation *Prop* (for proposition). In a derivational description of a given semantic structure we will use the convention of writing simply *Prop* $\rightarrow \langle Pred, Arg \rangle$, for example, or simply the equivalent logical notation *Prop* $\rightarrow Pred(Arg)$ or, in variables

$g(x, y, z)$. Some details of such logico-semantic derivations, that is of derivations of predicate logical formulae representing semantic structures, will be given in chapter 3. We will not discuss further the properties of these (semantic) rules and their place in T-grammars.

2.3.4. It would be premature to discuss here the precise MATHEMATICAL PROPERTIES of T-grammars. Their rules are constraints upon the combination of all possible sentences of a language, which form in turn a subset of all possible combinations over the vocabulary V_T. Thus the language L_S of grammatical sentences is a semi-group, and the language L_T of grammatical texts as well, since both satisfy the conditions of having a binary operation of concatenation, conjuncts of elements of V_T are elements of L and concatenation is associative. These conditions also hold for the macro-structures as intuitively defined above, although the notion of associativeness, here as elsewhere in linguistic theory, should be handled carefully (cf. Chomsky and Miller [1963] 274 ff.). Nor can we enter into a discussion of the formal properties of the types of rules admitted in T-grammars. Probably some basic semantic rules are context-free, whereas others are surely context-sensitive. Furthermore, the nature of macro-rules is still obscure, although we will adopt the hypothesis that they are formation rules like those of a (higher order) modal predicate calculus. Similarly, we cannot but speculate about the mathematical properties of the (presumably trans-formation) rules transducing macro-structures into micro-structures. Several mathematical models may be used to represent such one-many mappings as well as the relations between linearly ordered sentences in textual surface structure (cf. Palek [1968], van Dijk [1971g]), but no precise statements can be made at the moment about the mathematical foundations of the form of the grammar itself.

2.4. *"On the natural domain of grammar"*

2.4.1. The discussion in the preceding sections calls for some final methodological remarks. The 'extension' of the empirical domain of a linguistic theory and the corresponding extension of grammar must be founded not only on arguments, but these arguments must have been evaluated for their meta-theoretical relevance.

2.4.2. Gerald A. Sanders in a long paper, "On the Natural Domain of Grammar" (Sanders [1969]), has given such a methodological foundation for the extension of the scope of adequate grammatical descriptions. He tries to make explicit the notion 'natural domain of a grammar' and adduces many arguments to show that sentences and their structures cannot form such a natural domain. Neither are phonological, morphological, syntactic or semantic structures in isolation, like phonemes, words, etc., such natural domains. He claims that only "infinite sets of [what he calls] discourses" can be justified as natural domains of a grammar. A grammar/theory accounting for a natural domain is called a 'natural grammar/theory'. Other grammars/ theories are called 'non-natural'.

The criterion of 'naturalness' is made explicit by a set of 'conditions for reducibility'. If a sentence grammar can be reduced to a discourse grammar without loss of significant descriptive adequacy, such a sentence grammar can be considered to be a non-natural theory. The conditions for reducibility are purely formal and formulated by the general methodological requirements of philosophy of science (cf. especially Nagel [1961]).

A first criterion is the extension of the two theories. The set of theoretical statements of a discourse grammar is supposed to be included in the combined sets of a sentence grammar and an independent discourse grammar. Thus, a 'unified' theory is simpler than a non-unified theory. Moreover, their integration leads to empirically significant generalizations. The basic requirement, viz. that all theorems of an S-grammar are derivable within a discourse grammar, is satisfied under these criteria. This relation of reducibility is non-symmetric: a discourse grammar cannot be reduced to an S-grammar, because the set of its interpreted terms is not included in the set of interpreted terms of an S-grammar; similarly for the statements of a discourse grammar. Finally, to constrain the general condition for reducibility, the statements of a reduced theory must be 'jointly confirmable' in the reducing theory, and not just be part of them. This is the case for S-grammars and T-grammars.

2.4.3. We will not go into the methodological details of the formal criteria of theory reduction, for which we refer to Sanders' paper. To substantiate his claim, Sanders provides a set of linguistic structures which cannot be accounted for in S-grammars: differences between grammatical and non-grammatical sequences, ambiguous and synonymous strings, coordination and subordination, contrastive stress, completeness of discourses, elliptical constructions, pronouns with 'missing antecedents', etc. These problems encountered in S-grammar were, among others, also specified in the first be part of this section, and some of them will be treated in the next chapter.

2.4.4. The arguments of Sanders are correct and confirm our hypotheses. However, Sanders did not prove that an S-grammar extended with linear recursive rules or rule-schemata cannot in principle arrive at a satisfactory description of his problems. In fact, he has argued for a sequential grammar, not for a discourse or text-grammar. That is, if a linearly recursive S-grammar specifies the conditions upon sentence concatenation as understood by Sanders, it is weakly and strongly equivalent to a discourse grammar in Sanders' sense. He does not specify which theoretical elements, e.g. the initial symbol, are typical for discourse grammars. Still more important is his neglect of macro-structures and their rules and elements. His framework thus will not be satisfactory for the formulation of the global derivational constraints for sequences of sentences as a whole. We therefore consider Sanders' sequential grammar as a non-natural theory, because all its theorems are derivable in a text grammar. This reduction of sequential (or linear) discourse grammar to T-grammar satisfies the conditions formulated by Sanders himself. At this superficial level, a sequential approach will fail to formulate very important generalizations with respect to the structure of discourse (text), especially at the macro-structural level.

There is only one practical argument in favour of sequential grammars: actual feasibility. Indeed, with our present knowledge it is easier to study the general conditions for linear concatenation of sentences. Nevertheless, some fundamental properties (continuity, coherence, etc.) can be explained only in the framework of a T-grammar as outlined above.

2.4.5. Let us finally stress that even a T-grammar, having the traditional task of enumerating infinite sets of texts and of assigning one or more structural descriptions to each member of these sets, cannot be properly considered a NATURAL THEORY of a language. Earlier, and in more detail in chapter 9, we suggested that a complete theory of a language also comprises a formal semantics (theory of reference) and a pragmatics (theory of use). Without such components it is impossible to formulate a formal basis for an adequate theory of performance (acceptability), i.e. processes of verbal communication actualized in speech acts. Thus, a theory of language cannot be restricted to a formal study of the structures underlying the utterances, but must also provide the rules for the APPROPRIATENESS of such utterances in specified situations. Many formal elements of the utterances themselves can be described only in terms of such 'underlying' referential and pragmatic structures. It follows, then, that the only natural theory of a language is a text grammar having as components, or at least being associated with, a semantic (referential) and a pragmatic theory. Only then may a grammar provide the adequate formal basis of socio- or psycho-linguistic theories of performance, required by the transformational theory.

3. TEXTUAL LINGUISTICS: SOME CLASSICAL APPROACHES

3.1. *Introduction*

Having delineated some aspects of the grammar to be developed and the very diverse tasks it is supposed to fulfill we must give a very brief survey of some traditional approaches in this field of 'textual linguistics'. The search for 'sources' for our case is also important because at many points we are hardly more advanced than the traditional theories of textual structures and textual functions. A whole monograph, or several, would be required to examine in detail the different remarks about text/ discourse from classical rhetoric to modern structural and generative linguistics. In fact, the whole history of literary scholarship would be included in such a survey. We will limit ourselves, therefore, to a superficial account of the main directions of thought.

3.2. *Ancient rhetorics*

Before we deal with the attempts in our own time it is useful to stress here not only the historical role but also the conceptual relevance of classical rhetorics,[10] which today finds its often highly developed offshoots in such varied disciplines as stylistics, pragmatics, content analysis and the theory of communication. The reason for searching back that far is the very sophistication of rhetorics: its categories and classifications indeed seem to have given way to more explicit theorizing only in modern linguistics. The other disciplines mentioned are more adequate only in so far as they make use either of formal linguistics or of mathematical and psycho-social techniques. The proper description of texts has not advanced very much since antiquity.

It is well-known that the basic framework of rhetorics had a permanent influence on western civilization, especially from the 12th century onwards. This influence decayed only at the end of the 18th century, only to re-emerge at the beginning of our century and, finally, receive much attention over these last few years. This does not mean, however, that the complex of disciplines with which it was originally associated have kept the same close contact. For modern grammarians rhetorics and even stylistics is marginal if not irrelevant, and only the development of a textual grammar, and the study of performance and pragmatics in general might re-establish the broken bonds.

We have to recall, then, that grammar, rhetorics and poetics were closely associated. Grammar, as is well-known, originated in the description of sacred or poetic texts. Norms and rules were inferred from the exemplary use of language by some canonized *auctores*. The only difference between grammar and rhetorics was qualitative, the first dealing with the art 'bene loquendi'. Ancient grammar, although it was based on the description of texts, did not study the mechanisms and structures of these texts beyond the boundaries of the sentence and rarely beyond the boundaries of the word or the sign. This task clearly was left to rhetorics, whereas the term of 'text' itself was even unknown in classical antiquity and only the concept 'work' (of art) (ἔργον) was used.

The importance of rhetorics for our discussion concerns the following two aspects: its rather precise definition of the possible linguistic operations *(figurae)* underlying the production of specifically 'well-formed' texts, and the localization of the text in the entire communication process. The first aspect is mainly limited to micro-structural operations like permutation, different types of metaphorization and phonological repetitions. Macro-structural order in texts is discussed only in relation with the way

---

[10] For an exhaustive description of classical rhetorics cf. Lausberg (1960). A short survey is given by Barthes (1970). A structural re-interpretation of rhetorics is given by Dubois, *et al.* (1970). For the current re-evaluation of rhetorics see *Communications* 16 (1970), Genette (1969a), Steinmann, *ed.* (1967), Kibédi Varga (1970) and many current manuals of stylistics. For the historical role of rhetorics, cf. among others, Curtius (1948) and Zumthor (1971).

the material *(res)* is presented, especially in relation to narrative structures. The body of instructions given served however, as in classical poetics, not only an internal goal, but above all the external conditions of effectiveness on the public. In this respect rhetorics is not only a theory of texts but also a pragmatics *avant la lettre*.

3.3. *The Structural analysis of discourse*

3.3.1. The first modern approaches of textual properties can be subsumed under the broad and therefore vague label of structuralism, both in poetics and in linguistics. In fact, the development of the two disciplines in this domain can hardly be dissociated: the members of the Moscow Linguistic Circle were closely concerned with the work done by the Opajaz-group (cf. Erlich [1955]; Jakobson is still the main figure representing these common roots of linguistics and poetics in Russian Formalism).

Similar remarks can be made about the Prague School and Copenhagen glossematics, of which Ihwe (1972a) has given an elaborate historical and systematic survey. However, although formalist, structuralist and glossematic poetics mainly studied the different linguistic operations of literary texts, descriptions of texts as formal units were only occasional and *ad hoc*. The properties of 'literary language' were defined mainly as stylistic devices *(priëmy)* within the sentence or between successive sentences. Macro-structures were studied in narrative texts but their analysis was not founded on linguistic categories but on intuitively defined 'functions'. As we will see in chapter 3, the modern developments of this study of narrative structures has shown convergence with the tentative elaboration of macro-structural categories and rules for all texts.

3.3.2. Many of the different 'schools' of linguistic structuralism explicitly take texts or discourse as the point of departure for their analytic descriptions. However, we will see that the structuralist description of discourse is both linear and 'superficial', i.e. morpho-syntactic.

Hjelmslev (1943) explicitly conceives the linguistic object as a set of texts in which, by segmentation and inductive generalization, the regularities of grammar have to be found. The regularities thus discovered permit, deductively, a predictive description of all the possible texts of a language. So far his theory comes close to the ideas we have sketched above – of course taking into account the differences between his approach and our generative-transformational point of view. His grammar, however, does not provide very much evidence for this theoretical programme because it does not specify the explicit formal procedures for segmenting texts into smaller functional units such as chapters, paragraphs and sentences. Analysis actually starts at the level of the sentence and the structure of a text, for Hjelmslev, does not seem to be more than a sequence of serially ordered sentences. No restrictions upon this ordering or upon the possible syntactic or semantic form of successive sentences are given. The crucial Hjelmslevian concept of (inter)dependency is not defined for structures beyond the sentence. Segmentation of texts is operated along the two basic lines of 'expression' and 'content', but although Hjelmslev (1943) 87 stresses the difference in scope of his maximal linguistic units with respect to traditional theories, he does not give any conditions for the combination of sentences. Important for our discussion is his explicit statement that the macro-structural aspects of texts also belong to the object of linguistic description proper and not to the domains of logic or psychology alone. An infinite 'text', like language itself, can thus according to Hjelmslev be analysed in different types of texts, authorships, works, chapters, paragraphs, etc. Poetics therefore, according to Hjelmslev, has its natural place within an extended linguistics, i.e. conceived as the theory of all actual or possible manifestations of natural language.

It will be clear from our discussion above that, although a text in our sense may theoretically have infinite length, language proper will not be considered as such an infinite syntagmatic process *(forløb)*, but as an infinite set of texts.

Hjelmslev's concept of text is often close to, if not identical with, a performance notion of discourse (a corpus of 'realized' or 'realizable' language) and is not the purely abstract construct characteristic of a formal grammar.[11]

3.3.3. There can be no doubt that Zellig S. Harris (1952), (1963), (1968) was the first modern linguist who not only considered 'discourse' as a legitimate object for linguistics but who also realized his programmatic statements by giving the first systematic analysis of (given) texts. In this respect he definitely broke the Bloomfieldian tradition for which only the 'independent linguistic expression' of the sentence was relevant to the linguist, whereas discourse was only an undefined aspect of language use. The sentence, according to Harris, cannot be detached from the structural pattern in which it is integrated, and which he called 'connected speech'.

Rather than giving a theory of discourse Harris limits himself to analytical procedures. Discourse analysis is defined as a "method of seeking in any connected discrete linear material, whether language or language like, which contains more than one elementary sentence, some global structure characterizing the whole discourse (the linear material) or large sections of it" (1963) 17. Unlike Hjelmslev, Harris only describes the morphophonemic and syntactic structures of the text. Meaning or content is considered only in so far as it is realized in repeated or transformationally related morphemes (of which the equivalence, then, must be assumed intuitively, but which is motivated by similar distribution in similar contexts). There are other restrictions in the definition which unnecessarily limited Harris' analysis. Firstly, discourse is conceived of as a linear (surface) structure in which, apparently, no hierarchical relationships can be discovered. We will see that this point of view in

---

[11] Cf. Hjelmslev (1943) 16, 86ff and Hjelmslev and Ulldal (1957) 33. The ambiguity of the glossematic notion of text, sometimes simply equivalent to syntagmatic chain or process, has been noticed also by Siertsema (1965) 18, 41, 59 and especially 227. For a discussion of the glossematic notion of text in poetics, cf. Trabant (1970) 96–219.

fact characterizes the majority of work done in textual theory and analysis: dependencies are defined only within the sentence and therefore only at the level of syntactic structure. Secondly, Harris seems to exclude the large set of texts consisting of only one sentence, which appear frequently in daily conversation. This fact, *i.e.* the possible coincidence of text and sentence, will yield a heuristic argument for taking a grammar of sentence description as a model for the development of a text grammar (cf. however, chapter 3, § 3.3).

The most important factor in Harris' definition is his mention of the term 'global structure characterizing the whole discourse', which will be crucial in our generative account of textual structures. However, this 'global' structure turns out to have a taxonomic character. As is well-known at present, the discourse analysis resulted in a matrix of 'equivalent' structures, defined by identical co-occurrences and distributions of certain elements throughout the text. The procedure of descriptive reduction thus led to the fundamental notions of 'kernel sentence' and 'transformation', which, though in a modified sense, should play such a decisive role in Chomsky's grammar. Apart from the list of repeated morphemes or clusters of morphemes, the equivalences established were those characterizing the syntactic analogies between any two or more kernel sentences of the language. This implies that the method would apply to any set of arbitrarily concatenated sentences. What Harris discovered was not so much the structure of 'connected speech', but some basic properties of the English sentence. Morphematic recurrence and the syntactic categories in which it manifests itself only are a possible but not a necessary and certainly not a sufficient reflection of 'deeper' semantic relations. The methods of traditional (American) structuralism however did not provide the theoretical tools for analyzing these relations (cf. Klevansky [1967]).

In later writings Harris confirmed his programmatic viewpoint, but there also the relations between sentences are limited to typically 'short-term' relationships of morpho-syntactic surface-structure: "Finally, all grammars based on sentence, and not on discourse, miss the few grammatical dependencies among separate sentences of a discourse, such as between a pronoun and its antecedent in a different sentence" (1968) 36. He recognizes, however, that the conjunction of sentences is subject to additional constraints, which in principle are the same for compound sentences as for discourse, because a text can be described, according to him, as a long sentence constructed by means of a set of connectors (1968) 131.

We will try to demonstrate that this conception of a text cannot lead to adequate descriptions because some sequences of sentences cannot possibly be reduced to one structurally well-formed compound sentence (cf. Palek [1968] 131ff.), whereas, conversely, any compound sentence could probably be paraphrased as a text with *n* surface sentences (cf. Dressler [1970a] 209). This means, as we will see, that the optional formation of compound surface sentences is subject to additional constraints, but that the basic conditions of concatenation are those of texts. We notice that the consequences of positing the text as an initial major category have not been recognized by Harris. Like most other attempts at discourse analysis, discourse is 'constructed' from the sentence level upwards.

3.3.4. Our global criticism leveled against Harris' restricted theoretical view on textual structure applies as well *mutatis mutandis* to much work inspired by him, also within a generative-transformational framework. The notion of equivalence for example has played a central role both in linguistic and poetic studies on this and related topics. Jakobson's famous 'theorem' defining poetic function of language as the projection of the similarity principle of the paradigmatic axis onto the syntagmatic axis of combination, is only one example of this central concept of many 'structuralist' studies (Jakobson [1960]).

Similar ideas have been propounded by such linguists as Levin (1962) and Koch (1966), (1970). They certainly described one aspect of the structure of (literary) texts, but the rules underlying textual grammaticalness in general were not made explicit. All types of phonological, morphematic, syntactic or lexematic correlation between elements and structures in a (literary) text must be defined, as we shall see later on, with respect to these more general and more basic rules and structures. Moreover, they do not form a necessary aspect either of poetic or of non-poetic texts, i.e. they are the product of optional formation and transformation rules (cf. van Dijk, 1971a).[12]

3.3.5. Similar remarks can be made about other linguistic attempts to describe texts or discourse. Pike (1967) rejects the atomistic methods of Harris' discourse analysis, and correctly notes that structures beyond the sentence have been left to literary study and stylistics (145ff.). Linguistics, he says, has to provide the basis for such textual descriptions, and tagmemics therefore also defines a level of discourse in which smaller structures like paragraphs and sentences can fill a slot (484). Unlike Harris, he does not want to reduce textual structure to a set of sentences but to consider it a structure *sui generis* (146). Stating that discourse is necessarily a part of the 'verbal non-verbal behavioreme', i.e. explicitly relating texts with the utterance event, context and situation, Pike denounces the narrow American tradition, from

---

[12] The strict morpho-syntactic point of view of Harris has been abandoned by Koch (1966), (1970) and others. They use the term 'semantic discourse analysis', which essentially proceeds by searching topic-comment relations in a text. Texts thus having identical 'themes' in their subsequent sentences are considered as 'discourse', others as 'non-discourse'. The use of the notion of 'recurrence' indicates, however, that only textual surface structures, i.e. complex relations between sentences, are studied, not deeper underlying macro-structures. Interesting points in this respect have been made by van Holk (1968) about the analogy between text and sentence structures. No explicit semantic theory is applied to describe the different semantic relations of textual surface structure. Equivalences, therefore, are merely intuitive, despite their rather 'formal' treatment. Similar remarks may be made about our attempt (van Dijk [1969]) to describe textual semantic structure (of a poem) by recurrence-patterns of semantic features underlying the actually realized lexematic structure of the successive sentences. Cf. also Sparck Jones (1967). For an analysis (of a discourse by Russell) from a generative syntactic point of view, cf. the recent article by Smith (1971).

Bloomfield to Chomsky, which limits grammar to the formal study of sentential structures. The structure of the sentence depends on higher level structures, he argues, but – besides referring to much relevant work in anthropology – he only states that sentences fill 'slots' in these structures. We will see later that, unlike sentential constituents, sentences do not function like that in texts; only in some exceptional cases can we consider them as substitutable elements.

Dik (1968a) 169ff, whose functional approach is relevant for the description of semantic deep structures (cf. chap. 3), thus has *ile* (for 'independent linguistic expression') as an initial symbol. He rejects the view which considers the sentence as the highest functional unit, but does not draw the grammatical consequence of this view.

Most interesting applications and adaptations of Pike's theory have, as we saw, actually been given in numerous analyses of popular narrative, not because precise linguistic categories were used or introduced, but because typically narrative units and functions were constructed in order to give an adequate description of recurrent patterns in (narrative) texts. We will discuss the relevant aspects of these approaches in our later chapters, and we have to limit ourselves at this moment to a brief survey of the ideas propagated on the 'main roads' of modern linguistics.[13]

3.3.6. Lamb's (1966) stratificational grammar in many ways does not seem to present more than terminological differences with respect to Harris and Pike, although the study of discourse is also explicitly advocated by him and practised, again on narrative, by some of his followers (cf. Taber, 1966). Formally his system does not part from or end in a formal unit comparable to the notion of text.

3.3.7. An important and rather independent view of textual structures is developed by Hartmann (1964), (1968), (1970a), (1970b), (1971) and some linguists inspired by his work. More than any other linguist, Hartmann has advocated systematically the extension of the scope of linguistics, not only as a more reliable basis of literary descriptions but also as an internal task of modern theory of language itself. In a series of articles he has tried to make explicit the methodological criteria, the analytic instruments, elements, relations and categories with which texts should be described. He sums up a certain number of formal conditions for the formation of texts, and the distinctive features for differentiating in types the existing or possible 'universe of texts'. Not only anaphorical processes, the role of suprasegmentals and the intonation of dialogical texts are considered by him, but also the semantic properties defining textual coherence. He recognizes that before we are able to define the rules

---

[13] For bibliographical reference, cf. Hendricks (1967), Dressler (1970a), Pickett (1960), Waterhouse (1963), Wheeler (1963). Here discourse is studied from the point of view of 'transition' between successive sentences. Powlison (1965) tries to leave the proper linguistic frame of morpho-syntactic categories and sets up a system of 'actions' and 'actors', similar to units postulated in structural analysis of narrative (cf. chaps 3 and 8). Cf. Schnitzer (1971) for a tagmemic analysis of a philosophical argument, commenting upon an analysis of Pike.

for deriving texts we must first identify level and structure of its possible analytic categories. Important in his discussion of the topic is the fact that he clearly distinguishes between linear and non-linear (hierarchical) procedures of analysis and between a micro- and a macro-structural level of description. His work has thus laid the basis for further research in this field of 'textual linguistics'.

Similar remarks can be made about the work of Schmidt (1969), (1970a), (1971a), (1971b) whose textual approach is basic in his description of meaning in linguistics, philosophy of language and literary theory. Like Hartmann, he assumes the 'text' is the fundamental macro-unit in which meaning has to be defined (1969) 75ff.

3.3.8. One important detail of the formal conditions underlying the combinations of sentences in a text, *viz.* pronominalization, has been described in close detail by Hartmann's follower Harweg (1968). His monograph, together with Palek's (1968), see below, was probably the first in which pronominalization, as an object of linguistic research, was studied in the perspective of a grammar of texts. Pronominalization, according to Harweg, is the main if not the only characteristic determining the formation of sequences of sentences in a text. As many structuralist linguists have done, he thus limits himself to 'formal', i.e. morpho-syntactic surface structure, as if semantic relations between sentences could not have a formal character. In this way Harweg arrives at the following definition of texts: "a succession of linguistic elements constituted by uninterrupted pronominal concatenation". Obviously this definition is insufficient for 'texts' as we understand them, both intuitively and formally, because any sequence of sentences having appropriate pronouns would thus be text. We will see in the next chapter that pronouns only are aspects of textual relations and a surface structure manifestation of underlying continuity of semantic categories (cf. also Baumann's critical remarks [1969] 12, Dressler [1970a] and Brinker [1971]).

Following Hjelmslev, Harweg considers the text as a syntagmatic construction of the paradigmatic language system. In this respect the text apparently does not differ from the sentence. Its theoretical status is however not wholly clear, because it is situated in a 'universe of texts' *(Textkosmos)* which only can be considered, in his conception, as part of performance.

In fact, we have to note here the same fundamental shortcomings as in many of the approaches mentioned: no definition, by means of explicit rules or general descriptive statements, is given of the text as an abstract, theoretical construct. Texts or discourse are seen as the transphrastic realization of the system, as a set (if closed: a corpus) of utterances defined by a certain number of superficial properties of recurrence, substitution and co-occurrence.

3.3.9. We must here make brief mention of another approach to text structure, this time often undertaken from a semantic point of view, although mostly limited to the immediate transition from sentence to sentence: the different hypotheses of Prague structuralists or 'functionalists' about the 'functional sentence perspective (FSP)'. Linguists like Daneš, Palek, Firbas are interested in the serial concatenation and alternation of this functional perspective in the successive sentences of a text. They operate with traditional terms like thema (topic) and rhema (comment).[14] We shall see in our next chapter that these problems are important as expressions of sentential deep structure constraints on textual grammaticalness.

Most explicit is undoubtedly the work of Palek (1968) who studies cross-reference as a means of anaphorical relations in texts, i.e. as an aspect of 'hyper-syntax'. Few studies have provided more details about the constraints determining the ordering of sentences in a coherent text. 'Underlying text structure', as he calls it, is defined as a complex matrix of relations of identity, difference, inclusion and membership. This underlying structure, in fact, is identical with the subsequent underlying structures of the surface sentences. Further Palek explicitly limits himself, like most others mentioned above, to 'syntactic' relations: no semantic foundation is provided for the proper definition of the relevant relations. These have apparently been 'found' intuitively. Nevertheless, he is right to present his 'hyper-syntax' as only one part of textual grammar and is thus led to reject the different approaches of the leading transformationalists to the concept of discourse (Palek [1968] 128ff). We will come back to the cross-referential constraints treated by him in the next chapter.

3.4. *Generative-transformational approaches to text structure*

3.4.1. One would expect the theory of generative-transformational grammar to bring the necessary corrections to the often methodologically inadequate or just incomplete approaches to the text we have briefly treated above. As we have seen before, however, nothing is less true: generative grammar, at least in its standard versions, is not only essentially a sentence grammar, but it shared the shortcomings of the different 'structuralist' descriptions by limiting itself originally to morpho-phonological structure and to syntactic deep and surface structures. Since semantic 'interpretation' is based on syntactic phrase markers no interpretation can theoretically be provided for structurally independent but serially ordered sentences. Anyway, no projection – or other combinatory rules – were provided for the syntactico-semantic description of ordered pairs, triples, ..., n-tuples of sentences. Recursive embedding or conjunction, as we noticed, is merely a global surface aspect of texts: neither the conditions for conjunction nor the macro-structural constraints can be described in a simple, systematic, and empirically adequate manner in the framework of S-grammars.

These limitations of traditional generative grammars seem to be conscious: attention had to be focussed first on the structure of the sentence before more powerful

---

[14] For detail cf. Vachek (1966), Daneš (1964), (1970a), Beneš (1968), Firbas (1964), Sgall (1967). For the notions of topic and comment cf. the next chapter.

(contextual) grammars could be elaborated. On the other hand, however, it now turns out that many structural aspects of sentences can not be described at all independently of larger structures. Being aware of this fundamental incompleteness of the sentential (con-)text-free approach, various linguists have attempted these last five years, to find the ways of extending the scope of the grammar. The work of these linguists and theorists of literature will be mentioned and integrated in the following chapters. One could say, roughly, that the attempts of most linguists are still rather restricted, because they focus principally on the morphological and syntactic relations between sentences in the framework of discussions about such themes as pronominalization, relativization, coordination, conjunction, suprasegmentals, topic and comment, focus, etc. We will argue that these 'micro-structural' or inter-(intra-)sentential descriptions of textual surface structure must be based on a description of the sufficient and necessary semantic relations between sentences in a text. Furthermore, these semantic relations can only be described within a still larger and much more abstract framework of deep structures of whole texts. The following two chapters will try to give a systematic, though of course very tentative, account of these two aspects of text grammars respectively.

3.4.2. Although it is not possible to be complete, let us finally briefly mention the most recent developments in text grammatical research. It is striking to see that the interest for text structures is still absent in current generative grammar. Even if occasional attempts are made, they do not seem to draw the consequences for the most adequate form of the grammar. Bever and Ross (1967) only contains some, though very relevant, remarks, whereas recent work on presuppositions (cf. e.g. Lakoff, 1971b) also seems to suggest the relevance of a 'contextual' approach to semantic descriptions. As will be shown in the next chapter, most work close to text grammar is done in the domain of pronominalization, sometimes using – though not explicating – terms like discourse (cf. especially the work of Karttunen [1968a], [1968b], [1969a], [1969b]).

The development of text grammars is mainly restricted to European linguistics at the moment. Explicit attention to texts has been paid e.g. by Heidolph (1966) and Isenberg (1968), (1970) in Berlin (D.D.R.) where also research about related topics, like coordination (Lang [1967], [1971] and his forthcoming dissertation) must be reported. In Germany there are several approaches to be noted. At the University of Constance a research group develops models for text grammars. Aims, tasks and provisional results of this group has been reported in Ihwe, Köck, Rieser, Rüttenauer (1971), and van Dijk, Ihwe, Petöfi, Rieser (1971), (1972). Cf. the introduction to the subject by Hartmann and Rieser (forthcoming) and Rieser (1971). Ihwe (1972a) provides a critical review of earlier work in generative text grammar, and proposes himself some suggestions for textual derivations. Petöfi (1969b), (1969c), (1970), (1971), (1972a), (1972b), has extensively been occupied with the development of text grammars, in particular from a generative semantic point of view. He also paid attention to global structures of texts, formalized in so-called 'thematic nets' organizing the lexical items of the sentences of texts in explicitly related groups. His recent book, the first published introduction to text grammar (Petöfi, 1971c) reviews some earlier attempts in this direction. Other research on text grammars is going on in other universities in Germany (e.g. Bielefeld, Stuttgart), of which we did not yet see the results, however.

In the East-European countries there is also attention for the development of text grammars, be it often linked to problems about automatic translation, lexicography and sentential bases rules. Cf. Žolkovskij and Mel'čuk (1970), Larin (1971) in the Soviet Union. From Poland we should extensively report the early work of Irena Bellert (e.g. Bellert [1970]) which considers textual coherence especially in terms of presupposition, pronominalization (using iota operators). Partially inspired by her work, we finally have to close this brief enumeration of names by mentioning the recent work by Kummer (1971a), (1971b), (1972a) who studied several aspects of texts (identification of referents, pragmatical components, the establishments of chains of reference, etc.) and who uses several models from modern logic (theory of reference, pragmatics, etc.), to which we will briefly refer in the next chapter.

2

TEXTUAL SURFACE STRUCTURES: RELATIONS BETWEEN SENTENCES

1. INTRODUCTION: METHODOLOGICAL PROCEDURES

1.1. It seems natural to begin the construction of a text grammar at the point where sentence grammars normally leave off, *viz.* with the relations between subsequent sentences in a discourse. This decision is heuristic rather than systematic. It does not reflect order, direction or priority of rules in a textual derivation process, but it indicates the field where the first systematic descriptions are needed but still lacking and where the first positive results can be expected at this moment. That is, current grammars in principle provide the tools for describing at least some aspects of those relations between subsequent sentences, notably in the framework of the study of compound, coordinate or subordinate, sentences.

It has become common use to let generative grammars operate upwards from bottom (base) to top, i.e. from deep structures to surface structures, whereas – equivalently – derivational trees normally specify structure from 'high' initial symbol to 'low' derived strings. As we indicated briefly in the previous chapter, we see no reason to change this use and derivations of texts will therefore begin with the formation of 'deep structures', followed by the representation of these structures at the level(s) of 'surface structures'. The different notions of deep and surface structures involved here will be defined in the next section.

It must be recalled, then, that the directionality of the rules in generative S- and T-grammars is neutral with respect to 'analysis' or 'synthesis', terms often used to represent perception-models and production-models of performance respectively. The form of the grammar neither needs support from or lends support to psycholinguistic hypotheses which say, e.g., that both production and reception (interpretation) have a synthetic character, i.e. that the linearly perceived string is matched by a hypothetical process of reconstruction (cf. Neisser [1967]). We will further neglect the psycholinguistic reality of text grammars and the possible organization of competence and will briefly return to this problem in our last chapter.

There is no objection, therefore, to our beginning our observations at a level which comes last in textual derivation. We thus work 'down' to the rules and conditions of 'deeper' levels needed to explain or establish regularities at 'higher' levels. Our strategy does not imply, for example, the empiricist illusion that deep structure regularities or hypothetical rules may be 'discovered' simply by observing, systematizing and inductively generalizing surface structures of 'observable' utterances. Nothing is less true for our method, because at any point we will try to describe linguistic facts by hypothetico-deductive reasoning, i.e. by constructing underlying rules or conditions having a general character. We only prefer to begin at a level which is familiar to most linguists and try to resolve or to formulate progressively the problems encountered in this process of 'extending' an existing grammar by postulating more abstract and global regularities unknown, as such, in current linguistics.

1.2. The decision to start our observations on structures 'beyond the sentence' seems to imply that the description of the sentence is supposed to be 'given'. Although nothing is less true at the moment, this will indeed be our procedure, which in fact means that we leave typical intra-sentential problems of grammar as an indispensable permanent task for current linguistics. This rather bold procedure is not free of certain risks and motivated criticism. It may be argued, for example, that the establishment of relations between sentences requires preliminary knowledge of sentence structures proper and that any reference to structures of a larger scope is at least premature as long as this insight is only fragmentary. On the other hand, many of the problems of generative sentence description pertain to questions for which a satisfactory solution, in our view, can only be awaited in this broader framework. Historical analogies can in this respect be drawn between this step towards text grammars and the introduction of a semantic theory into an originally wholly syntactic grammar. That is, certain structures can only be described in a satisfactory way when others are described first.

Moreover, most of the actual problems of generative grammar are to be searched for at the level of semantics, and it is precisely here that the extension of the scope of the grammar has become necessary. We may even assume that the semantic description of sentence structure can be 'complete' only in so far as this sentence coincides with a text. Many aspects of the meaning structure of isolated sentences, like presupposition, entailment, conditions for lexical insertion, etc. are directly dependent on semantic inter-sentence relations in a coherent text.

If this assumption is correct, we still are confronted with the task of specifying which S-grammar is presupposed at this surface level of text structures. Decision on this point is difficult if not impossible at this moment. We will, however, provisionally adopt the model which is known as 'generative semantics'[1] because it postulates a

---

[1] For useful surveys of the different tenets of generative semantics, cf. Abraham and Binnick (1969), Fillmore (1969a), Lakoff (1971a) and the volumes edited by Kiefer (1969), Binnick, *et al.* (1969), Bach and Harms (1968) Wunderlich (1971), Steinberg and Jakobovits (1971), Fillmore and Langendoen (1971). A bibliography is provided by Krenn and Müllner (1970). One of the most consequent applications of generative semantics has been Rohrer (1971). For our discussion the semantic, and in general grammatical, ideas of Fillmore (1968), (1969a), (1969b) have been useful, as well as their

semantic base, although it is not yet fully clear what, in this model, semantic representations would look like, and how they are to be related with syntactic surface structures. We might say that much work in generative semantics is not semantic enough, and we will, therefore, add some suggestions borrowed from abstract case grammar.

We will thus narrow the scope of our possible sentence-models to 'generative semantics' including a modified syntactic standard model (Chomsky [1965]) for the representation of sentential surface structures, and should decide now which of the available 'semantic' approaches will be used. However, there is no proposal which in the actual state of semantics could pretend to be the 'best one'. In fact, they all are elaborating on different aspects of the semantic theory, sharing a rather uncertain but common core, with which can be associated the names of Weinreich, Rohrer, Postal, McCawley, Gruber, Lakoff, and partially those of Fillmore, Ross, Bierwisch, and others. Formalization, by most of them, is searched for in a specific adaptaton of (modal) predicate logic or 'natural logic' (Lakoff [1970b]) having a relational character. In this respect we will globally assume Fillmore's proposal as most propitious for further adaptation in our textual framework. Any proposal too closely relating semantic structures with syntactic (surface) structures is insufficient, we think, to describe abstract textual (macro-)structures. In our description of the relations between sentences, as will be clear, aspects of different theories will be traceable.

1.3. As we stated, there is no common agreement about the exact form of the semantically based grammars. Initially they kept rather close to rules and categories used for the derivation of syntactic deep structures. Thus McCawley (1968a), (1968b), following Weinreich (1966) simply interprets the syntactic category symbols as 'semantic'.

Base rules in such a generative conception specify well-formed semantic representations which are often identified with sentential deep structure. A series of syntactic transformation rules will represent these structures at the surface level. Lexematization, as opposed to the standard model and to interpretative semantics, can occur after some transformations have applied on prelexical configurations, which we will call LEXICOIDS. Lexicalized syntactic surface structures are finally represented at the morpho-phonological level according to the standard model (for some detail, cf. chapters 3 and 7).

Notice that the semantic formation rules first specify well-formed structures, that is they have a 'syntactic' character in the formal (semiotic) sense of that term (cf.

---

application or modification by Drubig (1967), Dahl (1969) and Petöfi (1969a), (1971). The first applications in poetics have been made by Ihwe (1972a), van Dijk (1970a), (1970b), (1971a), (1971b) and Petöfi (1970), (1971), (1972a), (1972b). For text grammars, cf. Bever and Ross (1967), Dressler (1970b), Bellert (1969), (1970), (1971), (forthcoming) and the work of Petöfi mentioned above. Further see especially Kummer (1971a), (1971b), (1972a), (1972b). For criticism of generative semantics, cf. Chomsky (1970), (1971), Katz (1970), Dougherty (1970b) among others.

chapter 9). They generate sequences of formal symbols which only in a later stage are assigned lexico-semantic 'content' in the form of feature matrices or lexicoids.

These deep structures can be described formally by means of formation rules from predicate logic (cf. Rohrer [1971]) and essentially consist of

– a nuclear proposition, structured as an *n*-place predicate and *n* arguments and having a 'specification' in terms of (pre-) lexical content of the variables of the abstract propositional formula.
– a modal part specifying aspects of the (nuclear) proposition as a whole like performative (pragmatic) elements, including
  (i)   speaker/hearer representation and time and place operators for the utterance,
  (ii) modal elements like Negation, Possibility and Probability,
  (iii) typological elements like Assertion, Question, Imperative, and finally
  (iv) quantifiers to bind the variables of the propositional structure.

We will specify this model in the next chapter because our hypothesis will be that this abstract structure does characterize not only sentential deep structure, but also textual deep structure. Argument-variables can be interpreted as functional elements, called actants (Tesnière [1959], Greimas [1966]). Predicate variables are interpreted as properties and relations: states, actions, events. At the level of deep structure syntax these actants can be compared to 'cases' (Fillmore [1968]), consisting of Preposition + Noun, *viz.* agentive, patient, objective, instrument, dative (benefactive). Details of these categories will be given below.

1.4. The global program of this chapter will be as follows:

We will first elucidate some important terminological problems of our theoretical language, because terms like 'sentence' are becoming more and more ambiguous, especially at different levels and in a larger scope of description.

We will then briefly treat different syntactic relations between sentences and their possible morpho-phonological implications. We will not repeat or try to elaborate work already done in this domain, but only point to relevant facts which seem to have been neglected.

We will then try to show that both syntactic and morphophonological properties of inter-sentential relations can, at least partially, be predicted from the structure of and relations between semantic representations of successive sentences.

Finally we hope to show that even this linear and superficial semantic description is incomplete without a hypothesis about underlying semantic (macro-)structures, i.e. about textual deep structure.

2. TERMINOLOGICAL ISSUES

2.1. This chapter aims at the description of some relevant properties of TEXTUAL SURFACE STRUCTURE(S). This last, complex, term needs some further specification since it is not wholly without ambiguity.

It could mean, first, those linguistic structures which are produced by the last sequence of transformations of a textual derivation. In that case they are roughly equivalent to traditional surface-structure as defined by generative S-grammars, that is they are formed of the surface-structures of the subsequent derived sentences S_1, S_2, ... S_n, plus the relevant surface relations between them, like for example serial concatenation.

A second, and less familiar, interpretation of this term would be: all sentential structures, both superficial and deep, i.e. morpho-syntactic and semantic, produced by 'intermediate' textual (trans-)formation rules operating the mapping of macro-structures onto micro-structures. This is the meaning we will normally use in our discussion, reserving the (included) concept of SENTENTIAL SURFACE STRUCTURE for the properly morpho-syntactic manifestation of this textual surface structure or micro-structure.

Strictly speaking, we here deviate from the traditional well-defined distinction between deep and surface structure as they are separated by a set of transformations (Chomsky [1965], [1970]). It might be the case, for example, that the formal means for representing (mapping) textual macro-structures at the sentential level does not necessarily require transformations (cf. chapter 3). Nevertheless, we will adopt the hypothesis that these rules are transformations of some kind, leaving it to further research to determine their precise theoretical status. For example, such transformations are only in a very special sense 'meaning-preserving'.

A third interpretation of the notion textual surface structure would, therefore, be the output of the (macro-)transformation rules operating directly on underlying semantic (macro-)structures. However, we will call this output TRANSFORMED MACRO-STRUCTURE, also because we do not know yet the nature of such macro-transformations.

Textual surface structure, then, will mean in this book: the structure of the sequence of sentences, *viz.* both sentential surface structures (morpho-phonological and syntactic structures) and sentential deep structures (semantic representations).

2.2. There is another theoretical notion which we would like to introduce here, and which pertains particularly to the phenomena treated in this chapter. It has become clear from our introductory remarks in the previous chapter that the notion SENTENCE is at least ambiguous. It has been used, just as in traditional grammar, to denote a 'complete', simple, complex or compound surface structure. Further it was also used to denote any S-dominated subtree of a sentential phrase marker, whether or not realized as a 'clause' in surface structure. We will conserve the traditional term 'sentence' to denote a surface structure as it is preceded and followed by sentential

BOUNDARY MARKERS. We will, however, use the term SENTOID for the abstract under-lying S-dominated (sub-)trees of a derivation. Thus, a sequence of such sentoids may be transformed either into a complex (or compound) sentence or into a sequence of structurally distinct sentences. When no ambiguity is possible we will sometimes use, instead of sentoid, the traditional term EMBEDDED SENTENCE (for a different use of the term 'sentoid', cf. Katz and Postal [1964], Staal [1967]).

Following other proposals (e.g. Petöfi, 1971) we will further use the term CO-TEXT to denote the sets of all sentences following and preceding a given sentence in a text, instead of the traditional but ambiguous term '(verbal) context', which is often used for co-text as defined above, but also for texts (or rather discourses) preceding or following (or overlapping) a given discourse. We will reserve the term CONTEXT for the set of all relevant factors of the communication process (or speech act) which are not properties of the text/discourse itself. In this respect our term 'context' corresponds to the traditional term 'non-verbal context'. The notion context will be made explicit in chapter 9. We will sometimes use simply the adjective 'textual' instead of 'co-textual' when we speak about the sequential relations of a given sentence in a text.

Finally, we have to stress again that the term 'sentence' is used only to denote a surface constituent of a text, *viz.* an element of a sequence. Such a sequence may consist of only one sentence, but the sentence then coincides with the theoretical notion of text. Only texts may underlie discourses, and only texts may be used to denote, to refer, etc. in processes of communication. Therefore, when we use such expressions as 'an uttered sentence' or 'the use of a sentence' or 'sentences in context', we always mean thereby texts consisting of one sentence. This distinction is crucial for an adequate text grammar, not only for grammatical reasons proper, but also for a correct description of the relations between texts/discourses and their pragmatical and referential functions in communication.

3. RELATIONS BETWEEN SENTENCES

One of the basic properties of natural language is not only the possibility of constructing complex sentences by recursive embedding or coordinating other sentences (sentoids), but also the possibility of producing sequences of syntactically independent sentences possessing certain RELATIONS between each other. We can have:

(1)   Mary lies in a hospital.
(2)   Mary was badly wounded in a car-crash yesterday.

and combine these two sentences into a sequence, i.e. into an ordered pair conceived as a coherent whole:

(3)   Mary lies in a hospital. Mary was badly wounded in a car-crash yesterday.

In this case we could also have produced:

(4)   Mary was badly wounded in a car-crash yesterday. Mary lies in a hospital.

At first sight the order of the two sentences does not seem to alter the meaning of the whole sequence very much. Closer analysis however will reveal important differences to which we will return below.

From the examples given we might conclude that we can freely combine two grammatical sentences into a sequence of sentences having the same intuitive grammaticalness (cf. Jacobs and Rosenbaum [1968]). Compare, however, the combination of the following grammatical sentences:

(5)   We will have guests for lunch.
(6)   Calderón was a great Spanish writer.

of which the sequence (7)

(7)   *We will have guests for lunch. Calderón was a great Spanish writer.

is definitely ungrammatical (unless it is used and interpreted as an enumeration of sentences). That is, any native speaker of English will consider this sequence, when presented in one utterance, as non-sense. This, of course, does not prevent the assignment of semantic representations to the individual sentences, but it is impossible to establish any semantic relation between them, that is, one can not assign a semantic representation to the sequence as a whole. The reverse order of the sentences does not alter this fact.

Typical of this sort of combination is the fact that we cannot thereby form complex sentences as we can do in (3) and (4) by using connectors as *because* and *now* or *therefore*, respectively. In this case the conditions for the combination of two sentences in a sequence seem to be parallel with those for combining 'sentences' (sentoids) in a complex sentence (we neglect here such further necessary conditions as pronominalization, etc., which will be treated below). Now consider two sentences like (8) and (9)

(8)   Yesterday John bought a car.
(9)   The car is very expensive.

These sentences can easily be combined into a grammatical sequence, but the difference with (1)–(4) is that sentence (8) has to precede sentence (9), because a combination like (10) does not seem to be grammatical:

(10)   *The car is very expensive. Yesterday John bought a car.

Coordinate or subordinate conjunctions of these sentences produce, as we noticed, grammatical complex (compound) sentences

(11)   Yesterday John bought a car, $\begin{Bmatrix} \text{but} \\ \text{and} \end{Bmatrix}$ it was very expensive.

(12)   The car John bought yesterday was very expensive.
(13)   Yesterday John bought a car that was very expensive.
(14)   Yesterday John bought a very expensive car.
             etc.

From these few examples one may conclude the following:

(i)   Some pairs of sentences may be freely combined into a grammatical sequence, or text.
(ii) Other pairs of sentences can be combined, but only in a fixed order.
(iii) There are pairs of sentences which cannot be combined into a grammatical sequence.
(iv) At least some conditions for the combination of sentences in a sequence are similar to those for combining sentences (sentoids) in a complex sentence.

We will require of any adequate grammar to predict which combinations (pairs, triples, ..., *n*-tuples) of sentences are grammatical and which are less grammatical or fully ungrammatical (cf. Heidolph [1966]). Such a grammar must further specify which sequences of sentences (sentoids) may be paraphrased as complex or compound sentences (and conversely) and which surface characteristics distinguish such semantically equivalent paraphrases. For the conditions for grammatical combinations of (embedded) sentences which have already been provided by current generative grammar, we may refer to the work done in this sentential framework (cf. e.g. the contributions in Reibel and Schane [1969]).

4. SURFACE RELATIONS BETWEEN SENTENCES

4.1. *Introduction*

The systematic study of the rules and conditions determining the grammatical combination of pairs, triples, ..., *n*-tuples of sentences in a coherent sequence will proceed at two main levels of textual surface structure, *viz.* at the level of sentential surface structure (morpho-phonology and syntax) and at the level of sentential deep structure (semantic representation). We will focus our attention first on the former level of sentential structure and consider in particular those categories the formal description of which is most directly dependent on inter-sentential relations: (in)definiteness of nouns (noun phrases) – and their articles –, pronouns, relative clauses, tense, sentential adverbs and conjunctions.

It will appear in the discussion that an adequate description of such categories will need a rather abstract characterization, e.g. in terms of underlying semantic categories and structures, which in part may be represented by formula borrowed from standard predicate logic. Since we are interested above all in inter-sentential relations, we will neglect in the following sections a precise transformational account of the resulting sentential surface structures as they are described in the standard model for morpho-phonological and syntactic descriptions.

4.2. *Noun phrases and (in)definite descriptions*

4.2.1. Let us consider first noun phrases and their structures: articles, nouns, relative clauses, etc. In the perspective of our discussion we are particularly interested in the conditions which make noun phrases definite, thus resulting in the formation of definite articles. We will see that here we touch directly upon one of the crucial aspects of linear coherence relations in texts: the process of definitivization cannot be studied within isolated sentences. Nor is it possible to account for it at the syntactic level alone, as we will try to show. It will be demonstrated, that an adequate description is necessary at the abstract level of semantic representations. Finally, we will need an insight into the well-known logical problem of definite descriptions.

4.2.2. The traditional description of the article is based on the feature specification of its head noun. Under domination of a pronominal category *DET* we derive definite articles when the noun is specified $[+ DEF]$ and indefinite articles when the noun has as a feature $[- DEF]$. Further specification comes, language specifically, from features like $[\pm SINGULAR]$, $[\pm PLURAL]$, $[\pm MASC]$, $[\pm NEUTER]$ and at the boundary of syntax and semantics from such features like $[\pm COUNT]$. We will not go into the precise forms of the article selection process based on these last sets of features.[2]

Generative syntax will normally leave unspecified the conditions under which only $[+ DEF]$ or $[- DEF]$ are generated in underlying structures. This is natural, in most cases, when we restrict ourselves to isolated sentences. However, as soon as we have to describe coherent sequences of sentences there are strict limitations upon their derivation. A T-grammar accounting for these specific constraints thus limits the class

---

[2] The transformational literature on articles and article selection is not very extensive, which may partially be explained by the intrinsic limitations of sentential grammars in dealing with these topics. For current description cf. Chomsky (1965) 107, Robbins (1968), Leroy Baker (1966), Smith (1969), based on syntactic feature specification. Of course the subject is implicitly based on the treatment of noun phrases in the grammar, for which we may refer to Chomsky (1965) Chap. 2, § 2, Smith (1969), Kaneko (1971), Bach (1968), Jacobs & Rosenbaum (1968) Chap. 7. We will refer below to work done at the boundary of grammar and logic, studying the properties of definite/indefinite, particular/general, etc. nouns or 'names'.

of well-formed sentences (in a text), and further has the methodological advantage, repeatedly stressed by Chomsky in the last few years (e.g. Chomsky [1970]), of providing a restriction upon the class of possible grammars of a language.

4.2.3. Consider, for example, the following text

(15)   (i)   Yesterday John bought a book.
          (ii) $\left\{ \begin{array}{c} \text{The} \\ \text{*A} \end{array} \right\}$ book is about theoretical syntax.

In the second sentence of this text *book* is necessarily definite, provided that it DENOTES THE SAME REFERENT as *book* in the first sentence. Note that this last condition is identical with the well-known condition determining pronominalization, which also distinguishes between definites and indefinites (in this section we will ignore possible pronominalization of nouns or noun phrases).

However, 'having identical reference' is not a syntactic condition, and therefore cannot properly be part of a syntactic deep structure description of a sequence. To describe the well-formedness of (15) we therefore either have to introduce other syntactic categories or look for relevant conditions at other levels of description.

Since the second occurrence of *book* is a token of the same lexeme-type *book* in the first sentence, we might think of a condition based on identical nouns. Such an *Equi-N* hypothesis leads to many correct predictions in pairs of immediately subsequent sentences. However, there are many cases where this condition is either too weak or too strong. Consider for example the following texts

(16)   (i)   Yesterday John bought a book.
          (ii) I also bought $\left\{ \begin{array}{c} \text{a} \\ \text{*the} \end{array} \right\}$ book yesterday.
(17)   (i)   John didn't buy a book yesterday.
          (ii) *He gave the book to his sister.
(18)   (i)   Peter is looking for a secretary to type his novels.
          (ii) *The secretary seems to be very pretty.
(19)   (i)   Peter met a pretty secretary in New York.
          (ii) The girl immediately fell in love with him.

The *Equi-N* condition does not hold in either of these sequences. That is, although there are two tokens of the lexeme *book* in (16,i) and (16,ii) we may not have a definite *NP book* in (16,ii), although indefinite *a book* is possible, provided it refers to another book. The identity-difference at the level of denoted individuals seems relevant again here. Clearly, then, the condition is too strong in this case. In (19), however, we may have a definite *NP the girl* in the second sentence (*a girl* is ungrammatical here), although this lexeme does not occur in the previous sentence. We know, however, that *pretty secretary* and *girl* denote the same individual, though the two lexemes are different. Here the condition, apparently, is too weak, and again 'identity of reference' seems to be the relevant condition, although this condition is still intuitive, and falls outside our syntax.

Finally, in both (17) and (18) the repeated lexeme does not produce a grammatical combination of the two sentences. Notice that when we consider the identical lexemes as referring to identical individuals, the two texts are ungrammatical. Obviously, neither *Equi-N* nor simple identity of reference is a sufficient condition here. That is, neither the lexico-syntactic nor the referential (extensional semantic) level of description is sufficient for an adequate account of grammatical 'continuation' in texts: we may have definite noun phrases without identical nouns (or noun phrases) preceding them, and conversely. 'Previous mention', thus, is too weak a condition.

4.2.4. This provisional conclusion excludes several procedures for enriching syntactic deep structures by different specific features, such as $[\pm\ m]$ for (non-)mentioned, $[\pm\ k]$ for (un-)known, or by referential indices attached to the relevant lexemes.[3]

Indeed, referential indices may be used to identify nouns or noun-phrases in further transformations, e.g. in pronominalization. These abstract numerical features however somehow represent at the syntactic level the identity and difference of individuals at the extensional (denotative) level. Their assignment therefore is problematic and their status doubtful.

Moreover, even if we assign identical indices to the identical lexemes in texts (17) and (18) we get false predictions: neither definitivization nor the whole following sentence is grammatical in that case. We must clearly look for more complex conditions. Note, for example, that (18) is perfectly grammatical as soon as we replace *seems to* by *has to*. A similar change can make (17) regular. This fact suggests that not only isolated (identical) lexemes or isolated referential individuals are relevant, but also other parts of the semantic (or referential) structures of which they form a part. Let us consider these conditions in some detail.

4.2.5. The processes involved here have been studied especially by Karttunen (1968a), (1968b), (1969a), (1969b) and Kummer (1971a), (1971b), (1972a) within linguistics and have further received attention in logical theory. Karttunen noticed that a discourse is characterized by DISCOURSE REFERENTS, and that heavy constraints restrict their introduction. If a noun (noun-phrase) applies to a discourse referent it may regularly be made definite in the sentences which follow. Its initial introduction however, if no specific pragmatic conditions are fulfilled (see below) is indefinite. In general, the introduction of a discourse referent is based primarily on 'identical

---

[3] Such syntactic features for identification have been discussed, among others, by Isenberg (1968), Kummer (1971a), Sampson (1969), Karttunen (1968a), and have been briefly introduced by Chomsky (1965) 145. Recent approaches mostly use different types of quantifiers, and base themselves on semantic and/or logical description (see below).

reference'. To explain cases like (17) and (18) however, we have to assume that negation, counterfactuals or intentionals may block the introduction of a discourse referent. In these cases the denoted individuals are either non-existent or non-actual, which is a requirement for further predication in subsequent sentences. This (semantic) constraint does not apply when the subsequent sentences are in the same counter-factual or intentional 'mode', as happens when we replace *seems to* by *has to* in (18). Here we touch upon an interesting feature of textual coherence: the establishment of discourse referents, and their ensuing definitivization (and possible pronominalization) is not only based on identical referents but also on 'existence' at the same modal level, that is within the same 'semantic world'. Semantic representations falling under the scope of specific categories, like negation, or predicates like *to wish*, *to hope*, *to look for*, *to imagine*, *to dream*, *to think*, etc. thus admit discourse referents within this textual scope. This difference in semantic representations can also be concluded from the inconsistency of implications of preceding sentences with presuppositions of following sentences. The first sentence of (18) implies *Peter does not (yet) have (such) a secretary*, which leaves the existence of (such a) secretary undecided. This contradicts her presupposed existence *(there is such a secretary)* in (18,ii).

In fact, it is not merely a question of 'existence', however. The book John didn't buy in (17) may well exist, but further predication is nevertheless impossible. We therefore have to require, as in (18), a type of 'specified existence', *viz.* a type of 'presence' in the referential domain denoted by the semantic representation of the two sentences. This 'presence' may, for example, have the feature of 'possession', as it is presupposed in (17,ii). If this presence or possession is not presupposed we may regularly introduce a discourse referent under the scope of negation or counterfactuals

(20)   (i)   The student could not buy a book on generative syntax.
           (ii) The book was too expensive for him.

4.2.6. The tentative conditions for definitivization may now be formulated as follows

(21)   A noun phrase in a sentence S_i of a given sequence is assigned $[+ DEF]$
           if it represents a semantic structure having identical reference, within an
           identical modal domain, with a semantic structure of a noun phrase in a
           preceding sentence S_{i-j} $(j < i)$.

We observe that the condition had to be formulated in terms of underlying semantic and referential structures; a purely syntactic formulation leads to false predictions. It is not clear, however, what the precise grammatical status of the expression 'identical reference' might be.

4.2.7. There are some apparent counter-examples to the conditions as formulated in (21). Firstly, we may have initial sentences, with no pragmatic conditions, apparently introducing discourse referents as definites and not as indefinites

(22)   Peter has at last found the secretary he has looked for for years.

In this text the definite description given by the embedded sentoid properly identifies a unique individual. This relative clause follows the noun phrase in surface structure. However, we will argue below that such definite descriptions, i.e. those represented by restrictive relative clauses, are transformationally derived from preceding sentoids. This means that (22) is derived from the structure underlying (23)

(23)   (i) Peter has looked for a secretary for years.
         (ii) Peter has at last found the secretary.

In this underlying structure the constraints normally apply, that is *secretary* in (23,ii) is regularly definite. Notice that this is not the case for (24)

(24)   Peter has found a secretary who is willing to type his novels.

which is derived from the structure underlying (25)

(25)   (i) Peter has found a secretary.
         (ii) The secretary is willing to type his novels.

Obviously relative clauses specifying indefinite *NP*'s are derived from sentoids following the matrix-sentoid in deep structure. We will come back to this feature of complex sentences below.

4.2.8. There is a large set of other apparent counter-examples. Take the following texts

(26)   (i) John always has troubles with his car.
         (ii) Today the motor broke down again.
(27)   When we arrived at John's house, he was just coming out of the front door.

From these examples we may conclude that not only semantic or referential identity identifies discourse referents but also inclusion or membership relations, provided these are unique. In these cases, the relevant relations are stated in the meaning postulates of the lexicon, which serve as presuppositions establishing necessary coherence

(28)   For each x: if x is a car, then x has a (one) motor.
(29)   For each x: if x is a house, then x has a (one) front door.

These meaning postulates are implied by the sentences introducing *car* and *house* respectively, such that *motor* and *front door* can be definite in following sentences. It is not easy to decide whether such postulates are part of our knowledge of the world, that is of the encyclopedia, and whether it is possible to make a distinction between semantic and referential implications. In any case, both somehow determine definitivization.

Besides a THEORY OF REFERENCE we will also need a PRAGMATICAL THEORY for the description of definitivization. Although discourse referents may be introduced in texts only by indefinite noun-phrases, there are many pragmatic conditions permitting the direct introduction of definite noun phrases. The general rule determining these pragmatic conditions is the following

(30)   Speaker of the utterance assumes that hearer of the utterance knows which object is referred to by the terms of the utterance.

This rule is valid for all individuals which are generally known as being unique, and represented simply by their lexical names or by definite descriptions: *the queen of Holland, the moon, the highway from New York to Washington D.C.*, etc.

As we shall see in chapter 9 the pragmatic structures include time and place categories, indicating the loco-temporal axes of the speech act. *The queen of Holland* thus implies the 'actual' queen.

Finally, general knowledge of unique individuals also applies to generic class names, *the workers, the students, the cat*, referring to a unique class of individuals.

4.2.9. We will not go further into these well-known pragmatic and referential aspects of definitivization. We have to try to find some formal representation for the intuitively formulated condition for grammatical definitivization in texts, that is, for a correct prediction of the identical referentiality of terms in a sentence S_i when $S_1, S_2, \ldots S_{i-1}$ are given.

Both semantically (referentially) and pragmatically the condition hinges on the identification or particularization of a UNIQUE INDIVIDUAL (or unique class of individuals). Modern logic has paid extensive attention to this problem of the definite description of unique individuals.[4] Instead of predicating over all or some individuals

---

[4] Increasing attention is being paid in modern logic to the problems related to (in)definite descriptions. Of course this work cannot be analyzed here and we will retain above all the studies relating the problem to grammars of natural language. One of the first to apply the traditional theory (of Russell and Whitehead's *Principia Mathematica*) to linguistic analysis was probably Reichenbach (1947) § 47. Further see especially Quine (1953), (1960) and Carnap (1958). The issue also receives much interest in the different modern systems of (modal) logic. Cf. Hintikka (1970a), (1970b), Donellan (1970), Rescher (1968) Chap. IX and the different contributions in Linsky, ed. (1971). Within linguistics proper definite descriptions are discussed by Lakoff (1970b) and Rohrer (1971). Relations with the grammar of texts have been established first by Bellert (1970) and Kummer (1971a), (1971b), (1972a). As we shall see below the problem of 'referential identity' is also crucial in matters

we may want to predicate over one individual in particular, that is, our quantification has to range over one thing.

To represent this uniqueness of an argument we might use an IOTA-OPERATOR ($\imath$), within a definite description. This operator can be defined with an existential operator, for example in the following way[5]:

$$(31) \qquad g\left[(\imath x)f(x)\right] = \mathrm{def}\ (\exists x)\ \{(y)\ [f(y) \equiv (x=y)] \wedge g(x)\}$$

The equivalence expressed here for the universally quantified variable y is the 'uniqueness condition' of the definition; it specifies that no other individual can have the property f without being identical with x. Thus an iota-operator as part of a predicate logical notation of underlying semantic structures of the sentences (sentoids) of a sequence, specifies which individual is selected for further specification. To represent text (15) we would have for example:

$$(32) \qquad \text{(i)}\quad (\exists x)\ [b(x) \wedge c(z_1, x)]$$
$$\text{(ii)}\quad s\ \{(\imath x)\ [b(x) \wedge c(z_1, x)]\}$$

of which (32,ii) may be paraphrased as follows: the one and only individual object which is a book (b) and which John (z_1) bought yesterday (c) – tense and adverbial analysis is neglected here – has the property 'to be about theoretical syntax' (s). In fact, (32,ii) thus provides a formalization of the complex sentence *The book John bought yesterday is about theoretical syntax*, containing a definite description as an *NP*. From (32) we can see, however, that the proposed description is redundant: we might

---

of pronominalization. For precise definitions of the different operators involved here we refer to the logical literature cited above.

Cf. also Vendler (1967) 33–69 who at some points in his treatment of 'singular terms' takes implicitly a textual point of view, by deriving definite articles from previous sentences in a discourse.

Note finally that referential identity is a condition which is formally dependent on temporal (pragmatic) aspects. Thus Prior (1957) Chap. 8 distinguishes between a 'weak' and a 'strong' definite article: *The president of the United States* may be a description for the actual president (a particular individual) or the president as a function (role) of a class of individuals. In fact this distinction may also apply to a particular individual when it changes in a way such that in some interpretation (world) it is no longer the 'same'.

I am indebted to Willem R. de Jong for suggestions, criticism and discussion related to the possible logical notations for representing (in-)definite descriptions in this section.

[5] There are several ways to represent formally definite descriptions. The formula as given in (31) is the 'contextual' definition borrowed from Russell and Whitehead (1962) 173 – who use a different, more complex, notation, however – and rather generally adopted by most logicians. Cf. however the discussion by Carnap (1957) 32ff. who discusses also the proposals of Hilbert/Bernays and Frege. (Cf. further Rescher [1968] 148ff. who introduces an implication to state the uniqueness). As Carnap rightly states, the problem lies in the possibility that none or several individuals satisfy the description. We will turn to the linguistic implications of this problem below.

Note that in this section we have simplified the logical problems pertaining to definite descriptions, because only their linguistically relevant aspects are considered here.

As a convention we will denote proper names by indexed variables (not by constants).

want to predicate something of the same individual as identified by the description of the previous formula, without in fact repeating the whole description. We could then write something like

(33) $(\exists\, x) \{[b\,(x) \wedge c\,(z_1, x)] \wedge s\,[(\imath y)\,(y = x) \wedge b\,(y)]\}$

which in fact is not much less redundant, but which shows – the linguistically relevant fact – that the individuals in the subsequent sentoids/sentences are identical and de-scribed both as *books* (we might have a different lexeme in the subsequent sentence to denote the same individual). This formula would represent the semantic structure of text (15). Note that the conjunction permits a permutation of the terms: for some x: there is some y which is identical with x and which is about theoretical syntax, and x is a book and John bought x yesterday.

Nevertheless, there are many problems with such a notation. In order to represent (19), for example, we may not use a simple logical conjunction, since, (19,ii) neces-sarily follows (19,i), because, normally, for some x to fall in love with y, presupposes x having met y. This ORDER of the propositions can be established by time operators or by time arguments together with event variables (cf. section 4.5 below and chapter 3 for details). Semantic conjunction in texts of natural language, apparently, is often a non-commutative relation. Formula (33) is not correct for another reason. The existential quantifier merely specifies that the property holds for AT LEAST ONE individual, not for ONE individual. We therefore may use an ÈTA-OPERATOR (η) for indefinite description, identifying a particular but unspecified individual (cf. Reichenbach [1947] 264ff.)

(34) $s\,\{(\eta\, x)\,[b\,(x) \wedge c\,(z_1, x)]\}$

This operator corresponds with the indefinite article and is required for each intro-duction of an individual into a text, whereas the existential operator generates an indefinite article but with feature 'non-particular', which may be represented also by *some* in English.

4.2.10. However, description in natural language is not as simply represented as would suggest the use of iota- and èta-operators. Let us briefly consider some specific problems related with definite and indefinite descriptions here which did not become wholly clear above. These issues have not yet received full discussion in linguistics and logical theory so that we cannot here overlook their full complications in textual grammar although they are very important for the establishment of linear coherence in text.

The problem at issue is the following: it has often been noticed, also in classical grammar, that indefinite articles/noun phrases are of two different TYPES. Bierwisch (1971) rightly observed that the traditional concept 'indefinite description' used in logical theory, and symbolized by an èta-operator, is misleading because the individual referred to by a sentence like *A man is waiting for you* is not 'indefinite', because the speaker uttering this sentence may well have identified the man as a particular individual. The very fact that he may continue his discourse with *The man...* or *He...* underlines this identification. The rule, apparently, is the one given earlier, *viz.* the use of indefinite articles/noun phrases in 'initial situations' (of texts or contexts) when 'picking out', 'specifying', a certain individual for further comment/predication. In such cases, thus, the speaker may pragmatically know the individual (or class) referred to, and may either judge further predication irrelevant, as in *Peter gave a present to his wife*, or may, once the individual in the text is identified, further specify it. We may assign to this case of 'indefiniteness' the two features [− specified] and [+ particular].

There is another possibility, however, for using indefinite descriptions. This time the unspecified individual is not referentially identified as a particular, hence the noun-phrase would have the feature [− particular]. In sentences like *A man cried at me from the audience*, the individual is not necessarily identified, which may be expressed by the subsequent grammatical clause: *but I didn't see which man it was*. Similarly, we may have indefinites in many cases where we have a non-actual mode, e.g. in 'possible', 'intended', 'searched for', etc. individuals like in text (18) and in sentences like *Sally would surely fall in love with a man who would be able to teach her Swahili*. In this case the individual is properly 'unidentified' and 'non-particular'. This may easily be seen by the possible substitution of *a* by *any*, and the substitution of the qualifying relative clause by preposed *such*. The description of the individual here referred to is in fact based on reference to a whole class of individuals satisfying the relevant description. However, it is not the class itself which is referred to, but only any member of the class. In the example given, Sally might well fall in love with *all* the men being able to teach her Swahili, but she would certainly not marry all men having this ability when we substitute *fall in love* by *marry*. As we saw also in (18), it is not possible in these cases to continue simply with *the secretary*, or *the man* in a subsequent sentence, without remaining in the same counter-factual mode. In a narrative taking the given sentence as data we would have to introduce a particular man having this ability with an indefinite noun-phrase: *One morning Sally met a man who adressed her in Swahili...*, which permits further definitivization of *man*.

These different types of indefinites can be characterized as REFERENTIAL and QUALIFYING respectively. In the referential use it is presupposed that there 'is' a particular individual satisfying a description, i.e. that such an individual is identified by the speaker. In the qualifying use it is only presupposed that an individual, not identified by the speaker and even possibly non-existent, is selected between all other possible individuals by his qualifications alone. In isolated sentences these different 'meanings' of indefinites may lead to ambiguity, as in *John wants to marry a girl who is hated by his parents*, in which the speaker either refers to a particular girl or describes any girl meeting the condition of being hated by John's parents. In the referential meaning of 'indefinite description' we may derive the relative clause from a subsequent sentoid: e.g. *John wants to marry a girl. This girl (She) is hated by his parents.* Here we would then have a type of non-restrictive relative clause. In the qualifying case, we are close to a CONDITIONAL: *If there is a girl such that she is hated by John's parents, then John wants to marry her.* The relative clause, then, is derived from a preceding sentoid having a modal operator for 'possible existence'. And, indeed, such a preceding sentoid, when embedded, produces a restrictive relative clause. The formal representation for this difference in logical notation would, as we suggested, be arrived at through an èta-operator for the referential (particular) meaning, and with a (modalized) existential quantifier for the qualifying (non-particular) meaning. In the first case we would have, then, a conjunction, in the second case a condition: e.g. $(\exists x)_{int}[g(x) \wedge h(y_1, x) \supset' f(y_2, x)]$ representing sentence *John wants to marry a girl who is hated by his parents*, where $h = $ *to hate*, $y_1 = $ *John's parents*, $g = $ *girl*, $y_2 = $ *John*, $f = $ *to marry* (for 'intentional existence', see below).

The interesting point is that the analysis given above also holds for definite descriptions (cf. Donellan [1970]). We even may have, in the qualifying use of descriptions, a definite article having roughly the same meaning as the indefinite, non-particular article: *Sally would like to marry the man who would be able to teach her Swahili.* The only difference lies in the (rather trivial) presupposition that she will only marry one man satisfying this description. Definites, clearly, and according to traditional logical theory, refer to UNIQUE or SINGULAR individuals. This is particularly obvious in the referential meaning of definite descriptions, where the presupposition is that only one individual satisfies the given description: *Sally met the man who is able to teach her Swahili.* In these cases, which are perhaps the most 'normal' ones, the definite noun(-phrase) represents a discourse referent which must have been introduced previously in the discourse as a unspecified particular: *There is a man who is able to teach her Swahili.* Following the rule, indeed, this restrictive relative clause can be derived from such a preceding sentence/sentoid (see below for details). In referential definite descriptions the description is only used as a complex 'name' for the individual, and the individual has been properly identified and specified. The presupposition, then, is that the description is applicable, or at least assumed by the speaker to be applicable. In qualifying definite descriptions the identification is based only on the description itself, the individual may be identified, e.g. by his actions (a murderer, a writer), but not known by the speaker. Hence the ambiguity of sentences such as *The man who wrote this book is a fascist.* The referential interpretation only 'uses' the description instead of the name of the author (e.g. 'the author of Waverley', instead of 'Scott' in the worn out classical example of Russell, Carnap, etc.). In the qualifying definite description this is not the case, because the author may be unknown and the fact that he is a fascist be a knowledge based on the content of the book in question. We may here insert such lexemes as *such*: *such a book*, and *surely*: *is surely a fascist*, which is not possible in the referential reading.

However, in many cases the distinction between 'reference' and 'qualification' is not strict in natural language. Descriptions may be used with both meanings in one sentence.

The formal description of these two types of definite description is not easy. The iota-operator is defined by a uniqueness condition, implying that only one particular individual satisfies the description, which is the case for both readings. We suggested above that the difference, then, may be established by using a conjunction for the referential reading and a conditional for the qualifying reading. However, let us try to specify this hypothesis by considering in closer detail the sentence used as an example above: *The man who wrote this book is a fascist*. We argued that this sentence is ambiguous (outside context or co-text), i.e. it has two underlying semantic representations. We assumed further that, in a text, noun phrases may only be definite (i) by pragmatical and referential rules (ii) when previously introduced as discourse referents with the aid of indefinites. Above we saw that indefinite noun phrases may be ambiguous: they may refer to non-specified particular individuals or to non-specified non-particular individuals. The ambiguity of definite noun phrases, therefore, seems to derive from the corresponding ambiguity of the indefinite noun phrases which they definitize. Let us therefore analyze first the underlying structure of this complex sentence.

We may derive the complex sentence from the underlying sequence *A man$_i$ wrote this book. The man$_i$ is a fascist* (for details about the derivation of relative clauses, see next section). The first sentence/sentoid of this sequence may have the two following readings for *a man*: (i) a particular individual, identified by the speaker, but non-specified in this initial sentence/sentoid of the text; (ii) a non-particular individual, non-identified by the speaker, but the existence of which is assumed/presupposed by semantic or empirical (encyclopedical) knowledge of the speaker, e.g. by the following rule (meaning postulate): 'for all x: if x is a book, then there is somebody who has written x', hence, by particularization: 'if this thing is a book, then somebody has written it'. Thus, if this implication is (assumed to be) true, we may assert that there is someone/somebody (some man, in the not exclusively 'masculine' interpretation) who wrote this book, and who is referred to by the expression *a man*. This second meaning of the indefinite noun-phrase is of course implied by the first, particular, meaning: if a speaker knows (has identified) an individual a with the property m, then there is some x having m, by general logical rule: $f(a) \supset (\exists x)[f(x)]$.

The problem at issue now is the following: which formal means may be used to represent this distinction in a predicate logical notation. Let us call *Indef$_p$* the 'particular, identified, non-specified' expression and *Indef$_{np}$* the expression referring to a 'non-particular, non-identified, non-specified' individual. In general we might use the existential quantifier to represent *Indef$_{np}$*, and the èta-operator to represent *Indef$_p$*. For *Indef$_{np}$* we may use in English, instead of the indefinite article, expressions like *some*.

The difficulty in our example is that this distinction seems to be blurred by the fact that it is normally presupposed that books have one author. Let us provisionally assume this presupposition to be true for our example. In that case the existential quantifier would provide too wide an interpretation: there is only one individual referred to, not at least one, although this single individual may be any member of a given set, e.g. the set of humans, or the set of authors. We assert in the first sentoid that some individual, member of the class of humans, is also member of the class of authors, but only one individual of this last class may be the author of this (particular) book. That is, we make a CHOICE of one individual from the set of authors, but this choice is random ('indefinite'). To represent this fact formally we will use an EPSILON-OPERATOR, and let $f[(\varepsilon x)g(x)]$ mean: 'one x, having the property g, has the property f'. In our example: one x, having the property 'man' (or 'human'), has the relation 'to write' to this book. We will not discuss here the set-theoretical foundations related with the use of an 'operator of choice'. It must be noted that often the èta-operator is interpreted in terms which are similar to those we used for the epsilon-operator. However, we will use the èta-operator for the more restricted case in which some particular individual is identified and singled out from a class. This brings it close to the iota-operator, because we seem to need a uniqueness condition in its definition to state the particularity.

The fact that the èta-operator is used for a more restricted domain than the epsilon-operator may be expressed in the implication $f[(\eta x)g(x)] \supset f[(\varepsilon x)g(x)]$. Note that the procedure of particularization which leads to the use of an èta-operator is based on PRAGMATIC factors: the individual is not identified by a linguistic expression, but is identified in the mind of the speaker.

The transition to definite descriptions is based on these two possible underlying logical forms of indefinite expressions. The preceding sentoid may by regular transformation be embedded in the subsequent sentoid (see below) as a clause modifying the head noun. Instead of pragmatically referring with the expression *man* to some (particular or non-particular) man, the speaker now uses a description. Such a description in fact restricts linguistically the class of possible individuals satisfying the assertion made by the whole sentence. Thus, *Indef$_p$* will lead to the use of *Def$_p$* for a 'particular, identified, specified' individual, and *Indef$_{np}$* will lead to the use of *Def$_{np}$* for a 'non-particular, non-identified, specified' individual. For the formalization of *Def$_p$* we normally use the iota-operator, defined as above. This iota-operator in a text, then, seems to 'continue' an èta-operator, which is used to introduce a particular 'discourse referent', to which is referred further by using the iota-operator. But how do we 'continue' a noun-phrase introduced with the aid of an epsilon-operator? In that case we may have recourse to an abstraction-operator, i.e. the LAMBDA-OPERATOR: '$(\lambda x)(...x...)$' being defined as 'the property or class of those x which are such that ...x... (Carnap [1957] 3, [1958] 129ff.). This is in fact the meaning we wanted to represent: anybody having the relation of 'being the author' to this book is a fascist. In general this would indeed be a class of individuals, but in our example, this class has only one member. The iota-operator seems to refer to this unique member, whereas the lambda-operator may be used to refer to the class, without identifying the member (the knowledge of the fact that the class has only one member is derived from semantic or referential presuppositions, see above). More exactly, we should say that in the non-identified interpretation of Def_{np} the lambda-operator is used to refer to a class of classes of which each class, having only one member, may – non-jointly – satisfy the description: $\{\{x_1\} \veebar \{y_1\} \veebar \{z_1\} \veebar ...\}$, where '$\veebar$' is used for exclusive disjunction. In the case where a book might have several authors the member-classes may have more members. The iota-operator excludes this disjunction: since one individual has been identified as satisfying the description, all others are excluded as possible candidates. Let us provisionally, then, note the Def_p-interpretation of the example-sentence as follows: $f\{(\imath x)[m(x) \wedge w(x, (\imath y)[b(y)])]\}$, i.e. the one and only thing which is a man and which wrote the one and only thing which is this book is a fascist. For the Def_{np}-interpretation we would like to state that for any individual (single) member: if he has the relation of having written this book, he is fascist, e.g. as follows: $(x)\{[(\lambda x)[m(x) \wedge w(x, (\imath y)[b(y)])]](x) \supset f(x)\}$.

We will not further discuss the logical implications and problems of this matter, nor try to find other possible notations. It was our aim to stress that in texts we may have two types of definite noun-phrases, based on (following) two corresponding types of indefinite noun-phrases. Note that only particular noun-phrases are definite descriptions in the strict sense: only they may therefore represent 'discourse referents' in the narrow sense. Neither epsilon-, nor lambda-characterization identify a particular individual. This is why we may not have definite$_p$ *the man* after *Sally wants to marry a man who will be able to teach her Swahili.* Thus the transition from epsilon-operator-sentoids to iota-operator-sentoids is not grammatical; we always need an èta-operator as an intermediary step. It is normal, however, to continue epsilon-operator-sentoids with lambda-definites, e.g. in *John is looking for a secretary. The secretary must be tall and blond,* i.e. we must remain in the same modal domain (see below).

We will see in section 4.3. that an important implication of our discussion is that pronouns, representing (in)definite noun phrases, may have the same ambiguous source, i.e. they may be 'referential' or 'semantic'.

4.2.11. We may try to find other means for representing the identity of individuals in a sequence of propositions. Recall that the uniqueness condition is given universally for all individuals having the same properties. For a text this condition is indeed restricted precisely to the 'universe of the text'. We may therefore introduce a more relevant RELATION-OPERATOR '$\yen$' denoting 'the individual previously referred to' (cf. Bellert [1970] for similar suggestions). The definition of such an operator is not easy to specify, because we seem to need concepts in it from the meta-theory, such as 'sequence' and 'to refer to'. In fact this formal device could be provided also when we introduce CONSTANTS in the expressions, once an individual has been properly identified. We will not go into this intricate problem here, and merely give the following pseudo-definition for the $\yen$-operator:

(35) $(\forall x)f(x) =\,_{def}(\imath x)[f(x) \wedge r(\Sigma, x)]$

where r is 'to refer to', and Σ the set of terms of previous propositions. We see that $(\forall x)$ is a meta-linguistic operator because its definition has a sequence of propositions as an argument and the notion of 'referring' as a relation. We now may write (33) as follows:

(36) $(\exists x)[b(x) \wedge c(z_1, x)] \wedge (\forall x)[b(x) \wedge s(x)].$

In the second term of the conjunction we repeat $b(x)$, because the individual is not necessarily referred to with the same name (lexeme), as in text (19). We will see that repeated names are a minimal condition upon pronominalization. The difference with the iota-operator should be noted here. The iota-operator requires uniqueness of extra-textual individuals and when this condition is referentially or pragmatically satisfied (see above) it may be introduced in an initial sentence. This is not the case with the relation-operator, which merely specifies uniqueness with respect to previously specified properties. Logical theory will have to make explicit the formal status of such operators or work out some other means of relating formulae with each other.

4.2.12. There is another aspect of current logical theory which bears upon definite noun phrases and the introduction of discourse referents: the LOGIC OF EXISTENCE.[6] For example, when we want to represent text (18) it is clearly inadequate to use simply an existential quantifier: there is some x, such that x is a secretary (...), since the existence of a secretary is not at all affirmed. Thus, if the existential quantifier commits us ontologically to the (actual) 'existence' of an individual, such an operator is clearly inadequate. In that case we might introduce, with Reichenbach (1947) 280 an 'intentional' operator of existence '$(\exists x)_{int}$' which expresses that the individuals only exist in the intention of the speaker. We here touch, in a simple form, on properties of MODAL SYSTEMS, using possible, necessary, probable, factual and other types of oper-

---

[6] The logic of existence is one of the central topics discussed in recent developments in modal logic (see also note 3). The problem at issue are the 'ontological' implications of quantifiers and the results of quantifying into modal contexts, an operation heavily criticized by Quine (1953), (1960); cf. especially the discussions in Linsky, ed. (1971). The semantics of modal systems, however, may abstract from such ontological bias and relate the problem to formal representations (models) of the different 'possible worlds' – and their mutual relations – in which such systems might be inter) preted. Cf., among others, Hintikka (1970a), (1970b), Scott (1970), van Fraassen (1971) and Rescher (1968) Chap. IX. Without entering into the technical details of such model theories, we adopt this non-ontological point of view for possible interpretations of text grammars and the structures they specify: 'existence' in texts – e.g. as established by 'discourse referents' (Karttunen) – is defined as 'textual' and not as 'ontological' existence. It is worth noting here that philosophical logic using terms like 'universe of discourse' has always presupposed – without further explication – the notion of discourse or text. In such famous examples as *Unicorns do not exist* we presuppose the textual existence of unicorns by selecting it as a topic for our discourse (cf. § 5.6. below): the topic of a sentence requires some sort of existential (actual, counterfactual, etc.) introduction of the noun phrase in a previous sentence.

ators. Here we may not only speak of modal propositions, but also of modally specified individuals, e.g. 'possible objects', although problems of quantification and semantic interpretation are notorious for such terms. *Secretary* in (18) thus refers at time t_0 of the utterance to a 'possible individual', which is usually bound with the operator $(/\exists x)$ (cf. Rescher [1968] chap. 9). As soon as an individual is introduced into the text with the aid of such an operator further predication must take place within the same logical domain, that is must be interpreted within the same possible world. In the same way we must describe the relations between counterfactual, impossible, probable, and virtual individuals referred to by the terms of the semantic structures. Logical theory about such modal notions is still in its first stages of development and we will not go beyond the intuitive remarks given above.

Just as was the case with the relational operator, operators or predicates of (mode of) existence have sentences (propositions) or texts as their scope. 'Actual existence', e.g. represented by the operator $(E!)$ (cf. Rescher [1968] chap. 9), may in that case be restricted to the 'universe of the text', for example the universe of a novel. Nothing within the text necessarily indicates that an individual is non-factual. Furthermore, the linearity of textual surface structure, often parallel with the linearity of temporal succession, may repeatedly change the mode of existence of certain individuals, with respect to a time t_i and a place l_i. It is premature, however, to investigate these very important properties of the MODAL COHERENCE of well-formed texts without knowing explicitly the semantic structure of the predicates defining these modes in semantic theory (*to think*, *to imagine*, *to believe*, etc.).

4.2.13. In concluding this section it is striking to see that when looking for the constraints determining such a superficial syntactic aspect as article selection, we had to descend first to feature specification of nouns, then to the semantic, referential and logical levels of definite descriptions of individuals.

We concluded that lexematic identity is neither a sufficient nor a necessary requirement of definitivization. 'Referential identity' seems to be a major criterion although many specifications of such an identity relation are necessary. Firstly, strict identity is not necessary, partial (part-whole, element-class) identities or relations may also be relevant. The semantic structure of the sentence, including the modal elements, has to specify the modal status of the discourse referents (existence, presence, possession, etc.), without which further predication is impossible. Similarly, presuppositions of a sentence S_i thus may not contradict entailments of preceding sentences.

From these general remarks we can already see that the conditions determining pronominalization are partially identical. We will consider these intricate conditions below, and turn now to the implications of our remarks about definite descriptions for the derivation of complex sentences.

4.2.14. In section 4.2.10 we saw that there is another important type of structure in which nouns may become definite and which falls under the specific scope of a text grammar: post-nominal modifiers, especially RESTRICTIVE RELATIVE CLAUSES.[7]

We have seen that definitivization is above all based on the principle of identification of discourse referents either through semantic relations between lexemes or through empirical relations between their referents. In principle, this process may also occur when the identifying elements follow the noun. We could speak, in that case, of a type of 'retro-specification'. Consider a sentence like

(37)   The restaurant next door is famous for its exclusive wines.

where the adverbial modifier *next door* identifies *restaurant* in the class of 'restaurants famous for their exclusive wines'. However, retro-specification has to be considered a surface phenomenon. The rule that only previous sentences (sentoids) may identify discourse referents does not seem to be broken. Take, for example, the following sentence which is grammatical as an initial sentence of a discourse

(38)   The girl I told you about yesterday will visit us next week.

This type of complex sentence having a restrictive relative clause and a definite noun can be traced back to the following underlying structure

(39)   I told you about a girl yesterday. The girl will visit us next week.

We see that the PRESUPPOSITION (see below) of (38) is a regular preceding sentoid of a text. *Girl*, then, according to the rules, can receive $[+ DEF]$ even when in surface structure the preceding sentoid follows the noun. It might be asked, therefore, whether we may have an indefinite noun in that case

(40)   ?A girl I told you about yesterday will visit us next week.

Indefinite noun phrases are normal however when the embedded sentoid is realized as a non-restrictive relative clause

(41)   A girl, who took a degree in physics, will visit us next week.

[7] Relative clauses have received much attention in recent transformational grammar, although the discussion is restricted to the effects of embedding upon pronominalization; no semantic considerations have been given in the formulation of the conditions upon grammatical embedding. For current treatment see Klima (1969), Smith (1969) and Kuroda (1969a). Recall that the traditional theory localizes embedding in the transformational component, whereas the standard theory defines it as a recursive property of the base (cf. chap. 1). Having introduced initial rule schemata for the generation of (possibly infinite) sequences of sentoids, we adopt a linear base and leave the process of embedding to the transformational component, in order to be able to derive linear surface structure of independent sentences from the same underlying structures as those of complex sentences.

One of the few linguists who derive relative clauses from a linear (conjunctive) base is Annear Thompson (1971) whose paper I saw after having finished this section. Cf. also Lang (1967).

Apparently this sentence will be derived from an underlying structure in which the embedded sentoid follows the matrix sentoid

(42)   A girl will visit us next week. The girl took a degree in physics.

The difference between restrictive and non-restrictive relative clauses, clearly, lies in their identifying and specifying natures respectively. Sentences with definite noun phrases followed by non-restrictive relative clauses may therefore not be initial sentences of a discourse:

(43)   *# The girl, who took a degree in physics, will visit us next week.

However, the problem is more complex than this, because, in opposition to (38), we may also not have initial sentences with definite nouns followed by a restrictive clause

(44)   *# The girl who took a degree in physics will visit us next week.

This sentence is grammatical as an initial sentence only when we have the pragmatic condition 'hearer knows the girl who took a degree in physics'. In (38) the pragmatic condition is satisfied by the realization of an embedded 'locutionary' clause, which expresses that the individual has been identified by 'previous mention'. This pragmatic presupposition, in (44), can also be considered to be a preceding sentoid: *There is a girl who took a degree in physics*, which is not the case in (43) where only *There is a girl* is the presupposition. In both cases such preceding sentences fail, hence their ungrammaticalness.

We may conclude, therefore, that restrictive relative clauses are derived from preceding sentoids in a text and non-restrictive relative clauses from following sentoids. In this derivation the normal conditions for linear coherence must be satisfied, with either previous indefinite introduction or pragmatic identification. Thus a sentence like

(45)   The restaurants of our town are closed on Monday.

presupposes a preceding sentoid *Our town has restaurants*.

The different types of relative clauses closely parallel the distinctions we made in section 4.2.10 for (in)definite descriptions:

(i)   a non-restrictive relative clause following a definite noun phrase provides a further specification of a particular individual, which has been identified (by èta-operator) in a previous sentence of the text; such complex sentences are therefore ungrammatical in initial position;

(ii) a non-restrictive relative clause following an indefinite noun phrase provides further specification of a particular, non-specified, individual, which is introduced as a possible discourse referent in the matrix sentence, where it is represented with the aid of an èta-operator;

(iii) a restrictive relative clause following a definite noun phrase identifies, by definite description, a particular individual in a class, such that this individual is the only member satisfying the description; to represent this description we need a iota operator, which requires that there must have been 'indefinite' identification (by èta-operator) in a previous sentence of the text;

(iv) a restrictive relative clause following an indefinite noun phrase identifies a class of individuals (possibly one) which may, non-jointly, satisfy the indefinite description; this indefinite description will be introduced with a lambda operator.

We may have also the following types:

(v) a restrictive relative clause following a definite noun phrase may identify a particular class (of possibly one member) within another class, as in type (iv); this type may be represented also by a lambda-operator;

(vi) a non-restrictive relative clause following an indefinite noun phrase may, in addition to type (ii), also specify a class (of possibly one member) introduced in the matrix sentence by an epsilon-operator; the difference with types (ii) and (v) will often be blurred in discourse.

For concrete examples we may refer to section 4.2.10 and the examples given below to illustrate types of pronominalization. Since we assume that embedded sentences (sentoids) are derived from preceding or following sentoids in an underlying sequence, we will study the other, e.g. semantic, relations between clauses and matrix sentences in section 5 below.

4.3. *Pronominalization*[8]

4.3.1. We tentatively remarked above that some conditions which make noun phrases

---

[8] We will assume as well-known the classical transformational treatment of pronouns, in which identical noun phrases are substituted by appropriate pronouns on the basis of 'referential identity'. Cf. Chomsky (1965) 145, 177f and the classical article of Lees and Klima (1969). In later work pronouns were introduced, as *PRO*-forms, in the base component, e.g. to explain the occurrence of isolated pronouns – especially personal pronouns – without explicit antecedents. Cf. Dougherty (1969), Langacker (1969), Ross (1969) and especially the recent work of Postal (1969a), (1969b), (1970), (1971); further Grinder and Postal (1971) and Grinder (1971). A structural approach is provided by Harweg (1968); see Chap. 1 for some remarks about this book. More general is Hiż (1969). Cf. also Lockwood (1970), Lowe (1969), Pike and Lowe (1969). For recent discussion about pronouns, reference and definite descriptions, see below.

In the pages which follow some conclusions are similar to those in Lakoff's paper on pronouns and reference (Lakoff, 1968a) which we saw only after having written this section. We believe that our textual approach to pronouns below has at least partially resolved some of the problems for which Lakoff could not find an adequate formulation.

definite are identical with those determining the pronominalization of nouns and noun phrases. The texts given as examples in the previous paragraphs even require in many cases a subsequent pronominalization of the definite noun phrases. Clearly, simple identity of reference does not allow pronominalization (cf. text (19)) without a difference of meaning. The additional condition requires lexematic identity.

Similarly, there are cases in which rules for pronominalization do not apply although the condition of referential identity is satisfied. We will turn to these cases in the next section.

Conversely, pronominalization may take place in cases where no referential identity seems to hold in the strict sense.[9] We have seen already that definitivization is possible with nouns referring to other members of the extensional classes designated by them. Similarly, pronominalization is possible in such sentences as

(46)   Would you lend your car$_i$ to that man, who stole it$_j$ from his neighbour?

where the individual cars referred to cannot be identical, i.e. they are discernables. Apparently, membership of the class of cars is a sufficient condition for pronominalization in such cases. Notice that pronominalization is normally permitted if the two cars referred to are identical. The 'identical reference' interpretation is excluded in (46) because *your car* and *your neighbour's car* are descriptions of different individuals.

An intermediate case of pronominalization which is not based on (strict) referential identity is possible for different tokens of the same type as in the following sentence

(47)   I gave Peter a book$_i$ on theoretical physics, but he had already bought it$_j$ himself.

Such examples demonstrate that rules for pronominalization do not always depend on referential relations of identity, but may also be based on purely semantic, i.e. intensional, identities. The use of identical subscripts or variables (bound by a iota-operator) in these cases would give rise to particular difficulties if restricted to referential individuals and if semantic identity as such is excluded as an insufficient condition. As the uniqueness condition for definite description with the aid of iota-operators is

---

[9] The discussion on the precise notions involved in the Identity Condition determining pronominalization is extensive at the moment. Cf. Dik (1968a) and Postal (1971) for critical remarks on the traditional formulation of this condition. Postal speaks in this case of Identity of Sense Anaphora, i.e. pronouns not based on referential identity but on semantic relationships. Palek (1968) studies these relations as representations of relations between elements of referential domains. For other criticism on referential identity, cf. Hall Partee (1970) § 2.

Furthermore, we need an investigation into the logical properties of the different notions involved in 'identity' or 'equivalence' relations in texts. When referring to an 'identical' individual in different modal contexts (possible worlds), which type of identity is involved then? Cf. recent work in modal logic, especially papers of Ruth Barcan Marcus (e.g. Barcan Marcus, 1967). For a brief discussion of some interesting linguistic implications, cf. Lakoff (1968b).

not satisfied in such cases of (lexico-)semantic identity, we might have recourse again (cf. section 4.2.10) to a lambda-notation. A λ-operator, as we have seen, provides exactly the abstraction from individuals we need in pronominalization of this kind; e.g. for (59): 'the property of x such that x is a book on theoretical physics'. That is, a variable y leading to pronominalization is predicated by the property assigned to its antecedent x: $(\lambda x)(Bx)(y)$, where B is the property 'book on theoretical physics'. Note that a referential definite description is given as soon as the semantic structures do not separate two individuals: *I gave Peter a book$_i$ on theoretical physics, but he lost it$_i$ the same day*, where the uniqueness condition is satisfied (at least for the universe of this text).

We conclude that pronouns are derivable from two different sources: from a referential base in the case of definite description of classes or individual identities and from a semantic base in the case of identical properties, if referential identity is excluded.

4.3.2. After these preliminary examples which show that the traditional condition of 'referential identity' is by no means without problems, we must try to adduce some evidence for a textual description of the processes underlying pronominalization. We will have to show that text grammars not only provide a more 'natural' framework for the description of pronominalization but also formulate explicit rules which are simpler and/or permit more satisfactory generalizations than those of S-grammars. We will see, for example, that the informal rule, given earlier, which derives restrictive relative clauses from preceding sentoids of textual surface structure, is only one example of a set of rules which also describe definitivization, pronominalization, presuppositions and topic-comment relations.

Before we start our argument with some examples, let us recall briefly the rules and conditions for pronominalization as formulated in S-grammar. Langacker (1969), in an important article correcting the results of, among others, Lees and Klima's early work (1969), stated that a noun phrase may be pronominalized if it has 'all relevant primacy relations' with respect to the noun phrase to be pronominalized. The notion of 'primacy relation' was an important generalization of the two relations of 'preceding' and 'commanding'. That is: pronominalization may take place if the antecedent *NP* precedes, and 'backward' pronominalization is possible if the following 'postcedent' occurs in a sentence which immediately dominates the S-symbol under which the pronominalizable *NP* occurs. The general conditions are that pronominalization is possible only if the two *NP*'s are members of different, but not conjunctive, *S*'s (and, which is made explicit by indices, if they are referentially identical). Thus sentence (48) is grammatical since it satisfies both of the rules and (49) is ungrammatical because the pronominalized *NP* has no primacy relation over its pronoun

(48)   Peter$_i$ is convinced that John will agree with him$_i$.
(49)   *He$_i$ is convinced that John will agree with Peter$_i$.

The given rules also permit a classification along several degrees of naturalness; the sentences satisfying both primacy relations being most grammatical and acceptable.

The Langacker-rules made good predictions, but recently some complications have been discovered known as the 'Bach-Peters-Kuno-paradox'. The problem concerns the precise part of the *NP*'s that should be 'substituted' by a relevant *PRO*-form. Take for example a sentence like (50)

(50)   The girl who fell in love with him kissed the boy who insulted her.

Here, at first sight and according to the rules, *the girl who fell in love with him* pro-nominalizes *her* and *the boy who insulted her* pronominalizes *him*. However, if this is true, the pronouns would reappear in the explicit definite descriptions substituted for the two respective pronouns, and so forth *ad infinitum*. Such infinite descriptions, of course, cannot be permitted in a finite grammar and another solution therefore must be found.

In a series of recent articles, e.g. Mönnich (1971), Karttunen (1971), Kuroda (1971), it was shown, however, that the paradox was only apparent. McCawley's (1970) solution, introducing indexed variables for pronouns, was rejected as inadequate, because it does not permit a differentiation between (50) on the one hand and (51) and (52) on the other hand, and because it does not recognize (50) as ambiguous, or as less grammatical

(51)   The girl who fell in love with the boy who insulted her kissed him.
(52)   The boy who insulted the girl who fell in love with him was kissed by her.

In order to determine the precise 'content' of the pronouns an explicit notation will be needed which specifies the definite description of the pronominalized nouns (or *NP*'s).

These notations are borrowed from predicate logic. They specify that, for this sentence, there would be 'exactly one girl who fell in love kissing exactly the one and only boy insulting this particular girl'. We use Kuroda's notation for indicating the difference between (51) and (52) respectively

(53) $\exists x\ \exists y\ \exists z'\ \{\text{kissed}\ (x, y)\ .\ x = (\imath z)[\text{girl}\ (z)\ .\ \text{fell in love}\ (z, (\imath w)[\text{boy}\ (w)\ .\ \text{insulted}\ (w, z)])]\ .\ y = (\imath w')[\text{boy}\ (w')\ .\ (\text{girl})z'\ .\ \text{fell in love}\ (z', w')]\ .\ (x = z')\}.$

(54) $\exists x\ \exists y\ \exists w\ \{\text{kissed}\ (x, y)\ .\ x = (\imath z)[\text{girl}\ (z)\ .\ \text{boy}\ (w)\ .\ \text{fell in love}\ (z, w)]\ .\ y = (\imath w')[\text{boy}\ (w')\ .\ \text{insulted}\ (w', (\imath z')[\text{girl}\ (z')\ .\ \text{fell in love}\ (z', w')])]\ .\ (w = y)\}.$

These rather complex expressions have to indicate the different identifications on the different levels. Kuroda (1971) found that pronominalization regularly takes place first in the most deeply embedded sentences with respect to their modified head clause nouns. We see that identity of full *NP*'s is a condition which is too strong for pronominalization.

Although the notations of (53) and (54) seem to render roughly the meanings of (51) and (52), such a way of formalizing is cumbersome and not easy to handle. Heuristic methods like the different 'data bases', as used for example by Karttunen (1971), give immediate insight into 'who insulted whom' and 'who fell in love with whom' and 'who kissed whom'. But how do we explicitly introduce such clear although informal 'descriptions' into our grammar?

There is another important point, which has been hitherto neglected in these discussions, *viz.* the other (semantic) relations between the sentences (clauses) thus combined in a complex sentence. Note first of all that the given example-sentences are mostly rather awkward, if not of questionable grammaticalness. As is well-known, double embeddings are often of a rather low degree of acceptability. To be sure, this is a question of performance, not of grammar, but our grammar has to specify at least which other expressions, synonymous with the given sentences, are also grammatical and which possibly have a higher degree of acceptability.

What has been neglected, then, are (for example) the different relations of cause and consequence between the different clauses in a complex sentence, and the (related) basic relations of time and mode. These may appear somewhat obscured in the formation of such complex sentences but an adequate grammatical description should make them explicit. Recall that definite descriptions, i.e. the introduction of 'discourse referents', depend on the semantic structure of the sentoid, e.g. its modal (negation, counterfactual, intentional) aspects. Similarly, the truth values of sentences determining their appropriateness are restricted by time and place properties of these semantic structures.

4.3.3. Since pronominalization is characteristic for relations between 'sentences' (or sentoids in our terms), a textual treatment seems to impose itself. A major advantage of such a textual description would be that both the structure of the mentioned complex sentence and the more 'normal' textual forms would be traced back to the same underlying linear sequence of sentoids. In that case complex sentence formation is, as formerly, a transformational process. Let us take as examples again sentences (51) and (52). We claim that they have to be derived from the following underlying sequences if we want to make their semantic relations (time, consequence) explicit:

(55)   (i)   A boy insulted a girl.
         (ii) The girl fell in love with the boy.
         (iii) The girl kissed the boy.

and

(56)   (i)   A girl fell in love with a boy.
            (ii) The boy insulted the girl.
            (iii) The girl kissed the boy.

These texts are grammatical apart from pronominalization, i.e. the initial sentences have indefinite articles and the sentences following have definite articles because they are referring to identified discourse referents. Further the linear order of the sentoids implies a different temporal order in the events described. Finally (55) seems to mean: A girl fell in love with a boy ALTHOUGH he insulted her, and in both (55) and (56) the girl kissed the boy ALTHOUGH he insulted her. These relations between sentoids will be described in section 5 of this chapter. We here limit ourselves at this stage to the process of complex sentence formation and pronominalization.

A first requirement will be that the linear order of the underlying sequence is somehow represented structurally in the complex sentence as well. If not, the relevant semantic relations (time, consequence, etc.) based on this relation will disappear, or ambiguities will arise, as in (50). We saw earlier that restrictive relative clauses can be derived from preceding sentoids. If there are more preceding sentoids, we will assume as a rule that the sentoid with the lowest index (i.e. the first sentoid of a sequence of which a sentence must be generated) is most deeply embedded in the matrix sentence, which is the sentence with the highest index (the last of the sequence).

We will assume further that 'sentientialization' takes place from left to right. That is, first sentence S_{i-2} is embedded in S_{i-1}. For (51) we thus have the intermediate step

(57)   (i)   A girl fell in love with the boy who insulted the girl.
            (ii) The girl kissed the boy.

in which the indefinite articles are replaced by definite articles, and conversely, according to the relevant rules for initial and following sentoids, and in which *WH*-transformations already applied. We then pronominalize regularly the second token of *girl* in (57,i): *girl* ⇒ *her*. In our next step this pronominalized (57,i) is embedded in (57,ii), yielding

(58)   The girl who fell in love with the boy who insulted her kissed the boy.

where the second token of *boy*, preceded by the *NP* 'the boy who insulted her and whom she fell in love with' may be pronominalized as *him*. There is no infinite regress here because *her* only pronominalized (*a*) *girl*.

We see that the depth of embedding of restrictive relative clauses mirrors the linear concept of precedence in deeper structures. The two primacy relations of Langacker, thus, here seem to be two manifestations of the same basic ordering relation between subsequent sentoids. Let us, then, consider the process transforming sequence (56) into one sentence. A first series of transformations (embedding, pronominalizations) yields

(59)   (i) A boy insulted the girl who fell in love with him.
        (ii) The girl kissed the boy.

The next step would require, for example, embedding of (59,i) after *boy*, e.g. as follows

(60)   *A girl*$_i$ kissed the boy who insulted the girl*$_i$* who fell in love with him.

However in this sentence *girl*$_1$ and *girl*$_2$ cannot have identical reference, and thus the meaning of the original sequence would change during this transformation. Such transformations therefore must somehow be blocked. That (60) under the identity-interpretation is ungrammatical is to be explained by the fact that the previous definite description of *girl* is lost during the transformation. Any definite description must be introduced by a relative clause (or similar postnominal modifier): *the girl who* (...). We are therefore obliged to insert (59,i) after *girl*. This insertion is possible only if (59, i) is first transformed such that *girl* is topicalized

(61)   A girl was insulted by the boy with whom she fell in love.

or as

(62)   The girl who fell in love with a boy was insulted by him.

Embedding in (59, ii) then produces:

(63)   The girl who was insulted by the boy with whom she fell in love kissed him.

However, (62) can only be embedded when first reduced to (61), since relativization requires that subject and verb-phrase follow each other immediately, (64) being ungrammatical

(64)   *The girl who who fell in love with a boy was insulted by him kissed him.

We may, conversely, topicalize *boy* in (59, ii) and then insert (59, i) as modifier

(65)   The boy who insulted the girl who fell in love with him was kissed by her.

Thus only (63) and (65) are grammatical products of the possible transformational embeddings.

There seem to be some general conditions for this sort of transformation. Firstly, the embedding of a complex sentence as a restrictive relative clause in another sentence seems to be permitted only when the topics/subjects are identical (cf. Lakoff [1968a]).

If this is not the case, we must first apply topicalization transformations, e.g. by passivization. Secondly, the transformation needed for this embedding (relativization) may not change the hierarchical structure of the complex sentence which represents the order of previous embeddings. This structure is respected only in the following ordering of arguments

(66) $\langle\langle x_1, x_2\rangle, \langle x_2, x_1\rangle, \langle x_2, x_1\rangle\rangle$

When, as in (56), this order is not respected, we first need topicalization before embedding is possible. This condition has to be explained by the necessity of having a full noun as head of a relative clause. Once pronominalized a noun cannot receive further 'definite description' by a following restrictive relative clause.

This requirement predicts that embedding in one sentoid of more than two sentoids, each with the same two arguments will be blocked. Thus, it will be impossible to reduce (without other transformations) the following ordered sequence into one sentence

(67)   (i)   A boy insulted a girl.
            (ii) The girl admired him.
            (iii) The girl fell in love with him.
            (iv) The girl kissed him.

Here we may have the following transforms

(68)   A girl admired the boy who insulted her.
(69)   The girl who admired the boy who insulted her fell in love with him.

but (69) cannot regularly be embedded into (67, iv) as a definite description for *girl*

(70)   *The girl who fell in love with the boy whom she admired (the boy) who insulted her kissed him.

The linear order, then, has to be represented by coordinative ordering, e.g.

(71)   The girl who admired the boy who insulted her fell in love with him and (then, therefore, etc.) kissed him.

Of course, when a sequence of four (or more) sentoids has three (or more) arguments, repeated embedding is possible. The sequence

(72)   (i)   Peter loves Mary.
            (ii) Mary hates Peter.
            (iii) Mary admires John.
            (iv) John likes Peter.

may be regularly transformed in several steps into the grammatical, although highly unacceptable sentence

(73)   John who is admired by Mary who hates Peter who loves her likes him.

Similarly, if there is no constraint upon the linear ordering of sentoids, e.g. in cases of non-ordered presuppositions, definite descriptions may be embedded freely after the arguments of the matrix sentence. In that case (67) might be transformed into e.g.

(74)   The girl kissed the boy who insulted her, whom she admired and with whom she fell in love.

or rather

(75)   The girl who admired him and fell in love with him kissed the boy who insulted her.

However, the meaning of such sentences is at least ambiguous because it is not clear which is the exact antecedent (postcedent) of the pronoun *him*: (*a*) *boy*, or *the boy who insulted her*? In the latter case, infinite regress re-appears, which seems to confirm that deep structures must indeed be linearly ordered. The restrictions formulated pertain to relative clauses modifying certain head nouns (arguments in deep structure), thus representing definite descriptions. Normally, all sorts of causal and modal relations connect the clauses so that adverbial clauses may easily be inserted between the relative ones. Thus (67) would naturally, in correct order, be transformed into the following surface structure

(76)   The girl who fell in love with the boy whom she admired, although he had insulted her, kissed him.

The required depth is achieved here because the first sentoid may be embedded as a clause of concession in the sentoid with less depth. This embedding may be continued for other categories (e.g. temporal) of the sentoids.

   At this point we should ask ourselves whether the transformational process is indeed 'progressive' and not 'regressive'. In the examples given, e.g. (55) and (56), we embedded the first sentoid into the second and the complex result into the final matrix sentoid. In this way definite descriptions are linearly 'built up', which enables correct pronominalizations without ambiguities of reference. When taking a given matrix sentence

(77)   A girl kissed a boy.

we may specify the indefinite individuals by definite descriptions e.g. first 'the girl fell in love with a boy'

(78)   The girl who fell in love with $\begin{Bmatrix} \text{a boy} \\ \text{him} \end{Bmatrix}$ kissed $\begin{Bmatrix} \text{him} \\ \text{a boy} \end{Bmatrix}$.

Next a sentoid like 'the boy insulted her' may further modify *a boy*

(79)   The girl who fell in love with the boy who insulted her kissed him.

However, there are two occurrences of *boy* in (78) and the following ambiguous sentence may also be generated

(80)   The girl who fell in love with him kissed the boy who insulted her.

In neither case is it clear which part of the first *NP* pronominalizes *her* in (79) and (80). In (79) *her* pronominalizes 'The girl who fell in love with the boy', but this was not the intended meaning: the boy did not insult 'the girl who fell in love with him', but an (indefinite) girl. This traditional, 'regressive', treatment leads to the well-known paradoxes and ambiguities in pronominalization. These problems may be overcome only when embedding, definitivization and pronominalization begin, cyclically, with the LOWEST sentoid, taking only the immediately dominating sentoid as its matrix

(81)

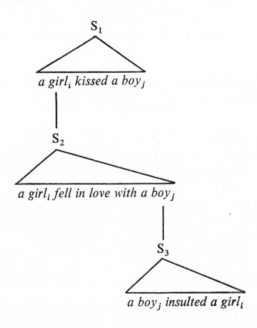

which will be transformed into the phrase marker of (82):

(82)

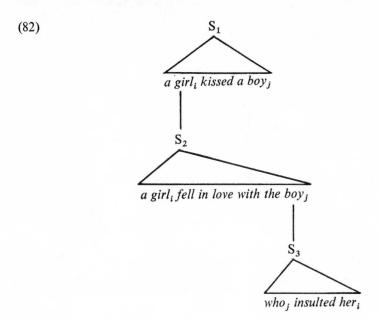

Finally this result is transformed into (83)

(83)

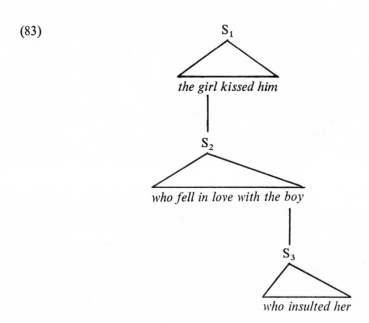

However, the phrase markers of (81)-(83) do not correspond to our operations: no embeddings take place before (83), so we must represent only S_3 and then S_2 with S_3 embedded in it and finally S_1 with S_2/S_3 embedded in it. This is just the linear process we have described above. We thus must depart from an ordered sequence Sq, with the following phrase marker

(84)

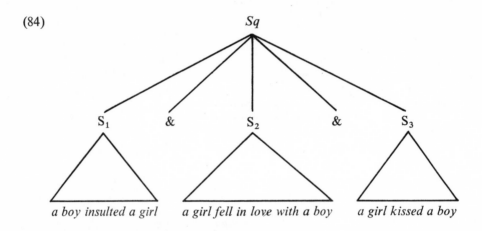

and then apply linearly the transformations producing the hierarchical structure such that the Sq dominates one sentence (S_3).

4.3.4. Finally, let us take another example in order to show that pronominalization is based only on the primacy relation of preceding. This time we shall take an adverbial clause, modifying the (implied) time operator of a sentoid, and derived from a preceding sentoid: whereas (85) is a grammatical sequence, (86) is probably ungrammatical because of topological presuppositions (see below)

(85)   (i)   Peter came in.
        (ii) Sheila smiled at Peter.

(86)   (i)   ?Sheila smiled at Peter.
        (ii) Peter came in.

A first transformation will place (85, i) at the end of (85, ii), i.e. at the place of temporal adverbs

(87)   Sheila smiled at Peter when Peter came in.

where the *WH*-transformation for temporal adverbs is applied. According to the

(Langacker) rules, we then have obligatory pronominalization of the second token of *Peter*:

(88)   Sheila smiled at Peter when he came in.

However, we may also have the following synonymous surface structures, both grammatical because the antecedent *Peter* bears all relevant primacy relations to the pronoun

(89)   When Peter came in, Sheila smiled at him.
(90)   When he came in, Sheila smiled at Peter.

On the contrary, we may not have

(91)   *Sheila smiled at him$_i$, when Peter$_i$ came in.

when *him$_i$* and *Peter$_i$* have identical referents. Now, how do we derive (88), (89) and (90) from the sequence in (85) and how do we prevent the derivation of (91)? We saw, first, that (88) is regularly derived from (87), i.e. by postposition and pronominalization. Note that here, too, pronominalization follows embedding (under the conditions of referential and semantic relations formulated earlier). After embedding and pronominalization, i.e. after (88), we may apply an optional adverb-preposing transformation, topicalizing the temporal clause, which produces sentence (90). In order to get (89) we first optionally prepose the adverbial clause of (87)

(92)   When Peter came in Sheila smiled at Peter.

and then apply the obligatory pronominalization. The order of the transformations, and the condition that, after linear embedding (post-position) only forward pronominalization is allowed, automatically excludes (91), which can only be produced by backward pronominalization. The Langacker-condition of commanding again seems reducible to the only primacy relation of preceding, when starting generation with linearly coherent sequences (for details, cf. Lakoff [1968a]).

It is worth noting that embedding represents the order of underlying sentoids, but that the same order can be obtained simply by coordinating the underlying sentoids in their original order, with the constraint of forward pronominalization

(93)   The girl loves the boy and kisses him.
(94)   ?The girl loves him and kisses the boy.

4.3.5. Although there is serious evidence for deriving restrictive relative clauses, adverbial clauses, etc. from preceding sentoids in a sequence (e.g. in order to explain relative depth of embedding, the restricted scope of pronouns, and – see below – of presupposition), the claim that the command relation is derived from the 'precedence' relation seems too strong. We are left with the set of well-formed, although sometimes rather awkward, sentences in which pronouns may precede their dominating antecedent

(95)   The girl who admired him kissed Peter.
(96)   The girl who admired him was kissed by Peter.
(97)   The girl who admired him thought that the woman who despised Peter was jealous.

Although such sentences are derived from sequences of sentoids, e.g.

(98)   (i)   A girl admired Peter.
         (ii) The girl kissed Peter.
(99)   (i)   A girl admired Peter.
         (ii) Peter was kissed by the girl.
(100)   (i)   A girl admired Peter.
         (ii) A woman despised Peter.
         (iii) The girl thought something.
         (iv) The woman was jealous.

the pronouns in the embedded preceding sentoids cannot be considered to be a result of linear (forward) pronominalization. Since embedding seemed to precede pronominalization, we must assume that backward pronominalization is possible in complex sentences under the well-known command condition.

However, there are some problems which are not yet quite solved for this type of 'backward' pronominalization. Langacker himself noticed that there are differences in 'naturalness' between the different possibilities of pronominalization. Clearly, the case in which the full *NP* both precedes and commands is the most natural case. Similarly, we may say that the primacy relation of preceding is more natural than the command relation

(101)   The girl who rejected Peter kissed him.

(101) seems more natural than (95). If this is true, how can we formally explain this fact?
In order to solve this problem, first consider the following sentences and texts

(102)   *The girl who admired him$_i$ kissed a man$_i$.
(103)   *The girl who admired him$_i$ was kissed by a man$_i$.
(104)   The girl who admired him kissed the man.

(105)   The girl kissed the man whom she admired.
(106)   (i)   Peter is jealous.
             (ii) He hates the girl who rejected him.
(107)   (i)   Peter is jealous.
             (ii) A girl rejected him.
             (iii) He hates the girl.

That backward pronominalization under dominance relation is not without problems is demonstrated by (102) and (103). Here the definite character implied by pronouns (cf. the preceding sections) prohibits an equireferential interpretation of *him* and *a man*. Similarly, in (95), (96) and in (104) we have the intuitive idea that *Peter* and *the man* have a definite character because of (deleted) previous sentences or pragmatic identification. This is not the case in (105), where the definiteness of *man* can be fully determined by the relative clause *whom she admired*.

Further, in (106, ii) we cannot say that *him* is pronominalized by the preceding and commanding *NP he*: both pronouns represent a preceding definite noun phrase *Peter*. (Notice that all proper names are definite *NP*'s, which in a sense might have biased much of the argument given e.g. by Langacker, since definite *NP*'s normally presuppose introduction of indefinite 'identical' *NP*'s, as we saw earlier.) Sentences like (95) and (104) are at least ambiguous as can be seen easily in such texts as

(108)   (i)   Peter is jealous.
             (ii) The girl who loves him kissed John.

where *him* is most naturally linked with *Peter*, not with *John* although in the same sentence as *John*. It seems as if preceding pronouns in a sentence are produced on the basis of deleted, or simply pragmatically omitted, preceding sentoids in which the noun phrase has been introduced. This would explain the acceptability, if not grammaticalness, of such sentences as

(109)   The girl kissed him, although Peter didn't love her.
(110)   The girl kissed him, but Peter didn't love her.

where backward pronominalization is excluded by the Langacker-rules.

Note that we here also touch upon the problem of presupposition, which is closely related to relative clause embedding and definitivization. In fact *A girl admired Peter* is a presupposition of (95) and (96) and the preposed pronoun *him* is probably derivable from *Peter* in the presupposition. Indeed, we will see that presuppositions must be treated as (deleted) previous sentoids.

However, we have not yet explained how and why full noun phrases may follow such pronouns, in a dominant position, and at least sometimes ((109) and (110)) in any position without themselves being pronominalized. A possible explanation might be that the matrix sentence in which the other (previous) sentoids are embedded must repeat a full *NP*-topic when the preceding sentoids are deleted or when their *NP*'s have been pronominalized. This is also why we may not have

(111)   *He$_i$ hates the girl who rejected Peter$_i$.
(112)   *He$_i$ kissed the girl, although Peter$_i$ didn't love her.

Notice that (112) is ungrammatical and (109) is probably grammatical, which must be explained by the difference in grammatical (semantic) function of the *NP*'s (arguments); in (112) *he* is subject/topic and in (109) *the girl* is subject/topic. In isolated sentences (matrix sentences) topics must be full *NP*'s, whereas other *NP*'s may be optionally pronominalized (for detail, cf. Lakoff [1968a]).

4.3.6. It is impossible at this moment to draw general conclusions from our discussion of pronominalization processes, let alone to formulate sufficiently general and simple rules. The predictions of the Langacker-rules seem to be roughly correct. Problems arise only in determining the precise 'scope' of pronouns, i.e. the part of the *NP* they pronominalize. The notion of command relations, furthermore, is a typical aspect of surface structure: embedded clauses are derived from preceding sentoids. Depth of embedding reflects the order of the sentoids in the underlying sequence. In some cases, preceding pronouns may command their *NP*'s. It might be asked, then, whether in general preceding pronouns in a sentence – when not obtained by clause permutation, e.g. in adverbial-clause preposing, and in passivization – should not be derived from (deleted or actually manifested) previous sentoids functioning as presuppositions. Such pronouns occur in relative clauses, realizing definite descriptions together with the head noun, i.e. always having the function of a presupposition of the matrix sentence (the last sentoid of the sequence). In isolated matrix sentences, finally, a pronoun may not occur as a subject/topic, whereas repeating full noun-phrases in other positions of the matrix sentence is optional, and obligatory when that noun phrase precedes in the same sentence.

In the next section we will consider some more specific exceptions to the rules.

4.3.7. There are some specific cases in which pronominalization may occur even when the rules are not respected, and also cases in which pronominalization is not possible although the general conditions are satisfied. Of course, this is not unusual in natural language and, especially in the rather abstract operations involved in pronominalization, there is much 'free variation', according to dialect or even idiolect, as divergences in the judgement on the grammaticalness of many sentences in which pronouns occur seem to indicate (cf. e.g. Labov [1970] 38ff.).

As we have noted for some examples given above, a correct interpretation of pronouns which are ungrammatical according to the mentioned rules of sentential grammars is possible in grammatical co-texts.

The same is true for all sorts of phenomena related with focussing, emphasizing, contrasting, etc. in texts, of which some will be treated in this section, although they need extensive separate treatment, e.g. in relation with a formal pragmatics which may formulate rules and constraints determining linear production/perception processes of the subsequent sentences of a discourse (cf. Kummer [1971c] for some suggestions).

Take, for example, sentences such as

(113)   Peter$_i$ saw hér$_j$ before Mary$_j$ saw hím$_i$

Here an *NP* in a subordinate adverbial clause (*Mary*) may be pronominalized, provided the pronouns are contrastively stressed (some other examples have already been given in the previous section; cf. also many examples given by Lakoff [1968a]). However, sentences like (114) are more awkward when denoting the same referents

(114)   *He$_i$ saw Mary$_j$ before she$_j$ saw Peter$_i$.

Recall that (113) seems to require a specific stress on the two pronouns in the coreferential interpretation. This fact probably has to be explained by both the parallel and the contrasting structure of (113). We will come back to these aspects below.

Conversely, there are certain specific conditions which block both forward (and permitted backward) pronominalization. Compare for example the following complex sentences, which of course could also have been realized as texts with two or more sentences

(115)   John has lost a pen$_i$ and a purse, but today he found the pen$_i$.
(116)   He decided to buy her perfume$_i$, but it turned out that she did not want perfume$_i$ but flowers.

Pronominalization would result in ungrammatical sentences here. In (115) a singular pronoun would have ambiguous reference. The addition of referential indices to the lexical structure of identical nouns having identical reference does not change this situation: syntactic deep structure cannot be specified thus to prevent pronominalization. We would need a rule blocking pronominalization when no antecedent can be unambiguously identified. In (116) the contrast between alternatives such as *perfume* and *flowers* is usually established only when the full nominal form is used. Phenomena like parallelism (as in (113)) and contrast appear to require specific constraints.

4.3.8. It would be false to conclude from examples like (115) that pronominalization of a noun is impossible when its antecedent in preceding sentences (clauses) occurs together with other nouns that could have been pronominalized. Take for example the following four texts having the same initial sentence

(117)   (i)   The statue in the park of that village has been damaged by a tornado.
                (iia) It could however easily be restored to its original state.
                (iib) The council therefore decided to close it to the public.
                (iic) It was by great good fortune that its houses were saved.
                (iid) In other villages it caused much more damage than that.

No ambiguity is involved in the interpretation of *it* in these different texts. This can only be explained when the semantic representations of the sentences (iia-d) completely determine which of the nouns must be selected as a further 'topic'. Referential indices for the correct interpretation of the pronouns are automatically assigned by semantic structure.

As in the selection of the features $[\pm \text{DEF}]$, it turns out here that possible features $[\pm \text{PRO}]$ can be predicted in a grammar built on a base of semantic representations of structures beyond the sentence. Well-known ambiguities resulting from the use of pronouns do not necessarily appear when the semantic structure of a sentence S_{i-1} is connected with the semantic representation of S_i. What was normally explained by complex deep structures or presuppositions is now part of preceding deep structures. A sentence like

(118)   John and Peter lost their book yesterday.

of which the ambiguity is normally reduced by deriving it as a complex sentence either from phrasal (*NP*)conjunction or from the conjoining of coordinate sentoids (leading to the interpretation *their common book* and *each his own book* respectively), can have only one regular interpretation when sentences like (119) and (120) precede them in a text

(119)   Putting their savings together John and Peter could buy this expensive book.
(120)   Both John and Peter could afford to buy this expensive book.

The influence of preceding sentences can be very complex. Ungrammatical combination of sentences (or sentoids) can become grammatical when additional semantic representations are given in these preceding sentences. A complex sentence like

(121)   Mary and Jane had to lend their textbooks to John and Peter, because they had lost $\left\{ \begin{array}{l} \text{*them} \\ \text{theirs} \end{array} \right\}$.

is ungrammatical when *them* (referring to the textbooks of Mary and Jane) is used, because the action *to lend* presupposes 'possession' which would contradict *lost*. For the same reason *they* can only refer to *John and Peter*. When a sentence like *The teacher gave a textbook to each pupil* precedes, the pronoun *them* can regularly refer to the *textbook* of this first sentence, thus meaning *each his own textbook*. Once again we see that simple referential identity is too strong a condition for pronominalization and that class relations are involved in the rule. When an appropriate semantic representation is available, pronouns may refer to different individuals of the same class, as we can see in the following text

(122)   (i)   The teacher has given some books$_A$ to each of his pupils.
          (ii) John read them$_B$ passionately.
          (iii) Peter immediately gave them$_C$ to his eldest sister.

where the referent of *them$_B$* is disjunct with the referent of *them$_C$*: $B \cap C = \emptyset$ and where $B \subset A$ and $C \subset A$.

4.3.9. Recent discussions in generative grammar have led to the hypothesis that surface structure, e.g. PHONOLOGICAL ASPECTS like stress, can contribute to the 'meaning' of a sentence by focussing upon a specific constituent (cf. Chomsky [1971], Lakoff [1970b], Bierwisch [1969b] cf. recent criticism by Kraak [1970]). Different stress upon the pronoun in sentences like (cf. Cantrall [1969], Akmajian & Jackendoff [1970])

(123)   John hit Bill and then George hit him.

would change the meaning of the second clause. Neutral stress would make *him* refer to *Bill* and a strong stress would make *him* refer to *John*. These phonological differences however seem to be fully determined by semantic deep structures, syntactic (deep) structures being identical in the two cases except for possible subscripts, which in turn – as we saw above – are predicted by semantic representations.

   Surface phenomena like these must be considered to be regular manifestations of different semantic relationships in deep structure (cf. especially Bierwisch [1969b] for details). Earlier these were represented in a simplified notation from predicate logic, where argument variables express different (individual) 'actants' of the semantic representation here including time intervals (see below). The two deep structures of sentence (123) may then be transcribed as follows

(124)   (i) $h(x_1, y_1, t_i) \stackrel{'}{\wedge} h(z_1, y_1, t_j)$
          (ii) $h(x_1, y_1, t_i) \stackrel{'}{\wedge} h(z_1, x_1, t_j)$
                $j > i$ (where t_i, t_j stand for times of the events)

where representation (124, i) results in the unmarked phonological structure and (124, ii) in the marked one. In the first case y_1 is patient in both sentoids, whereas the agents are differing. In the marked version the relations are inverted because agent x_1

becomes patient in the second sentoid, thus creating semantic contrast. This contrast is immediately recognizable from the logical representation of the semantic relationships. When we block pronominalization and repeat *Bill*, only neutral stress is possible. The only difference, then, lies in the different proper names used in the same agent-place. This weak contrast correctly predicts stress on *George*. When *Jim* is used instead of *him*, no contrast is established and no marked stress pattern can result.

Only the unmarked version permits deletion of *him* and further sentential conjunction. As we have seen above this is impossible in the contrastive case, because there is no way left to establish the contrast.

However, here the role of sentential conjunctions becomes important. Compare the following sentences

(125)   John hit Bill but then George hit hím.
(126)   *John hit Bill but then George.
(127)   John hit Bill and then George.
(128)   John hit Bill but George hím.
(129)   ?John hit Bill and George hit him.

Firstly, the use of *but*, representing contrastive structures alone, automatically selects the marked accentuation, without which (125) would be ungrammatical. In (126) *Bill* and *George* are both patients so that no contrast exists, consequently the use of *but* is ungrammatical, whereas functional parallelism correctly predicts *and* as grammatical in (127).

Up till now we have not mentioned the role of the third argument, denoting time of the actions. In the examples discussed the action of the second sentoid (immediately) follows the action of the first sentoid ($t_j > t_i$). This temporal succession is represented by *then* in surface structure. As soon as this difference of time is also eliminated, structures underlying (129) are wholly parallel such that pronominalization is not enough, and further reduction to *John and George hit Bill* seems necessary.

Similar phenomena can be observed when we use other conjunctions and adverbs. *Also* expresses only the parallel interpretation, while *therefore* (CAUSE) probably expresses the contrastive one.

In simple texts formed by juxtaposition like *John hit Bill. George hit him*, the contrastive interpretation seems natural, because of the consequences of the absence of *also* or *and (then)*.

Enumerations like *John hit Bill and (then) George hit him, and (then) Mary hit him (and) finally everybody was hitting him* only admit, by their parallelism, the unmarked surface structure.

The contrast represented by *but* seems to be neutralized by a negative element, such that in (79) *him* mostly refers to Bill

(130)   John hit Bill, but George didn't hit him.

The contrast expressed by *but* is now fully assumed by the change introduced by the negation operator. The further use of adverbs may, however, favor the one or the other of the two representations very well. Whereas stress on *him* in (79) is not wholly impossible, a sentence like (80) must definitely be assigned the parallel interpretation

(131)   John hit Bill, but George didn't hit him, he just stared at him.

Here the change of verbal predicate – other categories being equal – seems to 'draw' the contrast from these other categories.

4.3.10. From these few examples it has become apparent that surface structure does not 'contribute' to the meaning of a sentence but that different stress patterns are simply representations of differences (contrasts) and parallelism in the relations between semantic representations of sentoids and their functional elements like topic and comment (see below).

It follows that our remarks could also have been made for texts consisting of more than one complex sentence. The following texts are ungrammatical for the reasons made explicit above:

(132)   (i)   Peter doesn't like Richard Nixon.
        *(
        (ii)   John however doesn't like him either.

(133)   (i)   He planned to go to Italy this summer.
        *(
        (ii)   She also planned to go to France this summer.

The ungrammaticalness of these texts can only be explained when their whole semantic representations are compared, because conjunctions and sentential adverbs represent precisely the relations between the sentences of a text. We will see in section 5 how these semantic relations between semantic representations and their elements must be accounted for. We first have to see if there are other superficial constraints upon the combination of subsequent sentences, this time in the verb-phrase constituent of the sentences.

4.4. *Concluding remarks*

It may be concluded from the preceding sections that the rules and the conditions underlying such apparently diverse phenomena as article selection (definitivization), pronominalization, relativization, stress assignment, etc. are very similar if not identical. The constraints could be formulated adequately in terms of underlying semantic representations and their relations in a linear sequence of sentoids.

It was assumed that the introduction of discourse referents in a grammatical text obeys rather heavy constraints, which could be formulated in terms of different types of identity-relations between semantic representations and their terms. When no specific pragmatic (deictic, etc.) conditions are fulfilled, this introduction requires indefinite noun phrases and subsequent definite noun phrases. However, this assumption needed specification, because there are two different types of 'indefinites', and hence of 'definites', in natural language. Strictly speaking, indefiniteness only applies in cases were individuals (elements or classes) are not identified in a given class. Their formal introduction then required a provisional choice operator. The definite descriptions derived from such sentoids are therefore based only on (sets of) properties, such that 'identity' must be formalized with the aid of an abstraction operator. Similarly, definite descriptions based on strict referential identity must be derived from 'indefinite', or rather particular, non-specified noun phrases of which the underlying logical form contains an èta-operator.

The description of relative clauses hinges upon this analysis of co-referential/anaphorical relations in texts: restrictive relative clauses, and post-nominal modifiers in general, may receive a formal typology according to the way in which they identify a particular or non-particular individual for predication in the matrix-sentence. They may therefore be derived from preceding sentoids in a textual sequence. Since non-restrictive relative clauses are not identifying, but specify additional properties, they may be derived from sentences which follow the matrix sentence in deep structure.

Processes of pronominalization, which were assumed to be late transformations of substitution, were described in terms similar to those characterizing the different types of definitivization. The identity condition, therefore, requires specification as to whether identity is referentially or semantically (qualitatively) based. This presupposes a precise analysis of the scope of the definite descriptions involved, a scope which may seem to be blurred in complex sentence structures, but which may be made explicit in subsequent sentoids of a sequence. The different conditions for correct pronominalization are to be framed in terms of precedence relations in such a sequence. In the same way we may predict, by abstract constraints upon the ordering of arguments in the underlying semantic representations, which transformations of embedding and pronominalization are blocked. Similarly, relations of contrast or focus between subsequent SR's predict which noun phrases or pronouns may receive specific stress.

In this section we used sometimes a notation borrowed from a simple, standard predicate calculus and discussed some linguistic implications of recent work done in the theory of reference, philosophical logic, modal logic and formal pragmatics (intensional) logic. Our remarks, however, could not in this stage of (text) linguistic research be more than hints for future research; our attempt at elementary formalization was fragmentary and not always well-defined from a logical point of view. Moreover, it is certain that the current formal means available – of which at present we did not yet take systematic knowledge – permit an explication in more satisfactory terms of many of the relevant problems of formal relations in texts, although on the other hand even systems of modal logic are not yet flexible enough to model all relevant characteristics of texts in natural language. We will see below, and in the next chapter, that the relationship between abstract linguistic semantics and such systems of logic is, nevertheless, close enough to merit extensive future research.

4.5. *Verb phrases/predicates, tense/time*

4.5.1. In this section we will briefly touch upon the textual role of verb phrases and their underlying predicates, especially with respect to their aspects of tense and time respectively. It is impossible, in the actual state of our knowledge, to arrive at general rules and conditions in this reputedly ill-known domain of modern grammar. Still more ignorant are we about the temporal relations between the sentences of a coherent sequence, although we intuitively know that such temporal relations are crucial for textual well-formedness.

Several issues are involved here which are relevant for text grammar. Earlier we saw that the internal structure of the verb (or predicate) imposes constraints upon the ordering of sentoids in a sequence. Locutionary verbs for example are necessarily followed by their object sentoids, whereas we will see below that the presuppositions of a sentence are also determined by this internal structure of the verb. Another class of verbs, like *to hope*, *to dream*, *to wish*, *to intend*, etc. establishes the modal 'scope' in which the 'worlds' are specified determining the linear coherence of discourse referents. Furthermore, we will see that relations between whole sentences or propositions in a text, such as those of cause and consequence, hinge upon relations between their verbs or predicates. Finally, it will turn out that verb phrases or predicate phrases are normally assigned the function of 'comment' in a sentence, that is the part intuitively containing the new semantic information defining the 'progression' in the construction of the semantic content of a text. In that case identity and continuity is assured by the function of 'topic' which in normal cases is assigned to the subject noun phrase of the sentence (for detail and definition, see below). These still rather vague hypotheses suggest that verb phrases and their underlying predicates contribute in quite another way as do noun phrases to the coherence of texts, because their linear coherence is not primarily based on relations of referential or semantic equivalence, but on relations of contiguity or compatibility, such as those of order, consequence, etc. Intuitively speaking, thus, noun-phrases might be considered as the semantic 'constants' of a text, whereas verb phrases are the semantic 'variables'. Notice that these terms do not correspond with the logical notions of 'variable' and 'constant' respectively. This explains already the quasi-absence of genuine PRO-VERBS in natural language and their close relationship with PRO-SENTENCES, like *it*, *so*, or *do*. Their textual role, therefore, cannot be dissociated from the relations between whole sentences or propositions in a text, to which we will turn in the next section. There, we shall also consider some semantic relations between the predicates in a text.

4.5.2. At the level of sentential surface structure verb phrases seem to contribute little to the coherence of texts and especially here it will turn out that one aspect of their morphematic surface form, *viz.*TENSE, has to be considered as a manifestation of deeper temporal relations between semantic representations in a text.

The problem at issue is the following: which relations can be established between the tense forms of subsequent sentences in a text, and how do these relations correspond to underlying temporal relations between propositions? Our phrasing of the problem already suggests that there is no simple one:one relation between surface tense forms and semantic aspects of time. Indeed, these must be distinguished carefully: identical TEMPORAL relations may be expressed by a variety of tenses, and conversely. Similarly, it will turn out that the SEMANTIC notion of TIME has to be distinguished from the REFERENTIAL notion of real, denoted, PHYSICAL TIME. The interesting problem precisely lies in their respective correlation. It is well-known that events (actions, processes) develop in time, but how do we represent this temporal order in texts of natural language?

4.5.3. The different intricate problems involved here have been reflected in the current description of verbs, auxiliaries and tense in generative grammar. The standard theory derives tense as a constituent of a predicate phrase, dominated by the *Aux* constituent, which precedes *VP* and the two optional categories of *Place* and *Time*. Together with *Mode* and *Aspect* the different tenses, like *Past, Present, Future*, generate the tense morphemes of the verb and/or auxiliaries. We will not discuss here the precise base rules and transformations involved, but it has to be underlined that the status of *Aux* is still very problematic. It has been proposed that this category should be derived much higher in the tree, probably directly dominated by *S*. Especially the semantically orientated discussions stress that tenses, representing time in surface structure, characterize events, in which also the arguments/noun phrases and the adverbial *Time* constituents are involved. Auxiliaries, as well as time adverbials, are thus generated independently of the nuclear propositions and transformationally integrated in the predicate phrase in order to be able to account adequately of the selection restrictions between the verb on the one hand and tense, (in-)direct object and verbal phrases on the other hand (cf. McCawley [1968b], Verkuyl [1970], [1971] 84 ff, Wunderlich [1970b]).[10]

---

[10] Undoubtedly the most extensive treatment of tense and time in natural language has been provided by Wunderlich (1970b). Although his description is syntactically based, many hints for a semantic treatment are given. His book often refers to tense and time structures in texts or sequences of sentences, although it does not make these notions explicit in the grammar. A tense like pluperfect (in German) is thus characterized with respect to previous sentences. Furthermore, one of his main hypothesis is that time adverbials may be derived from subsequent *S*-nodes, which suggests their formal similarity with non-restrictive relative clauses. It was not possible to integrate his results in the present book already. For tense and time description in sentences we refer to his work, whereas the implications for text grammar require detailed special treatment in future research.

4.5.4. Neglecting, then, in our discussion the precise surface derivation of tense and its relation with verb and time adverbials within the sentence, we will confine our-selves to time and tense relations in sequences of sentences. We are confronted with the fact that some sequences are ungrammatical due to a wrong selection of tenses. Consider for example the following sequences

(134)   (i) *The old woman was buried in her native village.
             (ii) She is dying of a virulent pneumonia.
(135)   (i) *Peter will write an article for our review.
             (ii) It was published in a special issue.
(136)   (i) *Please try to come to Paris.
             (ii) I am sure you forgot to do so.
(137)   (i) *Harry has never been in Rome.
             (ii) He spent his last holidays there.

From these examples we conclude that there are constraints upon the selection of tenses in subsequent sentences of a text. It will often be the case for example that a given tense form requires the same tense form in a subsequent sentence, like in (134) and (135). Notice, however, that this requirement cannot be stated in general because it is based on the semantic structures of the respective sentences. It is easy to change the examples in a way such that different tenses are admitted in the sequences. In (134) we might have as a second sentence: *Her sons every month visit her grave*, whereas a future tense in (135, ii) will make (135) grammatical.

Obviously, the continuity/discontinuity in tense forms is wholly dependent on the underlying structures. Thus, in (135) the ungrammaticalness is caused by a contra-diction between the presuppositions of the respective sentences: (134, i) presupposes *the old woman is dead*, whereas (134, ii) requires as a presupposition *the old woman is (still) alive*. Put in other terms: the 'worlds' or STATE DESCRIPTIONS represented in these respective sentences are incompatible or ill-ordered. In (134) for example the presupposed death of the old woman excludes further predication about her as a living human being in a state description following temporally the state description presupposing her death. Conversely, it is ungrammatical to predicate something in (135) about an individual of which the (actual) non-existence has been asserted. The problem of time relations between sentences, thus, is closely related with the intro-duction of discourse referents discussed in the previous sections. The 'existence' of arguments is dependent on the temporal aspect of their successive state descriptions. Relevant here is the fact that the same holds true for the events designated by the verb/predicate, like in (136), where *try to* presupposes a future action and *forget* presupposes a past event such that the pro-verb *do so* cannot refer to the same event.

Conversely we may have in (135) a subsequent sentence *It will be published in a special issue* having the same tense as (135, i) but referring to a time point following the time of (135, i). This temporal succession, then, is wholly determined by the semantic representations of these sentences. Now, how do we make explicit the constraints upon these tense and time relations?

4.5.5. Notice first of all that the tenses are not directly related with the semantic time of the successive represented events. Crucial for the generation of tense is the relation of semantic or referential time of the events with the time of the utterance, that is with a pragmatic category of the speech act. We symbolize this PRAGMATIC TIME POINT as t_0. Since speech develops linearly in time, t_0 is a function of variable physical time, but for reasons of simplicity we keep it constant for the whole speech act.

Textual description of events is temporally related with t_0: events preceding t_0 thus have a time indicator (operator, argument) t_i smaller than t_0: $t_i < t_0$, and conversely for future events, whereas present events or states are contemporaneous with t_0. The general rule then, is that if $t_i < t_0$ a past/perfect tense is generated, if $t_i > t_0$ a future tense is generated and if $t_i = t_0$ a present tense is generated. A further rule is that a present tense considered as temporally neutral may also be generated if $t_i < t_0$ or if $t_i > t_0$ under some further conditions which will not detain us here.

More complicated, however, are the rules for 'compound' tenses like some past tenses, pluperfect, future perfect, etc. These tenses represent semantic relations between the events denoted by the propositions, relations which in turn are related with t_0. Traditionally, a time point/interval in past or future is selected as a focus with respect to which the other events are described in time. This SEMANTIC TIME POINT may be symbolized as t_f (for time focus). We, then, may formulate the general rules:

(138)   (i) $t_i < t_f < t_0$ → pluperfect
     (ii) $t_i < t_f > t_0$ → future perfect
     (iii) $t_i > t_f < t_0$ → past future

Notice that in fact in the earlier rule for past, perfect, present and future we should also have a time focus t_f, which in case coincides with t_0 (or with t_i):

(138)   (iv) $t_i = (t_f = t_0)$ → present
     (v) $t_i > (t_f = t_0)$ → future
     (vi) $(t_i = t_f) < t_0$ → past/perfect
     (vii) $t_i < (t_f = t_0)$ → perfect/past

These rather simple tentative rules are language specific; (138, vi and vii) for example are different for English, Dutch and French, at least in many cases of their use. Moreover, some languages do not have this differentiation in tense forms but express time relations with other morphemes or adverbs. Conversely, some languages may have specific tenses for other logical possibilities of ordering between t_i, t_f and t_0, e.g. $t_i > t_f > t_0$, which would be a 'future future', which is expressed with two futures, and possibly conjunctions like *and then (and next)*, in English, e.g. *He will inform you that he will not be able to visit us.*

Finally, we have neglected the close interaction with MODE and ASPECT, e.g. in conditionals, counterfactuals, duratives/nonduratives, perfectives/imperfectives, etc. In this respect we should have made the rules more precise by establishing more sophisticated relations, e.g. differentiated according to time points and time intervals. In *He had waited for her for five hours* and *He had seen her in the shop*, the events either wholly precede t_f, $(t_i < t_f)$, or are measured until t_f, which may be symbolized as follows: $t_i \gtrless t_f$. Similarly, we may want to denote that a (future) action starts at t_f: $t_f \gtrless t_i$, instead of occurring some time in future. In a possible axiomatization of these rules (cf. Wunderlich [1970b], Lieb [1970]; see note 10 above) we would then have to define not only relations such as *to precede*, *to follow*, *to be contemporaneous with*, and *to overlap* but also the notion *immediately (follows, precedes)*. These, and probably other, fundamental notions of ordering are necessary to generate such adverbs and conjunctions as *since*, *until*, *then/when*, etc. We see that time relations are expressed by complex combinations of tenses and other elements of surface structure. We will, however, not describe these interrelationships in detail, but turn to the specific textual implications of these brief remarks.

4.5.6. Firstly, the textual foundation of the tenses manifests itself in all compound tenses. In order to define such tenses, indeed, we needed a semantic time-focus, with respect to which events can be temporally related. However, it is clear that such a semantic time point or interval is not an isolated linguistic operator: it must be part of a semantic representation, or must be implied by referential and/or pragmatic knowledge available to the hearer(s) in a speech act. As we shall see for other semantic aspects like presupposition, topic and comment, etc. time-focus is only one of the possible elements of preceding sentoids/sentences. It is not possible to introduce times/tenses without letting them follow other propositions, if such times/tenses cannot be specified directly with respect to t_0 $(= t_f)$ like in *I'll come tomorrow*, *It rained yesterday*, etc. Thus, in order to have a sentence like *He had been waiting for five hours* we necessarily need a preceding sentence like *I met him at the corner of the street*. The same is true for future perfect and (in many cases and many languages) for past tenses. A rule therefore has to specify that a sentence S_i in a sequence Sq_i may have $\left\{ \begin{array}{l} \text{pluperfect} \\ \text{future perfect} \end{array} \right\}$ if S_{i-j} $(j < i)$ has $\left\{ \begin{array}{l} \text{past/perfect} \\ \text{future} \end{array} \right\}$. Analogous to the intro-

duction of discourse referents for nouns (arguments) we thus have discourse referents for temporal elements. This explains why we may have pro-temporal elements in a sentence, e.g. adverbs and conjunctions: *then*, *since*, etc. Any change of this temporal focus in a text is either implicitly defined by events linearly occurring after t_f, i.e. by their very semantic structure or the structure of the semantic representation *(shot → hit → kill)* or by explicit temporal phrases like *earlier*, *before*, *the previous week*, *after*, *later*, *the next day*, etc. Without such temporal modifications, t_f of a sentence S_{i-j}

remains unchanged as a temporal specification for its subsequent sentences: thus resulting in a state description.

All this is rather obvious but, until now, tenses rarely have in this way been related with ORDERING RELATIONS OF TIME IN SUBSEQUENT SENTENCES OF A TEXT. An intuitive or abstract time-focus like t_f, e.g. introduced by Reichenbach (1947), thus acquires an explicit status in a semantic description of a sequence.

4.5.7. In the previous paragraphs it has become clear that the problems related with constraints upon tense consecution in a text are to be formulated in terms of temporal relations between semantic representation in a sequence. Tenses are the language specific surface manifestations of such time relations and can be considered as the surface 'pro-forms' for deep structure time referents; that is, identical tenses represent – at their own – time continuity (either linear or contemporaneous) of the events/states described by the propositions of the subsequent sentences. Change of tense will normally occur only when other elements change the time referent.

The real problems precisely are to be sought for at the level of semantic relations between the sentences, and on the level relating semantic representations with referential structures (possible worlds). The issues involved here are common problems for linguistics and logic (and poetics): a 'tense logic' can be framed in terms of a 'time logic' for texts. That is: how do we represent, in a coherent text, e.g., a description of events, for example in narrative? (cf. Wunderlich [1970b]). In logical theory tense systems have been elaborated already in great detail,[11] but linguistic semantics still ignores a 'chronological logic' (Rescher [1968]) for the description of sequences of sentences.

In general we may postulate a mapping of referential/real time points and intervals upon semantically represented times. The very linearity of textual surface structure seems to admit such a simple one to one relation. We may represent each event by a sentoid and assign to them the corresponding time indicators. Thus the mapping would be $E_1 \rightarrow S_1, E_2 \rightarrow S_2, ..., E_i \rightarrow S_i, ..., E_n \rightarrow S_n$.

However, these relations are established between sentoids not between (complex) surface structures of sentences/clauses. We saw earlier that embedded clauses may be derived from subsequent underlying sentoids. Thus a sentence *Before S_i, S_j* would be derived from S_j *and (then) S_i* by a type of topicalization or focus transformation, in which the preceding clause establishes t_f, and in which S_j is a 'comment' (see below). Furthermore, events occurring at the same time are necessarily also mapped linearly on $S_1, S_2, ... S_i$. Since $t_1 = t_2 =, ... = t_i$ in this case we in principle cannot formulate

---

[11] We may refer to the classical work of Prior (1968ab), (1971) and, within the framework of recent systems of modal or intensional logic, to the advanced investigations of the 'Californian' school, e.g. Montague (1968), (1970ab), Kamp (1968) and further Rescher & Urquhart (1971), which we are, however, unable to apply at present in the description of temporal relations in texts of natural language. It is obvious, however, that these aspects of semantic relations in texts may be among the first to be formally modelled in terms of logical systems. For a brief review of some of these models, cf. Wunderlich (1970b).

constraints upon the order of the sequence when no other semantic relationships hold, such as discourse referents, presuppositions, entailments. Cf. e.g. the sequence: *John is not at the office. He must be ill.* Here the explanation given in S_2 has a time indicator t_2 which is identical with t_1. We may consider such a text as a permitted surface permutation of a relation of CAUSE and CONSEQUENCE between sentoids: *John is ill. Therefore he is not at the office.* The rule is that cause and consequence will imply temporal succession, thus constraining sequential ordering.

Labov and Waletzky (1967) have extensively studied possible permutations of (kernel) sentences in narrative. They arrived at a formalism in which the ordering of a sentence was defined by its deplacement sets, i.e. the number of positions it could be localized on the left or on the right of the place it was occurring. Of course, this important study, in fact, is dealing with the performance use of sentences in narrative, and therefore does not simply provide valid indications for the formal constraints. Moreover, replacement possibilities were rather loosely defined. A close description of the semantic structures involved would result in much more constraints upon the ordering of the sentences, whereas other replacements can be explained only as results of (narrative) transformations. These operations are especially used in literary narrative, to which we will turn in chapter 8.

We may conclude this informal discussion by repeating that the temporal elements of the sentence as represented in tenses, temporal adverbs and conjunctions, establish, together with discourse referents, presupposition and topic and comment, the main ordering conditions for sentences in a text. Subsequent events are marked with a linearly increasing time index, corresponding to linear sentence ordering (or in surface structure linear and hierarchical ordering). State descriptions and all types of general statements represented by the sentences keep the time indicators of a given sentence or sequence constant or abstract from them. Sentence ordering, then, is based on semantic relations of cause, consequence, concession, etc. for predicates/verbs and equivalence (inclusion, intersection) for noun phrases/arguments. The textual role of temporal relations can be characterized, thus, corresponding to (in-)definite descriptions for object-individuals, in terms of DEFINITE AND INDEFINITE TEMPORAL DESCRIPTION. (Rescher [1968] 200 f.). Adverbs like *sometimes, always, often, regularly*, etc. are temporally independent of the position in the text and do not require t_f. Definite time descriptions are provided by dates and by such adverbs as *then, now, since, during*, etc. which require a t_f in a previous sentence. The very analogy between time points/intervals and individuals seems to suggest that time points are to be considered also as arguments over which we may normally quantify.

Notice that these general constraints are further specified by more particular conditions. Thus, in subsequent sentences it will be necessary for momentaneous verbs that a time point is localized in a previous sentence and not a time interval. A text like

(139)   (i)   The whole afternoon Peter was working on his new book.
          ?(
          (ii) He lit a cigarette.

is of rather low grammaticalness without adverbs as *only once, sometimes,* which fix such (a) point(s) in (139, ii). Of course the converse also holds: we may not generate a sentence S_i having a durative predicate when contemporariness is asserted with a momentaneous predicate in S_{i-1}

(140)   (i)   A bomb exploded in the office.
          (ii) Meanwhile most of the employees quietly drank their tea.

Similar constraints hold here as between verbs and temporal adverbials in sentences (for detais, cf. Verkuyl [1971]).

Finally, we have to stress again that temporal consecution, and thus sequential ordering, is based on relations of cause, consequence, etc. Logical theory is able to give the explicit models for such temporal relations, provided the calculus admits connectives of a type relevant for natural language. Although logical theory is especially interested in valid deductions, i.e. in the conditions which make conclusions true or false, we may use such systems in texts for determining the grammaticalness of a derived sentence S_i with respect to its preceding sentences, which, then, can be considered as a sort of premises. Textual well-formedness, i.e. coherence, is also based on rules of temporal identity and change, like in tense logical systems. All types of process or event description may be framed in subsequent state descriptions for discrete time points/intervals (cf. Rescher [1968] 213 ff.). Thus the sentence *On Monday Peter said that he could not come the next day* may be followed correctly (implies) *Peter could not come on Tuesday.* Less trivial cases of derivational steps may be made and may provide adequate models for the study of a chronological logic in texts.

4.6. *Place adverbials and the topological logic of texts*

4.6.1. Whereas the preceding section at some length discussed time relations in texts as a main condition for ordering of sentences, we now might investigate the role of adverbials of PLACE. Clearly, textual coherence is not only defined over individuals and their relations, but actions and events also require a topological determination in a spatio-temporal 'setting'. Neglecting again pragmatic and referential factors (which may be formalized in logical systems) we here find the semantic constraints upon the selection of place adverbials in texts.

4.6.2. The systematic character of intersentential relations again enables us to introduce, here, notions analogous to those encountered before.

Firstly, we need a pragmatic zero-point l_0, formally representing the place of the utterance. This pragmatic category determines, besides the NUNC of t_0, the HIC of the text as a whole. It generates such adverbs as *here, until, (where), from (here), towards* and is implied in all DEICTICS like *this, that*, etc. (cf. Wunderlich [1971a]).

We will further need also a symbol indicating TOPOLOGICAL FOCUS: l_f, denoting the place at which or with respect to which actions, processes, states are localized. Thus, verbs may be combined with prepositions (or integrate prepositions) implying movement *towards* or *from* t_0 and t_f. Again intra-sentential constraints upon verb-place relations and presuppositions hold between sentences: **I was walking in the deserted forest. In the rooms the lights were burning (…)*.

Similarly, we may have DEFINITE AND INDEFINITE LOCAL DESCRIPTIONS: *everywhere, anywhere, somewhere, on some places*, are indefinite local descriptions which are independent of l_f, which is defined by previous sentences in a text, whereas *here, there, therefrom, in New York*, etc. are definite local descriptions.

The general rules for chronological relations also hold here: a sentence S_i has a place-indicator l_i identical with that of S_{i-j} if no explicit or implicit change has been introduced. In normal cases this place-indicator is present only in deep structure. In English there are no specific morphemes indicating obligatorily that an event takes place at the same topological point or area. Other languages, however, might have such topological 'loci'.

Finally, there are topological constraints upon the combination of sentences in a text. Thus, in the example used earlier: *When Peter came in Sheila laughed at him*, we may probably not have: *When Sheila laughed at Peter, he came in*, if it is presupposed that Sheila is in the room (and cannot see Peter through the window). The constraints are often implied by the internal structure of the verb, considered as an *n*-place predicate, often 'incorporating' a case or preposition (cf. Gruber [1965], [1967]) like *to leave = to go OUT, to enter = to come INTO, to pierce = to put THROUGH*, etc.

Based on such verbs and adverbs we find the normal logical constraints upon textual well-formedness: For example if S_i states *Peter left the room* we may not have in S_{i+1} e.g. *Peter was sitting at the table*, if it is presupposed that the table is in the room. By simple logical rule (excluded middle) individuals may not be in the room and out of the room at the same time. This is trivial, of course, but it matters to draw the consequences for an explicit formulation of the constraints upon textual coherence: a topological logic is one of the systems modelling this coherence (Rescher [1968]).

4.7. *Final remarks*

4.7.1. In the previous sections we have sketched systematically which categories of syntactic structures of sentences are dependent on relations with other sentences in a text. It turned out that all these relations have to be studied as manifestations of underlying relations between semantic representations. It has become clear, furthermore, that the same basic principles hold for the sequential relations of the different syntactic/semantic categories in the sentences of a text. The textual dependency of the respective categories manifests itself in a combination of identity and difference, i.e. in variables and constants. Definitivization is based on relations of referential and semantic equivalence or identity. Pronominalization is based on the same principles with the further constraint of lexematic identity. In both cases we met the relevance of discourse referents, i.e. definitely described individuals. These definite descriptions, in surface structure, may also be contained in restrictive relative clauses, although it was shown that these may be derived from previous sentoids. The different conditions on embedding (and its depth) for the possible order of pronouns and antecedent is explained on the basis of this linear introduction.

The same remarks may be made for verbs and adverbial phrases, where also indefinite descriptions and '*PRO*-forms' seem to exist, e.g. in the form of '*PRO*-verbs', adverbs, and tenses. These analogies are not at all artificial or far-fetched. They designate a fundamental generalization of the different types of relating sentences in a coherent text.

4.7.2. Although we now have a global picture of such intersentential relations which can be considered at the same time as a research design for detailed research on each issue, we had to neglect some important other categories and levels.

We left outside our scope, apart from the remarks in section 4.3.10., the systematic review of the PHONOLOGICAL CONSTRAINTS in textual surface structure. Although phonological structures are characteristic of the sentential level, there are several important features determining intonation and stress assignment in texts. We saw, however, that specific stress assignment in sentences can be predicted by deeper relations between semantic representations, such as emphasis and contrast. We will return briefly to these aspects in the section on topic and comment below. Besides these types of specific stress assignment in sentences there are features of intonation which may mark beginning and end of the text and between sentences and paragraphs in the text (cf. Dressler, 1970a). No explicit work has been done on phonological text markers, and we have to leave the issue without further comment. Let us stress however that such features are important as soon as we have to describe oral dialogical texts. Together with syntax and semantics they guide the processes of anticipation and feed-back in oral communication processes (cf. Harweg [1971]).

Similar remarks hold for the description of the GRAPHOLOGICAL STRUCTURE of texts, which lends itself more easily to detailed characterization. Textual boundary markers are explicit, whereas intersentential and inter-clausal markers are also manifested graphically, as distinct from phonological representation. It is well-known that these surface features are exploited in (modern) poetic texts, where typography is an important aspect of surface structure and its possible relations with deep structure.

4.7.3. We paid little attention to the eminent textual role of CONJUNCTIONS and SENTENTIAL ADVERBS. These categories are direct manifestations of the semantic relationships between sentences/propositions as a whole in a text. Together with pronouns they probably are the most direct surface morphemes of textual coherence. Since their derivation is predicted by semantic relations between whole sentences we will briefly discuss them in the next section of this chapter.

4.7.4. Finally, not only the syntactic categories themselves are placed under heavy textual constraints, but also SYNTACTIC STRUCTURE is dependent on intersentential relations. Analogous to stress assignment we may have transformations permutating categories in the sentence under the influence, again, of semantic deep structure relations in the sequence (cf. for detail, Drubig [1967]). Focusation and topicalization are processes resulting from these specific relations. We will give them more detailed attention below.

Having explained the surface phenomena of the textual coherence as manifestations of deeper relations, we now have to study the main properties of these relations in their own right. That is, first of all, it is necessary to study the relations between semantic categories of the underlying propositions, and then between these propositions as a whole. Especially notions like presuppositions and entailment, topic and comment, often used above, will now need explication.

5. SEMANTIC RELATIONS BETWEEN SENTENCES

5.1. *Introduction*

5.1.1. One of the major conclusions in the preceding sections was that a great part of the phenomena determining linear surface coherence of texts at the syntactic and phonological levels must be described in terms of more abstract relations between semantic representations of an underlying sequence of sentoids. The most important relation studied at this surface level was IDENTITY (or equivalence) and its different types: referential identity, semantic identity, lexical identity, the identity of individuals and of classes, etc. This relation determines to a large extent the linear continuity in texts, and closer examination revealed that there are several ways in which surface structure may actualize deep structure relations of identity. Many of our remarks of the section above, then, properly belong to this section, in which we will deal systematically with the (other) semantic relations between sentences in a grammatical text.

In the grammatical model we adopted for the construction of a text grammar, semantic relations between sentences are studied as relations between underlying semantic representations, including (pre-)lexical structures. We will first, then, make some brief remarks about the relations between (the more superficial) relations between lexical elements and then proceed to a characterization of relations between SR's. One of the important aspects of such deeper relations is known as presupposition (and entailment). Closely related to this aspect are such notions as topic and comment, which are also much discussed in current linguistic work, but which may be described adequately only in the framework of a text grammar.

We may of course try to study the different phenomena mentioned here in pairs or triples of immediately subsequent sentoids, abstracted from their co-text, but it is clear that an adequate text grammar must specify how the semantic structure of a text is linearly 'built up' in its successive sentences, i.e. how sentential phrase markers are combined in one very complex semantic phrase marker for textual surface structure. We will see that in this respect our knowledge of semantic processes is still very poor.

5.1.2. Recent research conducted in the framework of generative semantics has pointed to the fact that the insertion of terminal elements is by no means a simple operation taking place at the end of the derivation of syntactic deep structure. One of the reasons for abolishing these syntactic deep structures as the place of lexical insertion was precisely the fact that transformations already seem to operate on representations of pre-lexical configurations of features. That is, many lexical units, like the verbs *to leave, to kill, to buy*, and nouns like *entrance, bachelor, nephew*, etc. have to be (transformationally) derived from more elementary lexical structures (cf. Staal [1967], Katz [1970], Bierwisch [1969a]). This fact, of course, was already partially known from the first attempts in componential analysis and the formulation of projection rules and selection restrictions based on them, but it was barely noticed that the selection of terminal lexemes may be preceded by different derivational (transformational) steps. Gruber, (1965), (1967) showed, for example, that lexemes may be 'attached' to more than one pre-terminal category, and McCawley (1968a), (1968b) indicated that the ambiguity of such syntactico-lexematic unambiguous strings as *I almost killed him* can only be explained when transformations apply to pre-lexical deep structures. The insertion of lexical units, then, is a gradual process determined by properly generative semantic base rules. This more abstract view of lexico-semantic aspects of derivation also provides better instruments for the description of deep structures in diverse languages, of which the 'lexical mappings' of surface structure seem to be more language-specific, than the underlying rules.

The same can be said of the description of the relations between semantic representations in a text. Unlike traditional discourse analysis we regard the recurrence of identical lexical units (morphemes) in a text as a derived aspect of textual coherence, neither necessary nor sufficient, because only indirectly 'representing' basic deep structure equivalences. That is, it is possible that identical lexicoids in the subsequent SR's receive various lexematic surface forms (a fact which is crucial for the definition of the notion of 'style'). Furthermore, intersentential relations of 'equivalence' are not necessarily dependent upon identity of lexicoids: it is demonstrated below that also relations of predication, description, part-whole specification (and its converse), etc. establish such equivalences.

Moreover, this 'superficial' approach of semantic relations cannot possibly take into account semantic roles or functions of lexical units, because neither syntactic surface nor syntactic deep structures are able to define these functions, like (psycho-)logical subject or 'agent', etc.

5.1.3. Finally, some remarks should be made about terminological issues. Recent semantic theory has resulted in a proliferation of different proposals for names proposed for specific semantic units. For the basic units of semantic structures such different terms as 'features', 'markers', 'components', 'semes', 'sememes', etc. have been used. One rather coherent system has been elaborated by French lexicologists and semanticists, especially Greimas (1966), using '*sème*' for the basic features, *classème* for relational or contextual (selectional) features, *sémème* for the different surface 'meanings' of a lexical entry and *lexème* for the whole dictionary unit having a common core of basic features. In order not to confuse our argument with the extra burden of terminological innovations we will follow most current English terms: 'features' for the basic distinctive abstract elements, and 'lexeme' for an abstract lexico-semantic configuration defined by common features. Our use of 'lexeme' therefore does not include the morphological form defined by a phonological matrix, nor the syntactic features that can be associated with it. We will reserve the term 'lexical unit' for this whole dictionary entry consisting of a lexeme and its morphematic expression. The term 'semantic representation' (abbreviated as SR) will be used for the semantic structure of whole sentences or, later, of whole texts. Finally, the term 'semantic proposition' will be used for the basic nucleus of SR's, i.e. abstracted from such modifying elements as operators, quantifiers and other modal or performative constants and variables.

We will introduce only one new term, LEXICOID, which – as 'sentoid' with respect to sentence – is defined as a configuration of abstract features underlying the actual lexemes. Lexicoids may be realized by different lexemes at the 'surface' of the language, i.e. in the lexicon.

5.2. *Properties of relations*

5.2.1. The description of semantic relations between sentences, or rather, between semantic representations, requires some remarks about the term RELATION itself.

It is well-known that one of the most important characteristics of modern logic was the 'discovery' of many-place predicates or relations. The classical interpretation of predicates as inherent or accessory properties turned out to be insufficient, and the description of all transitive verbs like *to see, to buy, to give*, etc., of adjectives like *similar, tall*, and of nouns like *father, teacher, difference*, etc. cannot be adequate without postulating predicates having more than one 'place' for different arguments, i.e. without relations. These are binary, ternary, ... *n*-ary relations, respectively being defined as sets of ordered pairs, triples, ... *n*-tuples, that is of all the combinations of 2, 3, 4 ... *n* arguments to which this predicate can be assigned. We will see further that this logic of relations is basic to the description of semantic representations, of which the categories, unlike syntactic ones, can only be defined as functional relations between semantic argument terms, i.e. between lexicoids.

5.2.2. In a description of semantic relations we must make a distinction between several types of relations, that is relations themselves have certain properties. Relations may be reflexive, symmetrical, transitive, or irreflexive, non- or asymmetrical, intransitive and connected, relations may be ordering or partial ordering, etc. (for definition we refer to the standard handbooks in logic, e.g. Suppes [1957]). Further, relations may apply in different domains: between elements, between classes or sets, between elements and sets, between elements of different sets (functions), between abstract structures, etc.

We will see in the following sections how these different relations are used to describe the semantic patterning of textual structures. Because scarcely any systematic data about the very terms of the different relations, i.e. about the exact semantic structure of lexicoids or SR's is available, no formal description can be attempted at the moment to account for them.

5.3. *Relations between lexical elements*

5.3.1. The relations between the subsequent SR's in a text will be established, first, between the different semantic elements of these SR's, i.e. between lexical and pre-lexical constants, or more precisely: between predicates denoting properties and relations assigned to variables used to express the abstract structure of an SR.

5.3.2. We will first describe some relations between the arguments of these structures realized as nouns in surface structure.

As we observed, one major relation between lexical elements in a text is that of EQUIVALENCE, holding between different tokens of the same lexeme-type and for all proper synonyms (if any), i.e. between *table* and *table* and between *oculist* and *eye-doctor*. Of course, morphological identity does not matter at this level, although many semantic equivalence relations imply morphological identities. Our equivalence relation will often hold for several languages, if not, translation would be more difficult, if not impossible. This semantic equivalence can be defined by identical feature structures of lexemes.

We saw in preceding sections that semantic equivalences underly the process of pronominalization. It does not therefore imply in concrete sentences identical extension or reference of the equivalent lexemes or their possible difference in stylistic use. In sentences like: *I saw an old man and you saw a young man*, the meaning of the two lexemes *man* is equivalent, but not their actual referents. Abstracted from the texts, identical meanings might refer to identical 'ideal' classes, but in text individuals and subclasses are isolated from them, and combined with different predicates (properties). This is trivial but it is by no means clear whether semantic deep structures in generative grammars actually symbolize meaning or reference (cf. Rohrer [1971]). Selection restrictions are often based not on abstract features but on purely referential properties, and it is not easy to present a semantic theory clearly establishing a difference between them in actual description. We will come back to this problem.

5.3.3. A second category of semantic relations is that of INCLUSION. Two lexemes A and B are said to have an inclusion relation when either A is included in B ($A \subset B$) or B is included in A ($B \subset A$), that is if the feature-configuration of A is a part of that of B, or conversely. We can say roughly that the included lexeme is more 'general' than the including one and therefore denotes a referential class larger than the one denoted by the including lexeme, which is more specific. Thus the lexeme *furniture* is included in *table* (but, extensively, the class of tables is included in the class of all furniture).

5.3.4. We notice that our comparison of related lexemes in subsequent sentences in fact can be framed in terms of a logic of classes or sets. The elements of these sets are not unordered but have structural relations of dominance, connection, etc. as generative semantics has demonstrated. Lexemes can even be represented as phrase markers similar to those representing sentence structure (cf. McCawley [1968a], Lakoff [1971a], Bellert [1972], Agricola [1969], Leech [1969b]).

5.3.5. Within set theory another operation between sets is INTERSECTION ($A \cap B$). Two lexemes A and B intersect if at least one feature x is an element of both A and B. This relation between the lexemes of subsequent sentences is very important because most of the semantic relations holding in a text belong to this type. The lexemes *man* and *woman* intersect because they have the features [+ HUMAN], [+ ADULT] in common.

Of course, there is one important difficulty in taking intersection as a relevant relation between lexemes, because it will be very problematic to give criteria for determining how many and which features two lexemes must have in common to be considered as textually related. Any two subsequent sentences would probably have lexemes sharing [+ OBJECT] or [+ ABSTRACT], etc. Apparently, lexemes have to be related with less primitive features in order to have a significant relation between each other. Further, the rest of the semantic structure of the SR will decide about the relevance of the relation. In our specimen of description in the next section we will indicate some examples of these relations.

Like the relation of inclusion, intersection is relevant for the relation between other lexical categories like verbs and adjectives:

> *to go* $\cap$ *to come, green* $\cap$ *blue*

Notice that the notion of 'feature', and in logic the notion of property, is defined precisely in set theory as the 'name' of a class, *viz.* the class of the objects sharing that property. Thus, if we say that two lexemes intersect, i.e. if they have features in common, the abstract or concrete objects or processes denoted belong to the same class like 'green' and 'blue', both are elements of the class of 'colours'.

5.4. *Relations between sentences: presupposition and entailment*

5.4.1. The relations, roughly characterized above, between lexemes in the subsequent sentences of a text should be studied within the framework of relations between whole semantic representations or their nuclear propositions. We here touch the central part of the surface component of text grammar. All relations of cross-reference studied earlier were considered as aspects of relations between subsequent SR's in a text. Their morphophonological and syntactic manifestations have to be derived from these deeper relationships. Similarly, lexemes or lexicoids are surface elements in hierarchically structured sentence patterns. As was observed earlier, simple lexematic connections like equivalence, inclusion or intersection are probably necessary but certainly not sufficient conditions for intersentential coherence. Take, for example, the following sequence of sentences (cf. also Bever & Ross [1967])

(141)   (i)   John wants to buy a ring for his sister.
         (ii) The sister of our milkman had a baby yesterday.
         (iii) Small children internalize a highly complex grammar in a very short time.
         (iv) For the time being I refrain from giving them more money.

These sequences satisfy the conditions for lexematic relations between sentences, but these are insufficient to establish coherence. That is, the rest of the semantic structures are obviously semantically inconsistent with each other. Intuitively speaking, they are taken from completely different (universes of) discourse(s), manifesting different 'subject matters'. We will see in the next chapter that semantic relations between sentences are 'developing' within the bounds established by rules for macro-coherence. That is, the semantic structures of the subsequent sentences gradually have to build up a complex semantic macro-structure conceivable as an interpretable whole. Before elaborating hypotheses about these macro-structures it is necessary to gain some insight into the linear coherence between semantic representations of immediately subsequent sentences. Put more trivially: how may we significantly 'continue' a text when the sentence(s) $S_1, (S_2, ..., S_{i-1})$ is given?

5.4.2.1. The theory of text grammar may at this point have profit from a long experience of a highly exact nature with intersentential or interpropositional relations, *viz.* that of philosophy of language and of mathematical logic. Recent developments of semantics have made extensive use of such models, although the precise intertheoretical aspects are not yet solved: as was remarked earlier semantic descriptions of relations and representations in natural language are not necessarily DIRECTLY formalizable in a logical calculus, at least not within the framework of traditional, e.g. non-modal, systems. The use of logical notations requires extensive methodological discussion. Nevertheless, we may consider terms, definitions and rules from different logical languages both for their heuristic and their putative descriptive implications.

The set of terms most used for the description of relations between sentences, or even for the description of isolated sentences, comprises such important notions as PRESUPPOSITION and ENTAILMENT (or implication, or consequence). Other notions, e.g. equivalence, have already been studied in structural and interpretive semantics and cover such phenomena as synonymy and antonymy of sentences (cf. Lyons [1963]). These are however paradigmatic relations in the system, i.e. not relations between (subsequent) sentences in a text. We therefore will assume as a rule here that a text is coherent if immediately subsequent sentences/sentoids are not equivalent or contradictory. This rule asserts that texts in natural language, ideally, are linearly consistent and non-redundant. It seems to correspond with analogous derivational constraints upon logical coherence. Given a set of axioms we may, first, not derive theorems which are contradictory; second, though the basic property of equivalence between propositions is defined by the rules of deduction, this equivalence does not hold between the derived or derivable theorems of the system, e.g. in a theory.

5.4.2.2. More interesting for our purposes are such 'syntagmatic' connections between propositions as presupposition and entailment. Of course, in logic they also are characteristic of the system, that is, not all implications of a statement are used in derivations. Similarly, in formal semantics we are also interested in the possible (well-formed) presuppositions or consequences of certain semantic propositions and not merely in those realized in a given text. Only a small part of all possible presuppositions and implications of a sentence is realized in the text as we shall see below. On the other hand, text structure will rule out a great part of the possible presuppositions and entailments as 'irrelevant'. Finally, as we shall see, these notions also have important PRAGMATIC and REFERENTIAL aspects (cf. chap. 9). They determine the USE of sentences/propositions, in a text and in a situation. We are committed to some presuppositions and entailments only at a given time in a given place, that is, under given INITIAL CONDITIONS. These may, in part, be established by the preceding part of the text. We saw earlier that it makes sense to predicate something about an individual only if that individual textually 'exists'. The problem of definite descriptions underlying co-reference and cross-reference is one aspect of such conditions. Let us try to give a brief systematic account of this type of logico-semantic relations.

5.4.3. Let us first distinguish between FORMAL (deductive) and PROBABILISTIC (inductive) presupposition and entailment. A (linguistic) semantic theory will be interested especially in the first type of these relations, viz. in relations definable by the lexicon (and meaning postulates) and the semantic rules of the grammar alone. We can call them semantically NECESSARY. The other type is based on our knowledge of the world and will of course also heavily determine textual coherence. However, the grammar will not formalize such relations.

5.4.4. Defining briefly the two notions introduced above, we will say that a sentence S ENTAILS (or 'has as a consequence') a sentence S' when if S is true then S' is true, whereas a sentence S is said to PRESUPPOSE S' when S can only be true or false if S' is true i.e. when both S and $\sim S$ entail S'. (cf. Keenan [1970], [1971ab]; Kummer [1971b] and initially Strawson [1952] 175 ff.). Thus a sentence like *Peter is married to Mary* will entail e.g. *Mary is married to Peter* ('to be married to' is a symmetric relation), whereas its negation does not entail the second sentence. A sentence like *John knows he is arrogant* presupposes *John is arrogant* because its negation also implies the second proposition. There are, however, a series of theoretical problems which are still to be solved in this domain.[12]

Notice first of all that the traditional definition of presuppositions is based on the notion of truth value. That is, they are defined only within a theory of reference, i.e. within an extensional semantics or model theory. Intensional linguistic semantics is primarily concerned with the features of wellformedness, not with truth values.[13] But even in extensional semantics the definition would require further specification. Take, for example, non-declarative sentences like

(142)   Give me the book lying on the table.

(143)   Do you know when Peter arrived?

---

[12] The introduction of the notions of presupposition and entailment into modern linguistic theory has been due above all to generative semantics, although the subject was well-known in philosophy of language (Strawson [1952], Black, [1962]). An early linguistic attempt was Fillmore (1965). Cf. further McCawley (1968a), Morgan (1969), Lakoff (1970b), (1971a), (1971b) and the contributions in Fillmore and Langendoen, eds. (1971). It is striking to note that these two notions have been borrowed rather uncritically from philosophy of language. The main deficiencies of their theoretical introduction into generative grammar have been the lack of precise definitions of their theoretical status, e.g. at the level of semantics, their precise form, the consequences of their traditional definition in terms of truth values, the lack of differentiation between types of presupposition and the failure to make them explicit in the algorithm, e.g. by deriving them at the semantic level. For a critical survey, cf. Garner (1971). Undoubtedly the most satisfactory description of presupposition in natural language has been provided by Keenan (1970), who also recognized the textual aspects of presuppositional relations.

[13] *Pace* recent proposals, made by logicians only, for a truth functional linguistic semantics, e.g. Lewis (1970), Davidson (1970), Wallace (1970), and others. To be sure, we are convinced that a theory of natural language also needs a formal semantics (in the logical sense), i.e. a sound theory of reference or model theory, in which many problems of current linguistic semantics can be formulated more adequately (cf. chapter 9 for brief discussion), especially when based on powerful, i.e. flexible, systems of modal logic. However, up to the present, these attempts toward a truth functional semantics have not yet solved any relevant problem of the linguist (cf. Bar-Hillel [1970], Cohen [1970]), at least not problems of semantic structure. Intensional interpretations seem promising at the moment; cf. Lakoff (1970a) for some suggestions. The elaboration of a formal pragmatics, e.g. by Montague (1970ab), for natural language is still restricted to some domains of (rather superficial) syntax.

These sentences clearly have presuppositions, *viz. There is a book lying on your table* and *Peter arrived*, respectively, without (traditionally) being recognized as having truth value. We thus must either modify our general conditions of truth value of sentences or define other types of values for non-declarative sentences, or make our definition of presupposition independent of referential notions such as 'truth' or 'falsity'.

A first way out of this problem is the definition of presupposition on the basis of nuclear propositions instead of on whole sentences. In that case pragmatic or per-formative operators or 'hyper-sentences' dominate a proposition like *You give me the book lying on the table* and *You know when Peter arrived*, which can be assigned truth value. The complete expression, thus 'reduced' to self-descriptive declaratives: *I order you* (...) and *I ask you* (...), similarly has a truth value (being, in fact always true in ordinary communication situations) (cf. Lewis [1970]).

However, this analysis does not yield a satisfactory solution and does not conform to our traditional notion of truth value. That is, the truth value of a sentence like

(144)   John visited me yesterday.

is NOT determined by the fact that *I tell you* ... as representing a declarative is true or not (or at least not trivially: the utterance of the sentence being a self-confirmation of the truth of my uttering it), but by the truth or falsity of the statement I make by uttering that sentence, the statement being true when in fact John did visit me yester-day. Apparently the truth value of the statement is linked with the proposition domi-nated by the performative hyper-sentence. Although only texts may be used (as utterances) to refer to a certain state of affairs, their truth value seems thus linked to their nuclear proposition. This is trivial when we accept that any sentence (or text) is dominated by a performative 'sentence', which is always true (under normal communicative conditions, not in play-acting, etc.). This performative or pragmatic sentence refers to the speech-act, not to the state of affairs denoted by the sentential/ textual proposition, and is therefore not qualified by truth value but by (degrees) of APPROPRIATENESS. We may say therefore that sentences representing commands, questions, etc., like those in (142) and (143), are appropriate if their presuppositions are true. Or rather: If the speaker assumes them to be true, for the speaker might be mistaken about 'his' presuppositions. The truth value of presupposed sentences, clearly, is relative with respect to the pragmatic world of the speaker or to the common worlds of speaker and hearer. The presupposition *Peter arrived* is implied by *John knows (doesn't know) that Peter arrived*, if the speaker assumes that *Peter arrived* is true. Since the speaker may have wrong evidence about Peters arriving (or not), the sentence *Peter arrived* may be false, and yet be a presupposition. This fact is illustrated by possible answers to (142) and (143) as: *The thing lying on my table is not a book but a journal* and *But Peter did not arrive at all*, respectively. If presuppositions were 'absolutely' true sentences, texts consisting of these dialogues would be ungrammatical (inconsistent because of contradictory statements). This implies that the 'worlds' (or state descriptions) with respect to which sentences are true or false may change within one communication process or within one text. A presupposition may be false for sentence S_i having a time indicator (or predicate) t_k and true for sentence S_{i+j} having indicator t_{k+m}.

From this brief discussion it is clear again that the notion of presupposition requires detailed PRAGMATIC description. Not truth values in the strict (referential) sense are relevant here but always the set of assumptions of speakers and hearers. In discourse (dialogue) the set is permanently changing, a change which we might model ideally by providing formal semantic descriptions of relations between sentences in a text underlying this discourse. When thus integrating pragmatic categories (see chapter 9 for details) into an – informal – characterization of the example-sentence *Do you know when Peter arrived?* we would obtain

(a) Speaker tells hearer that he wants that hearer to tell speaker whether hearer knows when Peter arrived.

The presupposition of (a) would then be the following sentence

(b) Speaker assumes that it is true that Peter arrived.

Such pragmatic presuppositions may lead to a binary division of underlying structures into an 'assertion part' and a 'presupposition part' of the sentence, e.g. as follows

(c) (i) Assertion: TELL $(S, H, -)$
    (ii) Presupposition: ASSUME $(S, ---)$

We will show below, however, that such a binary representation of underlying semantic structures is not necessary and is even redundant in text grammar: presuppositions are equivalent with preceding sentoids in a text, even when they are properly pragmatic (contextual). Therefore, a sentence like the one given above might not be the initial sentence of a text (although in discourse we may begin a conversation with it).

The same holds for relations of entailment. A sentence S like *Peter will arrive tomorrow* entails S': *Peter will arrive*, but S' is necessarily true only when uttered 'today', and not (necessarily) true when uttered 'tomorrow', the 'day after tomorrow' and later.

5.4.5. From the observations made above, the precise theoretical status of presupposition and entailment has not become fully clear. Sentences without truth value may have (true) presuppositions, and false sentences may be presuppositions of (true?) sentences if these presuppositions are 'supposed' to be true. The problem for semantic descriptions is whether presuppositions are part of the 'meaning' of the sentences or simply conditions for the truth or appropriateness of (uttered) sentences.

4 9 8 5 1

A first step towards a possible clarification of this matter is to make a distinction between SEMANTIC (intensional), REFERENTIAL (extensional) and PRAGMATIC PRESUPPOSITIONS (and entailments). Pragmatic presuppositions determine the appropriateness of an utterance. Thus the question *When did Peter arrive?* pragmatically presupposes e.g. the assumption of the speaker that the hearer knows the answer and the fact that the speaker does not himself know the answer (in normal questions). These presuppositions are conditions for certain speech acts and may define their different types (cf. Keenan [1970] and [1971b] for details).

Referential presuppositions determine the truth value of an utterance. They specify the possible world(s) and its (their) elements to which statements made by utterances apply. The sentence *My sister gave me (did not give) her book this morning* referentially presupposes that *I* (speaker) 'has a sister', and that 'this sister had a book', 'was able to give the book', that *I* (speaker) 'was able to receive it', that the possible action preceded, on the same day, the time of utterance, etc. Notice that these presuppositions must be satisfied in order that the statement made by the sentence be either true or false. If, for instance, there is no such x that x is 'my sister', the sentence will fail to refer and hence cannot have a truth value. Such sentences may be called 'referentially inappropriate' (under specified conditions: time, place, etc.). This more general notion allows presuppositions for non-declarative sentences.

Finally, we must distinguish semantic presuppositions. These are defined by the semantic rules of a grammar (including the lexicon). Thus the sentence *Peter married the daughter of the Prime Minister* semantically presupposes 'Peter is a male human'. Such presuppositions determine the semantic well-formedness of sentences and are derivable from the meaning postulates of the lexicon.

Similar observations may be made for pragmatic, referential and semantic entailment, e.g. *I promise (you) I will solve that problem for you* pragmatically entails the moral obligation of the speaker to (try to) solve the problem; *This morning Peter found his pen*, semantically entails 'Peter is again in possession of his pen'; finally the sentence *I saw the morning star* referentially entails *I saw the planet Venus*. Referential entailment in this case also has a deductive (or definitional) character. Inductive or probabilistic referential entailment, which is based on (our knowledge of) certain relationships (e.g. causality) in our world merely leads to possible (probable) truth values of the derived consequences, e.g. *Peter is very ill* has as a possible entailment *Peter does not go to work*. Textual coherence is established on the basis of such inductive referential relationships. Their formal treatment can be only partially founded on pure semantic relations between sentences. Only when properties and relations in some possible world, e.g. 'Anyone who is very ill cannot work', are explicitly specified may we formally derive such inductive (or modal) consequences.

A second series of distinctions is more familiar in logical theory, but has often been neglected in the linguistic studies of presupposition. At the level of grammatical description, sentences (or texts) as formal objects may only be assigned degrees of syntactic, morpho-phonological and semantic well-formedness. Sentences (and texts)

– as types – do not refer and therefore do not have truth value. Only tokens of sentences (or texts) when uttered in a speech act may have pragmatic and referential values. A general theory of speech acts and of reference will specify the general conditions for these values. Sentences are further supposed to have semantic representations as deep structures consisting of a modified (compound or simple) proposition. Normally, the values assigned to the argument variables (e.g. as lexical constants) are considered to be (existential) presuppositions. E.g. *The boy reads a book* presupposes the existence of an (identified) *boy* and an (unidentified) *book*.

The 'existence' of denoted objects is not only physically (or even abstractly) presupposed, but also as intentional, imaginative, etc. objects; *The mathematician didn't find a solution for the problem* presupposes (weakly) the 'existence' of a solution, namely in the sense of the 'intended' existence of the solution sought for, even when (objectively, mathematically) there 'is' no (possible) solution to the problem in question.

The presuppositions involved in semantic structures most studied in grammar are, however, those which have 'propositions' as one of their arguments, either as 'subjects' and direct objects, or as presuppositional propositions of place, time, circumstance or manner. Strictly speaking these embedded structures are sentences (sentoids) and not (nuclear) propositions, for they may have quantifiers, modal operators, etc.

(145)   Peter (does not) know(s) that
$\left\{ \begin{array}{l} \text{All his friends left him} \\ \text{Some of his friends left him} \\ \text{His friend will probably leave him} \\ \text{His friends will not leave him} \end{array} \right\}$

In these cases the structure of the dominating verb (predicate) determines whether the truth or factualness of the content of the complement is presupposed.

To know may have as object a sentence assumed true by the speaker. The modal modification of that predicate has no influence upon the embedded sentence. Similarly, verbs like *to pretend* presuppose that the embedded sentence is false, whereas the object of the performatives *to say*, *to think*, *to ask*, *to suppose*, etc. is a sentence with undecided truth value. Notice that these specifications are part of the structure of the verbal predicates, not of the dominating sentences.

If sentences are objects in first argument places (as abstract agents/causes) they are sometimes presuppositions of the sentence in which they are embedded

(146)   That John is ill bothers me.
           ⇒ John is ill.

(147)   Whether Peter will come or not does not matter.
           ⇒ Peter will come or not come.

(148)   That Harry will come satisfies me.
           ⇒ Harry will come.

(where '⇒' means 'presupposes').

Such sentential *NP*'s, preceded by *that, whether*, etc. are however not always pre-suppositions, although they precede the matrix sentoid (main clause). A sentence like *That Harry will come is unlikely* does not entail *Harry will come*, and neither does its negation. The same holds for *That Peter will marry Laura is believed by everybody*, which does not entail *Peter will marry Laura* (for discussion, cf. Kiparsky and Kiparsky [1971]).

This difference in the behaviour of subject clauses with respect to truth value and hence to their presuppositional function can be easily explained in terms of our textual analysis of complex sentences. Sentences (146) and (148) have a subject clause which is derived from a preceding sentoid and which therefore forms a presupposition of the sentence as a whole. In the other examples the sentences have passed through sentential topicalization transformations because the preposed clause depends on the predicate (verb) of the main clause, as is always the case for performatives, locutionary and cognitive verbs, modal adverbs, etc. We saw earlier that such sentoids do not have a decidable truth value and hence they cannot be presuppositions.

It is becoming clear that a 'textual' treatment of presupposition can no longer be avoided.

5.4.6. The implications of these observations on presupposition for textual grammar are obvious. Since presuppositions are always represented as sentences, we may con-sider the set of presuppositions, followed by the sentence(s) presupposing them, to be part of a text. (cf. Keenan [1970] 101). The advantages of such a treatment are clear: presuppositions, can be studied on the level of semantic relationships of coherence. As with definite description, restrictive relative clauses, etc. we assume that presup-positions are preceding sentences, or rather preceding semantic representations, because some of them may be optionally deleted if implied by other preceding senten-ces. Thus any preceding SR which can be embedded in a given sentence S_i is a pre-supposition of that sentence. Cf. the following texts:

(149)   Peter is ill. John knows that.
(150)   *Peter is ill. John pretends that.
(151)   John pretends this: Peter is ill.
(152)   There is a book on your table. Give it to me!
(153)   John arrived. Do you know when?

Notice that (150) is an ungrammatical sequence because to *pretend* requires that – in deep structure – the sentence representing its object follows the verb, as in (151). We may conclude provisionally that phenomena like definitivization, relativization and presupposition are manifestations of the same basic phenomenon of ordering relations between SR's in a text. Such a textual description of presupposition also solves the problem of their status. Lakoff (1971a) and many others have considered the presupposition of a sentence as part of the meaning of that sentence. Such an 'overspecification' is not necessary as soon as we stop treating sentences in isolation that are clearly taken out of a text. Similarly, we will not need the notation of Lakoff (1970b): p/q, stating the truth (or obligation, etc.) of p when q, in such implications as $q \supset (p/q)$, a connection also rendered by the notation $q \overset{'}{\supset} p$ (Reichenbach [1947]). Entailment in natural language always depends on the connection with the sentence of the antecedent. This is one of the reasons why logical constants in representing inter-sentential relations in natural language have to be handled with care (cf. infra).

5.4.7. Lakoff (1970a) made some valuable observations about different types of presupposition, e.g. FIRST and SECOND ORDER PRESUPPOSITIONS, and about the modifications of the truth values of the embedded sentences dominated by performatives through these different levels. Take such sentences as

(154)   Peter pretends that John$_i$ realizes that he$_i$ is ill.
(155)   Peter realizes that John$_i$ pretends that he$_i$ is ill.
(156)   Peter knows that John$_i$ realizes that he$_i$ pretends that he$_i$ is ill.
(157)   John$_i$ pretends that he$_i$ realizes that he$_i$ is ill.

Normally, presupposition is a transitive relation. In (155) the first order presupposition *John pretends that he is ill*, presupposes the second order presupposition *John is not ill* which is also presupposed by the whole sentence. The same is true for (156). However, (154) and (157) are more doubtful examples of transitivity. Sentence (154) presupposes that John does not realize that he is ill which presuposes that John is ill. However, as in (157), it may be asked whether the whole sentence has the same presupposition. We may interpret such sentences in such a way that the pretence of the subjects also casts doubt on the truth of the (primary) presupposition. Strictly speaking, however, performatives like pretending only presuppose the falsity/negation of the sentoid directly dominated by them. This negation, according to the definition, does not change the presupposition of the second order presupposition: a presupposition is implied by both S and $\sim S$. Problematic, however, is the case in which verbs like *to pretend* are negated

(158)   Peter does not pretend he is ill.

This sentence is ambiguous: it may have as a presupposition 'Peter is ill', but also have no presupposition about Peters illness (Lakoff's and Keenan's zero-value). In the first case *pretend* is stressed for contrast, where 'not-pretend' is equivalent with 'speaking (acting) truthfully'. Thus, *Peter is ill* is not a presupposition of (158) because it does not hold true if the main clause is negated: *Peter pretends he is ill* implies *Peter is not ill*. In this case *to pretend* is classed with the other performative verbs (to claim, to think, to say, to argue) which do not have presuppositions. The negation of this performative *to pretend* means that Peter does not pretend anything at all, and that therefore neither his being ill nor his not being ill can be asserted. Finally, when stressing *ill* or *he*, we have the zero presupposition as a contrast stating that Peter pretends to be in another state of health or that another is ill, respectively; in both cases his being ill (or not) is not presupposed. The different interpretations can be made clearer in sentences like

(159)   Peter does not pretènd he is ill, he really ìs.
(160)   Peter does not pretend he is ill, he doesn't pretend anything at all.
(161)   Peter does not pretend that hè is ill but that his bròther is.
(162)   Peter does not pretend that he is ìll but that he is drùnk.

The different 'scopes' of the verbs mentioned and their transitivity relations can be made explicit more clearly in derivations from textual sequences of sentoids. Thus (155) would be derived from the sequence

(163)   (i)   John pretends $S_{(ii)}$.
            (ii) John is ill.
            (iii) Peter realizes this.

where $S_{(ii)}$, *John is ill* is under the scope of *to pretend* which makes $S_{(ii)}$ false, and where Peter realizes that both John's pretending and his not being ill are true. To be complete we should derive (155) from:

(164)   (i)   John is not ill.
            (ii) John pretends $S_{(iii)}$.
            (iii) John is ill.
            (iv) Peter realizes $S_{(ii)}$.

Sentence (154) can be derived first from the following sequence:

(165)   (i)   John is ill
            (ii) Peter pretends $S_{(iii)}$
            (iii) John realizes $S_{(i)}$

where pretending $S_{(iii)}$ presupposes that John did not realize that he was ill, which presupposes his being ill, which in fact is presupposed by the whole sequence because the sentoid $S_{(i)}$ precedes $S_{(ii)}$ and therefore does not fall under the scope of *to pretend*. When we derive the same sentence from the following sequence

(166)   (i)   Peter pretends $S_{(iii)}$
            (ii) John is ill
            (iii) John realizes $S_{(ii)}$

ambiguity arises as to whether $S_{(ii)}$ is under the scope of $S_{(i)}$ (which presupposes John is not ill) or under the scope of *to realize* which presupposes that John is ill, or under the scope of *does not realize* (presupposed by *pretend*) which also presupposes that John is ill. In fact only this last interpretation of (154) would be correct if *pretend* really always presupposes that its dominated sentences are false. That the negation of sentences with *pretend* change this truth value already demonstrates that *to pretend* is not a verb having presuppositions which are either true or false.

Notice that the performative and locutionary verbs have the specific property that they require their dominated sentences to FOLLOW the matrix sentence in deep structure. This explains why these sentences are not presuppositions of the matrix sentences, derived from preceding sentoids. That embedded clauses dominated by locutionary verbs follow the matrix sentoid and others precede it, is demonstrated by the following sentences

(167)   John is arrogant and he knows that.
(168)   *John is rich and he pretends that.
(169)   ?John is not rich but he pretends that.
(170)   John is not rich but he pretends he is.
(171)   *John is a brilliant linguist and he thinks so.
(172)   ?John gave me a dollar and he said so.

In (167) we may pronominalize the preceding sentence, which is a presupposition. In (168) and (171), however, pronominalization is not possible, whereas it is doubtful in (169) where *that* may refer to the neutral property 'to be rich' (pronominalization by lambda-abstraction). We see that a sentence like *John pretends that he is rich* cannot be derived from sequences such as those conjunctively manifested in (168) and (171). In (170) we observe that the negation may precede the matrix sentence and therefore serve as a presupposition (although *pretend* does not have presuppositions in the proper sense, i.e. being true when *pretend* is negated).

We may conclude that the notion of presupposition is also closely determined by the order of sentences in underlying sequences, and that different 'types' of presuppositions turn out to be merely differences of scope, with respect to these sentoids, of the predicates of the matrix sentence. These facts require extensive further research before definite rules can be formulated.

5.5. *Other semantic relations between sentences*

Presuppositions, as we saw, are formal conditions for the referential and pragmatic appropriateness of uttered texts. When made explicit in sentences they can be studied at the semantic level as conditions of textual coherence.

Within the sentence, the different arguments may have the presuppositional condition of their 'existence', i.e. their implicit or explicit previous introduction as 'discourse referents'. Here the usual set-theoretical relations hold between the different categories: identity, equivalence, inclusion, intersection, etc. leading to definitivization and pronominalization. Among the verbal predicates the relations are more complex. To be sure, we may say that the lexeme *to walk* 'includes' the lexeme (or rather the lexicoid) *to go*, but these relations are normally defined as entailment relations over sentences, e.g. $(x) [Wx \supset Gx]$, when $W =$ 'to walk', and $G =$ 'to go'. These universal statements are identical with the meaning postulates defining the structure of the lexicon. However, this type of 'paradigmatic' relations between sentences merely determine generalization and particularization within a text. In normal cases we have to deal with (all types of) entailment, with conjunction and disjunction at the inductive level of referential relations. In surface structure these relations are manifested normally in sentential adverbs and CONJUNCTIONS (cf. Lakoff, Robin [1971]). An explicit study of conjunction therefore requires preliminary formulation of the possible semantic relation between propositions. The majority of these relations specify the verbal predicate of a sentence, i.e. by determining time, place, cause, purpose, result, condition, concession, etc. of an action, process or state. It would be interesting to try to systematize these relations and find their possible properties (e.g. of transitivity). TIME RELATIONS, which can be formalized either as higher predicates or as arguments, can thus be defined for a temporal axis conceived of as a continuum or as a linear succession of time points with one pragmatical zero-point, indicating time of utterance, and a variable semantic zero-point indicating the time of an action or process referred to. This partial ordering has three main relations: 'to precede', 'to follow' and 'to be coextensive with', which may be defined in terms of each other. Thus if the predicate of S_i has a temporal specification t_i and the predicate of S_j a specification t_j, and when t_j is to precede t_i, then we generate either

(173)   (i) S_i *after* S_j

or

          (ii) S_j *before* S_i.

When the predicates (i.e. their time indicators) are continuously coextensive we have

(174)   (i) S_i *while* S_j

or

          (ii) S_j *while* S_i

and *the moment that* or *then (when)* when momentaneously coextensive. When the predicate has a time indication continuously following a given time point t_i (where $t_i < t_0$, where t_0 is semantic or pragmatic zero-point) we have

(175) S_j *since* S_i.

Similarly, when t_i continuously precedes t_j, we generate

(176) S_i *until* S_j.

Further we will probably need a term to define such conjunctions as *as soon as, just before/after*, etc., e.g. the term 'immediately', which can be defined as follows

(177)   when x, y, z are time points, then x 'immediately precedes' y, if there is no z preceding y and following x.

In a similar way we may study the TOPOLOGICAL RELATIONS generating the sentential adverbs *here, there, herefrom (hence), therefrom*, etc., and the conjunctions *where, whence*, etc. Taking a pragmatic zero-point (place of utterance, l_0) and a semantic zero-point (place of semantic focus) and a set of variable place points we can define such relations as 'separation' or 'approach', with respect to these points. We will not try to formulate the precise rules generating these topological adverbs and conjunctions, but merely stress that linear sentential coherence is based also on relations of identity and specified differences between the local elements of subsequent sentoids. The other set of intersentential relations, those of cause (reason), purpose, result, condition, concession, etc., might be defined by some primitive relations like CAUSE: CAUSE (S_1, S_2) generating *as, because, since*, etc. Result or consequence is then defined as follows:

(178) $\text{CONS}(x, y) =_{def} (\exists y)\, \text{CAUSE}(y, x)$.

The general conditions for these relations are the time relations *to precede* and *to follow*: if $\text{CAUSE}(S_1, S_2)$ then $t_{S_1} < t_{S_2}$, and if $\text{CONS}(S_1, S_2)$, then $t_{S_1} > t_{S_2}$. If t_{S_2} follows a semantic or pragmatic t_0 the consequence relation is intentional, generating *(in order) that*, etc. Conditional relations are also based on this cause (and consequence) basis, with the specification that t_i of the antecedent sentence S_i follows t_0 of utterance or semantic focus *(If Peter comes, I will go)* or if S_i has the modal specification $\sim$ [FACTUAL] *(I would have gone, if Peter had come)*.

Finally, relations of CONCESSION also combine causal, temporal and modal specifications. Both subordinational *though, whereas* and coordinational *but* are generated by this relation. This relation can roughly be defined as follows

(179) $\text{CONC}(S_1, S_2) =_{def} \sim \text{CAUSE}(S_1, \sim S_2)$.

which asserts that the fact stated by S_1 does not cause that not-S_2, i.e. does not prevent S_2. In this expression there is a pragmatic presupposition stating that the statement expressed in the concession will normally refer to a state of affairs which prevents a given event or state. We might symbolize this presupposition modally with the aid of the notion of probability (conjoining it to (179))

(180)   PROB(CAUSE(S_1, S_2)).

These few observations on relations between SR's and some of their surface manifestations have value only if we succeed in formulating them as explicit conditions for
linear coherence. It will be necessary to represent them further in some derivation or
corresponding graph. We will return to this problem in the last section of this chapter.

5.6. *Topic and comment*

5.6.1. There are two other notions relevant for the description of semantic relations
between sentences in a text, those of TOPIC (or THEMA) and COMMENT (RHEMA), a
distinction often made within the framework of Russian and Czech work on Functional Sentence Perspective (FSP).

Perhaps the topic/comment distinction within a sentence is determined still more
by intersentential relations than the phenomena described above. This explains the
inadequacy of the current treatments of these notions in S-grammars.[14] The linguistic relevance of the notion of topic and comment is intuitively clear when we
realize that our competence enables us to distinguish within a sentence a part which
is somehow 'given', or 'known', or 'assumed', and a part which is commenting upon
the first part. That is, we intuitively know which part of the sentence contributes the
'semantic information' it is intended to convey. A formal explanation by a grammatical explication of the concepts of topic and comment is therefore in order. We will have
to show, for example, that they are not surface concepts, to be related e.g. either with
NP's and *VP*'s, or, more traditionally, with 'subject' and 'predicate'. Any part of the
sentence may be topic or comment, depending on the structure of the preceding sentoids.

5.6.2. The notions of topic and comment have only recently been made explicit in
generative transformational theory.[15] Chomsky (1965) 221 briefly defines the topic

---

[14] In fact we here touch on one of the main explananda of generative grammar: the functional
description of sentence structure has been neglected in the current generative models which are based
on PS-rules restricted to IC-analysis. A reduction to such syntactic categories of the different functions of the sentence, e.g. as attempted by Chomsky (1965) cf. Lyons (1970), has not been successful.
Nevertheless such functions must somehow be represented in the base component of the grammar in
order to account for such intuitively relevant notions as subject and object, agent, patient, etc. and
topic and comment. For discussion about the functional aspects of the sentence, cf. above all the
Czech approaches, e.g. Vachek (1966), Daneš (1964), (1970a), (1970b), Beneš (1968), Firbas (1964),
Sgall (1967). Other functional approaches are Halliday (1967), (1970), Pike (1967) and Dik (1968a).
[15] Topic and comment have received brief attention by Chomsky (1965) and, especially since the
rise of generative semantics, by Fillmore (1969a) and Lakoff (1971a). This issue was one of the compelling arguments for Chomsky to modify the standard theory (cf. Chomsky [1970], [1971]). The
only monograph on topic and comment has been provided by Dahl ([1969], which is discussed below).
Cf. further Gruber (1969) and especially Kaneko (1971). Cf. the literature cited by Dahl (1969) and
in note 13.

of a sentence in terms of surface structure, *viz.* as the leftmost major category *NP* immediately dominated by S_1 and the comment as the rest of the string. Topics often but not always correspond with deep structure subjects (that is the relation $[NP, S]$). Such a context-free definition clearly leads to serious difficulties. First of all it excludes all other categories from being topics of a sentence. Many answers to questions have such structures

(181)   (i)   Who broke this glass?
        (ii) John (broke it).

where *VP* is the topic and *John* the comment. However, such topics are often deleted in surface structure. Already from such simple examples one may conclude that the function of topic can be assigned only within the structure of texts. That is, the topic of the sentence is determined by the structure of preceding sentences. A simple sentence like

(182)   My brother sold the book to his friend for 5 dollars.

intuitively has *the book* as its topic because the definite form of this *NP* presupposes its previous introduction into a text (or situation) (cf. the preceding sections). If we use *he* instead of *my brother*, probably both *he* and *the book* are topics. Finally, the possible assignment of non-regular stress to all (major) categories automatically gives it the status of comment, making the rest of the sentence the topic. An intuitive rule thus seems to identify the topic with that part of the sentence which was already present in a previous sentence. This formulation is extremely vague and needs explication. What does 'being present' mean exactly? And at which level (morpho-syntactical, semantical or referential) should it be defined?

A first characteristic of a definition of topic and comment seems to be confirmed here: it is a function of relations between (subsequent) sentences in a text. It further has to include such properties of relations as 'equivalence' and 'difference'. Finally, pragmatical (deictic) and referential aspects are involved, otherwise it would be impossible to decide for initial text sentences which part is the topic and which the comment.

5.6.3. Dahl (1969), who gives an early generative treatment of the issue, bases his approach upon semantic representations and their relations. He correctly observes that the basic properties of topic/comment relations between sentences are closely related with the conditions underlying pronominalization, emphasis, definitivization, etc. As in many recent discussions in generative semantics, he makes extensive use of the notion of presupposition. Topics, in this perspective, are those parts of the sentences which are presupposed by their semantic representation (cf. Lakoff [1971a]). Let us take the sentence

(183)   John comes tomorrow.

which has ordinary stress structure. The (pragmatic) presupposition is that 'there is somebody named John referred to by the speaker and known by the hearer'. If *comes* is stressed, John and some action of John taking place tomorrow are presupposed, and finally, if *tomorrow* is heavily stressed, John and the action of his coming are presupposed. This information, as usual, is said to be derivable from 'situation' or 'co(n)text', the last term being undefined although it is clearly linguistic. We have shown earlier that at least part of the set of necessary presuppositions of a sentence S_i is identical with the set $S_1, S_2, ..., S_{i-1}$ of the text. We may make this statement more precise by saying that the formal presuppositions of a sentence S_i, as opposed to its inductive or empirical presuppositions, are identical with the set P of the semantic representations of the preceding sentences plus the set of their logico-semantic consequences. This last addition is necessary because texts in natural language are not explicit: the semantic representations of their sentences for the most part have to be completed by propositions derivable by the semantic rules of the grammar, which are known by the native speaker. These well-known facts are important for the assignment of the property of topic and comment to the elements of a sentence in a text, since the identity relation between the topic and a preceding element can be based on non-realized but only implied elements of the preceding sentences.

Dahl proposes to identify the topic with the left hand term of an implication, clearly using *modus ponens* as the basic rule. He represents sentence deep structures as implications, following the base description of McCawley (1968a). Thus a sentence like

(184)   Peter bought a car

would have roughly the following underlying structure

(185)   Peter $(x_1) \stackrel{'}{\supset} (\exists y)[\text{car}(y) \stackrel{'}{\supset} \text{bought}(x_1, y)]$

of which the (first) antecedent is the topic of the sentence. In case we want to stress Peter buying a car (by stressing *car*) we have the following underlying form

(186) $(\exists y)[\text{Peter}(x_1) \wedge \text{bought}(x_1, y) \stackrel{'}{\supset} \text{car}(y)]$.

As we saw earlier, deep structure representation predicts stress assignment in surface structure together with topic/comment partitions of the sentence.

From these representations we see that the topic of the sentence is equivalent to its presuppositions. In (184) for example we might negate *car* by the stressed sentence *Peter did not buy a cár*; the cleft sentence *It was not a car which John bought*, having the same topic/presupposition: *John bought something*. Notice, however, that in the negation there is a pragmatic presupposition; hearer assumes that "what John bought was a car", or that "the proposition *John bought a car* is true".

In the same way we may take the verb as a possible topic. We may stress *bought* in (184) after such sentences as *Peter did not séll the car*. The topic in that case is something like 'Peter did something with the car'. In order to represent this topic/presupposition we should use predicate variables

(187) $(\exists y)(\exists f)[\text{Peter}(x_1) \wedge \text{car}(y) \wedge f(x_1, y) \stackrel{'}{\supset} \text{bought}(f)]$

(we omit further differentiation of time and aspect of the action verb here).

Finally we will have to represent the formal structure of sentences in which the whole proposition can be considered to be a topic, e.g. in sentences like

(188)   Peter bought a car yèsterday.

which can be paraphrased as *It was yesterday that Peter bought a car*. Here the time adverb is comment and applies to *Peter bought a car* as topic. The traditional account of such structures is known as 'event splitting', i.e. an operation in which we want to quantify over the whole propositional function: e.g. $(\exists v)[[f(x, y)]^*(v)]$, paraphrasable as: 'there is some event having the property that x bears relation f to y'. Adding a variable t for time, we may then represent (188) as follows

(189) $(\exists y)(\exists v)(\exists t)[[\text{Peter}(x_1) \wedge \text{car}(y) \wedge \text{bought}(x_1, y) \wedge [\text{bought}(x_1, y)]^*(v, t)]$
           $\stackrel{'}{\supset} \text{yesterday}(t)]$

We see that any part of the semantic representation of a sentence may thus become the comment of a sentence, the topic being presupposed in the form of an antecedent. The implicational notation correctly predicts that the implication is false if the consequent is false (i.e. if the comment is not true) and the antecedent true. Thus the negation of (188) is indeed

(190)   Peter did not buy a car yèsterday.

paraphrasable as 'It was not yesterday that Peter bought a car'.

5.6.4. However, there are some complications. An implication will be true also when the antecedent, or both antecedent and consequent, are false. That is, for (188), if it is not the case that John bought a car (sometime), the sentence 'John bought a car yesterday' would be true. The implicational notation would further have a series of other tautological consequences. Since implication can be dissolved or rewritten as follows

(191)   (i) $a \supset b \equiv \; \sim (a \wedge \sim b)$

(ii) $\equiv \; \sim a \vee b$

(iii) $\equiv \; \sim b \supset \; \sim a$

we would have to conclude that if the comment of a sentence is not true, e.g. '(Peter) did not buy a car', then the topic would be false, i.e. that there is no such x called 'Peter'. Similarly, it is certainly not the case that the sentence is equivalent to the sentence 'it is false that there is an x called Peter and that not Peter bought a car', which would mean to say that the existence of Peter is incompatible with his not buying a car. Conversely, when the whole sentence is true as an implication then the comment is true only if the topic is true (by *modus ponens*).

If we want to assign truth to a sentence if and only if both its topic and comment are true, we must represent it as a conjunction, which is false if one or both of its terms are false. For the unstressed normal sentence (184) we would then have

(192) $\text{Peter}(x_1) \wedge (\exists y)[\text{car}(y) \wedge \text{bought}(x_1, y)].$

However, this representation does not allow an automatic distinction between topic and comment since conjunction is an associative and symmetric relation: $a \wedge (b \wedge c) \equiv (a \wedge b) \wedge c$ and $a \wedge b \equiv b \wedge a$ are tautologies (at least: in logical theory). Before we try to provide a textual approach to this problem of topic and comment, consider the following difficulties.

Take for example the 'data base' in which a given boy and a given girl each may either sell or buy either a given boat or a given car. What, then, would be the topic of a sentence like (193) describing one of the possible issuing events

(193)   The boy bought the boat.

In this sentence the boy and the boat and the action of buying are antecedents of the sentence, which would leave us with no comment at all, all terms being topics. However, what is NOT given is the CHOICE of the relation *bought (boy, boat)*. It is not clear, though, how to represent this formally. The following expression comes close to it, but is clearly not fully adequate:[16]

---

[16] The problem of formalizing a sentence/text like (193) lies in the fact that it is not possible in the isolated expression to mark linguistically the 'topicality' of the verb (e.g. by definiteness as with the noun phrases). As we noted in earlier sections the (referentially) definite noun phrases should be represented with iota-operators, e.g. as follows: $\text{bought}[(\imath x)\text{boy}(x), (\imath y)\text{boat}(y)]$, where, however, the 'definiteness' of 'bought' is not represented, for example as $(\imath f)\text{bought}(f)$. We might say that it is just the 'definiteness', as expressed by the iota-operator, which is the comment of (193), because this operator requires an èta-operator in a previous sentence (cf. text (196) below). We may conclude, again, that it is not possible to determine topic and comment by isolated logical forms; we always need a statement of previous logical forms representing context (situation) or co-text in order to be able to infer from identity- and difference-relations which part of the sentence is topic and which part is the comment.

(194) $(\exists v)[(\imath f)\,\text{buy}\,(f)\wedge(\imath x)\,\text{boy}\,(x)\wedge(\imath y)\,\text{boat}\,(y)\wedge f(x,y)]^{*}(v).$

We might also, or rather, say that (193) consists only of comment(s), since all its elements, though present in the preceding (con-)text, are contrasted with (the) other element(s) of the respective classes of agents ('buyers'), objects and actions, such that no definite identification is given about 'who did what with what'. The topic of (193), then, has to be 'someone did something', or '(the boy ∨ the girl) bought ∨ sold (the boat ∨ the car)'. In the simpler case where we have a boy and a girl and only a boat to buy, we would get

(195)   The bóy bought the boat.

where stress upon *boy* is necessary to identify it as comment. We see that 'previous mention' (or similar concepts) are not sufficient to identify the topic. In the case where there are several (identified) individuals, the selection of one of them in a sentence assigns the function of comment to it, resulting in irregular stress assignment or cleft sentence formation.

However, irregular stress assignment does not necessarily represent underlying comments. In the following text

(196)   (i)   I met a boy and a girl.
             (ii) The bóy gave me a book.
             (iii) The gírl kissed me.

$S_{(ii)}$ clearly has *gave me a book* as a comment on *(the) boy*, and similarly *kissed me* in $S_{(iii)}$ is comment on *(the) girl*. This does not mean, however, that *the boy* and *the girl* are simply topics of $S_{(ii)}$ and $S_{(iii)}$ although present and identified by $S_{(i)}$. (Note that we may only pronominalize *boy* and *girl* if they are followed by stress assignment). As in (195) we might also assign comment value to *boy* and *girl* because, intuitively, we obtain semantic information about 'wHO did something'. Any type of differentiation either by contrast or by selection among other individuals thus results in the assignment of comments. We might call *boy* and *girl* in such texts as (196) SEMI-TOPICS.

5.6.5. From the preceding remarks it is becoming clear that the definition of topic and comment is a function of at least two sentences in a text. Only with the aid of specific topicalization operations of surface structure might we isolate the topic and comment of individual sentences. These operations however are automatically triggered when the deep structures of subsequent sentences are given.

From this perspective, let us begin with a provisional definition of 'topic'

(197)   Def. A topic of a sentence S_i is a subtree σ_i of its underlying semantic

phrase marker which is identical with a subtree σ_{i-j} of the *SR*'s of preceding sentences S_1, S_2, ..., S_{i-1} and which is not differentiated with respect to preceding neighbouring subtrees of σ_{i-j}.

This definition allows a sentence to have more than one topic. Indeed, the sentence

(198)   The boy stóle the car.

has as its topic both *(the) boy* and *(the) car*, which by their definite character were necessarily introduced in preceding sentences. Further, if *stole* is heavily stressed we may also consider the elementary action (e.g. DO) a topic of the sentence.

In defining a topic as an underlying subtree we obviously do not consider a topic to be a surface concept, defined e.g. in terms of identical lexical items. Take, for example, the following text

(199)   (i) Peter has found a pretty secretary.
           (ii) The girl just finished college.

where *the girl* in (199, ii) can be considered the topic (notice its definite article) although not lexically present in surface structure in the preceding sentence. Strictly speaking, then, *girl* can not be considered the topic here, but only the underlying subtree representing the predicate *Female*(x_1).[17] In a more loose and traditional way we might then identify as a 'surface-topic' the lexical items representing, together with the surface phrase marker defining their syntactic relations, the repeated subtree of the deep structure. That this description of the topic is not correct has been shown in the situation preceding sentence (193): we might still want to have a topic in a sentence although all lexemes of a sentence are identical with previous lexemes. In that case, the topic might reduce to an abstract underlying set of relations, i.e. a subtree without its lexical insertions.

Since in most cases the identical subtree of a sentence is transformed into the left-most *NP* of sentence, the topic is often associated with the subject. This might indeed be considered to be the 'neutral' form of introducing a topic. If the topic underlies other categories (predicate, object, adverbs, etc.) there are operations like passivization which may move an object (semantically object or patient of an action predicate) into subject position

---

[17] A more complete analysis of this example would have to mention that by lexical rule (or meaning postulate) secretary$(x) \supset$ human(x) and that *pretty* has a selection restriction [[+Female]−], hence female(x), and hence the conjunction human female (x). Since by semantic rule human$(x) \supset$ adult(x) $\lor$ non-adult(x), this human female is either adult or non-adult, and hence by lexical definition *girl* or *woman*. Sentence (199, ii), which specifies one of the members of the disjunction, thus has 'human female' as topic, and 'non-adult' as part of its comment. Apparently, the configuration 'human female' is sufficient − on lambda-basis − to definitivize *girl*.

(200)   The car was bought by a swindler.

5.6.6. Other operations are necessary to focus upon the COMMENT of the sentence. The general rule is that the comment of the sentence is assigned primary stress with respect to the topic(s) (cf. Kraak [1970], Schermer-Vermeer [1971]). As soon as a comment is manifested in 'normal' topic position, that is as the leftmost *NP*, it receives heavy stress. The same assignment takes place in cleft-sentence formation which is the usual way of focussing upon the comment

(201)   It was a swindler who bought the car.

The same operations are necessary to manifest not only differences but also contrasts between connected semantic representations. In a sentence like

(202)   It was the swindler who bought the car.

we presuppose that several identified (cf. the definite article) persons including the swindler were the possible buyers of the car and we express that none other bought the car. This might roughly be formalized as follows (see, however, note 15):

(203) $\text{bought}\left[(\imath x)\text{swindler}(x),\ (\imath y)\text{car}(y)\right] \wedge (\sim \exists z)\text{bought}(z, y)$

The definition of COMMENT now seems to be based on the notion of difference between underlying semantic trees of sentences in a text: the subtree which is not identical with some preceding subtree, which makes the definition simply derivable from that of topic.

However, we saw that the comment of a sentence may very well be part of previous sentences. In that case, however, the rest of the sentence has a subtree identical with some previous sentence and the comment only a partially identical subtree or an 'antithetic' subtree. Thus in (201) 'somebody' is a topic contained in the tree deriving the comment *swindler*. Comments which include partially identical subtrees or which are differentiated from other possible (expected) subtrees are assigned heavy stress

(204)   Peter did not arrive on Mónday. (but on Tuesday)
(205)   Jóhn will never make such a mistake. (but Peter will)
(206)   Did you know that car was stólen by him? (not bought).

The analysis of topic and comment, given above, defining these notions in terms of identity and difference relations between subtrees of pairs of underlying semantic phrase markers is closely related with the textual description of definitivization, relativization, pronominalization and presupposition, which are different phenomena of the same type of semantic relations between underlying SR's. In particular the analogy between presupposition and topic has become apparent. A presupposition is, however, a full proposition whereas a topic might be only a subtree of such a pre-supposition. Furthermore, the topic is a subtree of a given sentence S_i, whereas a presupposition is a member of the set of preceding propositions of S_i. Embedded previous sentoids (presuppositions) are of course in that case part of the topic of a sentence

(207)   The man who bought the car was a swindler.

where the whole *NP* including the restrictive relative clause is topic, whereas *a man bought the car* is the presupposition.

The given definition of topic further allows sentences of which no subtree is identical with previous subtrees. This is naturally the case for initial sentences in a text. These would then consist merely of one or more 'comments'. The intuitive notion of comment, as that part of the sentence 'applied to' or 'predicated of' a topic, is lost here. We might also say that initial sentences of a text (or of a text-sequence) 'introduce' topics not unlike the introduction of 'new' terms or the initial definition of terms in a theo-retical text. This description of an initial situation, indeed, can be compared with a formalized theoretical text, cf.: 'let there be an x, such that x ..., and a y, ...' on the hand and the initial sentence

(208)   A hitchhiker was walking along a highway.

which may be represented as follows

(209)   let there be an x, such that x is a hitchhiker
             let there be a y, such that y is a highway
             there be a relation w between x and y such that w is 'walking along'.

5.6.7. Again, we are touching here upon thorny logical and philosophical problems concerning the 'existence' of the individuals 'referred to' or designated. Clearly in 'true' descriptions, an initial sentence will, by indefinite description, 'comment' upon an initial extra-linguistic situation. However, in many texts (narrative, theories, etc.) individuals may simply 'come into existence' by introducing them as 'values of variables' into the initial sentences of the text. We will not go further into these matters and will consider initial sentences, according to the definition, to be 'comments', adding that any comment automatically can be used for further topicalization. The assignment of comment-value to initial sentences is to be explained also with respect to possible (future) referential and pragmatical structures of the grammar.

The introduction of a topic into a sentence is not always formal or based on explicit identity relations between subtrees. We may continue (208) with the following narrative

(210)   (i)   His feet were swollen and painful.
          (ii) The sun was right above his head, burning ...

where *his feet* and *the sun* (and *his head*) are normally considered the topics, although appearing for the first time. The definiteness of these lexemes however demonstrates that their 'existence' is somehow IMPLIED by previous sentences (cf. note 16). Thus, by lexico-semantic rules or postulates, subtrees may be derivable from actually realized propositions. Since *hitchhiker* has a feature $[+ HUM]$, we may semantically or referentially derive: for all x, if x is human, then x has feet, a head, etc. This semantic, referential or pragmatic knowledge permits the derivation of implied terms which may be introduced as topics in subsequent sentences. Again we see that also a notion like topic necessarily presupposes a set of explicit or implicit, deductive or inductive preceding propositions with respect to which it can be identified in a sentence. No implicational form is necessary in that case, to represent underlying structures of sentences.

It was observed that these 'preceding propositions' are not always realized as such as part of a text but may implicitly be presupposed. This is necessarily true not only for one-sentence texts but also for some sentences within a text e.g. those introducing a new paragraph or chapter. As was noticed earlier, linear coherence is not strict in the sense that immediately subsequent sentences necessarily have identical subtrees. This identity relationship may be indirect and established with respect to more global structures of coherence of the text if they are not determined by referential and/or pragmatic parameters. Topics, then, will normally be identified with the leftmost definite *NP*, although transformations (e.g. topicalization) and particular stress assignments may change the place of the topic.

There are a number of other cases in which the identification of topic and comment is problematic. Not only sentences merely actualizing indefinites but also complex sentences and questions, commands, etc. are not always intuitively clear examples of topic/comment combinations. Pragmatically *you* must be topic in such sentences as *Do you know what time it is?* and *Please, shut the door!* Thus, if we adopt the hypothesis of pragmatical hypersentences, any sentence would have *I* and *you* as pragmatical topics. In the second sentence we must further consider *the door* as a referential topic.

In a complex sentence like *John knows what time Peter will arrive* we will have *John* as the topic of the matrix sentence and further probably *Peter will arrive*, which is a presupposition. The embedded sentence, however, also has a topic: *Peter*. This may easily be concluded from the transformational history of such sentences. The given sentence may be derived e.g. from *Peter will arrive.* (and) *John knows at what time*. That in this case also previous sentences determine the topic is demonstrated by the fact that in heavily stressing *John*, the rest of the sentence is topic and *John* comment, as for example after a question like *Who knows what time Peter will arrive?*

Whereas presuppositions determine the linear coherence of a sentence with respect to previous sentences, the role of the distinction between topic and comment seems to be how from a given 'situation' (either textual or non-textual) we may appropriately generate following sentences. That is, a topic has precisely the function of a linguistic selection mechanism which isolates one or more particular or non-particular individuals from previous SR's (or state descriptions), repeats them (as definites or proforms) and assigns a, possibly complex, predicate to them. This is why the notions topic and comment were always associated with pragmatical theories of language and with the theory of communication in general. The topic-comment distinction is a formal linguistic means for what could be called the 'informational expansion' of a text: to the limited number of repeatable elements we can assign an infinite number of possible predicates.

5.6.8. These remarks may be made more explicit by elaborating a FORMAL TYPOLOGY FOR THE LINEAR EXPANSION of a text given an initial sentence S_1 or an intermediate sentence S_i. (cf. Daneš, [1970a]). Our theoretical remarks already suggest a first set of distinctions. Analogous with the differentiation of presupposition we may distinguish between, pragmatic, semantic and referential expansions, according to the type of topic introduction. Pragmatic topics will comprise speaker, hearer, place and time of utterance as (implied) topics to which may be assigned comments in many sentences, like *I am thirsty*, *Give me a dollar!*, *It is warm in here*, *It is five o'clock*, (notice that *it* often serves here as a surface representation of such pragmatical topics). Referential expansions are characteristic of any (non-formal) text and are determining its inductive (probabilistic) coherence. They are indispensable to the description of events and situations, in which the individuals do not always have (logico-)semantic relations among each other. Cf. such pairs as *After dinner John likes to read. Mary prefers to play the piano*, and *It was snowing. A man slowly crossed the slippery road*, which are connected either by identical situation (the same time indicators), referential relations between events and referential relations between events or objects and their properties. Topics, finally, are introduced semantically according to the rule given earlier: when a subtree of a previous SR is repeated. This is the only manner of expansion which may be accounted for, strictly speaking, within (text-)grammar, unless the grammar is supplemented with pragmatic and referential components.

Further criteria for a formal typology of textual expansions are thus to be based on these semantic relations. The (trivial) relationships, then, may be defined by the different categories which are repeated as a topic: arguments, predicates (properties or relations) higher predicates (properties of properties or relations), time and place indicators and the different modes. Furthermore, we may establish a differentiation according to the difference in categories (a patient in S_{i-1} may be topic and agent in S_i). Note that the most current form of expansion is the assignment of properties/relations to repeated arguments, which stresses the role of pronouns. The very fact that topicalization of verbs, adjectives, adverbs leads to specific stress assignment or transformations (like nominalization) and the rarity of pro-verbs, pro-adverbs and pro-sentences, seem to indicate the marked character of such expansions.

A final set of formal properties of expansion are those defining the semantic relationship between topic and its corresponding sub-tree in previous sentences. Not only identity, but also inclusion, membership, and entailment are relations which may introduce topics.

5.6.9. We will not investigate further the notions of topic and comment here, nor will we try to formalize the results of our discussion. We merely wish to stress that topics can be defined only for (at least) pairs of sentences and on the basis of pragmatic, referential and, within the grammar, semantic relationships between sentences/ propositions in a text, or between sentences and explicated state descriptions. Topics are those parts of the sentence which determine its linear coherence with the preceding text, whereas the comment defined the linear expansion of the text. Thus considered, 'topicalization' is defined analogously with 'definitivization' (definite description) and as the counterpart of presupposition. It is included in text grammar so that we may arrive at a unified description of such and related linguistic phenomena.

6. A SPECIMEN OF DESCRIPTION

6.1. Our remarks in this section have become more and more vague, because of the lack of systematic data. Our distinctions have been made from a logico-semantic point of view and need specification and testing on a concrete example.

This time we will choose an existing text of which we will try to localize the different elements relating sentence to sentence, in order to see whether the formulated constraints are respected.

The text is the beginning of an essay by Barthes from his *Mythologies* (1957). The French text is used to check whether the formulated constraints have a more general character.

We will limit ourselves to the first sentences only, because a full analysis of these two pages would take the length of this book. We will also neglect properties characterizing the individual sentences. Only the elements establishing and representing the different relations between the sentences are considered.

The description will finally have a schematic character, details are omitted. The text has been divided into elementary clauses supposedly generated by single propositions of the SR's of the sentences. What we do describe therefore are the relations between propositional SR's, and only secondarily the surface characteristics of the relations between the sentences.

Critique muette et aveugle

Les critiques (littéraires ou dramatiques) usent souvent de deux arguments assez singuliers. Le premier consiste à décréter brusquement l'objet de la critique ineffable et par conséquent la critique inutile. L'autre argument, qui reparaît lui aussi périodiquement, consiste à s'avouer trop bête, trop béotien pour comprendre un ouvrage réputé philosophique: une pièce d'Henri Lefebvre sur Kierkegaard a ainsi provoqué chez nos meilleurs critiques (et je ne parle pas de ceux qui font ouvertement profession de bêtise) une feinte panique d'imbécillité (dont le but était évidemment de discréditer Lefebvre en le reléguant dans le ridicule de la cérébralité pure).

Pourquoi donc la critique proclame-t-elle périodiquement son impuissance ou son in-compréhension? Ce n'est certainement pas par modestie: rien de plus à l'aise qu'un tel confessant qu'il ne comprend rien à l'existentialisme, rien de plus ironique et donc de plus assuré qu'un autre avouant tout penaud qu'il n'a pas la chance d'être initié à la philosophie de l'Extraordinaire; et rien de plus militaire qu'un troisième plaidant pour l'ineffable poétique.

Tout cela signifie en fait que l'on se croit d'une intelligence assez sûre pour que l'aveu d'une incompréhension mette en cause la clarté de l'auteur, et non celle de son propre cerveau: on mime la niaiserie, c'est pour mieux faire le public se récrier, et l'entraîner ainsi avantageuse-ment d'une complicité d'impuissance à une complicité d'intelligence. C'est une opération bien connue des salons Verdurin: «Moi dont c'est le métier d'être intelligent, je n'y comprends rien; or vous non plus vous n'y comprendriez rien; donc, c'est que vous êtes aussi intelligents que moi.»

Le vrai visage de ces professions saisonnières d'inculture, c'est ce vieux mythe obscurantiste selon lequel l'idée est nocive, si elle n'est contrôlée par le «bon sens» et le «sentiment»: le Savoir, c'est le Mal, tous deux ont poussé sur le même arbre: la culture est permise à con-dition de proclamer périodiquement la vanité de ses fins et les limites de sa puissance (voir aussi à ce sujet les idées de M. Graham Greene sur les psychologues et les psychiatres); la culture idéale ne devrait être qu'une douce effusion rhétorique, l'art des mots pour témoigner d'un mouillement passager de l'âme. Ce vieux couple romantique du cœur et de la tête n'a pourtant de réalité que dans une imagerie d'origine vaguement gnostique, dans ces philoso-phies opiacées qui ont toujours formé finalement l'appoint des régimes forts, où l'on se débarrasse des intellectuels en les envoyant s'occuper un peu de l'émotion et de l'ineffable. En fait, toute réserve sur la culture est une position terroriste. Faire métier de critique et proclamer que l'on ne comprend rien à l'existentialisme ou au marxisme (car par un fait exprès ce sont surtout ces philosophies-là que l'on avoue ne pas comprendre), c'est ériger sa cécité ou son mutisme en règle universelle de perception, c'est rejeter du monde le marxisme et l'existentialisme: «Je ne comprends pas, donc vous êtes idiots.»

Mais si l'on redoute ou si l'on méprise tellement dans une œuvre ses fondements philoso-phiques, et si l'on réclame si fort le droit de n'y rien comprendre et de n'en pas parler, pour-quoi se faire critique? Comprendre, éclairer, c'est pourtant votre métier. Vous pouvez évidemment juger la philosophie au nom du bon sens; l'ennui, c'est que si le «bon sens» et le «sentiment» ne comprennent rien à la philosophie, la philosophie, elle, les comprend fort bien. Vous n'expliquez pas les philosophes, mais eux vous expliquent. Vous ne voulez pas comprendre la pièce du marxiste Lefebvre, mais soyez sûrs que le marxiste Lefebvre comprend parfaitement bien votre incompréhension, et surtout (car je vous crois plus retors qu'incultes) l'aveu délicieusement «inoffensif» que vous en faites.

SR$_1$:
– *critiques* [+ DEF]: A definite *NP* can be used here for both extralinguistic and semantic reasons:
  (1) Literary critics are culturally well known.
  (2) The whole class of them is referred to.
  (3) The title indicates that criticism is involved.
  (4) The author is known as a writer on literary criticism.

SR$_2$

- *le premier:* Only a semantically based grammar can identify the relation with *deux arguments*, because no morphemes or lexemes are identical. Because *consister à* has [+ —HUM], *le premier* cannot refer to *les critiques*. Both *premier* and *deux* share a feature [+ NUMBER]; [+ DEF] and [+ TOPIC], here, presuppose only membership of the same class, not precise referential identity. Moreover, it is not the whole *NP* that is pronominalized but only, weakly, the head noun with the aid of the nominalized adjective.

SR$_3$ [in SR$_2$]

- *décréter* ... The infinitive requires a deep structure deleted argument (Agent) having [+ HUM] and [+ LOC] (of 'locutionary') which only can be related with *les critiques* in SR$_1$ as agent, and which intersects with the predicate of SR$_1$, of which it gives a specification.
- *la critique* is formed by nominalizing the habitual activity of *les critiques*. The lexicoidal relation is therefore that of equivalence (cf. also *critique* in the title).
- *l'objet* has [+ DEF] because it is determined by *de la critique*, and because it refers to the whole class of possible 'objects'.
- *ineffable*, having [+ LOC], [+ NEG], together with
- *la critique*, intersects with the lexicoids of the title. We see here that one of the functions of the title is to subsume briefly some semantic aspects of the text. We will see that these aspects, then, are normally those around which the text is organized.

- *par conséquent* in fact introduces a new sentoid within SR$_3$ of which the auxiliary verb has been deleted. The relation between SR$_3$ and SR$_3'$, then, is CAUSE (SR$_3$, SR$_3'$), and therefore one of implication. We notice that SR$_3'$ repeats the argument (Object) of SR$_3$: identity relation.
- *inutile:* stresses, semantically and stylistically, the parallelism with the preceding lexicoids.

SR$_4$

- *l'autre argument* ... similar remarks to those made for SR$_2$, and predicted by SR$_2$, because if two arguments are referred to, and if one is made explicit then the other must be made explicit. *Argument*, here, is identically repeated. Also the predicate *consiste à* is repeated. A modifying sentoid has been embedded after the *NP*.

SR$_5$

- *qui* pronominally repeats *argument*.
- *reparaît* intersects with the aspectual features of *souvent* in SR$_1$ of which it is a specification. Therefore a parallelism of the category *ASP* can be indicated by *lui aussi. Périodiquement* is the lexematic manifestation of this repetition.

SR$_6$
- *s'avouer*, like *décréter* in SR$_3$ has [+ HUM] and [+ LOC] (or [+ LING], or [+ EXPR], etc.) and also implies the argument-agent *critiques* of the preceding SR's.
- *trop bête, trop béotien* ... predication of agent, but again parallel to the attitudes of the object.

SR$_7$
- The relation with SR$_6$ is established by *trop ... pour + inf.*, expressing a relation of degree and its consequence.
- *comprendre*, again with [+ HUM] and [+ COGN], like in the other predicate of the argument-agent.
- *ouvrage* intersects with *objet de la critique* and has [+ LING] with a particularizing modification by *réputé philosophique. Ouvrage* is made explicit in SR$_8$: *une pièce d'Henri Lefebvre* ... etc.

6.2. We do not need to continue this description because it turns out that the more the text is progressing the more its lexicoids can be related by equivalence, inclusion or intersection with preceding lexicoids. The agent-argument *les critiques* remains constant and only a few modifying attributes are predicated to it. Its predicate-actions develop progressively but always include [+ HUM) and [+ LOC] or [+ LING]. Both modifiers and actions receive a negative feature [+ STUPID] in the original and the concrete sense of the term: *X NEG (SPEAK)*, or *X NEG (UNDERSTAND)* (...) *Y*.

We notice that in fact the most abstract deep structure of this sequence of sentences hardly becomes more complicated: only the lexematic surface manifestations become more differentiated. In deep structure the logico-semantic pattern Action⌢Agent⌢Patient⌢Object⌢Place⌢Time is gradually established by the generation of the lexicoids of these respective categories. The repetitions and intersections merely seem to point to the relevance-for-the-text of an introduced category.

There is no regularity in the topic-comment structure of this sequence. The only constraint is that topics are introduced as comments of preceding SR's, e.g. as argument-objects (*NP*'s of the predicate phrase in syntactic structure), whereas the argument-Agent *les critiques* can serve as a permanent topic, and can therefore be deleted.

Although, for stylistic reasons, Barthes' text employs many parallelisms and lexematic repetitions, we must stress the fact that the semantic coherence, especially for the different predicate actions, is established by such abstract deep structure relations as intersection, inclusion and implication:
$$\left\{ \begin{array}{l} \textit{décréter ineffable} \\ \textit{s'avouer trop bête} \\ \textit{faire profession de bêtise} \end{array} \right\} \overset{'}{\supset} \textit{(ne pas)}$$

comprendre $\overset{'}{\supset}$ *discréditer* $\overset{'}{\supset}$ *ridiculiser*, etc.

A precise analysis of the semantic structure of these lexemes together with lexico-semantic rules have to make these implications explicit. This will be one of the major tasks of a semantic theory.

In the next chapter we will see how these 'local' constraints in Barthes' text are only manifestations of more global textual constraints and rules.

7. CONCLUSIONS AND SPECULATIONS ON THE FORM OF THE SURFACE GRAMMAR

7.1. The aim of this section is to make some observations on how subsequent sentences are related in a text. It becomes apparent that surface relations and constraints such as morphematic recurrence, pronominalization, tense continuity and the use of specific inter-sentential conjunctions and adverbs, have to be considered as representations, often highly language specific, of deeper semantic relations between SR's.

The introduction of certain lexicoids or temporal and local indicators and modal operators in an (initial) sentence limits the choice of lexemes in following sentences. The selection of features like $[+ DEF]$, $[+ PRO]$ and $[+ TOPIC]$ turned out to be derivable from similar underlying structures of the sentence + those of preceding sentences.

Besides these aspects, manifested at the surface by syntactic and phonological elements (like stress), the selection of lexicoids determines lexematization of the terminal surface-sentence. Relations of equivalence, inclusion (generalization, particularization), and intersection are thus minimal constraints for the selection of new lexicoids. In one text sequence these are probably organized in the same basic pattern of sentential deep structure, made explicit at the surface by several different sentences. Finally, semantic relations exist between whole sentoids (or propositions of SR's). That is, sentoids can be equivalent with each other (resulting in stylistic variation, as in Barthes' text), or can entail each other as a logically necessary or inductively probable consequences. Furthermore, they will normally be conjunctions in which further specification of a given lexicoid will be made by commenting upon it as a topic. Disjunctions normally possess contrastive logico-semantic deep structure, that is $[+ NEG]$ and $[- NEG]$ or similar lexicoids in different functional categories (roles). These intersentential relations often are indicated by grammatical conjunctions (*and*, *but*, *although*) and adverbs (*also*, *not*, *similarly*, etc.) in the lexematic surface structure.

7.2. There is, however, one major problem left. We considered the constraints upon immediately subsequent sentences in a text, but it is intuitively clear that even when these apply we do not necessarily generate a coherent text. We might construct a text having features in common, or even lexicoids, between its sentences without establishing any GLOBAL COHERENCE. Intuitively, we can say that the selection of lexemes as agents, objects and actions, needs to be 'directed', that is to say guided by a more global semantic principle. We shall see in the following chapter that the global constraint for this transition from sentence to sentence is determined by the macro-structure which forms the deep structure of a text.

7.3. We might finally speculate about the possible FORMS of the sentential component of a text grammar. In the preceding sections we have informally described different aspects of the relations between sentences in coherent texts. The regularities which have been studied defined the linear coherence of text. The problem now at issue is how we introduce the provisional results into explicit textual derivations. Although, as we briefly touched on in the preceding paragraph, textual generation must start with the formation of abstract underlying macro-structures, it is necessary to integrate the formulated LOCAL CONSTRAINTS into the rules deriving coherent sequences. Let us assume, first of all, that the underlying macro-structure somehow controls the sequences of sentences for which it formulates minimal requirements upon semantic representations and their lexical manifestation, i.e. upon the 'context' of the sentences of these sequences. These requirements may be considered, as we shall see in the next chapter, to be global derivational constraints, e.g. upon the classes from which lexico-semantic elements may be selected. Let us further assume for the moment that these constraints are known. How, then, do we formulate in a grammar that definitivization of a specific noun, or rather its underlying argument, in a sentence S_i is obligatory, that some pro-forms are either obligatory or optional, that there are (partially) identical semantic subtrees, and that if subtrees differ in specific ways we have to generate stress or select specific adverbs or use syntactic transformations? And, which is perhaps still more important for the description of linear coherence, how do we represent the relations between sentences as a whole: causes, conditions, consequences, concessions, equivalences, conjunctions, disjunctions, etc.?

From the preceding discussions it might have become obvious that constraints for local (linear) coherence must be formulated at different levels and in different forms. Some of them are possibly part of 'formation' rules of sentences of the text, i.e. part of the base of the surface or sentential component of text grammar, whereas other constraints are probably specific conditions upon transformations and their ordering. We saw, for instance, that the process of embedding of previous sentoids into a given matrix sentoid, e.g. for the generation of restrictive relative clauses, is operated by transformational cycles in which the order of the sentoids and their semantic structure (e.g. identity, membership relations) play a role as conditions. At a deeper level, we must probably introduce (con-)text sensitive formation rules for underlying SR's of sentences. That is, two sentences S_i and S_{i-1} (or S_{i+1}) may only be connected by the sentential relation, e.g. of concession, if some conditions for the form of their SR's are fulfilled.

7.4. As a very tentative approach to a solution of these problems of formalization we introduced initially the base category Sq (for sequence) which may be specified in a rule schema by an ordered n-tuple of sentences

(211) $Sq \rightarrow S(\& \, S)^n$

with the condition $n \geqslant 0$. That is, a sequence may consist of one or more subsequent sentences (or rather sentoids) connected by an element '&'. Such a sequence might also be derived with an initial S-symbol (cf. Rohrer [1971]). However in this case the whole sequence is dominated by an S-symbol and must therefore be considered a formal unit called 'sentence'. In chapter 1 we adduced intuitive and formal arguments against such a conception of textual sequences of sentences: not every sequence may be reduced to one sentence, not even by simple conjunctive coordination, though the rule $S \rightarrow S(\& S)^n$ is adequate for the description of complex sentences. Starting with the sequence-symbol (which is not necessarily the initial symbol of the derivation) we derive linear structures which, at the surface, may be manifested either as structurally (syntactically) independent sentences or under certain conditions as complex sentences. Only in this way will it be possible to demonstrate that a surface sequence $S_i, S_{i+1}, \dots S_{j-i}, S_j$, may be a paraphrase of some complex sentence S_k having identical underlying structure of linearly ordered sentoids. The proposed rule schema must automatically assign indices to the subsequent sentences (sentoids), representing their linear order. These indices will be necessary for the formulation of the transformations and their conditions. When we assume that infinite length of texts is not only established at the level of the number of sentences of a sequence, but also at the level of sequences (a text may have, theoretically, an infinite number of delimitable sequences, realizing an infinite number of underlying 'textoids'), the given rule may be preceded by another rule schema, this time properly recursive

(212) $Sq \rightarrow Sq(\& Sq)^m$

where $m \geqslant 0$. We will see (in chapter 8) that in specific types of texts, for instance narrative, m may take certain minimal values, e.g. $m \geqslant 4$. We should probably introduce further specific boundary symbols (e.g. '#') for the delimitation of sequences. These do not always coincide with textual boundary symbols, and are necessary for the generation of specific surface manifestations, e.g. of written texts: chapters, (sub-)titles, white lines, etc. Without such symbols it will not be possible to represent the non-coherence between sentence S_n^i of sequence Sq_i and the initial sentence S_1^{i+1} of the following sequence Sq_{i+1} for which the normal condition of initial sentences might hold true.

Problematic, but extremely important is the status of the still unanalysed symbol '&', representing abstractly intersentential CONNECTION of some type. Following Rohrer (1971), using Ju as a junctor element between sentoids of complex sentences, we might specify '&', by the logical constants, e.g.

(213)
$$\& \rightarrow \begin{Bmatrix} \wedge \\ \vee \\ \supset \\ \equiv \end{Bmatrix}$$

However, this faces us not only with the completeness of this set for the description of SEMANTIC relations between sentoids (propositions) of a sequence in natural language, but also with the status of logical constants in a semantic theory and in grammatical base descriptions. In the first place modern mathematical logic does not presuppose (semantic or referential) connectedness between the terms related by these constants, but only formulates truth values for molecular formulae constructed with them when the truth values of the atomic formulae are given. This problem may be solved by adopting, with Reichenbach (1947), symbols indicating connective equivalence, conjunction, disjunction and implication, (e.g. $\overset{\prime}{\equiv}$, $\overset{\prime}{\wedge}$, $\overset{\prime}{\vee}$, $\overset{\prime}{\supset}$). Further, it is questionable whether such intuitively relevant relations as cause and consequence, condition result and concession can be reduced to these constants (which in fact are themselves reducable). We saw earlier that implications do not simply define cause and consequence, but that some formalism (e.g. Wright [1967b]) might establish the necessary connection between the sentoids/propositions. The relation of causation would then be defined as follows (cf. also Lakoff [1970b])

(214) $CAUSE(S_1, S_2) =_{def} S_1 \overset{\prime}{\supset} (S_2/S_1)$

that is: S_1 implies S_2 if S_1 (is given).

It is impossible to provide here a consistent solution to this general problem of the status and the role of logical constants in semantic descriptions. Provisionally it would be possible to introduce a number of semantic primitives like *EQUI*, *CONS*, *DISS*, *CAUS*, *COND*, *CONC*, for the generation of relations between sentoids

$$(215) \quad \& \rightarrow \begin{Bmatrix} EQUI \\ CONS \\ DISS \\ CAUS \\ COND \\ CONC \end{Bmatrix}$$

If these rules are correct we generate e.g. the following structure

(216)

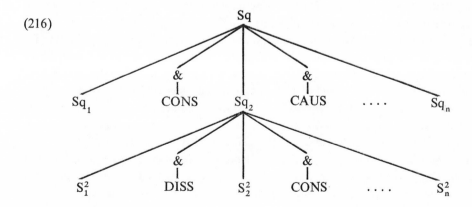

We shall see that at the level of macro-structures we may indeed describe a text (like the one by Barthes) as indicated by this graph.

7.5. A next step, then, will be the expansion of the S-symbols. In the next chapter we will go into some detail concerning this description of sentoids (textoids) in terms of abstract semantic propositions (n-place predicates, argument variables, operators, modal elements, etc.). The precise form of these semantic derivations is not a problem to be dealt with in this book. We merely want to know – once a rough formal description has been adopted in terms of recent suggestions from generative semantics and semantically/functionally interpreted case systems – how structures of sentoid S_i determine those of $S_{i+j}(j \geqslant 1)$.

We will assume that the basic formation rules for the derivation of well-formed semantic representations are context free: any sentence consists at least of arguments, a predicate, a quantifier and place and time arguments (or predicates). The textual conditions operate at the level of specific lexico-semantic assignments (of feature-configurations, lexicoids) to the categories of these structures. One of the textual conditions would be, for instance, that at least one lexicoid, or rather a subtree, is identical with one in a previous sentence or its entailments. We must therefore first derive S_1 before deriving S_2. The condition of partial identity (e.g. by inclusion, membership, equivalence) of subtrees, then, could be represented as follows

$$(217) \qquad S \to \dots$$
$$\begin{array}{l} X \to \alpha \\ Y \to \beta \\ Z \to \gamma \end{array} \Bigg/ \sqrt{\begin{bmatrix} R\equiv \\ R\subset \\ R\varepsilon \end{bmatrix}} (\delta(\subset S_i), \underline{\quad\quad})$$

where X, Y, Z are non-terminal categories and α, β, γ abstract semantic 'terminal subtrees', with the condition that at least one of the terminals has such a contextual relation as specified in the 'composed' two place predicate, where δ is a subtree of S_i. The notation of this rule recalls similar notations for RELATIONAL DESCRIPTION in logical theory, e.g. as given by Carnap (1957) 145 f., where $R'b$, meaning 'that individual having the relation R to b', is defined as follows $(\imath x)(Rxb)$. This notation is equivalent to the dash-notation $R(-, b)$ which is used as (co-)textual restriction in the given rule. The rule would be read e.g. as follows: a preterminal category A of a derivation Σ_i may be substituted by a terminal element φ if φ bears a relation of identity, inclusion or membership with an element φ' of a previous derivation Σ_{i-j} (where $i > j$). Note that φ and φ' may also represent 'terminal subtrees' of the derivations, i.e. (pre-)lexical structures. The proposed notations are related with the lambda-notation suggested earlier for the description of pronominalization based on abstraction, i.e. on intensional semantic identities between subtrees. Thus we may define the class of possible terminal elements of a semantic representation of a sentoid S_i by the property of having the specified relations with an element of a previous sentoid S_{i-j}, noted as follows: $(\lambda x)[(\exists y)Rxy]$; thus for each terminal subtree σ_i, we have $(\lambda x)[(\exists y)Rxy]\sigma_i$, or, when y is specified as a previous subtree: $(\lambda x)[(\exists y)Rxy \wedge \sigma_{i-j}(y)]\sigma_i$. This general property of a subtree is a constraint upon any sentential derivation in a sequence. Therefore it may be omitted in the individual cases and located in the meta-theory as a global coherence constraint for the derivation of sequences. There are, of course, several ways to represent obligatory and optional relations between subsequent sentences. However, these must fit the other rules of the sentential derivations. At the stage of present research it is therefore premature to propose definite formalizations of contextual constraints upon derivations which are still merely formulated in ordinary discourse, although many logical and mathematical models are available (cf. van Dijk [1971f]).

The relations of (partial) identity between subtrees, as generated by the base of the surface (sequence) component, serve in the next steps as conditions for processes of transformation. Firstly, the repeated arguments will lead to the assignment of [+ DEF]. Secondly, definite categories may be substituted by pro-forms if the base conditions are satisfied. Stress assignment and permutations will be the result of irregular topic-comment representation in sentential surface structure. Finally, embeddings will take place under more specific conditions: restrictive relative clauses require full-identity of lexemes and have obligatory relative pronoun insertion.

Nothing more precise can be said at the moment. As a matter of fact the exact nature of the transformational component depends on the form of the rules relating semantic representations and syntactic structures. So far, then, the intersentential constraints have to be formulated in rough provisional rules.

We may conclude this chapter by once more stressing that all elements and relations in the structure of a sentence are terms of intersentential relations, subject to linear and global constraints upon the derivation of sequences of sentences. Any description of the structure of isolated sentences, as practised in *S*-grammar, will therefore be incomplete if not inadequate.

3

TEXTUAL DEEP STRUCTURE: MACRO-STRUCTURES

1. INTRODUCTION: WHY TEXTUAL DEEP STRUCTURE?

1.1. In this chapter we adduce further support for our hypothesis that a text grammar is not limited to an explicit description of sets of linearly ordered sentences, but that a level of more GLOBAL and abstract structures must also be postulated. There are many reasons for considering this level, in analogy with generative grammar, to be the DEEP STRUCTURE OF A TEXT. This textual deep structure (TDS) is supposed to underlie the actual sentence structures and the interrelations between them which we studied in the previous chapter, and which have been considered the SURFACE STRUCTURE OF THE TEXT.

1.2. It is clear that this distinction must receive both formal and empirical confirmation, in order to avoid the danger of mere metaphorism. Taking generative grammar, and especially generative semantics, as a model might introduce serious bias in our theorizing about the macro-structures of texts. For example, if the notion of textual deep structure should turn out to account intuitively for a certain number of linguistic phenomena, we will have to formulate the rules for deriving such deep structures and, what is more, the transformational rules necessary to convert these underlying structures into a textual surface structure of sentences. The recent developments in generative semantics have pointed to the fact that a distinct level of deep structure might be dispensed with in a generative grammar. However this hypothesis was directed against the essentially syntactic deep structures of the standard model of generative transformational grammar. If a level of deep structure has to be postulated, this level, then, should be accounted for by the semantic component of the grammar. The output of the rules of this component, the semantic representation of a sentence, would next be mapped by transformation rules onto a syntactic structure and, finally onto a morpho-phonological and phonetic structure.

This model of a semantically based grammar has many different elaborations. Some authors continue to stress that some form of deep, shallow or intermediary syntactic structure must also be postulated in order to arrive at a systematic, general and relatively simple account of syntactic structures.

As we observed previously, the crucial drawback of semantically based grammars is the fact that no adequate and explicit formulation has been found to relate semantic deep structure representations with syntactic surface structures. Moreover, we are given hardly any consistent formulation of the rules generating these very semantic representations (cf. however, recently, Rohrer [1971]).

If, as many linguists maintain (Chomsky [1968], [1970], Katz [1970], [1971], Bierwisch [1970]), this model is only a 'notational variant' of an interpretative model, where syntactic (deep) structure serves as input to a semantic component, our position would not produce any theoretical difficulty. However, as we have tried to demonstrate in the preceding chapter, a certain number of syntactic phenomena seem to require underlying semantic structures without which very complicated syntactic rules and constraints must be formulated. Although many problems about the relations between semantics and syntax can be reduced to mere labeling differences of the theoretical categories used, there is very little evidence for taking a syntactically based generative grammar as a model for the construction of a text grammar. Textual deep structures have an essentially semantic character. Notice, however, that semantic structures are also purely formal, that is they have their own 'syntax' (in the logical sense), just like all levels of grammatical description. This syntax must be 'interpreted' as a semantic structure of relations. (cf. Wunderlich [1970b], Schnelle [1970]).

In forming this hypothesis about the semantic nature of textual deep structure, we are also motivated by reasons of formal simplicity. As we have noticed before it would be considered rather circumstantial if a T-grammar first generates textual deep structures (of an undoubted semantic character) and then rules which would map these global structures directly onto syntactic deep structures of sentences, which would finally be 'interpreted' semantically.

1.3. Instead of further debating the pros and cons of semantically based grammars, we will simply assume hypothetically that these are most relevant for our further argument. That is, we do not find any evidence, at the level of the text, of 'syntactic' structures in the strict linguistic sense of that term. Rather, the very abstractness of the underlying macro-structures brings them close to logical relations. Recent developments in generative semantics have repeatedly stressed this fact, and the result of these descriptions are certainly not less 'formal' or more 'fragmentary' than the traditional rules of interpretative semantics.

1.4. Before elaborating the different aspects of semantic rules for generating textual macro-structures, we may ask ourselves, as we did in chapter 1, whether we can also find empirical evidence for the notion of macro- or deep structure of texts itself. Why don't we simply consider a text as a series of sentences concatenated under a set of 'transitional' constraints as formulated in the preceding chapter?

Of course one must be careful with psychological 'evidence' as support for the form of a grammar. It has become clear in the last few years that our competence is not likely to be organized in a way postulated by a generative grammar. This is certainly true for the models of the strategies used by speakers and hearers to produce and perceive concrete sentences in a communication process (Campbell and Wales [1970], Wunderlich [1970a]; cf. chap. 9).

However, important arguments for the basic conception of generative-transformational grammar as a model for a mental device consisting of rules have been in psychological phenomena like verbal learning, processing, speech production, etc. Conversely, psychologists have used generative grammars to explain the problems with which they were confronted. (Cf. the contributions in Jakobovits & Miron, eds. [1967], Lyons & Wales, eds. [1966], Lyons, ed. [1970], Flores d'Arcais and Levelt, eds. [1970].)

1.5. Similarly, our text grammar is supposed to be a formal model for the competence of native speakers. Such a competence, which enables a user of the language to produce, interpret, process, paraphrase, etc. a virtually infinite number of texts, must be a rule-governed device. Such a textual competence, must first provide the rules, elements and constraints that permit a correct combination of subsequent sentences, for example according to the regularities formulated in chapter 2. These additional rules could be introduced into a sentence grammar without profound changes in the form of the grammar. The main reason for this assumption could be that these constraints are similar to those for constructing complex sentences. Apart from the formal difficulties (how do we formulate constraints for sentences that are structurally fully independent, what is the theoretical status, then, of an initial S-symbol, etc.?), probably no psychological objection would exist to the possibility of learning and manipulating such 'transition-rules'.

1.6. These rules are purely 'local' constraints which are essentially reapplied for every sentence connection. However, a text is not simply a set of well-formed pairs or triples. We intuitively know that a given sentence S_i is related in a certain way to several, if not all the preceding sentences of the text. That is, a text has a semantic coherence which surpasses the micro-structural or local constraints of its individual sentences. At the end of the previous chapter we saw, in a concrete sample text, that the selection of lexemes seems to be governed by an 'over-all' principle establishing a CONTINUITY in a text which precisely defines it as a structured unit, and not as a mere accumulation of binarily related sentences, i.e. as a set of well-formed pairs. The production of a given sentence in a text, then, seems to be determined at least by the semantic representations of the full set of preceding sentences, because lexical selection is made in accordance with the preceding SR's.

The program, plan, or strategy underlying actual speech (utterance) production would – among other parameters – be determined by the rules of a generative competence as has been demonstrated in psycholinguistics (cf. §2.7. below). It is highly improbable, however, that a native speaker manages to remember each previous SR in order to be able to generate a sentence which is textually related to them. At least for somewhat longer texts memory would not be able to perform that task. In fact, the precise form of a produced or received sentence is practically immediately erased from the short memory which has processed it quickly (Johnson-Laird [1970]). This is particularly true not only of the surface structures, which are only partially recalled, but also for the exact semantic representations. Memory tests can easily demonstrate this fact: the recall of a previous part of a longer text is only very fragmentary and global. Elements are 'recalled' which were not lexicalized in the text but which, for example as lexicoids, were present in several SR's of its sentences. Recalling, then, seems to proceed by (re-)constructing (Neisser [1967]) a global semantic framework: a 'plan', underlying the series of respective SR's. Such a global 'plan' has to be postulated in both productive and receptive processes (Hörmann [1967] 266, Dressler [1970a] 210). It is not relevant, here, whether this plan is the result of an analytical or a constructive process; probably both processes are involved (for details, cf. chapter 9). Important is the fact that a generative grammar has to specify how such plans can be formally constructed in order to provide an explanation of this linguistic ability.

Such a grammar should therefore specify a level of sufficient abstractness, generatable by a finite set of rules which determine the production and reception of the extremely complicated sequence of sentence of a text. This level can appropriately be considered a semantic deep structure of the text. In performance such a TDS would probably be formed first, at least in part, so that it can 'guide', in linear production, the selection of the lexemes of the subsequent sentences. Such a macro-plan can easily be memorized, which is not the case for whole sequences of SR's together with their semantic constraints of transition. Probably this global plan may be adjusted during the realization process either by changes of intention or by feedback phenomena from the produced surface structure of sentences.

For perception this process would probably not be very different, even when no global semantic plan can be present at the beginning. However, semantic information from the perceived and processed sentences probably has a 'projective' character. This means that in the gradual construction of a semantic deep structure the reader will often be able to predict roughly and hypothetically the further development of a text, such that a progressive increase of informational redundancy is formed. In order to construct these textual plans, a set of deep structure rules will be indispensable.

1.7. In the first chapter we have enumerated some further tasks a native speaker can perform with the aid of such macro-plans. The memorizing of a text essentially consists in recalling its deep structure, which has apparently been stored in long term memory. The abilities of abstracting, paraphrasing, commenting, etc. a text can only be accounted for in this perspective. The superficial surface structure, i.e. its sentences, are only indirectly relevant for all these tasks.

The hypothesis is in complete harmony with recent (and some classical) suggestions from cognitive psychology (cf. Neisser [1967]). In perception processes, learning and recall we essentially process with global patterns, not with collections of details.

The psycho-linguistic arguments for the existence of global plans in the processing of discourses do not necessarily lead to the hypothesis about the existence of linguistic macro-structures to be accounted for by a type of base rules. We do not exclude in principle that there may be other formal means to model macro-structures in texts. At the end of this chapter we will briefly discuss this possibility. The reason that we postulate semantic macro-structures is above all the linguistic (grammatical) possibility to relate such macro-structures with semantic structures of sentences. That is, even cognitive strategies of some kind which 'resume', 'abstract' or 'expand' and 'specify' towards or from macro-structures need formal semantic explanation.

1.8. All these facts, observations and hypotheses are linguistic and do not depend on situational or other performance factors alone. The production and reception of coherent texts, therefore, must be accounted for by models for which only a generative text grammar can serve as a formal basis. Further psychological confirmation has to be given, and it is the task of the linguist to investigate the nature and the form of the rules specifying global textual structures. Cognitive psychology will have to relate these structures to those of thought (intentions, knowledge, etc.) but grammar has to relate them with textual surface structure. This is undoubtedly the main task of a text-grammar, because mere speculation about alleged macro- or deep structures has only formal interest when we are able to state the still very abstract rules and constraints determining the generation of sequences of sentences that can be tested, as 'grammatical texts', on the linguistic intuition of native speakers.

This task however will be extremely difficult, and we have to limit ourselves, in this first stage of research, to a construction of possible deep structure rules.

2. SOME INFORMAL MODELS FOR MACRO-STRUCTURES

2.1. Having adduced some empirical arguments for the necessity of global underlying text structures, we now consider what these macro-structures could look like. There are several models which present themselves as possible, though, as yet, still very tentative candidates.

The first condition we have formulated for these possible models is that they specify structures in an algorithm, i.e. with the aid of explicit formation (and transformation) RULES. Without such rules, which will include recursive elements (texts may have, theoretically, infinite length), it would be impossible to explain how native speakers can process any text from the infinite set of their language. Any taxonomic model for the specification of these structures is therefore in principle inadequate: the possible textual deep structures are not part of a limited list, learned by the speaker and applied in appropriate situations. TDS can neither be a fixed 'schema' having sufficient abstractness to apply to any text, nor a differentiated set of such schemata underlying different types of texts. The infinite number of different deep structures must thus be accounted for by an algorithm. Before studying the possible nature of such rule systems, let us first consider other systems that have been proposed and applied to describe textual macro-structures.

2.2. We saw in the preceding chapters that traditional, both structural and generative, approaches to the structure of (co-)text were confined to the study of intersentential relations. Discourse analysis and its derived methods thus arrive at the establishment of matrices or schemata of the structure of a given text. In such matrices were introduced, mostly according to their grammatical category, the 'words' which recurred in the text and which established different types of equivalence structures.

Similarly, semantic approaches inspired by discourse analysis endeavour to find specific or general thematic or topic structures in a text. In this approach, equivalences are established by semantic (paradigmatic) relations between recurrent lexemes throughout the text.

In both approaches, about which we will be brief, the result is not a characterization of deep structures, but possibly only of (macro-) surface structure of the text, i.e. a structured taxonomy of its related morphemes and lexemes. Moreover, these structures are established ad hoc and intuitively and thus differ for each text: no instruction is given about the combinational possibilities of the schemata utilized. This lack of explicitness (and generality) and the taxonomic character of the textual structures analyzed can not lead to adequate models for the competence of native speakers to produce and to interpret texts. 'Plans' cannot possibly consist of lists, they must have a more abstract and structured (hierarchical) character.

2.3. Not wholly paradoxically, the most interesting suggestions seem to come from the domain of LITERARY THEORY, especially the theory of narrative structures, whatever the methodological weakness of these approaches still may be.

Traditionally poetics has been occupied by the structures of texts. Their global macro-analysis has, of course, also been practised. As we shall see in the second part of this book, attention has been paid especially to micro-structural operations for which rather complete lists are known from Antiquity onwards (as *figurae*). The description of macro-structures however has hardly been systematic: the 'organical' and later the 'structural' character of literary texts was (re-)constructed only in extremely vague terms. In recent times this description has taken the form of structural thematics, discussed above. We will return to these aspects in more detail in the following chapters.

In this perspective it has been, again, traditional rhetorics which offered most interesting remarks, though short and sketchy in comparison with the bulk of remarks about the *elocutio* of texts, in one of the *partes* of rhetorics, which was concerned with the art of the *dispositio* of texts. We might ask in what respect these normative and fragmentary remarks could be relevant for our discussion, but it will become obvious that a certain number of aspects treated here will be found, though in more explicit form, in recent discussion about textual macro-structures.

The *dispositio*, then, is the part of rhetorics that, coming after the *inventio*, regulates the ordering of the different functional parts of a whole text. Besides the possible numerical distribution of these functions, *viz.* as two antithetic parts, as 3 parts (initial, middle and final) and as 4 and 5 parts (as in dramatic texts), a 'natural' distinction is made between *exordium*, *narratio*, *argumentatio* and *peroratio*. Generalizing we can translate these terms as 'introduction', 'narration' or 'exposition', 'reasoning' or 'comment' or 'demonstration' and 'conclusion'. This order was considered 'necessary': all other distributions were taken to be 'artificial', and permitted only under specific circumstances (cf. Lausberg [1960] §§ 443–452).

This 'natural' order could of course be explained by the character of public address, but there is some point in interpreting these global categories from a more general semantic point of view, not only from that of stylistic 'well-formedness', for which rhetorics was established. We will return to this point below.

2.4. The theories of narrative structures, which were first developed in cultural anthropology and poetics, offered what was probably one of the first functional models for the textual macro-structure. We will treat the literary aspects of these narrative structures in chapter 8, but we have to stress here, firstly, that these hypotheses pertain not only to literary narrative texts but to all narrative, and secondly, that the functions which have been distinguished are analytical constructs which also apply to other types of texts.

Classical narrative theory normally operates with the intuitively well established notions of 'personage', 'character', 'action', and 'description', 'place' and 'time', that is, with the components which can be distinguished in any extra-linguistic event-situation (cf. chap. 8).

Structural analysis, mostly studying primitive narrative, in which 'personage' and 'character' are less relevant, has focussed upon the description of subsequent 'actions' in a tale or myth. These actions, called FUNCTIONS by Propp (1968) can be reduced to a fixed number of analytical primitives which can be found back, obligatorily or optionally, in any narrative. The order of these functions can be fixed in certain types of narrative or be more variable in other types. Greimas (1966), as we will see, reduced this number (31) of functions to more elementary categories and defined them with the aid of semantic features. Globally he distinguishes between the following functions

(i)   Disruption of a state of equilibrium.
(ii) Arrival and mission of the hero.
(iii) Trial of the hero.
(iv) Task accomplished by the hero.
(v)   Original state re-established. Hero recompensed.

There is striking similarity between these fundamental sequences of narrative and the parts of *dispositio* distinguished in rhetorics. Different scholars have thus arrived at basically comparable distinctions in narrative texts. Labov and Waletzky (1967) report that non-literary narrative also seems to have these fundamental parts

(i)   Orientation.
(ii) Complication.
(iii) Evaluation.
(iv) Resolution.
(v)   Coda.

These results may lead to hypotheses concerning NARRATIVE UNIVERSALS; and because a narrative is a type of text, we might assume that these distinctions could be transferred to other types of texts.

Isenberg (1970) explicitly tries to introduce the categories used by Labov and Waletzky into his textual derivation (see below).

2.5. What is the theoretical importance to be assigned to these inductively or hypothetically established FUNCTIONS of (narrative) texts? We may assume, for example, that they underlie a narrative ability of native speakers, but it cannot be maintained that this simple pattern determines all possible text structures. In fact, they also reflect a surface segmentation of specific texts into several stages of 'logical' development represented by sequences of sentences of the text. We could argue with Greimas (1966), however, that abstract constructs underlie these surface sequences, which, then, have to be considered to be manifestations of this abstract schema. Different texts are in that case generated by transformations applying to the elementary (neutral) pattern. No explicit rules are given to form this basic pattern, its structure is given as such, i.e. constructed (linearly) from its constituent categories.

For an empirically adequate model of text grammar these ideas are interesting but not sufficiently explicit. It must be impossible to generate a textual sequence determined by one simple category alone. That is, not only the whole text itself seems to have the syntagmatical functions discovered, but probably each 'function' of a text must be considered to be a certain relational structure. We could say, provisionally, that each function in fact must be viewed as an (embedded) text ('textoid'). We will elaborate this assumption in our chapter on literary macro-structures.

The importance of the distinctions referred to is in many ways similar to that of topic and comment in functional sentence perspective studies, because it assigns different functions to parts of a text/sentence. Before we are able to assign these functions we have to generate the proper semantic deep structures from which these functions are inferred. That is, we have to use models having a still more abstract and certainly more general character.

2.6. A more fundamental point of departure has been taken by Hendricks (1967), (1969b) and others, and their approach must be viewed as an intuitive preliminary step towards the deep structure hypotheses we will elaborate below. Investigating the nature of literary and in general 'connotative' macro-structures, he remarks that "the units and relations of the second-order system do not directly underlie the actually occurring sentences of a text" (1969b) 52. In fact, the underlying system can be viewed, according to Hendricks, as an ABSTRACT of that text, which is not directly manifested at the textual surface and its SR's. This abstract has to be accounted for with the aid of theoretical constructs and would determine the generation of the text. Hendricks rightly states that this speculation is not without theoretical and practical problems because we do not know how to arrive from this deep abstract to the surface text. He notices however that the hypothesis accounts for the fact that our textual interpretation is generated by our internalized 'theory of discourse'. An abstract, then, is a structural description of texts (Hendricks [1969b] 53–59; also Winburne [1964] 1097).

2.7. It is striking that Hendricks also refers to some concepts of psycholinguistics, especially the plan-notion we introduced above, following Miller, Galanter and Pribram (1960). This notion, though elaborated for sentence performance, apparently lends itself easily to interpretation at the level of macro-structures. We could say indeed that its real importance is still more relevant at this level, because the programming of verbal behaviour, as we showed, is totally impossible without the existence of abstract plans or strategies of which at least a textual deep structure has to form a part. Conversely, the authors established a relation between their hypothetical construct of 'plan' (which is basic in other cognitive domains) and syntactical deep structures as postulated by Chomsky's original model (1957).

These developments seem to point to the inevitable conclusion that textual deep structures can be compared with the deep structures of sentences. It is at this point that we can find a clue for a more explicit account of the possible form of textual deep structure.

2.8. Ideas similar to those of Hendricks had also been put forward by other linguists and literary theorists. Bever and Ross (1967), in a brief unpublished paper in which they investigate possible underlying structures in discourse, are also led to the conclusion that the 'cohesion' between the sentences of a text has to be explained by a formal construct of a highly abstract character: an abstract 'concept generator' which produces "some kind of abstract object which represents the maximal content of a whole set of discourse which derive from this concept" (7). In order to generate actual sentences this concept generator should be accompanied by a selection mechanism. The authors stress however that the coherence of discourse can certainly not be accounted for by linguistic devices alone.

2.9. At the boundaries of narrative analysis and linguistics these ideas about an underlying abstract generator can be traced in the work of scholars like Žolkovskij, Ščeglov, Mel'čuk, and other Russian linguists.

We will come back to the proper literary implications of this concept in a later chapter (cf. detailed discussion in Ihwe [1972]).

Mel'čuk and Žolkovskij (1970) in a recent paper explicitly devised a grammar working 'upwards' from text deep structure to the sentence level. Abstract semantic representations are mapped on lexico-syntactic structures which are realized as texts by syntax and morphophonology. The semantic representation consists of a structure of predicate-argument relations. Although the authors hardly treated 'texts' in our sense, but limited themselves to lexical (micro-)structures their model seems to be sufficiently general to be employed for texts.

2.10. Conceiving textual deep structures as (verbalized) abstracts of a text naturally leads to the theoretical foundations of paraphrasing.

As Ungeheuer (1969) has pointed out, paraphrase plays a predominant, but hardly explicit, role in generative grammar, because deep structures of a sentence have to be considered to be hypothetical and elementary paraphrases of the surface structure. The basic criterion, then, is the identity of semantic content, provided transformations do not change the semantic representations based on (syntactic) deep structure (cf. Nolan [1970]).

It might be asked, however, in which way we should understand the concept of textual paraphrase. If the current conception of paraphrase is also valid for texts, two texts can said to be paraphrases if their semantic structures are identical and if morpho-syntactic and lexematic surface structure differ. Textual paraphrase, in this sense, characterizes the semantic representations underlying the sentences at the surface of the text. In a more loose way of definition however this purely 'linear' conception of the SR's of a text seems to be irrelevant; texts can be paraphrased with sentences in another order, and with fewer sentences than that of the paraphrased text. In this more abstract sense a summary may be considered to be a 'minimal' paraphrase.

Formal models have also been elaborated within the theory of abstracting, especially in relation to computerized data processing (cf. Wyllys [1967]). It is clear that these developments can provide interesting suggestions especially because of their mathematical sophistication. However, an explicit linguistic foundation of the 'abstract' has not been given in this type of research, which concerns itself mainly with lexical surface structures.

3. TOWARDS A MODEL FOR MACRO-DERIVATION

3.1. The models presented in the preceding chapter have certain properties in common which seem to point to possible convergence about the basic idea: texts have to be conceived of as having a surface structure of sentences and a global deep structure which can be considered to be a semantic abstract underlying the text.

Until now, practically no explicit ways have been indicated of how this semantic deep structure should appear, or by which rules it could be formed out of more elementary semantic categories. Further, no elucidation has been given on the (certainly very problematic) rules relating such deep structures with sentential surface structures. Actually, such an indication would be impossible at the moment because we do not even have a precise idea of how the semantic representations themselves have to be structured. The problem is to construct a useful model that can be considered both as an adequate basis for a theory of (textual) competence and as a sufficiently simple and consistent framework for text grammars.

Instead of constructing a completely new base theory for text grammars, we will look for existing models in linguistics and logic, because the structures our grammar has to specify are supposed to have an abstract semantic character. Moreover, we have postulated that the grammar should be generative, that is contain explicit derivation rules.

3.2. It is natural, in that case, to consider generative grammars for sentences, in order to examine whether their rules have a character that is abstract enough to account for global semantic structures also. This hypothesis, then, is based on the simple assumption that the basic structures underlying whole texts and sentences can be considered to be isomorph. If this assumption should turn out to be correct, we can in principle use existing semantically based S-grammars as a point of departure. Of course, the difference in abstraction level will force us to make at least a number of formal adjustments.

This structural analogy between sentence and text is suggested also by their possible co-extensiveness. That is, theoretically – and also practically (as often occurs in spoken daily discourse) – a text can consist of only one sentence. If a text grammar would assign to such a one-sentence-text a structure which would be entirely different from that assigned by its S-grammar component the grammar could not be considered consistent. This trivial fact suggests that macro-structures, in principle, are not different from abstract structures at the sentence-level. If this is true, text surface structures can become gradually and linearly more complex, while their deep structure will roughly keep the form of a sentential proposition.

3.3. However, the text-sentence analogy postulated in the previous paragraph must be handled with care. The fact that a text may coincide with a sentence does not prove their structural isomorphism. Sentences may in turn consist of one word and yet not be similar in structure with a word. If sentences would simply be immediate constituents of texts, the analogy would certainly be misleading. This is why we establish the analogy merely at their abstract level of semantic representations, *viz.* at the level of their logical forms. We will assume that any 'minimal' meaning structure, be it micro-structural or macro-structural has the (modalized, quantified) 'proposition'-form. Such a form would correspond with a semantic phrase marker in linguistic descriptions. We will assume also that the general, abstract structure of semantic representations is somehow linked with the 'interpretability' of meaning in general, but we will not explore further the very important relations between structures of thought and reasoning and the abstract logical forms of linguistic expressions.

3.4. In a less systematic way this idea has also been propounded by several other authors, both linguists and literary theorists.

Hendricks (1969b) in his book draws the same parallel. The 'hyper-expression' plane established in (literary) texts at a higher tactical level, can be considered in terms of an 'idealized sentence' of the type Subject-Verb-Object. In that case, a complex one-many relation has to be established with textual surface structure (64, 82). Hendricks proceeds by analysis: he normalizes the sentences of a (given) text to the standard grammatical form (with the aid of transformations) and then puts these sentences into a matrix, not unlike Harris in his discourse analysis. The 'synopsis' thus may finally be phrased as a molecular assertion. No algorithm is given to describe these basic structures but one would expect that a normal grammatical derivation would generate this molecular assertion.

Less explicit are similar remarks from Barthes and Kristeva. Barthes (1966) 2ff. proceeding deductively, at least in his program, considers the narrative text (like Hendricks, Hjelmslev's followers and Russian semiotics) to be a message generated by a secondary language system. This message has a semiotic structure which is similar to that of a sentence, and, conversely, discourse, he argues, is a long sentence. It is not clear from this last remark whether he identifies sentence and textual surface structure (a concatenation of sentences) as was also propounded by Katz & Fodor (1964), 491 and Katz (1967) 177, or whether he just means global deep structure analogy (for criticism cf. Palek [1968] 130ff.).

Inspired by Šaumjan's combinatorial 'applicative' grammar, Kristeva (1969a) makes a distinction between 'geno-text' and 'pheno-text'. The first term can be considered as textual deep structure which generates the surface structure of the text. The possible components of this deep structure are specified but not its exact form or the generative or applicational rules forming it. From other remarks of Kristeva it follows that the formal part of this text structure is analogous to a predicate-argument pattern, of subsequent (embedding) modified and modifying categories. The (narrative) text, then, is supposed to have a structure similar to that of an elementary sentence of the form subject-verb-object, in which the subjects are the main actors *(actants)* and the predicate the action of the narrative.

However, she also notes that a narrative can thus be considered to be a long sentence (Kristeva [1969b] 442). We saw that the fundamental notion of 'actant' derives notably from the work of Greimas (1966) and others. It is in this perspective that we first have an idea about the possible categories of textual deep structure.

3.5. The preceding paragraphs in fact do not present more than intuitive confirmation of our hypothesis that textual deep structure is analogous to sentence deep structure. This analogy has been perceived especially by those confronted with the structural description of narrative. This can easily be explained by the traditional or current conception of sentence structure in terms of functions, both grammatical, psychological and logical. That is, a (psycho-)logical subject is associated with the 'actor' of an action expressed by the verbal predicate, the one who brings about a situation or the one of which an event process or state, is predicated. The similarity with analogous terms used for the description of whole narrative texts is striking in this respect, and therefore grammarians like Tesnière (1959), Greimas (1966), Halliday (1961), (1970) and Pike (1967) adopted a system of 'actants' (or actors) for the description of the functional structure of elementary (atomic) sentences.

Greimas (1966) in particular has elaborated this system for the description of texts. His actants are typical deep structure categories *(structure latente)* which can 'manifest' themselves as different actors in surface structure. His main actants are

(1) *destinateur*   (2) *adjuvant*   (3) *destinataire*
(4) *opposant*   (5) *sujet*   (6) *objet*

The antithetic categories of *adjuvant* and *opposant* are considered *circonstants* of this textual 'syntax' (Greimas [1966] 122ff., 173ff.).

Together with two types of predicates (static *vs.* dynamic) and the operators of mode and aspect these actants form the basic categories of the text as a whole. Some actants may be defined by the functions expressed in the predicate. If that is true, the categories set up may be reduced to more elementary ones, because it is clear that a subject + a verb denoting positive causation is automatically assigned a function like *destinateur*, and a subject combined with another subject, both having verbs denoting positive action ('aid') is similarly interpreted as *adjuvant*. These actants therefore seem to be derived from more elementary categories.

Numerous distinctions in Greimas' work are thus directly relevant for our model. Nevertheless, in his structural approach Greimas did not specify

(i)   the precise structure of this basic semantic syntax of textual functions,
(ii) the rules underlying the formation of well-formed structures of these categories,
(iii) the rules for manifesting actants and predicates at the surface of the text. This surface is independently described in semantic or thematic terms.

Finally, his methodological procedure was, at least originally, mainly inductive. His departure is the description by successive steps of reduction of a given corpus of texts. In later approaches he stresses that the postulated basic categories can also serve in a deductive description. Until now he has not given an explicit framework for such descriptions.

3.6. Common roots underlie an approach which has acquired more attention within generative grammar: Fillmore's case grammar (1968), (1969a), (1969b), (1970). We saw in the previous chapter that Fillmore intends to contribute to a more fundamental – and universal – description of the underlying structures of the sentence. These structures are defined by a relational pattern of abstract 'cases', which are not to be identified with the traditional (concepts of the) cases of classical grammar, which are restricted to the study of particular morphematic particles. Although in his different articles Fillmore uses different names or distinctions for his cases, his basic categories are essentially those of Agentive, Instrumental, Dative (the 'affected' animate being) 'Factitive' (the 'effected' object) Locative and a neutral case: Objective, defined by the meaning of the verb. The system, however, is not (or not only) set up in order to describe semantic representations. Rules are formulated to derive syntactic structures with them on the level of the sentence.

It has been shown by critics of Fillmore that the relations between his basic structures and those of the syntactic level are still problematic, either because the categories used are still too complex, or because their definition (like the one for Instrumental) is still too intuitive (Dougherty [1970b]).

The inevitable flaws in this interesting approach to the semantic 'syntax' of the sentence do not prevent accepting it roughly as the model for our textual deep structures. The abstractness and the textual relevance of this functional approach lend themselves very well to a description of macro-structures, as the less explicit but not less detailed work of Greimas has shown.

In our adaptation of Fillmore's ideas we will depart from the syntactic concept of 'case' however, because it seems to obscure, not in the least because of traditional associations, the basic semantic categories involved. For some tentative rules for these categories, cf. now also Chafe (1970).

Finally, we will introduce some new elements postulated in recent developments in generative semantics, not only with respect to the purely formal structures and their notation but also in connection with the role of some pragmatic aspects in (text) grammars.

3.7. The main theoretical problems in this stage of the discussion concern not only the identification or construction of relevant theoretical categories of textual deep structures, but also the form of the rules used to introduce, define and relate these categories with others.

The form of these rules, clearly, cannot be established *a priori* (Ihwe [1972]), that is they need not be traditional rewrite rules of the PS-type derivation. This can be understood from the very nature of semantic deep structures: unlike PS rules they do not specify categories directly intended to generate segments of morpho-syntactic strings, but, rather, different types of RELATIONS between semantic units of different levels.

Fillmore (1968) normally uses generative expansion rules of the rewriting type and represents his deep structures in labeled oriented trees having both binary and multiple branching. Similarly, McCawley (1968a), (1968b) first seemed to use normal rewrite rules for the semantically interpreted syntactic symbols of standard generative grammar. In his programmatic article of 1968 (McCawley [1968a]) he rejects rewrite rules and their order because certain parts of the terminal string can be ambiguously derived by means of more than one rule. Instead, he proposes, following certain mathematicians, the use of tree formation rules, in which nodes are replaced by lower nodes, under the constraints of node admissibility conditions. However, he has not worked out his suggestions in detail, so we cannot judge their possible relevance for textual deep structures. They do not seem to differ essentially, however, from the rewrite rules of a standard generative grammar, because the main difference is only that the instructions apply directly to graphs instead of to strings of theoretical symbols, structured by labeled bracketing.

The theoretical status of rewrite rules has not yet been wholly elucidated, especially with respect to their relation with 'formation' (and 'transformation') rules in logic and mathematics. We have to note for example that the formation rules (PS-rules) in generative grammar, which expand an initial, 'given', symbol, have at first sight the nature of 'transformation' rules in deductive systems, because they determine which string of symbols may be replaced by another string also being well-formed, thus deriving the 'theorems' which are the grammatical sentences of the language. However, in that case the role of linguistic transformation rules becomes unclear. Derivation rules are therefore indeed rules for the formation of the well-formed formula (wff's) of the language. For the relations between these linguistic wff's we then need transformation (deduction) rules which determine under which operations two wff's can be considered equivalent, for example, with respect to their semantic value, or in other words their meaning. It might be asked whether Chomsky's transformations can be considered to be such deductive rules. Moreover, no axioms seem to be provided from which well-formed formulas can LOGICALLY be derived (cf. Rohrer [1971] 108-121), although the system can be translated easily into a first order predicate logic (cf. Schnelle [1970], Wunderlich [1971b] Wang [1971a], [1971b]).

3.8.1. Within the framework sketched above we shall now try to formulate some tentative rules describing textual macro-structures. Our main hypothesis was that these rules are similar, at this level of abstraction, to those describing the 'logical form' of a sentence. One of the main differences lies in the character of the terminal categories of the derivation, and of course in the subsequent transformations.

The model most currently used for the description of sentential logical form is a first order PREDICATE CALCULUS (cf. Keenan [1970]). Within linguistics, these descriptions, however are still rather simple, and only restricted use is made of all the resources of standard predicate calculus, although its insufficiency for the description of natural language has often been underlined. We shall first roughly follow the lines of the logical standard theory as applied to the description of (macro-)semantic relations and indicate in the sequel where modifications, extensions, adaptations are necessary, or where the use of non-standard systems becomes inevitable.[1]

3.8.2. It has been demonstrated that the traditional formation rules of generative syntax can be translated into a first order theory. Conversely, we may use rewriting rules for the formation of the well-formed sentences of predicate calculus (cf. Rohrer [1971]), considered as formal representations of semantic structure. The abstract syntax of such a system, first of all, contains the usual argument variables ('x', 'y', ...), predicate variables ('f', 'g'), parentheses ('(', ')', '[', ']') and a comma. We will further need symbols as names for the different logico-semantic categories, viz. *Pred* for predicates and *Arg* for arguments. Subscripts and superscripts are used here to indicate the degree of the predicate higher than one: 2-place, 3-place, ... n-place predicates and similarly to indicate the number of the arguments respectively. We will use T as the initial symbol (interpretable as 'Text') representing the 'sentence' (or 'proposition') or more abstractly: the well-formed formula (*wff*). The rewrite arrow '$\rightarrow$' will be used as an equivalence relation between expressions of the system, specified as the substitutibility of the symbol occurring on the left by the symbol(s) occurring on the right of the arrow. Thus a *wff* like $g(x, y)$ would be generated by the following rules:

(1)   (i) $T \rightarrow Pred_2 \, (Arg)^2$
          (ii) $Pred_2 \rightarrow g(-, -)$
          (iii) $(Arg)^2 \rightarrow (x, y)$

The corresponding general rules would, of course, have subscript and superscript variables (i, j) and sets of predicate-variables and argument variables. The simple formula derived above may be interpreted when we replace the variables by the lexical constants of natural language: e.g.

---

[1] Even within logical theory itself the precise form of the different systems of modal logic has not yet been elaborated. Especially the construction of their semantics meets with serious problems; cf. Hughes and Cresswell (1968) and Rescher (1968) for introduction and bibliography. For their application to the description of natural language, cf. the contributions in Lambert, ed. (1970), *Linguaggi* (1970) and the two *Synthese* issues on Semantics of Natural Language (1970). For linguistic applications, cf. Lakoff (1970b) and Kummer (1972a).

The logical language used here is extremely simple and is reduced to a predicate logic with some necessary extensions towards higher order description and modal elements, considered as a tentative hypothesis about the structure of semantic micro- and macro-representations. Cf. Rohrer (1971) for similar descriptions of base structures. Notice that predicate logic has often been referred to by generative semanticists as a possible system for the representation of the logical form of the sentence, but as yet no explicit rules have been provided for its explicit derivation.

Up to the present the most explicit attempt to establish a base description in predicate logical terms has been made by Keenan (1970) whose work, however, could not yet be integrated into this book.

(2)   (i) $g \rightarrow$ *to read*
             (ii) $x \rightarrow$ *man*
             (iii) $y \rightarrow$ *book*

Note that the interpretation at the level of macro-structures would result in abstract prelexical constructs, not necessarily identical with the lexemes of sentential surface structure of a text. Further, also at this level, we have the familiar selection restrictions upon the choice of prelexical elements (see below). We see that the abstract structure of macro-semantic representations, until now, has been identical with the structure of the *wff*'s of a simple predicate calculus. This structure may also be represented by a labeled tree.

Already in these steps our logical notation seems to commit us to the traditional conception of predicate as 'properties' or 'relations', denoting e.g. STATES, ACTIONS, EVENTS or PROCESSES, and of arguments as abstract or concrete THINGS, represented by the surface categories of verbs (adjectives) and nouns respectively. We shall see that in a higher order predicate calculus these 'things' may, however, also be predicates or propositions (texts) or other categories. Similarly, when we consider the argument-variables simply as 'individual variables', the assignment of lexical 'values' might itself be of the predicative type: man(x), book(y), to read(g). Such an interpretation of the formula may be added as a 'specification' to its abstract logical structure (cf. [McCawley [1968a]).

3.8.3. A more important problem, hardly ever treated in logical theory, concerns the status of the arguments and their ordering relation. The difficulty here is that logical conventions for the notation of an ordered sequence of arguments are rooted in a rather superficial representation of the ordering of nominal categories in the sentences of natural language. Thus, the first argument is normally considered the subject, the second either as direct object or indirect object or even as a complement. In the two-place predicate *to read* the first argument is interpretable as the 'agent' of the action and the second as the 'object' of the action. The class of things of which the elements may substitute the x in our derivation, apparently, is restricted to those having the property 'agent', *The book reads the man* being ill-formed. Note that concepts such as 'agent' and 'object' are independent of syntactic surface structure: unlike a subject/ object (or NP_1, NP_2) conception of arguments, they are independent of such trans-formations as *The book is read by the man*, having a structure $h(x, y)$, where h is the two-place predicate *to be read by*. Although the active and passive sentences have (roughly) the same meaning, the predicate is different, whereas the individual vari-ables are interpreted as different lexical constants. Traditionally, the equivalence may be made explicit by considering g and h as converses, e.g. h as the converse $\breve{g}$ of g: $\breve{g}(y, x) \equiv g(x, y)$. However, the structure of the ordered sequence of arguments is now different, although abstractly speaking there are two individuals and one relation READ in both cases between these individuals. Such an equivalence would be rendered adequately by a formula such as *Pred (Ag, Obj.)* where the relation is not merely specified by its order, but also by its 'type'. That such a specification of the 'role' of the different arguments is necessary can already be concluded from the impossibility to represent formally the lexical 'converses' *to come* and *to go* with the traditional logical symbolism, e.g. $go(x, y) =_{def} come(y, x)$, while the 'converse' of *Peter is going to Paris* is NOT *Paris is coming to Peter*, but *Peter is coming from Paris*. Apparently, the 'converse' character of meanings cannot simply be represented logically with the order of the arguments, but should be rendered e.g. with a basic categorical difference between 'source' (or 'point of departure') and 'goal' (for descriptional detail cf. Gruber [1967] and the work of Fillmore cited above).

3.8.4. The question is whether the observations of the preceding paragraph are compelling reasons for reformulating our elementary base rules, and, if this is the case, how we have to introduce the relevant additional categories. The simplest way would be to specify the arguments as to their possible 'function' defining their mutual relations, e.g. by introducing *Ag, Pat, Obj, Instr, Source, Goal*, as primitives of the system

$$(3) \qquad Arg_i \rightarrow \begin{bmatrix} Ag \\ Pat \\ Obj \\ Instr \\ Source \\ Goal \end{bmatrix}$$

It is not yet known whether this set is closed, and if so, which fundamental categories should be introduced as primitives. Following the terminological usage introduced by Tesnière (1959) we may finally replace the traditional notion 'argument' by the functional notion of *actant*, represented as *A*. The first rule would then be:

$$(4) \qquad T \rightarrow Pred_m(A)^n$$

where the number of actants is indicated by the superscript *n*, which conventionally also indicates the value of the predicate (although the number of actants realized may be smaller than the possible number of actants of an *n*-place predicate: $m \geq n$).

A similar differentiation may be made for the predicate, for which a distinction between 'property' and 'relation' is already traditionally made. We may use, following Chafe (1970), such fundamental categories as *State, Process, Event, Action*, by the following rule

$$(5) \qquad Pred \rightarrow \begin{bmatrix} St \\ Proc \\ Ev \\ Ac \end{bmatrix}$$

This differentiation will be necessary for the selection of the possible actantial categories e.g. an action will require an agent or patient as one of its actants.

3.8.5. After this provisional extension of our system for deriving well-formed 'sentences' of the logical system describing textual macro-structure, we should consider the other categories to be introduced.

Firstly, all our atomic expressions generated above are too simple. We will need rules for the formation of complex propositions. This procedure can be carried out by introducing a general symbol for 'connection', '&', preceded and followed by at least one initial symbol. Such structures can be generated by the following rule schema (cf. § 5.8.3. of the previous chapter for 'independent' surface rules, and § 3.8.11 below for the problem of relating them).

(6) $T \rightarrow T(\&T)^n$

where n takes the values ≥ 0. The general symbol will then be used to specify the set of logical connectives

$$
(7) \qquad \& \rightarrow \begin{Bmatrix} \wedge \\ \vee \\ \supset \\ \equiv \end{Bmatrix}
$$

Note that we omitted negation as one of the relevant connectives: it does not connect propositions but modifies a proposition (see below). We have seen earlier that the logical connectives are certainly not sufficient for the description of the relations between sentences (sentoids) or, like here, between 'texts' (textoids) of a complex text: disjunction may be both inclusive and exclusive; conjunction may be 'joint' and 'non-joint'; implication is always material and connected, both logically and inductively (cause and consequence), etc. The terms of the complex formula in predicate logic being only considered for their independent truth values, we must change our symbolism so as to be able to represent the relevant propositional relations of dependency. Provisionally we will keep the sentential connectives as specified in rule (7) and introduce them with an accent, e.g. '$\overset{\prime}{\supset}$' (cf. Reichenbach [1947]) to indicate semantic or referential connections between the sentences (cf. Carnap [1958] 8f.). With the aid of the modal categories to be introduced later, we may then try to define other connections on the basis of these four primitives, e.g. a conditional sentence with the aid of non-factual sentences and an implication.

Embedding relations, or the corresponding recursive rules, are considered, just as were sentences (cf. previous chapter) operations of a more superficial character. The linearity implied by rule schema (6) may be transformed into hierarchical relations.

3.8.6. The basic structures for which we have formulated some simple rewrite rules were often called 'sentences', according to regular use in logical theory. Strictly speaking, however, they are merely PROPOSITIONS, which cannot yet be used as such to designate or to refer. They represent the abstract content of the underlying macro-structures. We may call them NUCLEAR PROPOSITIONS (cf. Seuren [1969]), which implies that other categories are necessary to complete them in such a way as to generate full 'sentences' (texts).

It is here, with these modifying categories, that the main problems begin to arise. Although they have the entire nuclear proposition as their scope they normally only apply to certain categories of this proposition. Thus QUANTIFIERS will be needed to restrict the domain of the argument variables, whereas MODAL categories especially affect the predicates or the nuclear proposition as a whole. Finally we may introduce primitives or another device for the representation of the SENTENTIAL ATTITUDES, which are the formal reflection of pragmatical categories at this level.

In order to separate this set of categories from the nuclear proposition we introduce them under dominance of a single category 'text-qualifier' (*Tql*), in analogy with the 'sentence-qualifier' used by Seuren (1969). The second rule would then be something like

(8) $T \rightarrow Tql\ Prop$

The choice of appropriate QUANTIFIERS for the representation of semantic structures has been the object of extensive discussion not only in logical theory, but also in linguistics. Introducing them as a deep structure category implies possible semantic changes in the transformational cycle: *Few men read many books* is not equivalent with *Many books are read by few men*. A further major problem is that the habitual universal and existential operators are far from sufficient to represent such notions as *few*, *most*, *several*, *many*, etc. although these might be reduced to some primitives. In order to formalize these notions we must depart from standard quantificational theory and introduce more diversified operators. The logic of such a quantification may suggest such obvious implications as

(9)   (i)   All men have a head $\overset{\prime}{\supset}$ Most men have a head
           (ii) Most men are poor $\overset{\prime}{\supset}$ Some men are poor

In set theoretical terms the sets denoted by the consequent are included in those denoted by the antecedent. The same is true for the following implications which, however, we would refrain from calling true in natural language

(10)   ? All men have a head $\overset{\prime}{\supset}$ Few men have a head

Of course we may try to define such notions as *few* and *many* by using the traditional quantifiers. We might, for example introduce *many* or *most* simply by negating the universal quantifier: *not all*, although a semantic difference (e.g. positive vs. negative) subsists. Similarly, *few* might simply be identified with an existential quantifier: *at least one* (or *some*), or equivalently, by double negation as *not none*.

Instead of trying to reduce so important a notion of natural language as *most*, we introduce an 'W' to denote provisionally (see below) *for most* ... in $(Wx) f(x)$, for which indeed the rules as given in (9) are valid (cf. Rescher [1968] 170f.). We might, then, try to define *few* in terms of this quantifier: $(Few\ x) f(x) =_{def} [(Wx) \sim f(x)]$, although a clear difference in meaning reappears. We therefore introduce an ('ꟻ' as the pluralistic quantifier corresponding to 'W', for which the following implications are valid (for detail, cf. the recent book of Altham [1971])

(11)   (i) $(\exists x) f(x) \supset \sim (x) \sim f(x)$
            (ii) $(\exists x) f(x) \supset \sim (Wx) f(x)$
            (iii) $(\exists x) f(x) \supset (\exists x) f(x)$

From this discussion on the introduction of additional quantifiers it did not emerge what the precise relation between *few* and *most* or rather between *most* and *many* and *few* and *some* might be. Clearly *most* implies that a subset of individuals of a particular set under consideration is predicated on. This is not the case for *few* and *many*. It would therefore be more consistent to use a *many*-quantifier, corresponding to 'ꟻ', and let 'W' denote now: *for many* ... The grammatical behaviour of *many* and *most* is rather different so that we may not simply consider them as quantifiers or 'scalar predicates' (Lakoff, 1970b) of different 'strength', e.g. by $(Most\ x) f(x) \supset (Many\ x) f(x)$, we have *There were many people in the room*, but not *There were most people in the room*. *Most* therefore seems the correlate of the existential quantifier.

(12) $(Most\ x) f(x) =_{def} (\exists x) \sim f(x)$

This system might be elaborated further but our aim was merely to point at the necessity of pluralistic quantifiers for the formal description of semantic (macro-)structures. Equally important, but accompanied by still greater problems, are the quantifiers used for ((IN)DEFINITE) DESCRIPTIONS. We will not repeat here the discussion on definite descriptions, the 'existence' of individuals, and related issues.

In the first place we will need a iota-operator (ι) for predication of unique individuals. This uniqueness condition is defined only for the 'universe of the text' we want to generate or rather for the 'universe of the speech act' in which a text is embedded as a token (cf. chap. 9). Without referential or pragmatic identification, this uniqueness can only be introduced, indefinitely, by preceding textoids: *There is a man who* φ. *This man* ψ. Formally, this uniqueness is specified by letting all other individuals possessing the same properties be identical with the unique individual. Similarly, we may introduce an èta-operator (η) for the description of non-specified individuals:

A man (or: *one of the men*) *was crying*, for which the same existential definition is given but without the uniqueness condition (cf. Reichenbach [1947] 264f. For epsilon- and lambda-operators, cf. chapter 2).

We are now able to specify one of the categories of the text qualifier of rule (8), viz. *Qu* (for quantifier), e.g. in the following manner: (*Qu* is optional – see rule 13 – because propositions may only have constants, e.g. proper names):

$$(11) \qquad Qu \rightarrow \begin{bmatrix} \forall \\ \exists \\ \text{W} \\ \text{ꓱ} \\ \iota \\ \eta \\ \lambda \\ \varepsilon \end{bmatrix}^{n}$$

with the convention that the number of quantifiers is identical with the number n of different argument-variables used in the proposition, and such that each quantifier is combined with a different variable. For reasons of simplicity we derive provisionally the operators as quantifiers, which of course is logically incorrect.

3.8.7. Once having left the first order level, we may also want to quantify over predicates by assigning properties to properties and relations. Although theoretically we may have n^{th} order predicates, we will restrict ourselves to higher predicates of the second and third level in natural language, in order to be able to generate semantic structures underlying adjectives and adverbs. By adding a superscript to *Pred* in the first rule of (1) we imply that one of the arguments may be itself a predicate, which again may contain a predicate as an argument: e.g.

$$(12) \qquad \begin{aligned} T &\rightarrow Pred_i^3 \ (Arg)^i \\ Pred_i^3 &\rightarrow \psi \\ Arg &\rightarrow (Pred_j^2((Arg), Pred_k, (Arg))) \\ Pred_j^2 &\rightarrow \varphi \\ Pred_k &\rightarrow f \\ &(\ldots) \end{aligned}$$

Recourse to higher order calculi will also be necessary if we want to quantify not only over predicates but over the whole proposition, i.e. the state or event described. In that case, the variable v representing the proposition might be put in relation to sentential modifiers like modal, temporal and local adverbs. Thus, if we want to indicate that some action g of individual x took place at time t_i we can write: $(\exists v)([gx]^* \ (v, t_i))$. Simply writing $g(x, t_i)$ would only relate the individuals and not the proposition itself with the time point: In the previous formula we are also able to quantify over the time and place points themselves.

3.8.8. The next complex category modifying propositional nuclei contains the MODAL OPERATORS, of which the importance for a semantic theory has to be stressed. Of course it is impossible to deal here with all the problems related to modalities or to integrate the results of recent developments in logical theory. Further, it is not yet clear which operators will be relevant for the description of natural language. For instance, it may be asked whether the necessity operator ('N' or '$\square$') cannot be dispensed with, at least if it is interpreted as logical necessity.

Important will surely be the ALETHIC OPERATORS, like those of PROBABILITY and POSSIBILITY, which we will indicate as *Prob* and *Poss* respectively. As a 'neutral' operator we will then use *Fact*, indicating the 'factual' or 'actual' character of the state of affairs designated by the sentence. Finally, we will consider negation as a propositional modifier, and not simply as one of the logical constants on the same level as the sentential connectives. We will use *Neg* to symbolize this operator although strictly speaking it is not a modal category (essentially the same categories have been distinguished by Seuren [1969], Lakoff [1970b] and other linguists). Preceding the other operators, it forms complex operators for 'improbability', 'impossibility' and 'non-actualness'. The other operators may also combine with each other. At the level of the sentence these operators not only underlie the generation of different adverbs, such as *probably*, *possibly*, *really*, but also counterfactual conditionals, modal auxiliaries (*may*, *might*, *should*, etc.) etc. Their role at the level of textual deep structure is more global. In order to generate texts which are counterfactual (dreams, lies, fictive narrative, etc.) we will need such modal categories dominating the whole derivation. This does not prevent the introduction, in sentential surface structure, of 'local operators'. We shall see in chapter 8 that textual operators of modality are of great importance for the description of narrative texts, both in deep and in surface structure. The rule schema introducing model categories might be something like

$$
\begin{array}{lll}
(13) & \text{(i)} \quad Mod \rightarrow & M \quad (Qu) \\
& \text{(ii)} \quad M \quad \rightarrow & \begin{bmatrix} Neg \\ Fact \\ Prob \\ Poss \end{bmatrix}^{m}
\end{array}
$$

where the superscript indicates that each operator may theoretically be combined m times with one of the other operators. Any complex structure may have different sequences of operators before its propositions, such that some operators may dominate others. The relations between modal operators and quantifiers is problematic and cannot be discussed here. It might be the case that rule (13 i) should have the form $Mod \rightarrow M\ Qu(M)$, or even $Mod \rightarrow Qu\ M$. In natural language all categories of a sentence may be modalized (negated, etc.) although normally, in the neutral case, it is the predicate which falls under the scope of the operator. If other categories are modalized, special operations like stress assignment, topicalization, etc. will be necessary: *Probably the bóys will be admitted (probably not the girls)* vs *The boys will probably be admítted (probably not be refused)*. Apparently the scope of modal operators is precisely the comment of the sentence, as defined in the previous chapter. If necessary, other, less conventional, modal operators may be introduced, e.g. to represent belief-statements, deontic statements (*it is permitted that p; it is obligatory that q* etc.) and similar categories. We will not discuss these operators here, although their role for textual theory is obvious.

Finally, we might introduce operators for TIME and PLACE, although these could already be introduced as arguments together with event splitting individual variables. These operators would follow the modal operators, e.g. as follows: $Prob(t_i)(\exists x)$ $(gx \stackrel{.}{\supset} hx)$. However, these possible time and place 'operators' may have indefinitely different values, which rather characterizes them as argument variables. Time and place points, although abstract, may also be considered 'things' over which we may normally quantify, although their 'scope' is the whole proposition.

3.8.9. There is one last category, the presence of which in this syntax of (macro-) semantics is controversial: the PERFORMATIVE category, representing the primary text qualifier, viz. the traditional 'sentential attitudes': affirmative (or descriptive), question, command, etc. These might simply be introduced as follows

(14)   (i) *Tql → Perf Mod*
        (ii) *Perf →* $\begin{Bmatrix} Aff \\ Ques \\ Imp \end{Bmatrix}$

Such categories, linguistically, are necessary to account for questions, imperatives and their specific syntactic behaviour (inversions, *NP*-deletions, etc.). In fact they define the basic formal 'types' of sentences/texts and formalize the attitudes of the speaker towards the nuclear proposition. Recent suggestions, e.g. by Ross (1970) and Sadock (1970), following in part the suggestions of Austin (1962), however, introduced, as we saw earlier, explicit 'hyper-sentences', instead of operators. E.g. *I declare you ..., I ask you ..., I order you ...*, etc. in which the further modified proposition would be embedded as an object *NP*. The reason for the 'existence' of such 'performative' dominating sentoids was the possible explanation of some deletions and contradictions in the behaviour of first and second person pronouns. Such an introduction, however, has some unpleasant consequences. First of all the *I* and *you* never change in such performative sentoids, which is a reason to transport them to the metatheory: universally any sentence will contain them. Further, the performative verb used in such sentences may probably vary, but perhaps only in such a limited way as to be deleted by transformation. Other locutionary verbs will necessarily be present in surface structure. In the case that we might reduce the performative verbs to some primitives, it would be easier to introduce them as operators. Recall, further, that embedding of any text into a performative sentoid would result in difficulties for assigning truth values which have the dominating verb (here performative) as their principal scope: any performative sentence is – in normal cases – always true. If the underlying structure of *Peter came at nine o'clock* would be *I declare you (that) Peter came at nine o'clock*, the sentence could not be false since declaring something is self-confirmative. In the case of operators only the modalized proposition is attained by truth and falsity. The whole question of performative sentoids merely results from the insight that somehow PRAGMATIC aspects are associated with grammatical description. The same is true, for instance, in the case of all deictically determined categories (pronouns, adverbs, etc.). A simplified semantico-syntactic representation of speaker, hearer, as *I* and *you* respectively and possibly t_0 and l_0 of time and place of utterance as *here* and *now*, is not sufficient anyway. The same difficulties were observed in early transformational theory, where obvious semantic categories were forced into the straightjacket of syntactic representations. Notice, above all, that both 'speaker' and 'hearer' and 'time' and 'place' are entities with respect to UTTERANCES, not with respect to formal objects such as sentences or texts. Clearly, another level of linguistic description is necessary to embed 'full sentences' into situational, communicational frameworks. In that case, other relevant categories which are not properly semantic will necessarily be introduced. The analysis of 'speech acts' (Searle [1969], Searle, ed. [1971], etc.) will thus be localized in a PRAGMATIC COMPONENT, which might be introduced, for its purely formal aspects – different from the aspects of performance – as a third component into the grammar. It will define the notion of 'communicative competence' and put formal conditions upon the APPROPRIATENESS of utterances. We will treat this question in chap. 9. This component, then, will in a more adequately detailed way perform the job of the operators of rule (14) or the hypersentences used elsewhere.

3.8.10. In the preceding paragraphs we have constructed a still very rough underlying syntax for semantic macro-representations. Our formal categories, introduced as primitives of a logico-semantic base, were interpreted in our explanations, supplying the informal interpretation of the system. We have roughly followed, rather trivially perhaps, the lines of an extended predicate logic (with many simplifications), in which semantic base structures can be appropriately represented if some important changes are made (e.g. in the truth functional character of the sentential connectives). It was repeatedly observed, that these structures thus derived are isomorphous with those specifying sentential deep structure. The difference lies in further components: the insertion of (pre-)lexical material and other transformations, to which we will briefly turn in this and the following section. Let a sentence

(15)   John probably will not give all books to Peter.

have the following tentative underlying structure, as specified by the rules given in chapter 2 and above.

(16)

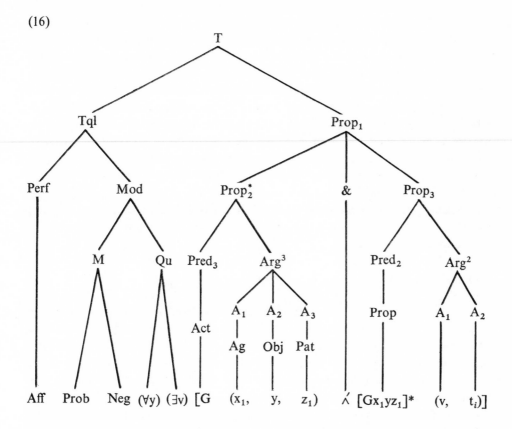

where $t_i \geqslant t_0$ (t_0 representing the zero time of utterance). We now have to assign a content to this logical form by replacing the variables by constants. These will not (at the abstract level of textual structure) be simply lexemes but probably abstract lexicoids. First the predicate-action variable will be substituted, since the other substitutions are restricted by the choice of the predicate constant. Thus the abstract structure of *give* requires the presence of at least three arguments, which are already indicated in the derivation, of which *Agent* and *Patient* are human and the *Object* is either animate or inanimate. By replacing *x* and *z* by proper names of humans this condition is fulfilled. *Prop₂* will generate a time relation *Fut*, representable as *will* in surface structure. *Prob* and *Neg* underlie the selection of *probably* and *not* and the quantifier identifies *book* as unique and makes it definite. At the level of textual deep structure we merely generate abstract lexicoids, e.g. $[[\alpha][\beta][+ - +\gamma]]$, not lexemes.

3.8.11. If the hypothesis, elaborated above, about textual base structures is roughly correct, we now have the important task of formulating the transformations which convert the highly abstract underlying sequence of textoids into a complex surface structure consisting of sequences of sentences.

The nature of such transformations is still obscure. Rather more familiar, though, are the deletion transformations, deleting theoretical symbols like *Aff* or *Neg*. We further have possible embedding or permutation transformations between *T*'s. An argument may receive as a predicate a whole textoid modifying it, which assures the recursive character of the base. However, as was demonstrated in the preceding chapter, such embedded textoids will be derived from preceding textoids in the base. Of course the ensuing normal sentential transformations (like definitivization, article selection, pronominalization) do not play a role at this level. Permutation will be necessary, as we shall see in chap. 8, for the description of all types of narrative structures (flash back, etc.). The semantic macro-transform, which is the output of the first cycle of (macro)-transformations, must then enter the cycle of what might be called a series of SPECIFICATION TRANSFORMATIONS. The exact nature, let alone the mathematical definition, of such transformations is unknown. Formally they are ONE-MANY RELATIONS which map an abstract macro-structure onto a set of sentence structures, ideally as follows

(17) $[XYZ]_T \Rightarrow \langle [x_1\, y_1\, z_1]_{S_1}, [x_2\, y_2\, z_2]_{S_2} \dots [x_n\, y_n\, z_n]_{S_n} \rangle$

That is, a macro-structure is converted into an ordered *n*-tuple of isomorphous structures. However, the structures of the different sentences of a text are not identical. They may individually be derived in a different manner according to the semantic rules. The isomorphism, thus, is only abstract, that is, it implies the similarity of the derivation rules. The one-many relation must thus be established between the 'macro-lexicoids' and the individual 'micro-lexicoids' of sentential structures. In this case, macro-lexicoids could be transformed by substituting them by the lexical classes they subsume and of which they are an abstraction

(18) $F(x) \Rightarrow \{x: Fx\}$

From this class will be selected the lexical elements of the respective sentences: either representing arguments or predicates and modifiers. Each individual sentence will supply the micro-semantic specification, by addition of features, in order to be able to select concrete lexemes. Not only is there thus a global constraint upon lexicalization in surface structure, but the different lexemes will also be selected – again globally – according to their semantic category: the subsequent sentences of a sequence have arguments in different grammatical positions which, however, correspond to the function of *Agent* or *Patient*, or *Place*, or *Time*, etc. It does not seem possible to give a formal representation of this process at the moment, at least not for non-idealized representation as suggested in rule (17). The constraint of lexical insertion would in that case be something like

(19) $[x]_{Ag} \Rightarrow \alpha \mid A_{Ag}$

that is: an *Agent*-variable is replaced by a lexical element α under the contextual restriction that it is taken from the class A representing the *Agent*-class of the text. It is however cumbersome to repeat such a constraint for each sentence. We might therefore specify it for the whole sequence, e.g. as follows

(20)   (i) $\langle A_i\, B_j\, C_k \rangle \Rightarrow Sq[\langle A_i\, B_j\, C_k \rangle]$
            (ii) $Sq \quad \Rightarrow (S)^n \mid \langle A_i\, B_j\, C_k \rangle$

where $\langle ABC \rangle$ is the ordered set of sets representing macro-structure, of which each set is associated with the functions i, j, k respectively. The global constraint will then for each sentence S_i of Sq_i have the same effect as rule (19).

Here we have arrived at a purely speculative level. The rules provided do not represent an algorithm which unambiguously selects lexemes and functions corresponding to them. In fact, as we remarked earlier, the rules are even too powerful, imposing exactly the same logico-semantic structure upon each sentence, which clearly is never the case. Apparently, stylistic freedom is great at this level, and the PARTICULAR choices cannot be determined individually. The whole sequence has to obey the constraint, with the effect that 'for at least one' or 'for many' sentences of the sequence the constraint applies. We will not try to solve prematurely all the problems here and leave the discussion at the level of intuition. For heuristic reasons a macro-description of Barthes' text may now illustrate some of the hypotheses.

4. A SPECIMEN OF DESCRIPTION

4.1. It would be useful if we could finally give a derivation of the macro-structures of a given text with the aid of the rules given above.

We will try to give such a derivation, in a somewhat rough and informal way, of the text of Barthes we studied in the previous chapter. Of course a complete derivation is totally impossible here. We will content ourselves with the derivation of its macro-structure and only indicate possible relations with its surface structure.

4.2. There are several ways of indicating the postulated deep structure of a text. As a hypothetical paraphrase it may, first, be represented by a structure of intuitively verbalized propositions, that is as an abstract. This abstract may then be formalized and the rules formulated to generate it.

Barthes' text may be considered as a combination of three textual propositions having a complex character, for example

Prop 1:   The critics say that if they don't understand a difficult philosophical work, this work is bad.

Prop 2:   This argument is based on a general 'terrorist myth' for masking one's own ignorance.

Prop 3:   But the philosophers understand the ignorance of the critics.

The text as a whole, like many essays of this type can be considered as a complete argument, having a syllogistic structure. Its semantic deep structure representation can thus be formalized according to the logico-semantic relations between its propositions (embedded or coordinated texts). We might first make *Prop* 1–3 more abstract, e.g. in the following manner

Prop 1:   IF *X* (CRITICS) SAY: *Prop* 1'

Prop 1':   IF(*X* NEG (UNDERSTAND *Y* (PHILOSOPHY))) THEN (*Y* IS BAD)

Prop 2:   THEN (*Prop* 1' SIGNIFIES ((*X* IS IGNORANT) AND (*X* IS TERRORIST)))

Prop 3:   AND THEN (*Y* UNDERSTAND (*Prop* 1')).

We can of course analyze the predicates in their basic semantic features but we will maintain the general lexicoids used here. This textual structure may finally be represented in a text-marker, e.g. as follows:

(43)

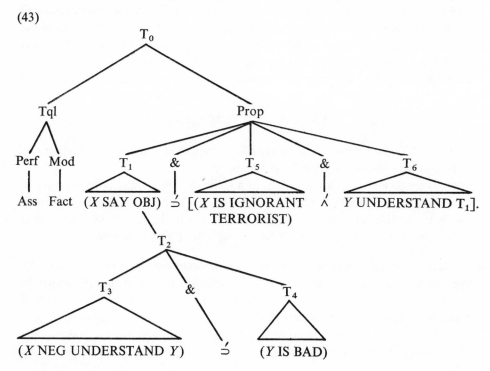

This very global derivation may even be reduced further to the implicational structure

(44)   IF $(X$ NEG $(UNDERSTAND$ $Y))$ THEN $(Y$ UNDERSTAND $X)$

which given the generalization in the second proposition can be noted as

(45) $(x)[\sim U(x, y) \overset{\prime}{\supset} U(y, x)]$

a formula which clearly underlines the symmetrical character of Barthes, argument.

4.3. The global structure represented in (43) has already been assigned the textual lexicoids at the end of the derivations of the embedded texts. But how can this interpreted structure be related to the surface of the text?

Firstly we notice that the three basic propositions, represented by T_1, T_5, T_6, coincide with three paragraphs of which the text of the first is again divided into two paragraphs corresponding with T_3 and T_4.

We will then have to rewrite the terminal macro-lexical categories CRITIC, SAY, etc. as sets of possible lexemes which may be used in the respective sentences of the text

(46)   CRITIC   → {*le(s) critiques, la critique, ...*}
         SAY   → {*argument, décréter, critique, s'avouer, faire profession, proclamer, confesser, ...*}
         NEG(UNDERSTAND) → {*ineffable, inutile, trop bête, ne pas comprendre, bêtise, imbécilité, impuissance, incompréhension ...*}

etc.

In these 'specification'-rules of textual derivation it becomes clear that functional deep structure lexicoids may be represented by different syntactic categories (nouns, verbs).

Finally, those surface constraints will be operating which have been formulated in the previous chapter: the formation of sentences is 'free' except for these local constraints and the global constraints given above. Further specification is determined by factors of performance such as intention, stylistic operations, etc.

5. CONCLUSION AND FINAL REMARKS

5.1. This chapter has led us to many often very speculative remarks and to few explicit rules, especially at the level relating macro-structures with sentence structure. Any definite conclusion, therefore, must remain on a hypothetical level.

We have adduced both formal and empirical arguments for the necessity of postulating global semantic deep structures in a text

(i)   texts cannot be mentally processed (produced and interpreted) as a coherent whole without underlying 'plans'.
(ii) the derivation of a semantically coherent sequence of sentential SR's can only be accounted for when global lexico-semantic constraints determine the selection of its lexicoids.

The form of the deep structure postulated was assumed to be analogous to those of (complex) sentences, such that sufficiently abstract models for sentential derivation can also be used for the derivation of underlying structures in texts. A functional (case) grammar based on modal predicate calculus provided the form of the rules and the categories needed for that derivation. One of the major tasks, then, for future research is to find the rules (functions) mapping the macro-structures onto the sequence of sentential SR's.

5.2. At the end of this chapter some remarks are in order about the feasibility of the program sketched above. We have repeatedly stressed the fact that sound linguistic theorizing about such an assumed abstract construct as a textual 'macro-structure' is still in a highly speculative stage. The main arguments adduced for postulating macro-structures, as we saw, are to be searched for in psycho-linguistics and cognitive psychology. In a sense it would be wise, then, to remain in these areas and frame the investigation in terms of cognitive processes and elaborate, for example, the much used notion of plan. However, there were compelling reasons to describe such macro-structures first at the properly linguistic level, *viz.* in terms which are abstract enough to permit a translation both into theoretical systems of cognitive psychology and into logical and mathematical models of all kinds. We therefore assumed that notions such as 'semantic representation' or 'logical form' may be abstract enough to interpret the global 'meaning' of a text as a whole. Moreover, semantic macro-structures are necessary to explain in sufficiently simple terms how it is possible that throughout a text the selection of lexical items and underlying formation of semantic representations is heavily restricted by some global constraint. Clearly, it is not possible to formulate, linearly, sentential formation rules with (co-)textual restrictions of possibly thousands of preceding (or following) lexemes and SR's. Such a task is certainly beyond the power of any grammar and, therefore, beyond the cognitive abilities of the human mind. This global underlying system, determining the macro-coherence, must therefore somehow be present, and the crucial point at issue is whether we seek some grammatical formulation for it, as we did, and/or whether such plans or programs are to be left over fully to the psychologist or the literary theorist. We do not think that this issue is in fact an alternative: we are convinced that a serious grammar must (once) contain the formal apparatus (rules) modelling the ability of native speakers to process discourses at two distinct levels: at the level of linear production/perception and at the level of global planning, programming, memorizing, etc. To be sure, as long as we are unable to formulate the rules relating the macro-structure of a text with the sentential structures, our assumptions might be qualified as plain metaphors, e.g. when taking the logical form of the sentence as a model and using concepts familiar in current grammars. Nevertheless, metaphors in scientific thinking may, besides the well-known dangers, have a very important heuristic role, and as long as many relevant phenomena fit well enough in the metaphorical schema adopted this may after some systematic and explicit work often be changed into a serious model.

Nevertheless, within text grammar it might be advisable to keep within the boundaries of the feasibility mentioned earlier and to confine ourselves to the concrete material provided by the sentential surface structure, leaving the amassed unexplained problems to the future macro-component. At this level and within psychological performance many rather explicit logical (pragmatic) and mathematical models are available (cf. van Dijk [1971f] for some brief suggestions). The production of discourse could be represented as a linear process, a series of subsequent actions in which cognitive states must be translated into linguistic expressions. In chapter 9 we describe perception in terms of hypothesis formation, and both production and perception may be considered as a type of problem solving: choices of appropriate pragmatic frameworks, of adequate (true) modalities, of well-formed propositions and surface structures and of intended (lexical, syntactic and phonological) 'style'. The processes involved could easily be modelled by logical (pragmatical) systems for state or action description, explicating all relevant factors such as time, place, speaker (and his knowledge), etc. Similarly, an inductive logic would be able to show how we might represent the linear process of argumentation and make explicit the relations between premises and consequences in coherent texts.

These models will show to be of great importance, but the linguist will be left with the problem how to relate the abstract categories and structures of the different logical models with the semantic, syntactic and phonological structures of the sentence or the text. And again there will be a gap between the abstract model and the 'real' processes determining verbal and cognitive behaviour. Of course, everybody will construct the macro-structure for a text which is relevant to him, personally, and these macro-structures will be different for the same text. However, the same is true for 'meaning' and 'sound' of a sentence, and nevertheless we do construct a grammar with phonological and semantic rules. The point is that without macro-rules the native speaker is not even able to construct his 'own' plan or interpretation of a text, whereas human communication with the aid of discourses would be impossible if their macro-structures would profoundly differ for one discourse.

The solution to the dilemma we seem to be captured in is not difficult: the theoretical efforts towards a sound description of linguistic macro-structures must be made from various points of view at the same time – logic, mathematics, psychology and grammar itself – whereas the concrete grammatical research may be conducted primarily at the level of sequence structure.

One of the problems is perhaps the 'generality' of the grammar as it was sketched in the preceding chapters: texts may be of very different types and it would be a more feasible task to write a grammar for a rather self-contained subset of them. One of these subsets is known as literature, and it will be the task of the second part of this book to see what sort of particular constraints define such a subset. At the same time such an attempt will show the possible relevance of text grammars in another discipline, for text grammars are certainly not only constructed to solve the problems of the linguist alone.

PART II

ASPECTS OF LITERARY TEXT GRAMMARS

4

THE FOUNDATIONS OF POETICS.
METHODOLOGICAL PRELIMINARIES

1. INTRODUCTION. ABOUT A DISCIPLINE

1.1. The first part of this book offered a sketchy framework for an explicit description of textual structures in general. We will now turn to a more specific problem, *viz.* the description of a special subset of texts: literature.

The very order in which we treat these subjects can be considered a valid indication of our rather unusual approach to the study of literature. We did not simply take literary texts as immediate data in order to 'find' the regularities underlying them, but first wanted to construct, within linguistics proper, the components of a formal notion of TEXT. Only then will we be able to proceed to the next stage, that of defining the specific properties of the subset of LITERARY TEXTS. This procedure, in our view, is the only one which is methodologically adequate, because any 'definition', i.e. delimitation, of that subset is normally considered relevant only in as far as characteristics are specified which do not define texts in general. The general properties, in traditional literary scholarship, had been assumed to be intuitively 'given'. This is not wholly incorrect, because native speakers may acquire the ability to distinguish, on the basis of the textual competence, between literary and non-literary texts, in a way that is defined below. However, this ability, in linguistics, must first be made explicit in the formal model called text grammar.

Because current linguistics hardly seemed to be interested in the formal description of general properties of textual structures, it was our task to contribute to these developments with some informal suggestions of our own.

Although we are far from possessing a complete insight into textual structures, we have at least some vague ideas of how texts are structured in general, so that we may now try to gain some understanding of the reputedly elusive distinctive traits of the literary text. We want to describe explicitly, for example, how literary texts like poems show very special ways of concatenating sentences (or semi-sentences) and how literary narrative on the one hand has macro-structures like any narrative or text in general and on the other hand operations defining its 'literariness'.

Our approach is further rather different also from the current methods of using linguistics in the study of literature (cf. next chapter). We do not limit ourselves to a characterization of the 'style' (use of the rules) in a given text, or a corpus of texts, nor to the description of real or alleged 'deviations' from the rules of grammar within the sentence. Ungrammatical sentences are not more grammatical in literature and they are not specific for literature: we daily produce a great number of ungrammatical sentences which are perfectly acceptable without being 'poetic'. We have argued in Part I that the grammatical status of sentences must be considered within the framework of textual structure. Similarly, in literature, the specific structure of sentences is wholly dependent upon characteristics of the whole text. There are no literary sentences, only literary texts.

This may appear rather trivial but it is important for us to explore the consequences proceeding from such a statement: the description of literature is the description of the relevant properties of a specific subset of texts. Any theory of literature will therefore automatically, in its formal parts, be based on a (general) text grammar. The aim of Part II can thus be understood as a further elaboration of some specific components of this general text grammar, i.e. the components precisely defining the underlying regularities of literature.

1.2. The characterization of literary texts, traditionally, has been the aim of the autonomous discipline of 'literary scholarship', not of linguistics. Very few linguists and practically no 'literary scholars' have hazarded to assert the converse (cf. however Jakobson [1960]). It will be our task, then, NOT to deny the right of existence of literary scholarship, but to investigate the precise relations, formal and practical, between this discipline, the disciplines of linguistics and those of the other social sciences.

In that case it will be important not to be misled by the still-dominant ideological conception of literature as a textual and social phenomenon deserving 'specific' treatment, e.g. on the basis of its esthetic functions. The subset of literary texts, then, though considered in its own right, is studied as one subset among others, differing from them in some textual structures and functions but situated on the same theoretical and 'ontological' level.

In this respect we must denounce, on purely methodological and on socio-cultural grounds, the still nearly exclusive preoccupation in practically any educational system with the study of literary texts.

Literary texts in any culture can only satisfactorily be described with respect to other texts produced in that cultural system, because their specific function also derives from this differentiation. Further, the role of literature in society is marginal with respect to that of other texts (in newspapers and other mass media).

This statement is trivial for the social scientist but iconoclastic in traditional literary scholarship as it is practised in the Faculties of Arts, of Philosophy or of Letters. We therefore, in this Introduction, place the study of literature where it belongs: amidst the study of texts (discourse, messages) in general. No educational program, either at school and at the University can afford to overlook these facts without losing its theoretical, scientific and social relevance.

Similarly, the role of linguistics, though fundamental in this respect (when it is extended to textual linguistics), will be seen in the perspective of that of the other social sciences. Conditions and functions of texts in human interaction must be studied by psychology, social philosophy, sociology, anthropology, etc. These relations are often crucial for the right understanding of the formal properties of language, texts and linguistic communication in general.

1.3. Having thus outlined the global but basic direction of our approach to the study of literature, we may now – first intuitively – try to give a rapid view of the phenomena we are dealing with. In the rest of this chapter we will then try to delimit the domain of the discipline of 'literary scholarship' by providing some terminological (re-) statements, a distinction of its different tasks, and some remarks about the methodological and metatheoretical foundations of theory formation in literary scholarship.

One of the first methodological tasks in delimiting the domain of literary scholarship must be the elimination of a series of misunderstandings among literary scholars about the nature of scientific inquiry in general. One of these misunderstandings is that of considering the 'object' of study in a discipline as immediately 'given'. Nothing is less true, however. The 'object' of literary scholarship, of course, might simply be defined as the (finite) corpus of existing literary texts. Such a simple delimitation however is misleading in many ways. First of all, it is impossible to describe and to explain all properties of all existing literary texts (cf. Nagel [1961] 4, Stegmüller [1969] Kap. IV). A choice has to be made of those properties considered as relevant within the description of literary texts. This choice is made by the scholar, guided by a set of criteria for deciding about the relevance of properties considered. These criteria are determined by a great number of scientific and pre-scientific factors
– the aims of a scholar investigating a given object,
– the aims of the other scholars working in the same discipline,
– the state of development of a given science or theory,
– historical, ideological and other socio-cultural norms, etc.

Similarly, the 'object' of literary scholarship is by no means given as 'evident', but is in a certain way the 'product' of the discipline itself, because the data studied are not indicated by the subject matter itself but by a hypothetical system, model or research design projected on it by the scholar. The development of a science, as is well-known, may show important changes in the 'object' it wants to investigate.

In modern literary scholarship, for example, we might intend to gain insight not only into a corpus of 'given' texts having some 'observable' properties, but also into all 'possible' literary texts, which have not yet been studied or which have still to be produced. Furthermore, we might be interested not only in the observable properties of all (possible) literary texts but also in their unobservable 'underlying' properties, their abstract structures, and in the different conditional factors which determine their production and reception (cf. Bach [1964] 3ff., Bierwisch [1966]). We finally might want to know something about the mental activities underlying this manipulation of literary texts and the psycho-social systems of which they constitute a part (Chomsky [1965] Chap. 1).

The object of literary scholarship, then, is not 'literature' as an undifferentiated whole, but rather a SYSTEM (cf. Harré [1960] 48ff.) of selected properties of literary texts and the relation between those properties and certain properties of their psycho-social 'environment', i.e. of their conditions and functions.

Within these restrictions we may say that our object is a subset of specific texts and a type of specific communicative situation in which these texts occur.

Clearly, two different aspects are involved here. First, we want to gain insight into the properties of an intuitively distinguishable set of texts, of which the existence may be accounted for by 'empirical evidence'. Second, we are interested in the specific functions of these texts in communicative situations, functions among which the 'esthetic' ones are normally considered as a basic characteristic of literary texts and communication.

We thus identify our object with the intersection of two sets: the set of all (possible) texts of natural language, and the set of all 'esthetic objects' of human culture.

In our approach we will consider the properties of this second set, i.e. the 'esthetic' character of literary texts, as 'given', although very little is known about them at present. We will focus our attention upon the study of the properties of the literary text itself and ignore for the present its esthetic (and other) conditions, effects and functions. We will briefly come back to these aspects of 'literary communication' in our last chapter. In fact, we claim that adequate knowledge about the different communicative aspects of literary texts can only be acquired through previous insight into the proper textual aspects of literature. We pay attention to the consequences of this claim in this and the following chapters.

1.4. Literary scholarship, like all disciplines, is not only defined by its object but rather by the different approaches to that object, i.e. by the type of investigation and the type of discourse produced by it. We may therefore, in our perspective of establishing the foundations of literary scholarship, consider the criteria, aims and methods of adequate research in this discipline, especially with respect to the criteria for scientific research in general. Like any other discipline, literary scholarship produces a set of texts: descriptions, explanations, hypotheses, theories, etc. It is important, in this chapter, to determine the possible forms of these texts, that is the 'language' of the discipline. This is one of the major tasks of a methodology of literary scholarship and of scientific research in general. Without such a methodological basis it is impossible to know how we must talk about the properties of the literary texts we want to study. And without using this common methodological 'language' or code, our scientific texts will certainly not be understood by other scholars in the discipline.

1.5. Finally, the discipline of literary scholarship cannot be considered in isolation from its historical development. The foundation of a modern discipline is necessarily rooted in its tradition. However, we will not be concerned in these chapters with the history of traditional and modern literary scholarship (cf. Wellek [1955] and Ihwe [1972a] respectively). Our attempt will rather have a systematic character: we will first try to determine the criteria and aims of adequate literary research and then give some aspects of the theory formulated from that perspective. Where traditional literary scholarship deviates from our methodological and theoretical procedures it is thus, implicitly, rejected as inadequate. Extensive criticism of the aims and methods of traditional and current research in literary study will not be given in such a more functional refutation. Moreover, many studies in this last decade have been devoted to a demonstration of the deficiencies of classical literary scholarship. We will see that the major defects concern its methodological foundations (if any), the (lack of) explicitness of its descriptions, definitions and explanations, and the form and interrelations of its theories (if any). The great bulk of traditional literary scholarship, or 'literary criticism', can easily be considered as pre-, if not anti-, theoretical, and therefore must be qualified as pre-scientific in the sense to be defined below. This does not mean, however, that many of its observations or intuitive generalizations could not be used, when made explicit, in the adequate theories to be developed.

2. TERMINOLOGY, SCOPE AND TASKS

2.1. After this general introduction about the discipline within which the second part of this book has to be situated, we may now consider in detail the scope and the tasks of that discipline.

What is needed to begin with, is a clarification of some terminological and conceptual issues. A discipline is not only statically defined, as we saw, by its objects, its methods and its assertions, but also as a set of activities. These activities have to be unambiguously labelled in order to be able to identify the different tasks of the literary scholar and the ways of necessary collaboration between scholars.

2.2. First of all the name of the discipline itself requires some comment. In the previous chapter we used the term 'literary scholarship'. This awkward complex term will be abolished and will be substituted by the term POETICS or 'general poetics'. With 'poetics' we intend to refer to the whole complex of empirical and theoretical study of literary texts and literary communication, both synchronical and diachronical. This term has been chosen not only for its shortness but also with reference to the classical, Aristotelian, meaning of poiètikè. We have to stress that it does not refer to the study of 'poetry' ('poetic' or 'lyrical' texts) alone, but to the whole discipline of literary studies. Poetics will have the same meaning as current European terms, like

German *Literaturwissenschaft*. In this sense it also replaces some Anglo-Saxon interpretations of the term 'literary criticism', which ambiguously refers both to a theoretical discipline and to the practice of reviewing and evaluating (new) literary texts in newspapers and periodicals. Of course, a theory of literary criticism may be part of poetics, while literary criticism itself, when based on certain methodological criteria of adequacy, may be considered to be a branch of APPLIED POETICS.

Poetics may be divided into a set of (sub)components. The basic part we are dealing with in this book can be called THEORETICAL POETICS. The aim of this subcomponent is the formulation of hypotheses and theories about abstract properties of literary texts in general, i.e. about the system(s) underlying these texts (see below). In this respect it has to be distinguished from DESCRIPTIVE POETICS, which is concerned with the description of specific texts or sets of texts, for example in a given language. It essentially provides the data on which theoretical poetics is based and on which the consequences of the hypothetical assertions have to be tested.

Both theoretical and descriptive poetics have a SYNCHRONICAL and DIACHRONICAL component. Traditional LITERARY HISTORY may be situated within descriptive dia-chronical poetics. General aspects of historical changes in literary systems ('literary evolution') form the object of study of theoretical diachronical poetics. COMPARATIVE LITERATURE, essentially, is part of descriptive poetics, although some of its components properly belong to theoretical poetics.

2.3. The branch of theoretical poetics with which we will be concerned here has different subcomponents, corresponding to the different aspects of its empirical object. We have to repeat first, however, that this object is not, or not primarily, a set of concrete literary texts, but rather the system (or systems) underlying the different properties of literary texts and literary communication in GENERAL. This means that theoretical poetics is essentially interested in the investigation of regularities and not in ad hoc features of given texts. Ultimately, it will try to establish the UNIVERSAL aspects of the cultural phenomenon of literature (cf. Ihwe [1972a] Chap. 1, for extensive discussion). In practice, however, examples of general properties of literary texts will often be taken from only one or a few 'literatures', i.e. literary systems manifested in particular languages. Further, in the actual stage of research, theoretical poetics will be mainly concerned with the elaboration of theories for specific 'types' of literary texts, e.g. poetry or narrative, often within a given culture and time.

We shall see below that the study of the literary system has important psychological implications, e.g. when we assume – in analogy with linguistics – that the general object of poetics is also the description and explanation of the ability of humans to produce and to interpret literary texts: the so called LITERARY COMPETENCE (cf. Bierwisch [1965], Ihwe [1972a] Chap. 1).

2.4. As we said, theoretical poetics will in practice, and actually, be divided into a series of subcomponents of which a THEORY OF POETICS must define the indispensable interrelations.

Thus different TYPES of texts have traditionally led to a 'theory of poetry', a 'theory of the novel', or more in general 'a theory of narrative' – which does not properly belong to poetics alone –, 'a theory of drama'. Subtypes of texts, like 'heroic poetry', 'realistic novel' or 'absurd drama' have led to more specific sub-theories. It is clear, however, that theoretical poetics must examine these traditional 'genres' critically and provide an explicit framework in order to arrive at a more satisfactory formal typology of literary texts.

Theoretical poetics further contains theories about the different aspects of the communicative situation, e.g. THEORIES OF LITERARY PRODUCTION which formulate the regularities, both psychological, semiotic, social and historical, determining the production of literary texts and their different structures. In a more strict sense a theory of literary production is concerned with the mental processes of writers of literary texts. In the same way we may study the conditions and effects underlying LITERARY RECEPTION, both psychologically and sociologically. These components of poetics can be united in THEORY OF LITERARY COMMUNICATION, which in a more specific way will include a THEORY OF LITERARY PERFORMANCE and a THEORY OF LITERARY CONTEXT (cf. Chap. 9).

2.5. When we focus attention upon the properties of the literary text itself, we may distinguish theories about its different LEVELS. Because our basic assumption was that literary texts are a subset of the set of all texts, we have to consider the same levels as those distinguished, within a linguistic grammar, for sentences and texts.

One can thus speak of LITERARY PHONOLOGY, and GRAPHOLOGY, for example, formulating the specific phono- and graphological units and rules characterizing literary texts, or some types of literary texts. The traditional and modern study of prosody, rhythm and meter belongs to literary phonology, and has even led to a part of poetics having its own name: METRICS, whereas literary graphology is concerned with the graphematic and typographical aspects of written/printed texts.

Similarly, we need a LITERARY SYNTAX defining the rules underlying the specific possible combinations of lexemes in literary texts. Notice that literary syntax, like the other components of literary grammar, does not (merely) describe 'deviations' from non-literary syntax but gives an autonomous (but not 'independent') characterization of all specific phenomena of ordering in the surface structures of texts. Phenomena of recurrence, for example, are not studied at all in linguistic syntax, so that literary syntax has to describe them in their own right.

LITERARY SEMANTICS probably forms the major component of literary (text) grammar because it must specify the rules for many characteristic aspects of literary texts, or aspects occurring under special forms in literary texts, like metaphor. Part of a (more general, linguistic) theory of metaphor then falls within poetics. Similarly, for other traditionally or recently postulated aspects on the semantic level, like 'theme', 'function', etc.

As we saw in the first part of this book, we must finally consider textual deep structures, defined by LITERARY MACRO-SEMANTICS, within which we may study the specific aspects of literary narrative.

One final part of literary grammar, which is often situated within a theory of literary performance, is LITERARY PRAGMATICS. This branch formulates the regularities underlying the relations between literary text structures and their 'users'. It is therefore concerned mainly with the general, abstract conditions defining the appropriate use of literary texts or their elements in literary communication.[1]

2.6. We may lastly distinguish, within poetics, subcomponents according to the methodological and theoretical constructs and models it uses from auxiliary disciplines.

Thus, the description of the specific linguistic properties of literary text structures may be practised within LINGUISTIC POETICS. This branch, which has received much attention the last few years has also been called 'stylistics' or 'stylo-linguistics' (Hendricks [1969b]). We will reserve the term stylistics, however, for the theoretical and descriptive branch of both linguistics and poetics, which studies the use (change, etc.) of the rules of a system in specific texts or sets of texts. It therefore practically coincides with a theory of performance and with pragmatics.

The use of terms and models from the social sciences for the theoretical formulation of the aspects of literary communication leads to the definition of branches like SOCIO-POETICS and PSYCHOPOETICS. In the first branch we can localize parts of what rather ambiguously has been called both 'literary sociology' and 'sociology of literature'. These last two terms will be considered now as belonging to the area of sociology proper, concerned with the study of literature as one socio-cultural phenomenon among others. The difference with sociopoetics lies in the different methods and aims applied: the sociology of literature is one part of a description of the structure of society, human interaction, etc., while sociopoetics is interested in establishing relevant relations between different aspects of social environment and specific properties of literary texts in order to gain insight into the structure of these texts and of literary communication. Like psychopoetics it aims, therefore, at an explanation of literary text structures. Psychopoetics, for example, will try to specify how we mentally process literary texts, how we store and recall them, and how we react to them. It therefore provides the theoretical basis for the branch of LITERARY ESTHETICS,

---

[1] As we shall see in more detail in chapter 9, the status of pragmatics is not yet clear. If a grammar purports to be a (semiotic) theory of a language it must have a pragmatical component. In the current interpretations of a grammar as an algorithm specifying only structures of formal objects like sentences or texts there does not seem to be place for pragmatics in general, only to some extent a syntactic or semantic representation of some relevant pragmatic categories like 'speaker', 'addressee', 'time of utterance', 'place of utterance'. Conceived as a linguistic rule system a pragmatic component, if internalized by all native speakers, is part of idealized linguistic competence and thus object for a grammar modelling this competence. In poetics a pragmatic component would formulate merely the general conditions and rules which – together with literary phonology, syntax and semantics – define the specific functions of literature in processes of communication: production, reception, evaluation, cognitive and/or esthetic effects, etc. Of course the concrete communicational and cognitive processes involved are object of psycho- and sociopoetics (see below). For detail, see chapter 9.

studying the specific effects, like evaluations, of literary texts, e.g. with respect to certain norm systems of given cultures and societies.

All these components of poetics, included in literary grammar and literary communication theory, may use mathematical methods and models for description and theory formation. We can state that these uses form a specific component of poetics: MATHEMATICAL POETICS. It would not only specify the statistical (stochastical) procedures for describing existing texts but also the algebraic foundations for specific grammars like literary grammars. Similar remarks may be made about a LOGICAL POETICS.[2]

2.7. Different criteria have led to the distinction of several component parts of the discipline of poetics. These components may each elaborate their own terms, hypotheses and theories. Little would be gained, however, if poetics could only be defined as a discipline by a set of heterogenous techniques and theories. We therefore have to make explicit the relations between the different components, i.e. between the different levels and aspects of description. Within a literary grammar for example we must relate the syntactic and the semantic theory, while the grammar itself must be related with possible theories of psycho-poetics. For the first relations we need a THEORY OF LITERARY GRAMMARS which belongs to the GENERAL THEORY OF GRAMMARS. This theory will specify, as will be seen below, the basic categories, the form of the rules and the necessary components of literary grammars. A THEORY OF POETICS, of which we consider, informally, the methodological aspects in this chapter, will finally determine the relations between the basic components of poetics like literary grammar, psycho-poetics, etc. It will specify for example which 'models' can be borrowed from other disciplines in order to be able to develop adequate literary theories, and which criteria of theory formation and testing must be satisfied by literary theories.

---

[2] Although applications of modern systems of logic have not yet been made in poetics, it may be expected that, again in analogy with their introduction into linguistic grammars (see chapters 2 and 3), such systems will play an important role in future attempts toward formalized literary theories, to begin with the theory of (literary) narrative (cf. van Dijk [1972d]). This application in some sense might even be considered as more specifically relevant than mere linguistic descriptions because they do not have the same 'reductive' tendency often felt in linguistic characterizations. That is, modern systems, especially from modal logic, may formalize notions which have traditionally been considered as particularly relevant in the study of literature, such as all sorts of referential aspects (fictionality; probability or likelihood; the representation, modelling of 'reality' and related truth values, etc.) and, more formally within text structure, relations of tenses between sentences/propositions and the related consecution of times of actions, etc. It is premature to specify all possible applications here before their possible use in textual grammar in general, but it is important to bear these possible applications clearly in mind. The difficulty of further elaboration is that there are nearly no literary theorists having profound knowledge of modern logic and hardly any logician interested in literary problems.

3. POETICS AND THE PHILOSOPHY OF SCIENCE

3.1. *Poetics as an empirical science*

3.1.1. This general survey of the domain of poetics must be considered also as a 'research program' (Lakatos [1970] quoted by Schmidt [1970c]). That is, it outlines the different tasks within a unified approach to literature. This rough sketch, however, can only have practical and theoretical results if it is elaborated in further detail.

Therefore, in this section, we make a closer examination of poetics as a scientific discipline among others. Although it may have a specific object and specific tasks, poetics does not necessarily have specific ways of describing these objects and specific methods for the construction and testing of theories. Moreover, even the specific aims of poetics cannot be isolated from the aims of the other social or human sciences, as can be inferred from the mere use of these disciplines as auxiliary components within poetics itself.

In opposition to traditional literary scholarship we therefore explicitly claim that the fundamental methods of theory formation, observation, testing, etc. are those of all other rational empirical sciences (Ihwe [1972a] Chap. 1, Schmidt [1970b], [1970c]). The methodology which has been elaborated for these sciences is thus also valid for poetics, and no adequate theory of poetics can be formulated without the basic criteria of general methodology, which will be supposed well-known here.[3]

Of course, poetics has its own specific problems and techniques of description and testing, determined by the character of its object, but these can only be resolved and applied within the general framework of the methodology of description and explanation in the social sciences, and in the empirical sciences in general (cf. Opp [1970]).

3.1.2. Some implications of the rather self-evident claim made above about the empirical basis of poetics and its place among other empirical sciences have to be considered now. Its implications for the theoretical aspects and the relations within the specific area of the social sciences will be treated below.

The major implication of the empirical character of poetics is that consequences and predictions which can be derived from its different theories must ultimately be tested on some empirical phenomena in the 'real world', i.e. the different aspects of concrete literary texts or literary communication processes, and of the reports of the native speaker (including the theorist himself) about the intuitive knowledge of his language and of literature. This procedure of testing can be very complicated since

---

[3] We will base ourselves essentially on the following works in philosophy of science: de Groot (1961), Hempel (1966), Popper (1959), Rescher (1964), Nagel (1961), Harré (1960), Rudner (1966), Apel (1967), Seiffert (1969), (1970), Opp (1970), Stegmüller (1969), (1970).

For methodological remarks in linguistics: Bach (1965), Chomsky (1965) Chap. I, Leech (1968), Bierwisch (1966), Botha (1968), (1970), Schnelle (1968), (1970). For poetics: Hanneborg (1967), Schmidt (1970b), (1970c) and especially Ihwe (1972a) Chap. 1

terms, rules, and other hypothetical constructs of our theory, are only very indirectly related with empirical reality.

We argued in the first section of this chapter that poetics is not concerned with the description of concrete texts alone but rather with the abstract systems underlying these texts. We therefore need complex operational definitions and transition rules to relate our theoretical terms defining these systems to the aspects of concrete texts, i.e. to the empirical terms of observation.

These relations can probably be established without great difficulty for phono-logical and syntactic surface aspects of texts. But how do we test a theory about the underlying mechanisms of metaphorization or of semantic operations (interpretation!) in general? How do we test, further, predictions or explanations of the alleged mental 'reality' of literary grammars, of the complex socio-cultural conditions determining the different aspects of texts, and of the processes of interpretation and evaluation of literary texts in readers? (cf. Mooij [1963]).

These problems, of course, are not easy to resolve. Actually they are common problems of linguistics and poetics and of the social sciences in general, and many of them are related with our knowledge of cognitive processes. This means that our procedures of validation will always remain indirect, for example through utterances of 'users' of literature (writers, readers) about their reflected but intuitive knowledge of the processing of literary texts. It goes without saying that reliance on such intro-spective data can only be valid within the perspective of possible intersubjective control.

From these utterances we can under specific conditions infer certain mental structures, or conversely we may construct a formal model (e.g. a generative text grammar) about these mental structures and use the 'observable' utterances as one source of possible confirmation of the consequences derivable from the model.

As for properly textual aspects such as the structure of metaphor, the formal theory can only be tested on internal coherence and simplicity (if a certain degree of formalization can be attained and if other theories are comparable) and on the adequacy of predictions about derivable surface structures of underlying mechanisms.

From this short discussion it might have become clear that the testing of literary hypotheses will constitute one of the most awkward problems of a modern empirical poetics. That is, we first need the hypotheses and the theories before we can test the consequences derivable from them. The main criterion, of course, will remain: the hypotheses and rules must in principle be sufficiently explicit to be testable. In this stage of research, therefore, we cannot do more than formulate some aspects of a formal theory of literary texts. Their validation is provisionally based on intuitive knowledge of (existing) literary texts or rather on our internalized knowledge of the rules of the systems of literature and on (degrees of) 'literariness' of texts.

3.1.3. Let us consider in more detail the different empirical aspects of poetics. Two basic tasks of any empirical science are probably the DESCRIPTION and EXPLANATION of a set of related empirical phenomena. Similarly, in poetics, we first want to gain insight into the structural aspects of literary texts and literary communication, e.g. by formulating the rules underlying their formation. An adequate description thus leads to predictions about the structure of well-formed texts of the same type, i.e. about the FORMAL 'literariness' of these texts with respect to an assumed literary competence of users of literature. In analogy with the distinction, made by Chomsky (1965) Chap. 1 between observational, descriptive and explanatory levels of adequacy, a theory of literature or a grammar of literary texts must first reach the basic level of OBSERVATIONAL ADEQUACY. The poverty of systematic observations of literary texts and of their different aspects indicate however that even this level has not yet been attained. Extant observations (also called 'descriptions', or 'analyses') are often fragmentary and ad hoc, i.e. limited to single literary texts or to rather arbitrarily selected aspects of text structure. The same holds true for the observation of processes of literary communication, the study of which has a still less systematic character.

Observational adequacy in poetics can thus be reached by a literary grammar, if it succeeds in correctly accounting for the structure of literary texts, and by a theory of literary communication if it correctly represents the factors of text users, channels, codes and situations involved in literary performance. Clearly this last theory, and the levels of adequacy definable for it, include literary grammar which only specifies one aspect of the communication process: the structures of the 'message' itself.

At the level of DESCRIPTIVE ADEQUACY a grammar of literary texts must perform formally what can be performed by any reader of literary texts: it has to distinguish between literary, less-literary and non-literary texts, by specifying the structures underlying observable literary data. As such it provides a model for the ability of 'native speakers' to perform these specific tasks, e.g. the task of recognizing a text as a novel or as a lyrical poem, and to recognize differences and similarities in texts of the same type.

For a correct description of phenomena like production and reception the psychological implications of a theory of literary grammar are crucial. We could of course simply limit ourselves to a description of an abstract underlying 'system', but no 'external' way of testing the empirical basis of our predictions about that system will be possible when no relation is established with mental properties of text users. The system is not only an abstract product of the linguist, it may somehow also be present, unconsciously, in the readers of a given literature. Without such an internalized literary text grammar they would not be able to compare literary texts, to make abstracts from them or to 'remember' them. They would even fail to read them as a coherent text or recognize them as literary.

Finally, a general theory of literary grammar must explain, among other things, how speakers of a language acquire the specific text grammar(s) which enable them to read, to interpret and evaluate literary texts, how rules are learned which may deviate from the rules underlying non-literary texts, how these rules may change in different cultures or times, and how 'deviant' structures can be assigned well-formed semantic representations. More generally, a (universal or simply general) theory of literature must also explain why literary texts having such or such properties are produced under given socio-historical circumstances and why texts with these properties have such or such effects on readers or have such or such functions in given cultures and times. This task however is of such complexity that at present we could hardly pretend even to elaborate details of it without explicit insight into the nature of linguistic and esthetic communication in general, of a general theory of human interaction, and of a general theory about the influence of historical, sociological and cultural factors upon linguistic and esthetic products. We have therefore adopted a strategy-design which first intends to establish the underlying and manifest properties of texts with which these extra-poetic and extra-linguistic factors are supposed to be related. When these terms of the extra-poetic and extra-linguistic relations have been made explicit, we may try to formulate the regularities underlying these relations.

3.2. *Poetics as a theoretical science*

3.2.1. Leaving the crucial problems of its empirical foundations we will proceed to concentrate on the theoretical aspects of poetics. That is, we will be further concerned with the possible forms of literary theories and with the relations between these theories. Which criteria have to satisfy adequate theories of literary texts and of literary communication?

The general requirements for theories, formulated in the philosophy of science, are also valid in poetics: a literary theory must be general, as explicit as possible, consistent, systematic and complete. As we saw above, it further has to lead to testable consequences (predictions).[4] We will not comment upon these well-known criteria – to which others may be added – but we have to stress that, again, our argument must be programmatic rather than descriptive, because no literary theory seems to exist at the moment which would satisfy these conditions.

Firstly, no functional and hardly any operational DEFINITIONS are given of the terms used in the formulation of most literary hypotheses. Intuitive knowledge of terms like 'event', 'personage', 'action', 'character', is used in the theories of narrative. Probably only metrics has until now succeeded in defining rather explicitly its theoretical terms. Without such empirical or theoretical definitions no assertion can be explicit, which prevents thorough testing of its implications.

3.2.2. This lack of explicit definitions is related also with the lack of RULES in literary theories or with the absence of literary grammars in general. To this more specific formulation of regularities in texts we will come back below. For the moment we only want to stress that the requirement of GENERALITY is not satisfied in poetics. We do

---

[4] For detailed discussion about these and other requirements for scientific theories, cf. Nagel (1961) 90ff., de Groot (1960) 42ff.

not have laws or rules formulating properties of a general, let alone universal, character, and even if we have some of them, e.g. in the theory of narrative, they are hardly explicit enough to be tested.

The requirement of generality seems to have problematic implications in poetics, because of the often alleged 'uniqueness' of literary texts. Any generalization, as was argued by the traditional branches of hermeneutics and by the classical methodology of the humanities in general, has to be considered as a neglect of precisely those phenomena which are essential in literary works of art.[5] These and similar arguments have been used also in psychology, sociology and esthetics and need not to be refuted here.[6] It is clear that the demonstration of 'uniqueness' is a fully ad hoc procedure which can only be valid if it is based on an explicit knowledge of common properties of literary texts from which the 'unique' ones would then be differentiated. Moreover, in a sense no object is strictly 'identical' with other objects so that any object would be 'unique'.

The intuitive perception of the 'unique' character of a given text, then, derives from an implicit knowledge of the literary system of a certain culture and age and from the concrete experience with other literary texts. It is precisely the task of poetics to formulate the rules or 'regularities' underlying this knowledge. The demonstration of uniqueness, then, would simply coincide either with the non-derivability of a given text by the rules valid in that culture and age, or has to be defined in terms of different use of rules.

Although this statement is methodologically correct, we are faced in poetics with some implications of the problem of generality which do not appear in linguistics, for example. The main difference derives from psycho-social facts; that is: natural language and its rules are determined as systems of conventions in large groups of people and its general character is a direct requirement of rapid and effectful communication between the members of the group. No individual member, or small group, may normally change the rules of the grammar underlying the language system of a whole society: idiolects rarely influence the language. In poetics this situation is fundamentally different, for individuals or small groups may sometimes rather abruptly change, actively and consciously, a system of rules (norms, conventions, codes) independently of immediate positive or negative sanction of the group of readers of literary texts. That is, literary systems are characterized not only by rule-governed, but also by rule-changing creativity.

It would be false, therefore, to neglect these basic properties of literary systems, because evaluation procedures often closely depend on this mutation of the rules of the system by a set of individual texts (of one or more authors). This change, unlike general linguistic change, is not always gradual, as can be seen in the transition from

---

[5] For a survey of these theses, cf. Gadamer (1960), Abel (1953), Apel (1967), Seiffert (1970).
[6] This refutation has been given by Rudner (1966) and Stegmüller (1969) 360ff. among others. A short comment in van Dijk (1971a).

the symbolist system to dadaïst and surrealistic systems of poetry in a few years between 1915 and 1925. Poetics therefore will have to include a very important theory of diachronical 'transformations' of underlying systems.

These changes in literary systems have to correspond somehow with changes in the literary competence of native speakers, otherwise they would not be able to interpret texts derivable in that new system. This situation of a constant learning process of course requires specific intellectual abilities and social conditions, which explains the fact that revolutionary changes in the system are immediately acceptable only for very small cultural groups. This can be seen very clearly in the diachronical development of poetic (lyrical) systems, which is determined by still smaller groups, i.e. smaller than the groups which, in our age, accept changes in narrative texts. Important differences, as in the nouveau roman (from Joyce onwards), are however also socially restricted in the narrative system. We will return, briefly, to the psycho-social implications of these changes and learning-processes of literature in the last chapter.

These remarks do not intend to demonstrate that 'generality' cannot be reached by assertions (hypotheses, theories, predictions) in poetics, but only that this generality is less deterministic as in natural language. In this respect literary systems probably behave like other esthetic systems, and a general theory of diachronical change therefore must be formulated probably for all esthetic products.

The establishment of regularities in poetics will take place on several levels of description and differs for the different parts of the literary process of communication.

First, the change of literary systems itself is probably determined by a set of regularities. The well-known intuitive 'action-reaction' trend characterizes almost any change such that properties of a system B at time t_j are often opposed to properties of system A preceding it at time t_i, while system C of time t_k $(k > j > i)$ might realize again properties of A or another previous system. Nevertheless, this type of change does not prevent a certain continuity in the development of the literary (sub-)system as a whole: i.e. we do not now produce medieval heroic poetry or allegory, and we will probably not return to narrative systems of the 17th century. This hypothetical, but intuitively acceptable, statement is an important indication for the fact that there are certain regularities and that we have an implicit knowledge of them. Both the perception of very 'old' texts and of very 'new' texts is 'difficult' for inexperienced readers because these have acquired only the dominating, traditional, literary (mostly: narrative) systems (for detail, cf. Wienold [1971]).

The second type of generality therefore characterizes each literary system, that is the set of literary rules defining the texts of a given culture and age, for example the behaviouristic novel of the thirties, or medieval *chanson de geste*. This is probably the range theories in poetics will often have to limit themselves to at the moment, that is: the explicit formulation of the regularities of a given spatio-temporally restricted subset of literary texts. At the same level we also need both a grammar of rules (and a lexicon) deriving globally the abstract structures of these texts, and a theory of socio-historical environment which relates the grammar with the conditions of the age or culture. Many properties, especially at the semantic level of the text ('themes', 'concepts', 'narrative functions') can be closely related with other textual or semiotic systems, of a given time and a given society or culture.

A third type of generality mostly characterizes the definition of certain general 'types' or 'languages' of literary texts, traditionally called 'genres'. Thus medieval epic shares many narrative properties with the novel of our modern times, and a general theory of narrative might formulate these general, if not universal, properties for such different 'languages' of literature. Similarly we might try to formulate the rules of poetic (lyrical) and dramatic systems. Descriptive adequacy is attained if we are able to account thus for the fact that native speakers can differentiate narrative texts from non-narrative, e.g. lyrical ones, or establish correspondences – intermediate forms – between those systems when realized in one text (some modern novels).

Similarly, we may want to formulate the more specific regularities of some subtypes, like tragedy or fantastic fiction, or even of types only defined by specific morpho-phonological or graphical surface regularities like sonnets.

Finally, poetics has to establish the possible universals of literature, both on the formal level of rules and on the substantial levels of literary categorial 'vocabularies' of 'themes', 'motives', or 'functions'. Such universals are probably very rare for all types of literary texts, and might be reduced to some basic types of literary (trans-) formation rules like repetition and permutation, and to general properties of literary communication like 'foregrounding' and 'desautomatization' (cf. chap. 9).

Notice that all these regularities as formulated by rules of different types of grammars only define IDEALIZED ACCEPTABILITY of the texts derivable from them. In concrete situations of performance an author may, individually, deviate from a given system, often by establishing ad hoc rules or 'stylistic' rules characteristic of one text or the set of all texts written by him. An adequate theory of literary performance must, however, formulate the regularities underlying specific uses (applications) of systematic rules by individual writers and readers. Such a theory would partially coincide with a theory of stylistics (cf. chap. 9).

3.2.3. Generality in theoretical poetics, as we saw above, is formulated by means of RULES where properties of text structure are concerned. The methodological status of rules is not wholly clear (cf. Black [1962], Quine [1970], Safran Ganz [1971]). Unlike general laws they may be broken by individuals because they only 'record' global, idealized conventions of semiotic systems. Unlike rules in logic these conventions are implicit and as such are used unconsciously by users of the system. Rules can thus be considered to be formal conditions for the production/reception (interpretation, recognition) of literary texts.

Descriptive poetics and the theory of literary performance may also formulate inductive generalizations in terms of statistical probabilities. In that case we characterize the concrete empirical use of rules and elements of the system (frequencies of certain words, certain transformation rules, embedding ratio's, etc.) which have been studied extensively in quantitative stylistics. We will not discuss these empirical performance generalizations here. Their methodological flaws, both in linguistics and in poetics, are mainly due to a lack of theoretical foundations such that the linguistic or literary relevance of elements 'counted' and the formal regularities underlying these counted surface structures could not be accounted for (cf. chap. 9).

Similarly, in a theory of literary communication we will deal mostly, at this moment, with probabilistic statements. It is rarely the case that a condition X always determines a text property Y, and a text property Z an effect or function V. We share here the methodological and theoretical shortcomings of the social sciences in general (cf. Nagel [1961] Chap. 13, Topitsch, ed. [1965]).

3.2.4. The other (methodo)logical criteria for the well-formedness of theories, decidability, consistency and completeness, follow of course the requirements of explicitness and generality, and can only be attained in formalized theories. Existing literary theories do not therefore satisfy these conditions. They imply for example that, within a literary grammar, we are able to predict unambiguously which texts are well-formed and which are not. That is, a grammar may not formulate rules such that the same text is characterized both as 'grammatical' and as 'ungrammatical' in the same literary system, i.e. as literary or as non-literary. Further, it may not fail to specify texts which are – intuitively – considered 'grammatical' (literary). We'll treat some of these formal requirements of (literary) grammars below. Notice however that grammars themselves are not axiomatic systems possessing a set of axioms and deduction rules in the logical sense. Grammars only contain formation rules which define which string (texts) belong to the language and which do not. Formal proofs of consistency and completeness normally require the axiomatization of a theory (of language, of literature) in which two contradictory statements cannot be derived if deductive rules are applied correctly.

It is clear that for a theory of (literary) communication full formalization and axiomatization cannot be attained at present. Maybe only a few more general statistical theories about textual surface properties (distribution, frequencies, redundancy, transition probabilities) are the first candidates for formalization.

The formal property of consistency can be assessed under certain further conditions, for example when we are able to construct MODELS for the axiomatic system (cf. Badiou [1969], Nauta [1970], Nagel [1961] 95ff., Apostel, [1960]). These may be formal and empirical under the conditions that their formulas satisfy the axioms of the first system. Thus we may use an axiomatized theory of sentence structures (a theory of S-grammars) as a model for a theory of text structures (a theory of T-grammars). Empirically we can normally take or construct a well-formed (literary) text and see whether it is derivable from the system. If this is not the case the system is incomplete, and if it derives both literary and non-literary structures it is inconsistent. Notice, however, that these models in deductive sciences are associated with the concept of truth which plays no role in linguistic and literary grammars. Interpreted linguistic structures are grammatical or ungrammatical or, within pragmatics, appropriate or inappropriate. The same holds, of course, for literary grammaticalness. We'll come back to this problem of models for literary grammars.

The grammar itself is a (formal) model of a linguistic or literary system or of the internalized mental form of that system: competence. For these (generative) grammars themselves different mathematical (algebraic) models have been constructed, for example within the theory of (semi-)groups. We might however use other logical or mathematical models for the description of textual structures in literature (modal logics, set theory, topology, etc.). For the description of corpuses of concrete texts stochastic models have often been used (in information theory) to describe the distributions and frequencies of certain elements. It may be shown, with the aid of such models, that the ratio's of information and redundancy differ in some types of literary texts, like poetry, with respect to non-literary texts (cf. chap. 9).

Thus, in a theory of poetic surface structures we may use the very elementary model *a b a b a b a b c d c d e e* for the description of rhyme structures in a specific type of sonnet. Metrics makes extensive use of such models (especially matrices) for the description of abstract structures underlying the prosody of lyrical texts.

We will not consider the different mathematical or empirical models which may be used for the description of literary text structures, but focus upon the aspects of linguistic (grammatical) models.

3.3. *Poetics as a social science*

3.3.1. Our discussion in the previous and following chapters might obscure the important fact that poetics, just like linguistics, is a social science. The extensive use of formal deductive models in modern linguistics for the description of sentential structures has been the cause of a flaw in the study of the relations between language and society. These studies have mainly been undertaken in anthropology, sociolinguistics being only a poorly developed discipline, where requirements of explicitness or generality are hardly attained at the moment (except, again in statistical studies). Generative grammar, intended precisely as a formal model of a postulated mental competence and as a basic mechanism underlying speech production and reception, naturally focussed attention on psychological problems of cognition: learning, memory, etc. Hardly any relevant relations between that theory and possible theories of human communication and interaction could be established. This fact must be considered a serious drawback of modern theories of language when we realize that language constitutes precisely a basic system of interaction in human society. The mere assertion of this fact is trivial, if not banal, but it is curious to notice that general models of linguistic communication have hardly changed since Bühler (1934), cf. Miller (1964). One important reason for this lack of explicit relations between linguistics and sociology is the nature of traditional and modern grammars. It is clear that very few relations can be established between the structures of sentences and those of social systems. Text grammars, as was argued in Part I, may provide a more adequate basis for establishing these relations, because people do not communicate with the aid of words or sentences but with the aid of coherent (or often incoherent) texts. Verbal interaction like conversation, discussion, speeches, propaganda, articles, books, etc. therefore must be defined as essentially textual. The structures, functions, and conditions of communication can thus only be based on theories of language which take the text as a basic formal unit. All smaller units having a specific (e.g. rhetorical) role are functions of the structure of the whole text.

3.3.2. Similarly, in poetics, we only can arrive at adequate explanations of literary phenomena if a theory (grammar) of textual structures is related to theories of verbal interaction from social psychology. The recognition of certain textual properties as 'literary' is also determined by our knowledge of the properties of other types of texts and by the relation existing between texts and extra-linguistic context (situation, 'reality'). The ultimate aim of poetics, then, is a specific contribution to our insight into the mechanisms (systems) underlying verbal, and in general semiotic, communication in human society. As such, it provides theoretical understanding of one important type of text in these complex networks of communication. Poetics might even provide the models for the study of other types of texts such as propaganda, the language of politics and advertising, psychiatric reports, etc., which are now mainly studied in the theoretically rather poorly developed interdisciplinary content analysis (Holsti [1969], Gerbner, *et al.*, eds. [1969]).

From these remarks it follows that poetics is based on methodological principles common to other social sciences. The theory of literary text grammars is probably most developed at this moment and can be partially formalized, especially when linguistic models are used. Not so, however, for the description of the aspects of literary communication. As we shall see in the last chapter we may use statistical (cybernetical, etc.) techniques and models for the study of encoding and decoding processes, but hardly anything is known about the socio-historical conditions for literary text production. Socio-poetics (which covers only part of the domain of traditional sociology of literature) has arrived either at ad hoc statements about the social or political determination of structures of a given text or at intuitive untestable 'generalizations' about the socio-historical 'roots' of literature. Any explanation which aims at methodological adequacy in this domain must be based on deterministic or probabilistic laws about the general conditions of literary production and reception. Such laws are not yet formulated. Under similar conditions very different literary texts may be produced and, conversely, under different conditions very similar texts can be produced. This fact can only be explained if users of literature (writers, readers) are rather free in producing (interpreting) their texts, under the condition that the general rules of the literary system are globally respected.

The representation of social phenomena in literary texts can of course be studied, for example in relation to non-literary texts representing these phenomena. This representation however is optional and has undergone different modifications on the semantic and referential levels. Conversely, most literary texts do not have direct referential relations with historical events but with fictive events. This does not prevent us from studying the properties of (fictive) texts in relation to the properties of socio-historical reality or rather of the description of that reality.

We will return to the problems of psycho- and socio-poetics in our final chapter.

4. FOUNDATIONS OF A THEORY OF LITERARY TEXT STRUCTURES

4.1. Central to the actual development of poetics is the description of the structural properties of literary texts. Priority therefore will be given to the attempt to make these descriptions as explicit as possible. Only then may a satisfactory explanation of psycho- and socio-poetic phenomena of production and reception be awaited.

Among the possible FORMAL MODELS for a theory of literary text structures we have adopted a generative grammar, or to be more precise a GENERATIVE-TRANSFORMATIONAL TEXT GRAMMAR, as it has been roughly outlined in Part I of this book. We must briefly consider here, at the end of this methodological chapter, what the form and the aim of such a literary grammar could be. In the following chapter we will, then, more generally consider the relations between literary and non-literary grammars and between the aims and methods of linguistics and poetics in general. The subsequent chapters will try to formulate some rules and define some categories of the different components of literary grammars.

4.2. One of the basic arguments which have led to the assumption that a description of literary text structures has to be formulated as a generative grammar is provided by the empirical fact that at least some groups of speakers of a language can produce and interpret a potentially infinite number of different literary texts. A theory of literary texts therefore requires descriptive systems which are able to specify an infinite set of 'grammatical' i.e. literary, texts. A similar task had to be performed, according to us, by an adequate linguistic description, with respect to all possible texts of the language. Below, we will try to make explicit the exact relationships between the sets of all literary texts and the sets of all texts, but we may intuitively assume already that the first set is properly included in the second one if we consider linguistics and generative grammars in a sufficiently wide perspective. The first formal requirement of such a generative grammar of literary texts will be that it distinguishes between the set of literary and the set of non-literary texts of a given language. The second requirement will be that it assigns a structural description to each member of the set generated by the grammar. A third formal requirement will be that the grammar assigns a possible index of 'literariness' to each member of the set it generates and to the set of texts which are not generated by it, but are acceptable as literary under specific conditions.

This last requirement prevents too strict a binary approach towards formal literariness and provides a formal basis for more adequate empirical predictions.

4.3. Drawing further consequences from our decision to use modern generative theory of language as a valuable heuristic and formal source of models and heuristic techniques, we may consider our literary grammar as a formal model of an IDEALIZED COMPETENCE of all speakers of a language which enables them to recognize texts as literary, and to recognize intuitively the differences between literary and non-literary texts. (cf. Bierwisch [1965], Ihwe [1972a]). These activities, and other similar ones, can only be appropriately explained when a 'speaker of the language' (a notion to be made more explicit below) has at his disposition an internalized knowledge of the rules which generate these different types of texts. Without specific rules generating literary texts it would not be possible to identify as literary an infinite set of literary texts.

Because literary texts can be very different from each other, the differentiation of properties probably has a rather general character. There is no simple abstract 'schema' inferred from previous reading of literary texts which could apply in the production, reception and interpretation of all the members of the set of possible literary texts. Productive rules as provided in a generative grammar are therefore indispensable to account for that knowledge. Further, the limits of human memory do not permit a full or partial storage of 'learned' literary text structures, for these structures are infinite in number, because, theoretically, there is no upper bound to the length of (literary) texts.

Of course, the actual application of the rules of competence in processes of literary communication, i.e. in literary performance, can result in structures differing from those formally specified in the grammar, under the influence of mainly psychological and sociological factors. One important fact of a theory of literary performance is for example the empirical phenomenon that only a restricted group of individuals seems to use their literary competence in active literary production (cf. chap. 9).

It has to be asked, therefore, whether a postulated literary competence can have psychological reality when only comparatively few individuals seem to master it actively, and when it is not sure whether any native speaker of a language can interpret literary texts as such. This psycho-social fact, however, does not prevent the functioning of a literary system within at least one group in society, i.e. a group of experienced writers/readers who are able to qualify oral and written texts as literary (or 'fictional'). This knowledge, as we showed, is productive, and therefore must be rule-governed. These rule-systems can be learned and therefore acquire a cognitive status. It might be the case that a specific literary competence is either a subcomponent of general linguistic competence or a derived competence which has been formed by special training. The abilities underlying writing and reading of other specialized (non-literary) texts such as newspaper-articles, reviews, etc. would also be explained in this way. We will come back to these relations between literary, 'normal' and 'general' competence in the next and in the final chapter.

Notice that in a strict sense 'literary competence' is defined only for the members of the class of 'users of literature', that is those native speakers having acquired in a normal learning process the rules and categories underlying literary texts. We may say however that all native speakers have an ability for learning such specific languages.

4.4. There is another aspect of the theory of literary grammars which needs elucidation. Until now we have rather vaguely used terms like 'literary grammar', the 'theory of literature', etc. without indicating the scope of these terms. That is, grammars are theories, or rather partial theories, about the (formal) aspects of particular languages. Thus a literary grammar will only specify literary texts (and their structures) in a given language. This is certainly correct, but clearly, in poetics we are not primarily interested in a theory of French literature or in a theory of Chinese literature. Just as in linguistics we are interested in the properties of literature in general, that is, in possible UNIVERSALS of literature, or of some general types of literary texts like narrative and poetic texts. The properties of the 19th century novel in France are practically identical with those of the contemporaneous novel in Russia, England, Germany, etc. The same holds true for medieval epic and modern poetry in different literatures. The definition of the rules of literary systems hardly seems to be literature-specific. We might conclude, therefore, that very few literary rules are dependent on (specific) natural languages, although – as we will see in the next chapter – they need the rules of natural languages as a basis. Of course, specific natural languages may have influence on some literary aspects, especially at the surface level of prosody. Specific metrical systems depend on sentential stress structure of specific languages: a meter based on long and short syllables cannot, without abstraction and generalization, be used in languages where the length of syllables is phonologically irrelevant (cf. Greek vs. French). Similarly we may explain the early abolition of rhyme in England by the poverty of lexico-phonological rhyme-words.

Literary grammars, then, specify literary texts 'in' a specific language and we may therefore adopt the hypothesis that the relation with grammars of natural language is at least connective (inclusion or intersection). The typically 'literary' rules of these grammars, however, are necessarily of a more general character. A general theory of literary text grammars, or rather a general theory of literature, will specify these more general rules and categories common to all literary text grammars. The tentative rules we will define in the following chapters are not specific for French or English but have in principle a general character. Although literature is probably universal it would probably be too speculative for us to assume an innate character for these general literary rules. What might be innate however is the general ability for learning (extending) new (derived) grammars.

4.5. A general theory of literary text grammars not only specifies the task and the scope of such grammars but must also indicate the exact form of such grammars. We have already postulated that such a grammar must be generative, that is, it must be complete and have explicit rules. They must furthermore be T-grammars for reasons given in the first part of this book. The description of literature is *a fortiori* not a description of an infinite set of sentences but of texts. We do not normally speak about 'literary sentences'. Even sentences in isolation having an apparent 'lyrical form' may be a grammatical or ungrammatical part of any conversation or newspaper article. Moreover, literary texts have transphrastic structures with a very manifest character, such as repetition, rhyme schema, fixed verse forms, narrative structures, etc. And, of course, because they are texts, they normally satisfy the rules of general text grammar. Deviations or specific rules have to be precisely accounted for in literary text grammars.

It follows from this short discussion that literary grammars probably will need a set of ADDITIONAL rules which do not underlie non-literary texts and which enable speakers to differentiate these texts. We will further need specific theoretical categories (symbols) in the non-terminal vocabulary of our grammars to be able to derive specific structures like rhymes, alliterations, metrical units, etc. These could of course be defined by rules defining operations on linguistic categories alone. However without specific symbols it will be impossible or too circumstantial to generate literary structures.

Still more than the textual rules of 'ordinary' grammar the specific rules of literary T-grammars are context sensitive. Nearly all surface structures, especially in poetry, are generated under the influence of contextual correlations (alliteration, rhyme, repetitions, etc.). Context free rules probably only characterize textual macro-structures, both phonological/graphical (fixed verse forms: sonnets) and semantic (narrative structures).

A literary T-grammar, furthermore, must be TRANSFORMATIONAL, not only because any T-grammar has to include rules having a transformational character for representing semantic structures at the morpho-syntactic surface, but also because nearly all typical literary operations can be considered to be transformations of underlying 'normal' structures. Thus, the process of metaphorization needs certain transformational steps to represent well-formed semantic representations as (linguistically) ungrammatical lexico-syntactic structures. However, for some rules at least, we might adopt a more direct way of derivation, by considering them proper formation rules.

It is becoming clear from these few examples that the specific rules of literary grammars must be defined on all levels distinguished for texts in Part I. We can therefore distinguish between phonological/graphical, syntactic, semantic (and if necessary pragmatic) literary rules both in textual surface structure: micro-structure, and in textual deep structure: macro-structure.

It is not yet apparent how these specific rules should be integrated (or *if* they should be integrated) in generative T-grammars. This intricate formal problem, which is also partially empirical, will be treated in the following chapter. There we will endeavour to make explicit the precise relationships between linguistic and literary structures of texts and between the grammars describing these structures.

5

LINGUISTICS AND POETICS

1. GRAMMARS OF NATURAL LANGUAGE AND THEIR EMPIRICAL SCOPE

1.1. One of the empirical weaknesses in current generative grammar is the lack of a methodologically adequate characterization of languages as systems of social conventions. It has become clear from recent discussions in sociolinguistics (cf. Labov [1970]) that a notion like 'homogeneous speech community', used by Chomsky (1965), is not without problems. Although formal theories like grammars will always be related to idealized language systems and thus will abstract from ideolectal and even dialectical differences, it is primarily based on the system of a specific 'standard language'. This notion has to be defined in sociolinguistic terms, e.g. as the language of a certain social (middle) class, normatively used in educational systems and prevalent in mass-media like papers, radio and television. Formally speaking, however, any dialect can be considered as a language in its own right, having its own grammar. The use of different linguistic forms is not necessarily a 'deviation' with respect to the standard language, but may be the result of interference between two systems (cf. Weinreich [1963], Labov [1970]). It is not always easy to determine whether certain language forms must be considered to be permitted variations of the first system, e.g. the prestige standard language, or as elements of the other, dialectical or sub-cultural system. Furthermore, differences between 'recognized' languages may be smaller than those between dialects 'covered' by the same language. The criteria for these differentiations are cultural, historical, political and sociological, which considerably weakens the empirical ground on which generative grammars are built. The more so because these grammars are normally tested against linguistic intuition, i.e. the ideal knowledge of a (particular) language, which means – implicitly – knowledge of the standard language and, secondly, knowledge of the system used by parents and others taking part in the socialization processes of the child.

It goes without saying that an adequate theory of (a) language may not fail to disentangle such and related problems of empirical scope because notions like standard language may be either too restricted or plainly ideological. Instead of making occasional remarks such as 'in my dialect', it might – at least for some cultures – be inevitable to write sets of (related) grammars for 'one' language.

1.2. The discussion in the previous paragraph is relevant for another reason. We recalled that, once having established a grammar of hypothetical rules, we need to test its consequences, *viz.* its derived sentences, against some empirical instance. In generative grammar it has been stressed that this empirical basis is formed by the very linguistic intuition of native speakers (for discussion, cf. Botha [1968] 69 ff.). Empirically this intuition is not confined to concrete production or reception of a given utterance (sentence), defining the notion of ACCEPTABILITY, but it also comprises isolated judgements of native speakers about the (degree of) grammaticalness of given sentences. The basic hypothesis underlying these procedures of testing is that global consensus about 'grammaticalness' or 'well-formedness' is a sufficient indication of the correctness of the hypothetical rules postulated for deriving the sentences in question (Quirk & Svartvik [1966], Botha [1970], Leech [1968]).

Strictly speaking, however, we do not test a formal notion such as grammaticalness (derivability) but the notion of acceptability. That is, testing a grammar is always an indirect procedure, because it is based on reliance upon the actual knowledge of individuals about their language and not upon the hypothetical construct of 'ideal' knowledge. It might be asked, then, whether relevant testing of our predictions can be isolated from the real empirical situations of application of the rules by native speakers, *viz.* in concrete communication processes. This problem of course is well-known in psychology, because it is a fact that the behaviour of test-persons may deviate significantly in laboratory situations from the behaviour in situations we want to acquire knowledge about.

The judgements of native speakers about the grammaticalness of sentences of their language is therefore only a very rough indication about correctness of rules. Native speakers are either not even able to perform the required task because they do not know the concept 'grammatical' or 'correct', or their judgement is biased by their knowledge of traditional grammar, learned at school, a fact which clearly leads to circularity in our demonstration.

1.3. Before we try to formulate the implications of our foregoing remarks for the status of 'literary grammar', we must consider another notion of 'language'.

Somewhat metaphorically the term 'language' is also used to indicate specific CODES within a given particular language, such as the 'language' of propaganda, the 'language' of the court, the 'language' of the nuclear physicist, etc. Many of these 'languages' cannot be understood by all native speakers of the language within which these specific 'languages' are used. In many cases the specific character of these languages is based only on an extension of the vocabulary with a set of technical terms. Because a vocabulary is in principle an open set, i.e. includes categories defining open sets (verbs, adjectives and especially nouns), these technical terms are simply 'additions' to the standard language, of which active or passive use, i.e. performance, is limited to a small group. We can best refer to such 'languages' as LEXICAL CODES because they do not normally imply different syntactic or semantic rules (only certain selection restrictions derivable from the specific lexemes by which they are defined) (cf. Bier-wisch and Kiefer [1969] 60).

Notice that we are dealing here with codes of natural language, not with formal languages of science, which clearly have their own syntax, phonology (or 'graphology') and semantics. These languages are however in most cases – and ideally – independent of natural languages, and therefore need to be translated into natural language.

Somewhat different however is the use of the term 'language' in such expressions as 'the language of propaganda' or 'child-language'. In these cases we may also have an extension (or reduction) of the vocabulary but the distinctive properties are above all determined by a specific USE of the rules, by the establishment of new rules and by specific selections of certain lexemes. Therefore we are dealing here with aspects of performance, that is with the use of grammar and lexicon, in specific situations, for the production of specific semantic representations ('subjects', 'topics') in order to produce specific effects (persuasion) etc. These aspects belong to pragmatics and a theory of performance. No formal justification can therefore be given for the use of the term 'language' in that case. Child language is characterized by specific rules (for example for topicalization, cf. Gruber [1969] and flection of verbs) and in that case we could probably speak of a 'language'. This language is, nevertheless, derived from the standard language (or dialect) spoken by the parents and has to be defined as a set of 'mistakes', e.g. incorrect generalization, or of specific strategies in learning or cognition (topicalization). The specific grammar we might construct for child language has therefore also to be defined with respect to the rules of the grammar of the (standard) language, which provides the 'primary linguistic data'.

1.4. We may conclude that a definition of 'standard language' is a first, rather complex, step of abstraction in linguistics, which, however, has certain empirical, that is sociological, correlates as 'generality', 'consensus', and 'norm'. It is not equal, therefore, to an intersection of the sets of rules and the sets of vocabularies used by individual speakers or groups, nor is it identical to the union of the sets of all utterances produced by the members of a group.

We will not make an attempt to give a definition of standard language and will simply consider it as 'given' in sociology or sociolinguistics, letting it denote 'the system underlying the normified use of language in a given speech community'. This system, then, is defined by an open vocabulary, including a 'basic' part known by all speakers of the language, and a set of semantic, syntactic and morpho-phonological rules also implicitly known by all speakers of the language.

2. LANGUAGE, LITERATURE AND GRAMMAR

2.1. In the previous section we tried to indicate some problems concerning the empirical scope of grammars. We now want to consider the empirical and formal status of the set of texts in a language we normally call 'literature'.

Notice, first of all, that the delimitation of that set is subject to problems similar to those met before. Although we may say that there is a very global consensus about the membership of given texts of the set of literary texts, there are large subsets which cannot unambiguously be assigned either to the set of literary texts or to the set of non-literary texts. This well-known fact can be observed not only for all sorts of 'popular' texts like myths, *Trivial-literatur*, detective stories, etc. but also for philosophical essays, or historical narration. The criteria involved in these decision procedures depend on historical, cultural and ideological factors, and not only on textual properties. We see that any definition of literature necessarily includes sociological components, because, also here, rather small groups in society seem to establish the membership of given texts of the set of literature. The traditional criterion applied in that case is ESTHETIC: a given text can be assigned to literature if it has a certain esthetic 'value'. The criteria of this evaluation procedure are, however, intuitive and are roughly confirmed by consensus within a group. This consensus can of course change from culture to culture and from age to age. From these well-known facts we conclude that an empirical notion of literature is a function of (i) certain cultural groups in society (ii) the differentiation of textual functions in a given society and (iii) historical developments of systems of esthetic norms as applied to texts.

Any test-procedure of the predictions derived from a theory or grammar of literature must take account of these sociological and historical factors.

2.2. In the following sections and chapters we will, however, abstract from these empirical problems, which must be resolved in sociopoetics, diachronical poetics and esthetics. We will therefore take as our object an IDEALIZED notion of literature, and assume that some groups of native speakers of a language can distinguish globally between literary and non-literary texts. This ability is of course the product of a learning process and it is our task to distinguish and make explicit its different components.

One important part of this ability, which may be called 'literary competence', is pragmatic and defines the knowledge of native speakers about the general properties underlying the process of literary communication, that is the relation between textual properties and their appropriateness (cf. Wunderlich [1970a]) in certain communicative situations. This pragmatic part of competence, which will be treated in Chapter 9, is clearly a part of the pragmatic component of our general textual competence, which enables us to relate texts with their possible functions.

Leaving both the sociological and the pragmatic components of the underlying system, we will focus upon the textual properties of literature, and assume that the knowledge and recognition of these properties is a basic factor in the communicative processes of reading and evaluating. We want to know, then, which system of rules determines the structural characteristics of all literary texts.

As we noticed before, reasons of empirical adequacy will force us to postulate several systems underlying different TYPES of literary texts. This procedure further enables us to assign a specific status to those types (myths, detective stories) for which no general consensus about 'literariness' can be assessed. In these cases, if they are relevant examples of 'semi-literariness', we may use the concept DEGREE OF LITERARI-NESS. This notion would be formally defined by an index representing for example the number of literary rules applied or not applied (Bierwisch [1965]). Observe that this notion is formal. It is not necessarily correlated with possible high or low evaluation scores for given (types of) texts.

This purely formal character is defined by the literary grammar(s) we want to construct. 'Literariness' is meant only as a concept equivalent to 'grammaticalness' in linguistics and denotes derivability with the aid of literary rules.

2.3. Even if we accept the hypothesis according to which the system underlying the set of literary texts is defined by a generative text grammar, it is clear that the generation of literary texts in a given language is not defined by literary rules alone. We empirically recognize in literary texts a great number of lexical units and grammatical constructions which are common to those in other texts of the language. It will be our task in the rest of this chapter to elucidate the precise relations between literary structures and general linguistic structures in literary texts, i.e. between literary text grammar and text grammar in general.

In order to be more explicit we will therefore first introduce some symbols. We will use L_i to denote a particular natural language, defined as an infinite set, $\{T_1, T_2, ...\}$, of texts belonging to that language. Let G_i denote the (text-)grammar enumerating all and only members of L_i and assigning to each member one or more structural description(s). G_i is defined by a quintuple, $\langle V_N, V_T, R, T \rangle$, consisting of a set V_N of non-terminal, theoretical symbols denoting grammatical categories, a set V_T of terminal symbols denoting members of a lexicon, a set R of derivation rules, a specific symbol T or 'initial symbol', member of V_N, and a boundary marker '#' for texts, also member of V_N.

The problem at issue now is the status of an assumed distinct set of literary texts L_L^i, and a specific grammar, G_L^i, enumerating and describing all and only members of L_L^i, a status to be defined in relation to L_i and G_i. This problem is rather complex, because in empirical reality we have many texts of which literariness, i.e. L_L-grammaticalness, is not easily decidable. In order to be able to clarify the issue, it is necessary, therefore, to make a distinction between the formal set of texts as generated by G_L^i, which of course are only abstract constructs, and the empirical open set of all texts belonging to 'literature', that is all texts ACCEPTED by a certain cultural community as 'literary'. These two sets do not exactly correspond, i.e. not every member derivable by G_L^i is necessarily also accepted as formally representing a member of the empirical set called 'literature'. And conversely, not any member belonging to literature is necessarily also represented by a formal construct derivable from G_L^i. We here meet a familiar distinction, viz. the distinction between 'grammaticalness' (or derivability) and 'acceptability'. Both notions admit measures of graduality. The first notion is purely abstract and denotes a formal property of an abstract textual construct, the second notion is an empirical, *viz.* cultural and psycho-social property: membership assignment to a corpus. This distinction is theoretically very important because it is the only way to arrive at an explicit account of literary structures. Thus the membership of a concrete text to the literature of a language is not only decided on the basis of its textual properties as specified by G_L^i but also by a set of factors of textual communication: intentions of writers, knowledge of readers, systems of esthetic and ideological values, etc. (see chapter 9). A complete theory of literature, therefore, requires also the elaboration of a theory of literary performance or communication, stating the factors and laws which determine how and why the members of a given community accept or reject texts as literary or non-literary, and how these procedures of acceptance or rejection may differ in function of time, culture, social class, personality, etc. By using notions like G_L^i and L_L^i we therefore merely provide an approximative, formal, insight into rules and structures of literature.

2.4 If our hypothesis is correct according to which it must be possible to differentiate also at the formal grammatical level between literary and non-literary texts of a language, we adopt a symbol L^i for the language as a whole and a grammar G_N^i specifying all and only members of L_N^i, i.e., the non-literary part of L^i. (We will further omit for reasons of simplicity the superior index i denoting a particular language.) It is our task then to make explicit the relations between L, L_N and L_L and between G, G_N and G_L.

Our first assumption is that the binary distinction between L_N and L_L is exhaustive with respect to L

(1) $L_N \cup L_L = L$

Of course this is trivial because L_N is merely referred to negatively, *viz.* as the difference $L - L_L$. Nevertheless, this expression symbolizes that we consider literary texts as texts of a language and that it somehow makes sense to divide the set of texts of a language into two sets.

The binary division implies furthermore that the two sets are exclusive

(2) $L_N \cap L_L = \emptyset$

Observe again that the exclusive distinction is formal: it might be the case that a non-literary text is acceptable in a given society or time as belonging to literature.

The formal reason to distinguish L_N and L_L is not only our aim to characterize L_L, because this would also be possible when L_L were simply a subset of an indifferentiated set of all texts of a language, but the fact that the grammars for L_N and L_L should be distinguished. G_L seems to require categories and rules which do not belong to G_N. That is, certain structures of texts of L_L are ungrammatical in L_N. This assumption is supported by the existence of regular syntactic and semantic 'anomalies', e.g. in modern poetry. Furthermore, it is the case that certain structures of texts in L_L are not grammatical with respect to G_N but simply not specified at all, although considered as relevant structures of L_L: metrical structures, narrative transforms, etc. In order to describe them we would need a set of EXTENSIONS of G_N, such that V_N of the quintuple defining G_N would be replaced by V_N' and R by R'. We will assume that these extensions are relevant and regular only for the description of literary texts, such that an extended grammar G_N' is either properly or improperly included in G_L

(3)   (i) $G_N' \subset G_L$
       or (ii) $G_N' \subseteq G_L$

Since we assumed that G_L has to specify also structures which are ungrammatical in G_N and possibly also in G_N', the relation must be one of proper inclusion, and a fortiori, then

(4) $G_N \subset G_L$

which means that any category and rule (and the lexicon, and the initial and boundary symbol) of G_N also belongs to G_L.

We may consider, in a next step, G_N to be roughly equivalent with a 'normal' (text)grammar of a language, specifying all texts of that language but not the literary texts.

It might further be the case that L_N is a set of sets of texts, i.e. that it should be differentiated into TYPES of text. We will assume, however, for reasons of simplicity, that these typological differences between subsets of L_N are not grammatically, but pragmatically and referentially founded, that is based on the use of the rules, possible varied choices from the lexicon and specific factors of speech acts or communication processes.

We must now draw some formal consequences of the assumptions made above. Since the separation of L_N and L_L is exclusive and exhaustive with respect to L, we may conclude that the grammar G, describing L, cannot have categories or rules excluded from G_L, when $G_N \subset G_L$ is true. This leads to the result that the ideal construct G is formally equivalent with G_L

(5) $G_L \equiv G$

This implies that a grammar of literature is powerful enough to describe any text of a language L. However, this does not mean that any text of L is a literary text, i.e. that $L \subseteq L_L$ – although again, at least many texts of L not belonging to L_L can be accepted as 'literary'. We therefore have to assume that membership for a text of L_L requires the application of at least one SPECIFIC rule of G_L, that is a rule not belonging to G_N. Now, it is the task of theoretical poetics to formulate precisely this specific set C of categories and rules which do not belong to G_N

(6) $G_L - G_N = C$

We leave the specification of G_N as a task for (textual) linguistics and we will focus on the explication of C and its relations to G_N. We will call C the set of COMPLE-MENTARY RULES or specifically literary rules (and categories) of G_L.

The status of complementary rules, with respect to G_N, is not wholly clear. Above we mentioned the possibility of EXTENDING a grammar G_N to a set of POSSIBLE GRAM-MARS $\{G'_N, G''_N, ...\}$ which may be called CONNECTED when they share, by intersection, sets of rules, categories and a lexicon (cf. Bierwisch and Kiefer [1969] 61–64). Although native speakers will normally first acquire the rules of G_N, it is possible that they extend this BASIC OR NORMAL COMPETENCE with sets of complementary rules, such that they are able to distinguish e.g. between literary and non-literary texts (formally speaking). We will assume, then, that any native speaker has a mechanism to change or extend his 'primary' competence and to acquire a 'secondary' or 'derived competence', or 'subcompetences' for specific languages such as the set of literary texts. If, indeed, we have to consider specific literary rules as extension rules with respect to a basic, normal or primary grammar G_N, we may assume that they some-how DEPEND on those of G_N, and that any literary text also needs rules of G_N in order to be generated. That is, we define the relation $\langle C, G_N \rangle$ as one of dependence, such that any rule of C is based on at least one category or rule (or structures generated by these) of G_N. One may say, then, that C, and hence G_L, PRESUPPOSES G_N.

2.5. Let us now examine in more detail the structure of C, that is, e.g., the TYPES of rules and other elements characterizing it. First of all we will distinguish two subsets C_M and C_S. C_M is the set of those rules of G_L which can be considered as MODIFICA-TIONS of rules of G_N. We will see in the next chapter that such rules may be either modifications of formation rules or specific transformation rules. C_S, then, is the set of rules/categories which are specific, in their FORM, for G_L. That is, such TYPES of rules are wholly unknown in G_N. We here think, e.g., of metrical rules and rules for specific recurrence structures which are not described by G_N, although an extension of G_N to G'_N, i.e. $G_N \cap C_S$, would account for them. One of the differences between the rules of C_M and C_S is that the specific rules of C_S operate not only on the 'normal' categories of G_N, but also on specific LITERARY CATEGORIES, such as RIM or ALL for the generation of rhyming and alliterating structures. The rules of C_M only operate on linguistic categories and therefore are considered as 'modified' rules with respect to the basic grammar G_N. We see that the difference between V_{N_N} and V_{N_L} is due to C_S and the difference between R_N and R_L to both C_M and C_S. The set C_M is often considered as a set of DEVIATION RULES with respect to 'normal (text) grammar'. This view, however, although formally not incorrect if we accept a certain primacy of G_N, is misleading.

It might suggest that such rules, in fact, are not rules in their own right but, for example, 'rules' of performance. Describing structures generated by the rules of C_M as 'deviations' reduces the description of literary texts to a description of SEMI-GRAMMATICAL structures which are indeed normally characterized with respect to levels and categories of the rules of G_N which are not applied or ill-applied. Notice that the structures specified by C_M are not conceived by the native speaker of literature, i.e. 'the experienced reader', as 'deviations' but as structures grammatical within the literary system. The converse is true: a text presented/intended as literary, but with no rules either from C_M or C_S is considered as L_L – ungrammatical, and will probably be assigned to L_N.

2.6. In the next chapters we will investigate in some detail some of the hypothetic rules and categories of the complementary set C of G_L. Their general character however is not yet clear. Bierwisch (1965) and Ihwe (1972a) have made extensive preliminary remarks about the status, form and effect of 'literary rules'. Bierwisch first postulates a selection mechanism P' which should select all those structures generated by the grammar which have a certain degree of 'poeticalness'. However, he then rejects such a recognition procedure and proposes a system P which has to assign to the structures generated by G specific literary features or markers. This system would probably produce the same strings as our system C_S, and is therefore weakly equivalent with it. He further postulates a set of 'deviation rules' formulating regular structures in literary/poetry which can be specified with respect to a 'normal' system like G (our G_N). Above, we have indicated that such a 'negative' characterization may be misleading, although at first sight it is weakly equivalent with C_M.

The major difference between Bierwisch's and our views is that Bierwisch seems to be committed to an exclusive TRANSFORMATIONAL conception of literary rules. Such a position is not *a priori* impossible and has some advantages and possibly even psycho-linguistic/psycho-poetic correlates when we consider 'transforms' indeed as derived from more 'normal' or 'basic' structures. However, the assumption according to which we first need 'normal linguistic structures' which, then, are transformed either by P (our C_S) or by 'deviation rules' (our C_M) into literary structures, seems highly doubtful. Given the condition of RECOVERABILITY it is not at all sure that we arrive at the establishment of the 'normal' underlying structures. It might be the case that certain specifically literary structures are directly generated in the base of G_L. In order to generate metrical structures, for example, we do not first generate a normal deep structure and then assign a metrical pattern to it. The selection of lexical elements and even of syntactic structures is restricted by the metrical pattern (see next chapter). Such rules apparently have the character of ADDITIONAL SELECTIONAL CONSTRAINTS, similar to the 'global (and trans-) derivational constraints' defined by Lakoff (1970a).

We have to conclude from these remarks that the rules of C_M and C_S are both formational (base) and transformational rules. It is possible that the syntactic and semantic rules of C_M are transformational, i.e. have structures generated by G_N ($\subset G_L$) as input.

We may assume, furthermore, that G_L not only contains specific rules but also specific RULE-SCHEMATA, RULE-SEQUENCES and GLOBAL DERIVATIONAL CONSTRAINTS of ordering, etc. Especially in metrical structures the selection of a specific rule may lead to the obligatory application of other rules. The choice of a global metrical schema like *SONNET* requires the generation of a fixed number of lines (14) having a specific distribution, e.g. $\langle 4\ 4\ 3\ 3 \rangle$, and with a specific metrical pattern (e.g. iambic pentameter or alexandrine) and a specific rhyme scheme, e.g. $\langle a\ b\ a\ b\ a\ b\ a\ b\ c\ d\ c\ d\ c\ d \rangle$.

2.7. Until now we assumed that only the sets of non-terminal category-symbols and the set of rules of G_N and G_L are different. It might be the case, however, that also the set of terminal elements, the LEXICON, is different in both cases. We will assume however, that in principle the lexicon of G_N and the one of G_L are identical, at least in many literatures. This is not necessarily the case, however. The possible use of archaisms in literary texts, for example, shows that elements of diachronically different lexica may be added to V_{T_L}. The same is true for neologisms and the use of lexemes from other languages. However, such extensions of V_T are not specific for G_L and also exist in texts of L_N and may be considered as a stylistic phenomenon which can be described as 'lexical code shifting'. The use of neologisms is a normal procedure also belonging to the productive possibilities of G_N, since V_T is an open set, or rather a set with open categories, like verbs and nouns. Some literatures, nevertheless, seem to have a proper lexicon of specific metaphorical readings to normal lexemes, e.g. in Old-Icelandic and Petrarquist poetry. If these extensions cannot be regularly explained by specific rules (metaphorization, for example) they may be considered, indeed, as specific for G_L, *viz*. of C_S.

At the level of phonological matrices, we may further sometimes have optional differences in phonological structures under specific, e.g. metrical conditions, (the pronunciation of *e-muet* in French metered verse, and of *-ig* as /i:g/ instead of /ęj/ in reflexive pronouns under the rhyme in Swedish poetry). For some detail, cf. next chapter. Similar lexical changes are possible in the (ortho-)graphical forms of morphemes in (modern) poetry. All such differences in the lexicon are, however, rather marginal and rarely regular. They will no longer detain us here.

Finally, we will assume provisionally that the INITIAL SYMBOL T is identical for both grammars since both are T-grammars. The differences in derived strings result from specific rules in G_L. It is not clear how these rules are 'triggered', however. We might adopt specific 'performative' categories, like *POET*, although it is not sure whether such labels represent pragmatical primitives (cf. chapter 9). We will therefore not exclude a possible distinction of an initial symbol T_L, in order to mark from the beginning of the derivation which rules are admitted in the derivation and which are not. Similar remarks may be made for the BOUNDARY SYMBOLS of G_N and G_L. Especially for the generation of metrical structures it will be necessary to use specific boundary symbols for metrical strings. They will be treated as normal elements of V_{N_L} and need not acquire specific status.

2.8. The comparison between the 'normal' or at least 'non-literary' grammar G_N and the literary grammar G_L leaves us with some complex problems at the level of the THEORY OF GRAMMAR. We assumed that all the rules of G_N seem to be admitted in G_L and that the set of non-terminal categories of G_N is included in the one of G_L. It is not obvious, however, whether – especially when the initial symbols are different – these relations of proper inclusion also mean that the whole grammar G_N is included in G_L, although if $V_{T_N} = V_{T_L}$ and if $R_N \subset R_L$, then $(V_{N_N} \cup R_N) \subset (V_{N_L} \cup R_L)$ seems correct, and if $T_N \in V_{N_N}$ and $T_L \in V_{N_L}$, then $G_N \subset G_L$. This implies that if of G_L only the non-literary rules are applied we merely generate a non-literary text, hence $L_N \subset L_L$, which could be interpreted as: any text is a literary text. However it only means that G_L is superior in weak generative capacity to G_N because it generates more strings. We therefore formulated the condition that the set of specifically literary texts, viz. $L - L_N$, requires that at least one rule of G_L is applied in the derivation. Different initial symbols might contain the information for this condition to be applied. The difference thus also lies at the qualitative level: G_L does not merely specify a more extensive language, it also provides more adequate structural descriptions. It is possible that G_N generates a text belonging to L_N which is superficially identical with a text of L_L. However, G_L provides a description of certain structures in this text which are not specified by G_N. This is especially the case for rules of C_S, the rules of C_M being defined as modifications or alternatives of rules of G_N, thus resulting into structures which cannot be generated by G_N. A rhyme, repetition, etc. is 'possible' in a text generated by G_N but only the random result of application of normal rules. Intuitively, then, G_L assigns 'more structure' to the string it specifies than does G_N, since at least one rule of C_S or C_M has to apply for a literary text. Hence G_L is also superior in strong generative capacity to G_N, due especially to C_S, whereas C_M seems to explain the higher degree of weak generative capacity of G_L.

2.9. Finally, we should consider the theoretical status of the concept of DEVIATION, often associated with the concept of STYLE. This concept, clearly, is a relational term which can be defined only with respect to systems like grammars, or in general 'conventions', 'norms', etc. It is important to stress the difference between particular, or ad hoc, deviations and general or systematic deviations. The first are considered to be interfering factors of individual realizations, that is: of performance. The second type might either be considered to be a performance-system (cf. Ihwe [1970]) or a specific (competence-)system. In that case they are not ungrammatical, but grammatical with respect to another underlying system, which allows its own performance-derivations (use, style).

   Thus, it is a task of a theory of language to define grammars which are also able to assign structural descriptions to strings not normally generated by them: SEMI-

SENTENCES. The current theory (Chomsky [1964], Katz [1964a], Ihwe [1972a]) defines degrees of grammaticalness for such semi-sentences according to the number and the rank of the G_N-rules that have been violated or not applied. A theory of semi-sentences is very important, both in linguistics and poetics, because its task is to make explicit the mechanism which enables speakers/hearers to assign semantically well-formed representations to ungrammatical surface structures, which occur frequently in daily conversation. Part of the complementary rules of G_L therefore have to be explained within a general linguistic theory of semi-sentences. This theory is related to, but distinct from, a theory (grammar) for NONSENSE STRINGS (Katz [1964a] Ihwe [1972a]). Such strings cannot normally be assigned a semantic interpretation and therefore only function at the level of their surface structures. This fact is important, especially in poetry, for the definition of the theoretical status of interpretation in literary theory.

We will return to these two types of 'deviance' in detail in our following chapters.

2.10. From the discussion in this section we can now draw some provisional conclusions about the theoretical status of literary 'language' and literary 'grammar'.

Current conceptions of literature as a 'dialect' must be rejected as misleading (cf. Thorne [1965], [1969], [1970], Fowler [1966], cf. Hendricks [1969a] for critical remarks). For the generation of L_L we rarely need a lexicon that is different from that of standard language. Furthermore, all the rules of G_N are perfectly admitted in G_L, which is not true for dialects.

Similarly, it is an important mistake to think of literature as a 'style' of the standard language, defined only by a specific 'use' of the rules of the normal grammar. First, the regularities underlying the production of literary texts are not ad hoc products of performance and they are not conditioned by situational factors. Second, many rules of G_L do not occur at all in G_N so that we cannot speak of a specific 'use' of these rules. Third, rules of G_L are also ideal abstractions which admit their proper use in processes of literary performance (style of novel A vs. style of novel B). Fourth, structures of L_L 'deviating' from those generated by G_N have to be considered possible grammatical realizations of specific rules formulated by G_L, that is as rules in their own right, characteristic of a different language. These rules may have their own (performance) deviations (cf. Ihwe [1970]). All approaches to a definition of literature that try to reduce it to a specific 'use' of standard language or to a specific 'function' of language (Jakobson [1960]) thus overlook the important fact that it is a SPECIFIC LANGUAGE-SYSTEM, WITHIN A LANGUAGE L BUT DIFFERENT FROM L_N, DESCRIBABLE BY AN AUTONOMOUS BUT NOT INDEPENDENT GRAMMAR.

This grammar is improperly included in G but properly includes G_N. The rules of G_L, however, necessarily co-operate with those of G_N. Some rules of G_L have well-formed linguistic strings as input, other directly form strings which then serve as input to further 'linguistic' rules, operations and constraints. Similarly, the theory of the set of possible literary grammars $\{G_{L_1}, G_{L_2}, ...\}$ is not included in the theory of grammars of standard language: some non-terminal symbols and probably some types of rules (such as those defining all sorts of recurrence) do not belong to the theory of ordinary grammar. They do however belong to a general theory of grammar, because they are indispensable for a correct account of perfectly acceptable (grammatical) texts in any language.

The specific rules and categories postulated have to be made explicit in the following chapters. Before that, however, let us consider the more general relations between linguistics and poetics as distinct theoretical disciplines.

3. LINGUISTICS AND POETICS

3.1. Much work dealing with the relations between linguistics and poetics has been biased by ideological arguments rather than theoretical and methodological ones. The so-called 'formal' description of literary texts, of which some roots can be traced back to Russian Formalism, was often rejected as an approach missing the 'essentials' of literature. It is not our task, however, to refute these viewpoints, but to give a sketch of the framework in which the description of literary texts can be made explicit according to criteria of sound theory formation.

Similarly for the role of linguistics in literary theory, which has received much attention these last ten years.[1] This role has in many cases been minimized, not in the least because many applications of the 'auxiliary discipline' were indeed theoretically and methodologically feeble. It is in this sense that we should interpret Schmidt (1970c) when he says that 'linguistic poetics' turned out to be a failure. Such an assertion however is premature when we notice that the full implications for poetics of the aims, models and methods of linguistics have only recently been fully understood (cf. especially Ihwe [1972a]). Nevertheless, it goes without saying that the

[1] We will not give a survey of these developments of 'linguistic poetics', or of 'stylo-linguistics', as Hendricks (1969b) called it. Of course most studies in literary scholarship have traditionally used 'linguistic' notions, both in hermeneutic approaches (Spitzer, and the whole 'school' of 'romance stylistics') and in 'formalist' approaches. The most systematic studies go back to Russian Formalism and Czech Structuralism, but are often restricted to the main core of early structural linguistics: phonology. For an extensive survey, cf. Ihwe (1972a). Uitti (1969) also investigates earlier relations between language and literature, from Antiquity onwards.

One can consider the (first) *Style in Language* Conference of 1959 as a major initial landmark in the development of linguistic poetics (Sebeok, ed. [1960]). Numerous anthologies about language and literature, language and style, linguistics and literary theory have appeared in this last decade. We will confine ourselves to giving the most important ones: Davie, *et al.*, eds. (1961), Spencer, ed. (1964), Kreuzer and Gunzenhäuser, eds. (1965), Fowler, ed. (1966), Chatman and Levin, eds. (1967), Barthes, ed. (1968), *Linguistique et littérature* (1968), Love and Payne, eds. (1969), Freeman, ed. (1970), Chatman, ed. (forthcoming) and finally Ihwe, ed. (1972a) which is undoubtedly the most complete survey of current work in this domain.

For bibliography, cf. Milic (1967), Burton and Bailey (1968). Surveys are provided by e.g. Baum-gärtner (1969), van Dijk (1971b), (1971c), (1972b), Carstensen (1970).

role of linguistics in literary theory is important only in so far as it helps to resolve the problems of poetics proper. We therefore must indeed be critical with respect to possible false analogies and to the use of irrelevant methods of description.

One of the aims of this book is precisely the textual extension of linguistics, not only as a necessary development for grammar itself, but also as a more adequate basis for a description of literary texts. The relevance of linguistics is crucially linked with this extension. The description of sentence structures in literature is only of marginal interest without a textual foundation. Specific sentential structures are nearly wholly limited to certain types of modern poetry. It was in this domain that most applications of generative grammar were made (cf. van Dijk [1971c]).

Although these methods of description were more explicit, the loss of relevance with respect to many good structural descriptions (discourse analyses) of texts is beyond doubt. The rather trivial conclusion that many sentences of poems could not be generated by the grammar did not lead to the construction of hypothetic rules accounting for the regularity of these 'deviations'. Descriptions thus remained fully ad hoc (as in Levin [1962]).

The major reason for the fundamental incompleteness of this type of application of linguistics in poetics was not only the uncritical acceptance of the sentence as the maximum structural unit, but above all the lack of consciousness about the explicit aims and tasks of poetics proper. Hardly any attempt was made to insert analyses or descriptions within a theoretical framework.

Having made these preliminary points we now have to consider briefly and systematically the general relation between linguistics and poetics. Such an investigation is inevitable within the perspective of this book, which has a linguistic foundation and 'applications' in the establishment of the aims, tasks and descriptions of poetics which are heavily inspired by those of linguistics.

3.2. The relations between linguistics and poetics must be established, first, at the most fundamental level: the level of PHILOSOPHY OF SCIENCE. In this respect they are linked not only with each other but with any other science because they share the same fundamental methods of inquiry. In the same way as we have rejected, in the previous chapter, the traditional hermeneutic distinction between the methods of the natural sciences and those of the social sciences, we now reject a distinction between the most fundamental methodological procedures in linguistics and poetics. That is, although the epistemological objects of 'language' and 'literature' have different properties, we claim that the description and explanation of these properties follow the same methodological paths. Criteria for theory formation and testing therefore do not differ (for detailed discussion of these matters, cf. Ihwe [1972a] Chap. 1, Schmidt [1970c], Hartmann [1970a]). It is not the case for example that linguistics is mainly concerned with the formulation of rules representing abstract underlying regularities and systems of natural language, whereas poetics is rather concerned with a set of 'individual descriptions' of singular texts. We have seen that poetics is also interested in the underlying regularities and in the explicit account of them in generalized expressions, although many of these regularities have a much less stable character than those the linguist is dealing with.

In both cases the fundamental approach is hypothetico-deductive, especially for the description of textual structures. Rules are postulated on the basis of some observational data and the strings derived by them tested against the empirical evidence of linguistic intuition and acceptance by native speakers.

These and other basic methodological grounds common to linguistics, poetics and all other sciences are still rather programmatic for poetics. In the actual state of our research hardly any testable hypotheses or rules have been formulated in poetics, let alone the construction of complete, coherent theories. Formalization and axiomatization are necessary tasks of poetics but at the moment far beyond our reach.

We will see below that identity of methodological basis does not imply that linguistics and poetics have identical problems of description, explanation and testing.

3.3. The next set of relations between linguistics and poetics concerns the place of both of them within the complex of the SOCIAL SCIENCES. With them they share not only the basic scientific methods referred to above, but also a certain number of specific descriptional and explanatory techniques and a common task.

One practical difference with respect to many natural sciences is probably the lack of possibility of experiment in many branches of the humanities. Human (inter-) action has an essentially irreversible and historical character and behaviour is only rarely identical under similar conditions. These facts, and many others, require several steps of idealization and generalization which bring any theoretical formulation rather 'far' from the concrete empirical objects. The emotional and ideological implications of these methodological problems have led to the well-known 'Methoden-streit' and other 'crises' in the social sciences.[2] Such 'crises' have only marginally characterized the developments of modern linguistics but become habitual in poetics.

These difficulties of abstraction and generalization, caused by the heterogeneity of the studied empirical data, underlie the restricted and probabilistic nature of most social theories, which in turn were the cause of the well-known difficulties of validation, explanation and predictions derivable from the hypothetical statements.

Similar methodological differences from the natural sciences can be inferred from the mental roots of all human behaviour. In opposition to positivistic behaviorism modern linguistics has stressed that complex surface structures must be hypothetically derived from deep structures and that the system of rules underlying them must somehow have a mental reality (cf. Chomsky [1959b], [1968], Katz [1964c], [1966], Botha [1968]). These references to the structures and processes of cognition also

---

[2] These discussions characterize above all the development of sociology in Germany. For a global documentation, cf. Topitsch, ed. (1965), Seiffert (1970), Jaeggi (1968), Adorno (1970), Habermas (1970).

characterize modern psychology and should underlie many social processes of verbal and non-verbal interaction as well (cf. Hörmann [1967], Neisser [1967] and the contributions in Lyons and Wales, eds. [1966], Jakobovits and Miron, eds. [1967], Lyons, ed. [1970]; cf. chap. 9). It is clear that no direct observation of this mental black box is possible and that only explicit predictions from hypothetical constructions (like grammars) about the possible output can yield insight into the structure of language and mind.

We discover at this point that the basic aims of the social sciences, including linguistics and poetics, coincide. That is, they must both provide descriptions and explanations of the structure and processes of, on the one hand, the human mind and of the behaviour which is controlled by it, and on the other hand, of the structures and processes in human interaction, communication, culture and society in general.

These aims are very general and it seems trivial to adduce them here to demonstrate the relationship between linguistics and poetics. However, it leads to the consequences of the still rather recent understanding of the role of language both for processes of the mind (thought) and for social interaction. Linguistics therefore is not only fundamental for poetics but for all social sciences.

We have tried to show repeatedly that the importance of this role of linguistics is considerably enhanced when it takes the text, or the infinite set of texts, as its formal object of description and the underlying textual competence as the psychological correlate of this description. Thinking, reasoning, memory, and speaking on the one hand, and communicating, persuading, informing, etc. on the other hand, are thus based on texts and their underlying structures. If not identical with it, linguistics thus conceived is a central discipline in the large network of the 'science of texts' (Schmidt [1970c], [1971c]) that accounts for these different structures, conditions and functions of texts and textual communication.

Poetics here finds its natural place, either within this broad discipline of linguistics or, at the side of linguistics, within a 'science of texts'. The specific cultural (esthetic) function of literary texts in both cases is studied like the functions and effects of any type of text (or non-verbal human artefacts). It is also within this range of social sciences and specifically in relation to linguistics that we are able to study the conditions, both psycho-social and historical, and the specific functions of the literary text, i.e. of the cultural phenomenon of literature in general. Only when its theoretical relations with different social theories and those of poetics proper are made explicit, can poetics become a science aiming at valid explanations of its object.

3.4. Together with psycholinguistics, sociolinguistics, and linguistic anthropology, poetics thus forms a cluster of disciplines around linguistics, all interested in the structure of verbal (textual) behaviour and its formal and psychological underlying conditions and functions.

In this respect it is now easy to understand that many aims and tasks of linguistics and poetics are similar if not identical. It is misleading, then, to reject extensive use of linguistics by alleging possible bias of 'analogical thinking'. Linguistics as a discipline could thus become a MODEL for poetics both by the similarity of their basic aims and for the historical reason that linguistics is far more advanced in descriptive and theoretical techniques. Linguistics, therefore, is more than a simple heuristic device which might provide some theories for the formation of hypotheses in literary scholarship. It cannot be but the GENERAL FOUNDATION of theoretical poetics, because it provides the description of text structures in general, of which those studied by poetics have only a specific form and function. This specific character authorizes a specific approach, which defines poetics as an AUTONOMOUS DISCIPLINE, but not as an independent discipline. Linguistics, we repeat, cannot therefore be reduced to one auxiliary discipline among others. It describes and explains in general that which is described by poetics in particular: texts and their structural properties. Linguistics thus conceived, i.e. including poetics, is in its turn included in the social sciences, first in psychology and then in social psychology and anthropology, of which it, however, forms a central discipline because of the importance of the communicative aspect of the human society it must study.

These extremely general remarks are necessary to clarify the methodological status of the relations between linguistics and poetics, on which the debate has often been obscured by a fundamental ignorance about the aims and tasks of both linguistics and poetics and of the social sciences in general. We may now study in more detail the exact role of linguistics as a foundation for poetics.

3.5. The traditional and still central function of linguistics in poetics is to provide DESCRIPTIVE DEVICES (grammars and their rules and categories) for the characterization of the properly 'linguistic' aspects of literary texts. Texts have sentence structures constructed with the aid of 'normal' linguistic rules and these are therefore describable with these rules. A similar case applies for structures beyond the sentence. Those sentences and texts not describable with the 'normal' grammar G_N thus acquire, negatively, a specific status. They can either be conceived – a view which we rejected – as deviations from the rules, i.e. as determined by ad hoc stylistic operations characteristic of all performance processes, or as the product of SPECIFIC RULES, those of another grammar. Description is meant here as the structural characterization of existing literary texts. *Stricto sensu* we then describe language USE, and our linguistic description will automatically lead to a definition of the 'use of language' in literature. This use of 'normal' language has often been identified with the 'language of literature' or 'poetic language' as such, thus confusing use and the underlying (specific) system. Linguistic description of this type can be identified with (descriptive) stylistics and lies naturally within the domain of linguistic performance.

In a more general and abstract sense, linguistic description implies the use of the rules of G_N to generate texts of L_L together with the specific literary rules of G_L (see above).

Here we see that a specific linguistic grammar, e.g. generative text grammar, is 'built in' in a grammar of literary texts. The interesting role of linguistics consists here in providing the formal basis for the construction of the complementary rules of G_L, by which, as we saw, they are presupposed.

Linguistics, or rather grammar, is applied here to the description of SPECIFIC LITERARY STRUCTURES like rhymes, prosody, metaphors and narrative plot. These descriptions are possible because the CATEGORIES used in the construction of these structures are linguistic besides a set of specific literary categories. The rules describing them however are not linguistic but belong to literary grammar, because these rules do not underlie the textual structures possible in all texts of a language. That is, more precisely, these specific structures do not have a FUNCTION in other types of texts. Rhyme, for example, can be described by a rule selecting a lexical unit having (partially) identical phonological structure with some other word in the text. The categories like morpheme, phoneme (and 'identity'?) are part of any grammatical description, and only the SPECIFIC CONDITIONS for these types of context-sensitive phonological rules make it 'literary'. Essential therefore is the following difference: linguistic grammar G_N provides the instrument for describing some ad hoc relations with no general linguistic significance, whereas literary grammar describes this relation precisely by formulating a rule for their algorithmic description, that is by characterizing them as regular, grammatical structures within another (semiotic, linguistic) system. It is in this sense that the literary system has often been qualified as a secondary (or 'connotative') system with respect to that of the (ordinary, primary, denotative) language system (cf. §2.6. above).

3.6. The very fact that we describe certain literary structures by RULES is a further implication of the function of linguistics in poetics. Linguistics not only provides general or specific descriptions but also the FORM of these descriptions. These rules in literature need not to be identical with those used in generative grammar, but if such a grammar is incorporated within G_L it is possible that specific literary rules have to satisfy the same formal conditions as all grammatical rules. We may use for example the rewrite-rule type of generative grammar which, under several modifications, seems to be generally accepted. In the following chapter we will see how these literary rules can be constructed.

3.7. The use of rules is implied by the very use of a GRAMMAR to describe literary texts, which is a further suggestion adopted from linguistics. This step has been made possible only by extending grammar to a text-grammar. Without such a T-grammar we would be able to describe only sentences in literary texts, not the multiple deep- and surface relations between them. Because such a grammar is a partial theory of a language, it should be considered to be a formal model in theoretical poetics. It provides an abstract algorithm which under specific modifications can be interpreted as a 'literary grammar'.

The consequent application of the model requires at the same time that both its axioms and its components are satisfied by literary grammar. We therefore distinguish also in literary texts between surface- and deep structure, and between different levels of description (syntax, phonology and semantics). The model is adapted only in so far as the literary grammar requires a certain number of non-terminal (theoretical) symbols to denote categories for the derivation of literary structures.

The use of a generative-transformational grammar can be justified on the basis of its very explicit character with respect to other grammars for the description of sentences and, as we assumed, of texts. As we have seen in Part I this generative T-grammar does not necessarily have a base component identical with the one postulated in traditional generative grammar.

Like a generative grammar in linguistics a literary grammar will thus be asked to perform the double task of, firstly, enumerating all and only the texts belonging to a literature, and, secondly, of assigning a structural description to these texts.

3.8. Finally, a generative grammar and its rules have been used as descriptive, heuristic and theoretical models for theory formation in poetics because they ultimately provide a tentative model of linguistic competence. If we assume that groups of native speakers also have something like a LITERARY COMPETENCE, that is an ability to produce and interpret a virtually infinite set of literary texts, we are obliged to take a generative grammar also as a model for a literary theory about that specific competence.

We here rejoin the general discussion about the fundamental descriptive and explanatory goals of both linguistics and poetics (cf. chapter 4).

3.9. At the end of this rather general chapter we must observe an important phenomenon of feed-back from poetics to linguistics. Text-grammars were shown to be a necessary extension of a theory of grammar within linguistics proper. Hardly any models seemed to be present for the description of textual macro-structures. Now, at this point, a specific branch of poetics, the theory of narrative, seemed to provide a useful model, though still very intuitive and unexplicit, for this description. This model, the semantic relational model of functional actants, showed convergence with extant sentence (deep structure) descriptions. This combination could thus suggest ways for deriving deep structures of texts in general. We may speak here of a sort of 'inductive modelling'; knowledge about general linguistic structures is obtained from knowledge about more specific (literary) narrative structures.

In much the same way we may hope that the fundamental ways in which we try to describe the specific TYPE of text which is called 'literature', can in their turn provide the heuristic and theoretical models for the description of other types of texts in society.

3.10. Before we proceed to the formulation of the hypothetical rules and categories of literary grammars, we must finally consider briefly the problem of the relation of

REDUCIBILITY between linguistics and poetics. Can poetics be considered a discipline formulating NATURAL THEORIES as defined by Sanders ([1969]; cf. chapter 1)? Can poetics be reduced to linguistics and is this reduction scientifically relevant, i.e. does it lead to a more systematic and simpler description of a given empirical domain?

From the discussion above we inferred that poetics is an autonomous discipline with respect to linguistics, though it has certain relations of theoretical dependency with it. However, the possibility of reduction cannot be ruled out *a priori*. Actually, it depends on our conception of the tasks of linguistics and of the empirical domain defined for linguistic theories. If, indeed, linguistic theories have to account for the structures of all texts in a given language, there seem to be no reasons to exclude literary texts from that set. Grammatical description in that case implies the description of structures specific for literary texts. In a more strict sense of the notions of linguistics and grammar, however, the task of linguistic theories is not so comprehensive, especially when grammars are limited to specification and description of sentences. In T-grammars specific literary structures would be qualified either as ungrammatical (less grammatical) or as functionally irrelevant for a linguistic description of textual structure. As we saw, a basic grammar G_N is then included in a literary grammar G_L. This relation seems to indicate, rather paradoxically, the reducibility of linguistics to poetics. However, poetics is interested in the difference-set C of $G_L - G_N$, not in the formulation of categories and rules defining G_N. Poetics, then, is typically a COMPLEMENTARY discipline formulating regularities for a specific (sub-) domain of empirical reality, in much the same way as chemistry in relation to physics, biology in relation to both chemistry and physics, and psychology in relation to biology, neurology, etc. The complementary rules are intended to define units and to describe structures relevant ONLY in that sub-domain, not in others related with it. This means that rules of literary theories are not JOINTLY confirmable in linguistic theories (Sanders [1969] 8) and therefore reduction is impossible following general criteria for reducibility of theories.

The relation between poetics and linguistics can therefore further be characterized as NON-MUTUAL, because literary elements are not used in (general) linguistic description. Poetics uses (borrows) elements and rules from linguistic theories as GIVEN, i.e. conclusions made in grammar are initial statements in literary theories. Poetics thus formulates with the aid of the borrowed statements its OWN theoretical statements and defines its OWN theoretical elements, by giving a specific interpretation of them. We conclude, then, that the relation between linguistics and poetics is one of NON-MUTUAL DEPENDENCY.

Linguistics therefore cannot reduce poetics because its sets of statements and elements cannot include those of literary theories. Although the empirical domains seem to be identical at first sight, or at least intersecting, both disciplines study different aspects of texts and textual communication. Because literary statements use linguistic statements, poetics can be called SECONDARY with respect to linguistics, but this does not mean that the specific statements are automatically DERIVABLE from the more general ones (for details of these aspects of reduction, cf. Nagel [1961]), and a short discussion in van Dijk [1971c]). A strict reduction of literary theories to linguistic ones would signify either a reduction of relevant literary categories or an extension of linguistics. Both possibilities, especially the first one, seem undesirable for an adaquate account of the respective domains of both disciplines.

Nevertheless, it is possible (cf Sanders [1969]) to reduce both disciplines to a more general THEORY OF TEXTS, a unified discipline formulating the general (universal) statements about all possible texts of natural language, and therefore defining the possible relations between linguistics, poetics and other disciplines concerned with verbal behaviour. This is precisely the aim of this book.

6

SURFACE OPERATIONS

1. INTRODUCTION

1.1. After the general remarks of the previous chapters about the linguistic and methodological foundations of theoretical poetics we now have to consider the different levels described by the components of a tentative LITERARY TEXT GRAMMAR. These components, as we saw before, are those of any text grammar of natural language.

It is evident that it would be impossible to give, in the few remaining chapters, a full-fledged literary grammar. Our task consists in designing the foundations of such a grammar and in sketching only some aspects of its possible form and rules. We will go into some detail, with the description of semantic operations like metaphorization, but surface and macro-operations will only be dealt with in a very rough manner. It can not be expected that we should arrive at a satisfactory formalization of literary regularities. The rules (if any) will be of a very informal character. More important, at this moment, is the classification of their general theoretical status, their location between other linguistic rules and the categories on which they must operate.

1.2. The first component we want to consider can be termed roughly the 'surface-component'. We hereby denote the literary rules characteristic of both textual and sentential surface structures, *viz.* of PHONOLOGY (and GRAPHEMICS), MORPHOLOGY and SYNTAX. Textual surface operations characteristic of sentence deep structure, accounted for by semantic rules, will be treated in the next chapter.

This order of presentation has no particular significance but only practical impact. We go from surface to deep structure because the operations at the surface are best known at the moment, whereas micro- and especially macro-semantic operations have only recently very tentatively been studied, because of the lack of an adequate semantic theory.

We have to stress however, as in the first part of this book, that surface operations may be formally conditioned by underlying structures and rules. The assignment of textual FUNCTIONS ('meanings') to some specific surface operations seems to operate before the general phonological rules of G_N. It is not the case, as it seems to be, that fully derived linguistic (grammatical) strings serve as input for literary rules. These have to operate first in order to explain the different types of constraints and restrictions upon lexical insertions.

1.3. The rules defining the specific literary operations in principle have a rather GENERAL character. They do not describe structures peculiar to a literature in one language. When we take examples from English and French, this is only for practical reasons. Our hypothesis is that their basic properties are common to all literatures. In actual derivation they generate texts of a particular language often together with the language specific linguistic rules necessary for such a description.

Since literary rules co-operate with these linguistic rules, some specific implications of the operations are, however, restricted to particular languages. Syntactic permutations in Latin and also in German (and in general in languages with overt case systems) are of course syntactically, though not stylistically, less important than those in French and English. Some literary rules are therefore absent or less frequent in some particular languages because of the non-specific character of the structures generated by them.

The language specific literary rules occur above all in surface structure. Semantic operations, if we assume universality of deep structures, have a still more general nature. This is especially the case for textual macro-operations, e.g. in narrative texts.

1.4. For reasons of simplicity and coherence we further will often take our examples not only from English and French texts, but also from a rather restricted historical period: 'modern literature'. This rather vague label will not be defined. For poetry we refer to examples from its development in France since Rimbaud, Mallarmé and especially since Appolinaire and Surrealism. In English literature we take some examples from poetry since Eliot. German examples are also taken from the system established since Expressionism. For narrative structures we will take a much more general view, although we will refer especially to narrative since Sterne, Balzac and the Russian novelists of the 19th century.

We will not give specific rules for dramatic texts. These are considered to be narrative structures having specific performance implications, which we do not treat at the moment. Observe that we do not want to provide rules for the description of specific poems or novels, however. We will only occasionally give some concrete examples to illustrate our argument, which will essentially be abstract and general and guided by our global knowledge (intuition) of the conventions determining the literariness of certain structures and texts.

1.5. From this very rough delimitation of our material to a global synchronic part of modern literature, we can already see that the differentiation of different basic TYPES of literary texts seems inevitable. That is, many literary rules seem to be specific for distinct types of literary texts, and hardly define literature in general. These rules therefore make up specific SUB-GRAMMARS for these different 'languages' of literature. We will see that surface operations primarily define poetic texts, whereas semantic macro-operations above all underlie the generation of narrative (cf. van Dijk [1972d]).

We will treat, however, the different structures from a general point of view without systematic reference to the formal definition of literary types. Moreover, there are many types of literary development of which the texts must be generated by rules which in later or earlier periods seem to be restricted to specific types. Prosody for example, until the middle-ages and later in seventeenth-century drama, co-occurs with specific narrative structures (epic, 'heroic poetry').

The precise diachronical distribution of the rules will not concern us here, we must limit ourselves to their general abstract properties.

1.6. It is impossible to define *a priori* the FORM of the rules of a literary grammar. As we saw, often they are even merely limited to specific CONSTRAINTS and (con)textual restrictions upon formation rules of G_N. In principle we will try however to use, first heuristically then systematically, the expansive rewrite rules of generative syntax and phonology. Deeper rules will be formulated in accordance with proposals from generative semantics (cf. Part I). Macro-rules will have the form of those rules suggested for macro-derivation in chapter 3.

Apart from these formation rules, constraints, selection restrictions and 'extensions', we'll use TRANSFORMATIONAL RULES to account for literary structures. Many of them have already been described more or less explicitly in classical and modern rhetorics (cf. Lausberg [1960], Dubois, *et al.* [1970]), which stresses their universal character as linguistic extension or complementary rules. The basic types of transformations are similar to those of linguistics: (i) ADDITION, (ii) DELETION, (iii) SUBSTITUTION (which might be defined by (i) and (ii), and (iv) PERMUTATION. We might add REPETITION as a fifth basic operation, but it is uncertain whether we can consider it transformationally, instead of as a specific (recursive) property of formation rules.

2. PHONOLOGICAL OPERATIONS

2.1. *Introduction*

2.1.1. The phonological operations underlying literary texts have probably received the most explicit treatment of traditional literary theory. Prosody was, from classical periods until the 20th century, a comparatively exact part of normative poetics and the classification of metrical 'figures', like 'feet', 'verses', 'stanza-forms', etc. is still part of the education programmes in literature at school.

In this domain, then, we have sufficient observational and taxonomic data to attempt a characterization of the rules on which the prosodic structures are based.[1]

2.1.2. First of all, phonological operations in modern literature seem to be dominantly restricted to what is known as poetry, that is to 'verse', although modern poetry has abolished most of the prosodic systems of classical literature.

As we remarked earlier, prosody was by no means restricted to lyrical texts. Classical epic and drama, as well as all medieval texts, also have systems of versification. The rules, in general, are therefore independent of specific semantic representations determining the 'subject' of the text. Conversely, this does not prevent the choice of specific prosodic elements of meter and rhyme both determining and being determined by lexical selection.

2.1.3. We should recall, further, that many phonological operations in literary texts depend – at least in the majority of cases – upon the phonological systems of given languages. A metric system based on stress cannot as such, underlie surface structures based on vowel length. Similarly, languages having only vowels in initial positions cannot have assonance and consonantal alliteration.

This statement is roughly true, but it does not imply a total dependence of literary rules upon the exact phonological structure of the language. Especially in classical literature could the metric system dominate the structures of G_N, creating deviations from intonational and stress pattern of normal phonological structures. The use of metrical systems in French literature, for example, imposes a stress distribution which goes counter its normal clause stress. In such cases two different consequences are possible: either the metrical system is – at the surface – adapted to the phonological structure of normal language, thus creating specific rhythmic 'deviations' of performance (which could lead to certain degrees of esthetic evaluation), or normal phonological structures are submitted to the metrical system. The choice between these two possibilities depends on the historical development of the literary system. The trend of most modern literatures has followed the first possibility.

2.1.4. Phonological and graphemic operations can be described by METRIC and NON-METRIC rules. The first type is very unusual for texts of natural language because it implies NUMERICAL elements, i.e. variables that can take fixed values in the derivation of specific types of texts. To generate a sonnet for example we will probably have to use the integer 14 to be able to stop the derivation exactly after 14 lines. Numerical

---

[1] A modern survey of traditional work in metrics has been provided by Chatman (1964). Research in this domain ranges from linguistics and phonetics to literary theory and musicology and cannot be mentioned here. Many modern studies have already been prefigured by formalist work, e.g. Žirmunskij (1966). Cf. *Poetics* etc. 2 (1966) and Levý, ed. (1966). Further the contributions in Sebeok, ed. (1960), Chatman and Levin, eds. (1967), Doležel and Bailey, eds. (1969), Kreuzer and Gunzenhäuser, eds. (1965) and Freeman, ed. (1970). For generative approaches, see below.

214   SURFACE OPERATIONS

elements thus impose restrictions on the theoretically infinite length of lines, sentences, stanzas and whole texts. Phonological and graphemic rules co-operate here.

Non-metric phonological rules can also imply certain regularities of recurrence, but these are not numerically fixed by an existing prosodic system. Alliteration and non-metric rhymes belong to this category.

We can say that non-metric phonological rules seem to dominate in modern literature. Metrical structures are now considered too artificial, because the lexical constraints they can imply are too heavy for the construction of an intended semantic representation. The knowledge of the exact nature of these constraints can serve as an explanation of the performance aspects which have led to a change of literary systems, a problem of diachronical poetics which will remain outside our scope.

The presence of numerical elements in literary rules (not in ad hoc types of constructions, especially in the Middle-Ages), indeed, recalls some aspects of artificial languages (cf. Nebeský [1971]). In this sense the extension rules of G_L seem to intersect partially with some rules of algebraic languages. This can also be noticed in the pictorial and especially in the architectonic arts. We will not go further into the general semiotic relevance of 'number' in the arts, but only wish to stress the very exceptional existence of numerical elements in rules for text generation. We may even say that such metrical rules are in a sense those which are most specific for literary systems in general. All other rules, somehow, are also possible in non-literary texts. This is one explanation for the fact that in periods having only written texts with a prosodic-metrical structure, the very concept of 'literature' could not be opposed to non-literary written texts but only to spoken discourse.

2.2. *Non-metrical structures*

2.2.1. Let us consider first some NON-METRICAL structures of literary texts, like alliteration, rhyme, assonance, etc. We should observe from the outset that these structures are not wholly restricted to literary texts. They also characterize some forms of affective speech, some fixed non-productive expressions of L_N, and advertisements. This sort of boundary crossing between textual types does not matter for the general description of literature, because it is not the case, mostly, that only one of such structures characterizes the literary text. Occasional non-metric surface operations are hardly decisive about the literariness of texts. If they do occur, however, they are assigned a specific literary function, because their presence in non-literary language is considered a non-systematic aspect of performance.

2.2.2. The basic property of both metric and non-metric structures is undoubtedly RECURRENCE. To account for this, we have to construct rules that, under specific conditions, generate strings with identical elements. Such rules will be needed at many levels of description. They are not unknown in G_N, where rules exist that require identical elements in previous clauses or sentences: cf. the conditions for pronominalization and other surface coherence constraints discussed in Part I. Similarly we have, for example in French, rules for congruence between adjective and noun, and in many other languages between verb and noun (subject), or between other constituents often resulting in repeated endings, etc. The types of context-sensitive rules used for the description of such DISCONTINUOUS structures are mostly placed in the transformational component, where the required identity of parts of the structural description can be explicitly given in the conditions. It is not impossible, however, to introduce these specific conditions on well-formedness at a deeper level, because the constraint of identity often has to operate before lexematization. Lexematization in principle takes place within the limits defined by textual and sentential semantic representation. That is, in literary derivation there is no substitution of an already inserted appropriate lexeme by another having partially identical morphophonological structure with previous lexemes. Such a substitution probably would lead to semantically and syntactically ungrammatical strings.

2.2.3. We shall not discuss traditional problems denoted by such terms as 'sound-symbolism', etc. These do not seem to have systematic character on the competence level. Any type of psychological association based on certain sound patterns or individual sounds belongs to the study of literary performance. Moreover, the experimental data in this area are theoretically hardly significant (but cf. especially the work of Fónagy [1965], [1966]) while most extant work in this field is wholly based on unexplicated intuition (cf. Delbouille, [1961]).

Let us stress only that no semantic representations can be formed with the aid of isolated or discontinuous sounds alone. Whether such sounds, that is specific recurrences or specific feature qualities of phonemes, can 'underline' independently (lexically) established semantic representations may be doubted. This is a problem belonging to psycholinguistics (psychophonetics) and to psychopoetics.

2.2.4. We will first try, then, to study the rules determining non-metric rules based on the principle of phonematic recurrence. The abstract condition for such structures is very simple and can be defined for all linguistic categories as follows

P_1. $\quad$ RECUR$(x) =_{def} (\exists y)[\text{PRECEDE}(y, x) \wedge (x \equiv y)]$
$\quad$ where the variables may be substituted by constants, representing phonemes, morphemes, etc.

The connection established in this case is equivalence, which is of course symmetric and transitive. We cannot therefore define operations like alliteration, assonance and rhyme as 'units' or 'properties' but have to consider them as RELATIONS. The often noted specifically structured character of literary texts is not only derived from the 'normal' textual relationships between sentences (cf. Part I) but is also established by such 'complementary' relations, which belong to C_S (a subset of G_L).

For reasons of simplicity we will further assume that the equivalence constraint in a derivation will be formulated for the second, third ... n^{th} term of the relation and not for the first term which will be considered as linearly preceding and therefore 'given' in linear derivation of the (pre-)terminal string. Thus in P_1: if x precedes y and if x has phonological properties P, then y must also have the phonological properties P.

A rule introducing for example an alliteration relation, will then be inserted roughly as follows in a derivation:

P_2 (i) $X \to a$
          (ii) $Y \to b | ALL(a, -)$

where X and Y are pre-terminal (syntactic or semantic) categories and a and b morphophonologically represented lexemes (we here neglect the exact matrix schema of a and b); '|' denotes 'with the condition that'; a followed by a horizontal line denotes '(of) preceding a'; and the hypothetical complex symbol 'ALL' denotes 'in alliterative relation with', which clearly SPECIFIES THE CONTEXTUAL CONDITION.

We could further analyse the complex symbol ALL into a set of features, roughly as follows:

$$P_{DEF_1} \qquad ALL \to \begin{bmatrix} + \text{ INITIAL} \\ + \text{ IDENTITY} \\ + \text{ CONSONANT(S)} \end{bmatrix}$$

This rule, however, does not belong to the grammar itself because it gives a (universal) definition of alliteration, and therefore belongs to the theory of literary grammars. Its 'content' is automatically implied by the use of symbol ALL. The result is that in P_2 (ii) a morpheme b is selected having identical initial consonant(s) with a preceding morpheme a (cf. for detail, Valesio [1968]).

Notice that P_2 is an abstract schema for a SEQUENCE OF RULES. Rule (i) and (ii) for example do not necessarily follow each other immediately; other morphemes having different initial consonants may be inserted between them. Theoretically the 'distance' between the two related terms can be infinite, but it goes without saying that performance conditions are necessary to define the range of perception of the relation. This range is larger if the elements repeated are larger. Repeated words or whole sentences are memorized and perceived better than repeated phonemes, also because this last recurrence does not have any semantic function.

Similar rules can be used for the description of assonance and rhyme. We will need, then, the specific symbols ASS and RIM, which can be theoretically defined by the following rules:

$$P_{DEF_2} \qquad ASS \to \begin{bmatrix} + \text{ EQUIVALENCE} \\ \pm \text{ INITIAL} \\ - \text{ TERMINAL} \\ + \text{ VOWEL(S)} \end{bmatrix}$$

P_{DEF_3} $RIM \rightarrow$ $\begin{bmatrix} + \text{ EQUIVALENCE} \\ + \text{ TERMINAL} \\ X \ \{[\text{CONS}]^n \\ \text{VOWEL } [\text{CONS}]^m\} \ Y \end{bmatrix}$

In the definition of assonance we notice that it applies both to initial and to non-initial vowels. It might be the case that initial assonance is considered a form of alliteration. These are matters of convention which we will not discuss.

The definition of rhyme is somewhat more complex and traditionally depends on such language specific phenomena as stress and value of vowels. Recurrence patterns are based on a terminal vowel but optionally n consonants may precede and m may follow this vowel; X and Y denote any preceding and following string of phonemes, which may also have the same recurrent pattern. A further convention will be that the vowel is stressed, and may be followed in some languages (e.g. Italian) by another syllable with an unstressed vowel. Small curled brackets indicate syllable boundaries.

The definition of rhyme is very general and has to be restricted when rhymes in final verse position have to be described. We could then introduce a feature $[+ \text{TERM}_{\text{verse}}]$ for example. Another, simpler, solution is to use boundary symbols necessary to define verselines, e.g. '$\dashv$', as a complementary contextual constraint, optionally coinciding with the sentence or clause boundary '$\#$' when no enjambement has to be generated

P_3 $(...)$
              (i) $X \rightarrow n|RIM(m,-)$
              (ii) $Y \rightarrow \#$
              (iii) $Z \rightarrow \dashv$

with the condition that X immediately precedes Y and Y immediately precedes Z.

We should finally notice that the repeated elements are not necessarily phonemes, i.e. whole feature configurations, but may also be smaller feature configurations, thus defining WEAK versions of the relations described. Thus /p/ and /b/, /t/ and /d/ might produce weak alliteration, and /i/ and /e/ weak assonance and rhyme. In order to be able to operate therefore, the given rules, must contain feature matrices, from which the rule not only reads identity (equivalence) of two phonemes but also semi-equivalence. The variables in P_1, P_2, P_3 represent these matrices, according to the usual rules of generative phonology (cf. Chomsky and Halle [1968]).

2.2.5. In the preceding paragraph we generated equivalence of two elements in a string (text) by a specific context restriction upon lexematization of a second element, the first element then being considered already inserted. Intuitively, however, this description does not seem to be wholly satisfactory. More in general, we would like to have a constraint upon a given string, i.e. upon two or more elements of the string, not upon one element of it. We want to represent formally this intuitive, hypothetical structure, for example with the use of dummy symbols dominated by the labels of the

operation: *ASS* or *ALL* or *RIM*. In that case the selection of the first lexeme (morpheme) is also determined by the second. The specific dummy symbols will dominate
both morphemes, and the convention to be formulated for them would be: select a
morpheme having a phonological structure equivalent, as specified by the features of
ALL, *ASS* or *RIM*, with another morpheme also dominated by the same dummy
symbol (where Greek letters represent features and Roman letters represent phonemes).

(1)

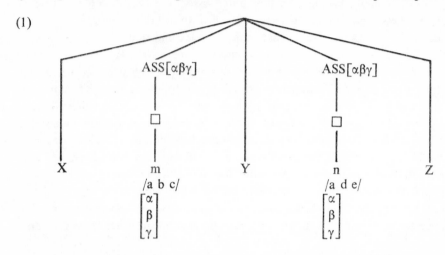

A third possibility is probably equivalent to the previous one: specify for both *m*
and *n* a specific (recurrence) context restriction, as in P_2 and P_3. No dummy symbol
would then be necessary. In fact symbols like *ASS*, *ALL* and *RIM* themselves function
as such 'restricting' symbols for correct lexical insertion.

2.2.6. It might finally be asked whether a further step of generalization should not be
made. That is, the generated structures all share the fundamental property of RE-
CURRENCE (repetition of identical elements). We could probably DERIVE the described
structures from this basic category, instead of formulating several additional pre-
terminal symbols in the theory of literary grammar. In that case we would have to
specify in the derivation the contextual rule by a COMPLEX SYMBOL *REP*, for repetition
and then choose between the different possible realizations of *REP*: [+ INITIAL] or
[− INITIAL], [+ CONSONANT] or [+ VOWEL], [+ TERMINAL] or
[− TERMINAL].
   This type of description will probably have advantages over the more specific ones
given above, because it allows for the derivation of other types of recurrence: alternation of elements, antithetic repetition, etc. applied also to other elements: syllables,
morphemes, etc. These types also have specific names in classical rhetoric, and it
seems too complicated to introduce each time a new pre-terminal literary (prosodic)
symbol. This type of rule would also account for recurrence at other levels: morphological, syntactic and semantic. It is not yet clear where this general rule would have to

be introduced into the derivational process. It is obvious, however, that rules repeating whole lines or stanzas and rules repeating semantical elements have to be applied deeper than phonological rules, which need only operate after the formation of semantic representations and before concrete lexematization. We will come back to these rule-ordering problems below.

2.3. *Metrical structures*

2.3.1. Some types of non-metric structures, such as rhymes, can be inserted into METRICAL SCHEMATA, which must be described by complex METRICAL RULES and rule sequences, to which we will now turn. In opposition to non-metrical rules, these rules probably should be considered to be CYCLICAL. That is, they also indicate specific constraints upon the selection of morphemes, upon the length of clauses and sentences, etc., but these constraints re-apply regularly for each morpheme, and/or syntagm, and/or clause, and/or sentence of the text. For example, when we want to derive a text which has a perfectly regular iambic structure we either apply the schema $X\acute{X}$ (where X is an unmarked element and $\acute{X}$ is a marked element) arbitrarily such that a phonetic representation is marked in that way, independently of normal stress distribution, or the schema underlies lexical insertion such that only morphemes and morpheme combinations, i.e. strings, are derived with this schema cyclically applied. This latter case will normally be the most natural 'integration' of the metrical structure into the normal phonological pattern.

Metrical schemata can have different scope. They normally apply to syllables, verses and stanzas. In all these cases we have to use a variable to indicate the number of times it should apply. Fixed values of the variables are thus associated with fixed verse types (e.g. alexandrines) and fixed text types (e.g. sonnets). The differences depend on the literary system of a given period and culture. Certain of these periods have highly sophisticated systems; others, like the modern periods in poetry, practically have no metrical systems.

2.3.2. Some metrical systems apply not only to one line, but to a whole text. The terms SCHEMA or PLAN, already used to denote underlying semantic structures of texts, can also be used for these macro-phonological (and macro-graphematic) structures. These underlie the whole text and impose rather severe constraints upon lexical insertion. The resulting structure thus receives a 'hyper-structural' character. Apparently, we must assume that textual derivation is dominated both by a semantic 'plan' and by an (optional) metrical 'plan'. In fact, we therefore might use the term 'metrical deep structure', although this structure seems immediately observable in surface structure. If no transformation rules change these structures they may also be MACRO-SURFACE STRUCTURES, determined by a schema having linear surface structure as its scope.

However, the proper metrical schemata must be thought of as underlying plans. They are very abstract in their 'canonical' forms. Moreover, their realization in linear surface structure may undergo different transformations, e.g. in the combination with the normal stress pattern of the sentence. The resulting structure, then, is usually referred to as 'rhythm'. Furthermore, metrical elements may be added or deleted by transformation under specific phonological conditions: position in the verse, at the caesura or in initial or final position. These complex conditions are well-known in traditional metrics and the transformations can easily be formulated[2].

The part of the literary phonological component generating these structures will be assumed to follow the semantic component, but it is not clear whether it also follows the syntactic component, because the (trans)formation of syntactic structures seems to be at least partially dependent upon the boundaries imposed by the metrical component.

2.3.3. Before we can say more about the ordering of these metrical rules among or before the rules of syntax, and 'normal' surface phonology, we should consider their possible form.

A preliminary question is the hypothetic introduction of METRICAL CATEGORIES such as 'stanza', 'verse', and 'foot', or 'metrical segment', as the immediate constituents of metrical text structure.

We could begin a tentative derivation with simple expansion rules of the rewrite type, with an initial symbol T. However, this symbol was expanded by macro-semantic rules and is not characteristic for phonological structures of texts. Let us therefore first try to introduce independently a provisional initial symbol M indicating a macro-textual metrical structure. This notion is fully abstract and does not depend upon a specific text, it is merely a formal system which must be mapped onto textual surface structures. Such a 'metrical derivation' would have a form roughly as follows

$$(2) \qquad P_4 \quad \begin{array}{ll} \text{(i)} & M \rightarrow (STR)^m \quad (m \geqslant 1) \\ \text{(ii)} & STR \rightarrow (VS)^n \quad (n \geqslant 1) \\ \text{(iii)} & VS \rightarrow (P)^o \quad (o \geqslant 1) \\ \text{(iv)} & P \rightarrow \begin{Bmatrix} X\ \acute{X} \\ \acute{X}\ X \\ X\ X\ \acute{X} \\ X\ \acute{X}\ X \\ \acute{X}\ X\ X \\ \acute{X}\ \acute{X} \\ \dots \\ \dots \end{Bmatrix} \end{array}$$

when $XX(X)$ is a metrical segment. These segments may group into specific combinations, but often the same segment type is recursively applied. Depending on the

[2] Recent studies in metrics have been based on generative phonology and make use of transformational notions. The exploratory article in this field was that by Halle and Keyser (1966). First reactions were Beaver (1970). Cf. also the work of Keyser (1969), Kiparsky (1970), Valesio (1971). A special issue on this topic of *Poetics*, edited by Ihwe and Beaver, is in preparation. Cf. now also Halle & Keyser (1971), Halle (1970), Roubaud (1971), Beaver (1971).

language, $\acute{X}$ may in surface structure be represented as a stressed syllable or as a long syllable, and X as an unstressed syllable or as short one (see below for some detail).

2.3.4. If such an 'independent' derivation is roughly correct it is crucial to relate metrical structures thus derived with the phonological and graphical structure of the text. The theoretical difficulties one meets here are considerable and are similar to those encountered in the formal relations between semantics and syntax. The problem is additionally complex because, as in G_N syntax, the metrical rules do not apply in only one order but seem to interrelate at different levels with syntactic rules, lexematization and phonological rules of G_N.

We might consider M and its specification as a component of the textqualifier *Tql*, because this symbol has the whole text as its scope. In that case the operations not only affect semantic representations but also a global phonological surface structure. If Assertion, Question and probably also *NARR* and *POET* might be introduced to define basic TYPES of texts, we may optionally associate with these last (two) categories the symbol M of which the specification would then operate as a TEXTUAL CONSTRAINT upon the derivation of *Prop*. Pre-lexical structures are then transformed into syntactic and morpho-phonematic strings with the required form.

We could represent this structural description in the following graph

(3)

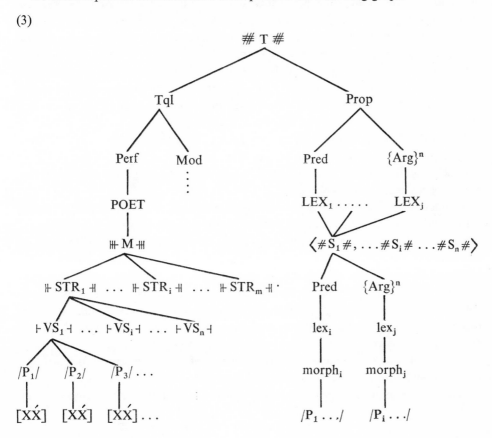

Where ' ⧺ ', ' ⊩ ', '⊢' and '/' indicate metrical text, stanza-, verse-, and foot boundaries. When the variable subscripts of the categories dominated by M have been assigned specific values, we can begin with the generation of the morphematic strings dominated by the linearly ordered set $\langle S_1, \ldots S_i, \ldots S_n \rangle$. A set of specific conventions will then operate, for example to establish coincidences between the sentence boundaries '$\#$' and the verse boundaries '⊣'.

Notice that the symbols of M may have both a phonological and GRAPHEMATIC function. Verse boundary symbols thus may coincide with line boundary symbols. These do not always coincide however: metrical verses are not necessarily restricted to one line. After the boundary symbol ' ⊪ ' for stanzas we will automatically have at least one graphematic zero sequence, that is one 'white line'.

2.3.5. In specifying underlying metrical structure as part of Tql we in fact evaded the problem of the precise RULES relating such structures with phonological and graphological surface structure. Recent developments in generative metrics precisely endeavour to formulate such rules, of which the status and place have roughly been described above. In these approaches, however, there are no formation rules for underlying metrical structures as we tried to formulate them in (2). The problem there was that apparently no sufficiently general conditions can be formulated for the syntax of metrical 'morphemes', i.e. the traditional feet, in the verse-line or 'metrical sentence'. Some metrical systems, e.g. the classical hexametre require six dactyls of which the last may optionally be also a spondaeus. Other forms of alexandrines permit combinations of other feet, like anapaest or amphibrachus. Although the possible combinations are high in number, they are certainly finite at the level of the verse. Theoretically, however, the different combinations throughout the whole text structure are infinite, as is asserted by the rule schemata.

The problem, then, consists in relating these underlying metrical schemata with surface structure. Generative metrics has called such rules 'mappings' and we may consider them therefore as a type of transformations substituting metrical elements by phonological/graphological elements.

The main mapping rule, in fact, substitutes a non-marked metrical element (X) by a non-marked syllable and a marked element ($\acute{X}$) by a marked syllable. More precisely the mapping relates the metrical structure with the prosodic (suprasegmental) structures of the phonological representation: we do not select an independent syllable, but we require as a condition that lexemes are generated and a syntactic structure constructed of which the phonological representation has features like stress, length, tone, etc. which may be considered as marked or unmarked. Like semantic macro-structures, metrical structures thus have syntactic and phonological surface structures: the meter is not (or rarely) imposed *a posteriori* on phonological structures.

Bearing this general problem of the organization of our grammar in mind, we may then formulate the rules in which metrical elements are mapped onto phonological structures. The interesting problem here is precisely that not every metrical element corresponds one to one to a phonological element like the syllable. Some elements may be set into correspondence with more than one syllable, whereas, conversely, more metrical elements may correspond to one syllable. Thus the metrical system of French classicism requires merely two marked elements in the verse: at the caesura and at the end: $XXXXX\acute{X}/XXXXX\acute{X}$. Similar constraints upon a minimum or maximum number of marked elements exist in other metrical systems, e.g. in Germanic and Scandinavian versification. Often these constraints, which are looser than the strict metrical system of Greek and Latin verse, can be explained by the phonological structure of the language: in principle a language will adopt or tend to favour the systems corresponding best to their stress distribution regularities. In French verse a marked element may only coincide with the stressed syllable at the end of a phrase or clause. In the same system we must assign one metrical element to each syllable, including *e*-muet but not to *e*-muet followed by an initial vowel (elision) and not to *e*-muet at the caesura (if admitted) and at the end of the verse. This is only one (complex) rule of the system, which however may be still more complex in more sophisticated systems. Diachronically, the general tendency of such systems is to drop many constraints, such as 'counting' the *e*-muet or the place of a marked syllable at the sixth position.

Metrical schemata not only regulate phonological structure, such as number of syllables, number and distribution of marked (stressed, long, etc.) syllables, but may also underlie the structure of stanzas and whole texts, as was seen in the initial rules of (2). Such schemata determine the number of lines and stanzas but may also determine the distribution of line-lengths throughout the text. They further may determine the distribution of phonological equivalences at the end (or sometimes at initial) positions of the lines: metric rhyme, known from the traditional rhyme schemata. We will not discuss these schemata here and it would not be too difficult to formulate explicitly their rules. They are different for many types of metrical texts and, as was said earlier, we are interested here in their status and in the organization of a metrical component in G_L. The different categories and rules involved automatically lead to formal TYPOLOGIES of metrical structures and metrical texts (Lotz [1960]).

It can be concluded that this relatively explicit part of G_L formulates the rules which traditionally are considered the most specific part of the extensions with respect to G_N. As was remarked above, in modern ('western') literature most metrical systems are abandoned in literary, and in particular narrative, texts, being replaced by less regular rules, such as non-metric phonological and graphological rules, by syntactic rules and by specific semantic rules.

2.4. *Morphematic structures*

2.4.1. In the previous paragraph it has become clear that the phonological rules in fact operate on MORPHEMES, and it would therefore be appropriate to use the term morpho-phonological rules. The abstract features $[\pm$ INITIAL], etc. refer to aspects of the morphematic structure of strings. The recurrence relations were based however on phonemes and/or feature configurations and matrices.

Similar rules, as we saw, can be used for recurrence relations between whole morphemes, either without further restrictions or with specific restrictions on the position (e.g. verse-initial) of the repeated morpheme. It must be stressed that morpheme recurrence is a normal surface phenomenon of textual coherence (cf. Harris [1952] and other structural research in discourse analysis). Only specific types of recurrence, therefore, might be specific for literary texts, e.g. when identical lexemes are not deleted or represented by pronouns or proverbs (for morphematic recurrence in literature cf. Levin [1962], Koch [1970]).

2.4.2. Other types of literary morphological rules are exceptional. Morphemes in literature are in principle those which also characterize the lexicon of G_N. Some types of dada- and other experimental poetry however admit certain transformations of generated morphemes, for example some graphical permutations, deletions and substitutions. Similarly, different or even ambiguous graphematic representations may be used to realize grammatical phonological representations. These operations are *ad hoc* and should be considered specific performance aspects of some writers. Our linguistic and literary competence, however, enables us to 'retro-transform' such surface structures into grammatical morphematic strings, which can be assigned an interpretation. This fact is a further indication of the systematic presence of the abstract (trans-)formational rules in our competence. Such strings are thus often acceptable, even when they should be considered as ill-formed according to G_L, which may be an accidental lack in the system of literary rules.

3. SYNTACTIC OPERATIONS

3.1. *Introduction*

3.1.1. Less systematic than the metrical rules is the set of specific SYNTACTIC OPERATIONS occurring in literary texts. Again, they above all apply in poetic texts. The main traditional account was limited to *ad hoc* descriptions of inversions, which were considered G_L-grammatical in classical metricized texts. In that case they were normally used for metrical reasons or for reason of normal topicalization. They are more frequent in modern poetry, where more extensive use is made of them than in the few permitted cases of inversion in classical literature.

3.1.2. Syntactic operations are relatively easy to describe because of the sophistication of modern syntactic theories. Many systematic syntactic structures of L_L which cannot be described by the rules of G_N can thus be specified with respect to these rules. New rules must, then, be introduced in order to account for the complementary regularities.

The most interesting aspect of these specific structures is probably their theoretical status. It is rather difficult at this level to separate *ad hoc* deviations with respect to the rules of G_N from rare applications of certain postulated rules of G_L. We will therefore treat only those types of rules which seem to have sufficient empirical relevance (conventionality) to be integrated into the literary (poetic) system.

Linguistically, these types of structures, called SEMI-SENTENCES, can also be accounted for by the grammar. This task has been introduced only recently into the theory of generative grammar (cf. Chomsky [1964], Miller and Chomsky [1963]).

The notion of semi-sentence is related to the important notion DEGREE OF GRAMMATICALNESS which had to be introduced to account formally for perfectly acceptable, i.e. interpretable, sentences which do not have a derivable syntactic structure. A generative grammar must assign an index for the degree of grammaticalness of such strings. This procedure has been founded essentially upon the number and rank of the rules of G_N that are NOT applied to derive the string. The characterization of semi-sentences is thus purely negative. Rank is based on the DEPTH and scope of categories. Thus, a rule $S \rightarrow NP\ VP$ is considered as more fundamental than a rule like $VP \rightarrow V$ $(NP)(PrepP)$. Rank is thus defined by relations of dominance. The degree of grammaticalness of semi-sentence S_S is higher if fewer and less important rules are violated (for details, cf. Chomsky [1964], Miller and Chomsky [1963]).

It can be asked next whether this description has theoretical relevance for the description of the relations between syntax and semantics. That is, are semi-sentences of a higher degree of grammaticalness 'easier' to interpret? Take, for example, the following sentences

(5)   The boy is writing a letter to his mother.
(6)   *Boy is writing letter to mother.
(7)   **Boy the writing letter a to mother his.
(8)   *?A letter is writing the boy to his mother.
(9)   ?To his mother the boy is writing a letter.
(10)   *The boy to his mother a letter is writing.
(11)   ***Mother boy letter the a his writing is to.
etc.

According to the rules sentences (6) and (7) should have a higher degree of grammaticalness than sentences (8), (9) and (10), because lower rules are violated in the first set. However, sentences like (7) are much more ill-formed than a sentence like (6). Degrees of grammaticalness also seem to depend on the kind of deviation: deletion is less disturbing than permutation in the lower rules. Further, as we see in (8) and (11), permutation of major categories (NP, VP) seem less disturbing than permutation of minor categories (Art, Aux). A rather grammatical sentence like (6) further shows that the number of violations of the whole sentence do not necessarily change interpretability, since (6) has undergone three deletions and (9) only one permutation.

These few remarks indicate that formal semi-grammaticalness, described by the number and depth of rules and categories involved, is not necessarily related to the degrees of semantic interpretability. Whereas some violations like (6) and (9) are acceptable under certain conditions (in headlines in newspapers, topicalization, emphasis), violations like (7) and especially (11) are fully unacceptable. Precise psychological tests are necessary to find the regularities underlying these degrees of acceptability and interpretability. These seem to be highly correlated, because the acceptability of sentences is probably wholly based on immediate interpretability, even when presented semi-sentences are 'marked' by the hearer as 'awkward', 'baby-language', 'stranger-English', or as 'poetic' (cf. chapter 9).

It is becoming clear that it is impossible to measure different degrees of grammatical-ness only at the level of one sentence. As we will see in the next chapter the degrees of semantic well-formedness seem to be much more important in linguistic communi-cation than degrees of syntactic well-formedness. Strings may be fully grammatical at the sentence level (*colourless green ideas sleep furiously*, etc.) but have to be marked as NON-SENSE STRINGS (if no process of metaphorization applies) because of their semantic ill-formedness. We will come back to this problem in the next chapter. We will assume however as a working hypothesis that syntactic rules in G_L in principle cover well-formed representations. That is, any operation must be relatable either through normal syntactic rules of G_N or directly through rules of G_L with interpretable underlying structures (cf. Patton [1968], Butters [1970]).

3.1.3. There are two different ways of describing syntactic structures that are specific of literary texts. In the previous paragraph we implicitly described sentences (6)-(11) in TRANSFORMATIONAL terms as if they were derived from a grammatical structure like (5). In that case some permutations and some deletions must be postulated (cf. van Dijk, [1970b], [1970f], [1971a], [1971b], [1971c], [1972b]).

The advantages of such a transformational description should be clear. First of all, the specific structures can thus be reduced to regular underlying structures, which in turn can be assigned well-formed semantic representations according to the rules of G_N. The 'automatism' of our knowledge of the rules of L_N would, in performance, force us to reduce irregularities to the regularities of our L_N-competence. This must certainly be the case for readers not having acquired specific literary rules. Specific structures are then simply marked as deviations. Although psychological tests can hardly provide evidence about the internal organization of our grammar, we might try to find some empirical correlates for this secondary and late generation of literary syntactic structures (cf. Fowler [1969] who considers the interpretation of ill-formed structures to be a performance-skill).

However, a full transformational account also has serious drawbacks, both of a formal and of an intuitive nature. Although form and order of the rules of a grammar are probably not directly related to the exact cognitive processes of production and reception, it might be doubted whether, in literary texts, we must always first generate (and produce) regular structures and then transform these into the deviating or literary structures. It seems more 'natural' that irregular syntactic forms are directly related to semantic representations.

In that case the specific rules would be FORMATION RULES (according to the standard-syntax) or transformational rules among all other syntactic transformations necessary to represent semantic representations at the surface (according to generative semantic models). Such rules have to be considered optional among the G_N rules of G_L, because the normal rules are always admitted and because the literary rules are not obligatory. This more 'direct' conception of literary operations underlines the linguistic equivalence of the two types of rules: literary syntactic structures need not be conceived of as 'derived' or 'secondary' in this formal sense but are surface structures in their own right, that is, possessing their own specific relations with semantic deep structures. This is possible, linguistically, because of the often irrelevant language-specific syntactic surface structure for the construction of these semantic representations.

There is another formal argument in favour of a formational description. It prevents us from generating categories and lexemes which are not realized in surface structure and of which the presence in deep structure cannot be assessed. A transformational description, or any other description first generating well-formed strings according to G_N, would require specification of these categories and selection of lexemes which need not be present. Especially when it should turn out that the requirement of well-formedness at the semantic level does not hold, this transformational syntactic account is not possible, because 'normal' semantic representations are needed as input to 'normal' syntactic rules. An interpretative semantic component, operating after the syntactic component, would not resolve this difficulty, because in its turn it does not account, or does so only inadequately, for the probably more important fact that ill-formed syntactic structures can be assigned well-formed semantic representations (interpretations).

Though this last series of arguments is relevant, we will provisionally assume that the syntactic rules of G_L are TRANSFORMATIONS (which is no problem, of course, if it should turn out that all syntactic rules are transformational, i.e. mapping deep structures onto surface forms). The reasons are those given above and we hope that they lead to greater simplicity in our description. The many different types of literary syntactic structures can thus be reduced to some simple but specific transformational operations, whereas otherwise many different base rules would have to be optionally introduced. One transformation TYPE, like permutation, can thus account for per-mutation at all levels of derivation, that is both of *NP VP* and of *Det N*, etc.[3]

---

[3] The analysis of literary syntax in generative transformational terms has been a major development of modern poetics and stylistics. Although many discussions of principles were presented, the status of these structures has never been made explicit. In most descriptions they are considered to be stylistic deviations from the grammatical norm. Only in some cases is an autonomous specific syntax advocated. Cf. the work cited in the previous chapter and especially Fowler (1966), Ohmann (1964, 1967), Bezzel (1969), Levin (1963, 1964, 1965), Thorne (1965, 1969, 1970), Baumgärtner (1969), Hendricks (1969a), van Dijk (1971c).

3.2. *Some syntactic rules for modern poetry*

3.2.1. We will now give examples of some syntactic transformations. Examples are taken at random from modern poetry, especially French modern poetry, of the last fifty years. The status of such examples is of course problematic, because they might be individual stylistic realizations of the rules of G_N. Their general and systematic character has to be established by extensive empirical observation. This is necessary, because it is hardly possible, in modern poetry, to construct relevant counterexamples to the rules, as if ANY syntactic structure occurring in a poem would take a 'literary' character.

This point is crucial for the validation of the predictions of our grammar of course. However, we know, from intuition and from observation, that some operations occur regularly in poetry, and others do not. We will base these rules therefore on observed and postulated regularities, without trying to construct counter-examples i.e. sentences with them, which definitely do not possess a literary character. As we have seen earlier, this literariness is decided for the whole text, and not for isolated sentences. It is more precise, therefore, to speak not of literary structures, but of specific syntactic operations of literary texts.

3.2.2. A first type (cf §1.6. of this chapter) of syntactic transformation is PERMUTATION. It applies, first, to those categories like temporal adverbials which already tend to have a rather unstable position in sentence structure. Consider the following lines

(12)   L'éclaire toutes les nuits son nom silencieux
                                (Pleynet [1963]15)

where the verb with preceding pronominalized direct object has been topicalized. The rule generating this structure would be something like

$$S_1 \qquad \left\{ \begin{array}{l} NP\ VP\ Temp \\ Temp\ NP\ VP \end{array} \right\} \Rightarrow VP\ Temp\ NP$$

We may generalize such a rule and consider it a permutation of *NP*'s having subject function and (in)direct object + *V*:

$$S_2 \qquad NP_1\ NP_2\ V \Rightarrow NP_2\ V\ NP_1$$

or still more generally

$$S_3 \qquad NP\ PredP \Rightarrow PredP\ NP$$

For reasons of thematization any (in)direct object following the main verb may thus be placed in initial position as like in the following lines (in which also, a subject is deleted and represented by an infinitive, which is an admitted rule in some cases of G_N)

(13)   (i)   La simplicité même écrire
            (ii) Pour aujourd'hui la main est là
                        (Eluard [1968]I:298)

These lines are ambiguous and several descriptions are possible: either *simplicité* is direct object of *écrire* (an infinitive without apparent subject, a construction permitted in L_N) or the copula is deleted first (*écrire c'est la simplicité même*) and then the predicate-nominal preposed like in the first case. Deletion of auxiliaries is treated below. The rules for direct object or predicate-nominal preposing would be something like

S_4 (i)   *V NP* $\Rightarrow$ *NP   V*
            (ii) *Cop PredNom* $\Rightarrow$ *PredNom Cop*

Cf. also:

(14)   When that intemperate life I view
            From this temperate October
                        (Barker [1965]97)

This sort of permutation was habitual in classical metrical verse. Although we cannot treat here the specific (*ad hoc*) textual functions of the operations, we can say that syntactic parallellism and semantic antithesis with the next line is established, which is another poetical rule. The rule for (4) could be something like

S_5 NP_1 V $NP_2 \Rightarrow NP_2\ NP_1$ V

Notice that other immediate constituents seem to exist in poetry, for example the combination of subject and verb (NP_1 V) which as a whole may undergo specific transformations.[4] We do not know however whether in a permutation of a string

---

[4] Our analyses in this chapter follow roughly the standard-syntax of Chomsky (1965) and these may be justified independently of the generative base conception in the rest of this book. The literary transformations, therefore, are based on well-known IC-input. In the Direct Object Preposing transformation of S_5, however, it is not wholly clear what should be considered to be the final surface structure. When such a rule in a sense 'extracts' an *NP* from a *VP*, we cannot simply identify *V* as the *VP* of the derived structure, but NP_2 X V would rather form a discontinuous *VP*. Here, as in other examples from modern developments in generative syntax, the status or even the existence of a *VP* node becomes questionable. In such cases a deeper approach to literary syntax may be more adequate. If we follow the formation rules proposed by generative semantics, we would first have an unordered string $\{V, NP_1, NP_2, ... NP_n\}$ on which would apply a specific linearization transformation. Notice that topicalization of direct objects is also possible in L_N. The formational approach to literary structures, as was observed earlier, presupposes identical semantic deep structures to the 'marked' and the 'unmarked' surface structures. The rules in this chapter could, then, be read as follows: on the left of the double arrow we have the unmarked structure and on the right the marked structure.

X Y Z into *X Z Y* we must describe it as if *Z* is placed before *Y* or *Y* after *Z*. This formal uncertainty (which is irrelevant for the resulting surface form) is similar to the problems of the precise theoretical description of transformations in generative grammar, a question which cannot be treated in the framework of this book. We therefore use the general but unspecified term of 'permutation'.

We will not give more examples because the general schema of this type of transformation presents no difficulty. The rules, as was observed before, mainly operate on major categories like *NP*, *V* and *VP*, but not on the combination *Aux V*, nor on lower constituents like *Art N*.

3.2.3. More important are the different DELETION transformations in modern poetry. They are characteristic of many lyrical structures in which a process of 'nominalization' can be observed: i.e. the deletion of verbs in favour of nominal constituents. This type of rule is not excluded in G_N, where it describes exclamations (*Fire!*) and enumerations. The most elementary form of this rule is

S_6 $NP\ PredP \Rightarrow NP\ \emptyset$

applied, for example, in the following lines:

(15)   Sur le train des ailes
              la voix qui s'éteint
              (Reverdy [1964]92)

(16)   Un mouvement de bras
              Comme un battement d'ailes
              (Reverdy [1964]111)

Deletion transformations like these create specific theoretical problems, especially concerning the relations between syntactic and semantic representations. Normally, the deletion of the verbal element heavily truncates the structure of a sentence of which it constitutes the relational nucleus with respect to which the actants have their functional roles. Action and event descriptions, in all cases where no normal nominalization took place before verb deletion, as in (16) (see below), are thus impossible. Such rules can therefore only actualize simplified semantic representations where predicates are reduced to attributions or complements. Verbs like *to be* or *to become* are often automatically by catalysis (Hjelmslev [1943]) supplied in interpretation. The mere occurrence of a noun seems to presuppose (without negative operators) textual 'existence', which can also be concluded from the logical representation of the deep structure of such sentences: there is an *x*, such that *x* is *f*, for instance. We may consider this type of verb deletion to be possible by such elementary presuppositions. As for their general communicative function, we might describe them as cases of reduction of redundancy, i.e. as information productive operations in the statistic sense. The precise psychological, e.g. esthetic, correlates of such operations are not yet clear and belong to a theory of literary performance, to which we will turn in chapter 9.

Very frequently modern poetry realizes a type of verb deletion like the one in (15). The transformational process is more complex here because it is linked with embedded structures (sentences manifested as relative clauses for example) and/or several types of adverbial complementation (*Prep NP*, etc.). In the former case we automatically interpret the verb of the relative clause as the predicate of the noun in the dominating sentoid: *Sur le train des ailes la voix s'éteint*. The rule underlying this operation can be represented as follows

S_7 $NP\ S\ PredP \Rightarrow NP\ S\ \emptyset$

or more precisely

$S_{7'}$ $_{s_i}[NP_i[_{s_j}\ NP_j\ PredP_j]_{s_j}\ PredP_i]_{s_i}] \Rightarrow NP_i\ PRO\ PredP_j\ \emptyset$

where $NP_i = NP_j$, such that $NP_i\ PredP_j$ is interpreted as a propositional unit.

A good example of this operation can be seen in the following lines

(17)   (i)   Le feu qui danse
            (ii)   L'oiseau qui chante
            (iii)   Le vent qui meurt
                 (Reverdy [1964]90)

There are also less strong versions of this rule, for example when not the entire predicate or verb but only auxiliary elements are deleted as in the following example

(18)   (oiseau ...)
            (i)   Et dans le miroir
            (ii)   Son vol touchant le mur
                 (Pleynet [1963]14)

where *PRO* in $S_{7'}$ is presented as a present participle, a construction that can also often be considered to be based on deletion of *to be*.

Sometimes, the predicate function of the deleted verb can be assumed by adverbial elements instead of by a relative clause. Consider the following lines

(19)   Le même courant d'air dans l'œil et dans l'oreille
                        (Reverdy [1964]97)

(20)   (i)   Voyage de silence
            (ii)   De mes mains à tes yeux
                 (Eluard [1968]I, 239)

(21)   Lois sur la vente des juments. Lois errantes
Et nous-mêmes (Couleur d'hommes.)
(Perse [1960]148)

(22)   Cri de corbeau des yeux qu'enfoncent les poings en deuil
(Deguy [1961]87)

We can thus generalize rule S_7 in the following manner:

$$S_8 \qquad NP \begin{Bmatrix} S \\ Prep\ NP \\ Adj \end{Bmatrix} PredP \Rightarrow NP \begin{Bmatrix} S \\ Prep\ NP \\ Adj \end{Bmatrix} \varnothing$$

where all the possible categories between the curled brackets assume the semantic function of a determining, modifying predicate.

Finally, we have already seen that this form of verb deletion can be based on a normal nominalization transformation. In that case the surface form is ungrammatical because there is no *VP*, but the deep structure representation regularly has as predicate the nominalized verb. This is possible because the 'logical form' (Lakoff) of a sentence does not specify grammatical (syntactic) categories at all, only predicates (properties and relations) and bound variables. Thus examples (16), (20) can be considered specific literary nominalizations of the following form (we give only a very rough rule)

$$S_9 \qquad NP\ VP \Rightarrow V_{NOM}\ de\ NP$$

3.2.4. Deletion transformations may also affect NOMINAL constituents, though less frequently. Conditions similar to those for verb deletion seem to hold here: presupposition or (con)-textual presence of the deleted noun. Of course this is trivial because otherwise we would not even know which noun was deleted. The deleted *NP* is mostly subject and is a semantic Agent of the Action denoted by the Verb Phrase. The implied pragmatical *I* of any text may, for example, serve as the deletable category, for example in co-occurrence with infinitive verbs

(23)   Ne pas dire son nom sous la voûte au tréfonds
(Reverdy [1964]347)

(24)   N'avoir rien vu rien compris
(Eluard [1968]I, 244)

(25)   La simplicité même écrire
Pour aujourd'hui la main est là
(ibid. 298)

This type of construction is not excluded in L_N where it serves certain affective stylistic goals. Focus is thus directed towards the verb and its semantic content, as well as to the (in)direct object normally serving as Object or as Patient. Again, the communicative function of this operation is based on redundancy reduction, which is possible due to the underlying presence of a textual Agent. The provisional rule for such deletions is

$$S_{10} \qquad NP_1 \; Aux \; V \; NP_2 \Rightarrow \emptyset \; \emptyset \; V_{INF} \; NP_2$$

or more generally

$$S_{11} \qquad NP \; PredP \Rightarrow \emptyset \; PredP$$

as in the following examples

(26) (i) Fut embaumée, fut lavée d'or
      (ii) Mise au tombeau dans les pierres noires
                    (Perse [1960]I, 116)

(27) (i) Once it was the colour of saying
      (ii) Soaked my table the uglier side of a hill
                    (Thomas [1952]89)

(28) (i)   hat sich geöffnet, nach luft gerungen
      (ii) hat etwas warmes gekannt
      (iii) ah gesagt überm kalten löffel
      (iv) was weiss ein mund
                    (Enzensberger [1967]18)

The absence of an explicit *NP* (*N* or *PRO*-form) – in French – has archaic implications because, as in Latin, in Old French the subject is present in verbal flection. In the lines of Enzensberger, the topic *Mund* need not be repeated, for example under pronominalized form, in order to represent the semantic deep structure of the respective sentences of the poem. The verbal predicates alone are relevant (as comments or themata) for the semantic information development.

3.2.5. Finally, we find both in poetry and in newspaper headings (cf. Rieser [1971]) the deletion of DETERMINERS, especially of the article, of which the partially redundant character is well-known and which is fully predicted by semantic deep structures (cf. Chap. 2). The simple rule can be stated as follows

$$S_{11} \qquad Art \; N \Rightarrow \emptyset \; N$$

and is realized in lines like

(29)   Fragmentation est la source
                (Pleynet [1963]17)

(30)   Présence exacte qu'aucune flamme désormais ne saurait restreindre; (...)
                                                          (Bonnefoy [1953]28)

(31)   My world is pyramid
                (Thomas [1952]31)

(32)   Cri de corbeau des yeux qu'enfoncent les poings en deuil
                                              (Deguy [1961]87)

In many cases article deletion is manifesting itself in typical lyrical exclamatory constructions (cf. (30)) where the verb phrase is also deleted.

3.2.6. Not only elements occurring within the structures of the sentence but also intersentential elements like CONJUNCTIONS, ADVERBS, etc. can often be deleted in modern poetry. That is, surface constraints for textual coherence can differ from texts in L_N. The modern poem, in general, has few conjunctions because long complex sentences with many embeddings are mainly characteristic of narrative. Where they are necessary in the lyrical text they may be omitted according to the general principle of reduction of redundancy, because conjunctions are at least partially predictable from the SR's of the text.

Conversely, we also meet the realization of conjunctions, e.g. the selection of *and* at the beginning of a sentence, which does not correspond to the semantic relation between the subsequent sentences (sentoids).

The general rule may be formulated as follows

$$S_{12} \qquad S_i \ \& \ S_{i+1} \Rightarrow S_i \ \varnothing \ S_{i+1}$$

where '&' represents any connective lexeme (*and, but, because, if, though, ...*). Some examples are

(33)   (i)   La solitude l'absence
             (ii) Et ses coups de lumière
             (iii) Et ses balances
             (iv) N'avoir rien vu rien compris
                      (Eluard [1968]I, 244)

(34)   Fut embaumée, fut lavée d'or
             Mise au tombeau dans les pierres noires
                            (Perse [1960]I, 116)

In (33) both processes occur, deletion of *et* in (i) and (iv) and addition in (iii). These operations are well-known in classical rhetorics under the names of asyndeton and polysyndeton. They both result in different types of PARALLELISM, a structure typical of literary texts (see below).

3.2.7. There are some general CONDITIONS for this type of literary operation. Deletions are normally possible only if

(i) the deleted element is semantically redundant or syntactically implied in the sentence: auxiliaries, articles, verbs like *to be* and *to have*,
(ii) the deleted element is semantically redundant in the text, like the deep structure Agents normally pronominalized in surface structure,
(iii) the deleted element is not relevant when other elements of the sentence are to be placed in special focus.

In general we may conclude that L_L at this level of syntactic surface structure permits a more direct manifestation of semantic deep structures, without the numerous constraints on well-formedness prescribed by G_N. We could even say that in many cases the transformations are RETRO-TRANSFORMATIONS to more 'primitive' stages of the derivational process. If this is true, it is obviously misleading to speak of literary operations as 'secondary' with respect to the 'normal' grammatical rules. It would be more adequate, then, to say that L_L has more possibilities of representing well-formed SR's at the surface levels than L_N. In performance this larger set of possibilities makes choice more 'difficult', such that the information of the surface forms increases. This fact shows convergence with the general tendency of redundancy reduction, characterizing literary deletions in general (cf. chap. 9).

3.2.8. In the previous paragraph we have already seen that the converse operation of ADDITION takes place in literary texts. However, the literary character of this transformation is less decisive than that of the other operations, because additions hardly seem to produce structures which are ungrammatical in L_N. They may contribute to certain types of irregular redundancy, as in polysyndeton, which may often be formed by cancelling normal deletion transformations or substitution transformations. The repetition of nouns instead of *PRO*-forms is a well-known instance of such a structure

(35)   Lois sur la vente des juments. Lois errantes (...)
                      (Perse [1960]148)

We will see below that this type of identical addition leads to general operations of recurrence.

3.2.9. A final literary transformation, SUBSTITUTION, is not only characteristic of the syntactic level but also defines semantic transformations like metaphorizations. We may describe, first, all sorts of categorial transformations in this perspective. Such a well-known example as the line by Cummings studied by Levin (1962)

(36)   He danced his did

may be considered as a substitution of a $N(P)$ by a $V(P)$ (for G_N re-categorization, cf Lyons [1968]282). In many cases the operation is ambiguous and takes place at several levels: morphological, syntactic and semantic, because categorial substitutions imply both morphematic and lexical shifts. Consider for example

(37)   I fellowed sleep who kissed me in the brain
                              (Thomas [1952]26)

(38)   Once it was the colour of saying
                              (ibid. 89)

where a noun takes verbal flections and where a verb occurs as an NP (it is possible that the last example is only semantically irregular).

This sort of operation, again, is ungrammatical only at the surface level of L_N and is language specific. As we saw, logico-semantic deep structures are not categorically specified. A given semantic configuration, for example as realized in *fellow*, may then very well take the form of a verb, especially when no verb with that content seems to exist in that language.

Substitutions of subcategories as in

(39)   Love's function is to fabricate unknownness
                              (Thomas [1952])

are already metaphorical because feature transformations are involved. The substitution of N_{CONCR} by $N_{ABSTR.}$, therefore, is a semantic operation rather than a syntactic one. However, it is often the case – especially in dadaïst and similar texts – that when both levels are affected NONSENSE STRINGS are being formed, i.e. strings to which no interpretation can be assigned. Clearly, no explicit derivations can be constructed for them, because they seem to be the result of pure random choice in the lexicon, i.e. generated by unrestricted rewrite systems.

3.2.10. Whereas most operations treated above must be described by rules deviating from related rules in G_N, there is also an important group of syntactic rules which do not exist in the basic grammar, or which are normally considered to be aspects of performance: REPETITIONS. Especially at the phonological level are such operations frequent. Thus, when whole morphemes or syntactic structures recur we are dealing with fundamental aspects of recurrence, as have mainly been studied in well-known structuralist studies (Jakobson [1960], [1965], Levin [1962], Koch [1966]).

Jakobson (1960) even considered recurrence of identical elements to be a major feature of poetic language, or rather of the poetic USE of the language. He describes these structures by defining them as a projection of the principle of equivalence of the paradigmatic axis onto the syntagmatic axis.

Levin (1962) studies similar phenomena under the heading of 'coupling'. We clearly deal here with a general principle of literary (or more in general: stylistic) operations of all levels of description. Of course a distinction must be made with respect to normal recurrence, which results from G_N grammatical constraints. In any text we will find sentences with the same syntactic structure – a discovery which led to Harris' and Chomsky's transformational views – and identical lexemes manifesting semantic coherence. Similarly, typical literary recurrence must be distinguished from normal distribution (which of course is a performance phenomenon) such as for the phonological structure, studied earlier.

3.2.11. Because observations of these structures are numerous in the extant work of structural poetics we omit extensive quotation of examples. Moreover, from classical rhetorics onwards, these operations are very well known as 'figures of speech' (cf. Lausberg [1960], especially §975; and Dubois, *et al.* [1970]). What we want to know is how we have to describe these structures in explicit processes of derivation.

In the preceding section on phonological correlations we have already noticed that they have to be viewed as specific types of (con-)textual restrictions upon syntactic and lexical manifestations, at the surface, of semantic deep structures.

The operation resulting in syntactic recurrence, which is generally known as PARALLELISM, might probably be described with the aid of RULE SCHEMATA which specify repetition of identical structures (see chap. 1). Thus lines like

(40)   (i) Le feu qui danse
            (ii) L'oiseau qui chante
            (iii) Le vent qui meurt
                 (Reverdy [1964]90)

which were already studied for their verb deletions, can most adequately be generated by a simple FORMATION rule of the following form

$$S_{12} \qquad X \rightarrow (\varphi Z \varphi')^n \ (n \geqslant 2)$$

where φ and φ' may be null and where Z may be X such that recursion may result, for example for S itself. In this case we generate continuous sequences of recurrent categories. Often, however, these structures are more complex and discontinuous. The instructions, then, are contextual, for example in the following way

$$S_{14} \qquad X_{S_i} \rightarrow (\varphi\ Z\ \varphi')_{S_i}/(\varphi\ Z\ \varphi')_{S_{i-j}} \text{\_\_\_\_}$$

that is: a structure X of sentence S_i may be expanded as $\varphi\ Z\ \varphi'$ if and only if a preceding sentence S_{i-j} also has a structure $\varphi\ Z\ \varphi'$. Such constraints are inserted early in syntactic derivation of course, and they operate before lexematization when no lexemes are to be repeated.

4. CONCLUDING REMARKS

4.1. From the examples given and the very tentative rules provided describing their specific structures it has become evident that two main types of literary operations must be distinguished at the level of sentential surface structures in texts. It is assumed thereby that sufficient arguments can be adduced to establish a relevant formal distinction between them.

Specific FORMATION RULES assign to 'normal' sentential structures a dimension of 'super' structuration which is redundant in ordinary language or which is characteristic of specific language USE. They always operate early in the derivational process because they are optional contextual constraints upon literary well-formedness. They are most regular and specific at the metrical level of phonological description, where their specification directly or indirectly pre-determines the whole textual derivation. These constraints are less obvious on the syntactic level, because identical syntactic structures (without lexematic recurrence) are too abstract to be perceived consciously and/or are a normal aspect of the structure of sentences in general.

4.2. The other type of literary rules results in G_N-ungrammatical structures and probably should be described TRANSFORMATIONALLY (according to the standard version of a generative grammar). The general ability to interpret these structures, that is their connection with well-formed representations, is explained by the universal character of the transformational TYPES (deletion, permutation, addition, substitution) necessary to generate these structures. We have already concluded that many of these operations simply seem to cancel the language specific rules of G_N by establishing other relations with the SR's of a sentence.

In performance, the principle of REDUNDANCY REDUCTION appears to govern many of these literary operations. In this respect they are apparently opposed to the REDUNDANCY PRODUCTIVE literary formation rules treated above (cf. however chap. 9).

We do not claim that the transformational account of the specific syntactic structures in literary texts is correlated directly with performance processes of perception and interpretation. Because we do not yet know how syntactic structures are paired with semantic representations, it is impossible at this moment to determine how 'irregular' structures receive well-formed interpretations or, conversely, how well-formed SR's are transformed into irregular surface structures. In the next chapter we will study in more detail this notion of well-formed semantic representation, because it might be asked whether it is a necessary condition for the generation of sentences in literary texts.

7

SEMANTIC OPERATIONS.
PROCESSES OF METAPHORIZATION

1. INTRODUCTION

1.1. Among textual surface operations in literature the semantic ones are probably the most interesting. Their description, however, faces us with intricate linguistic problems. Whereas our knowledge of phonological and syntactic structures of L_N, especially of English, is already rather explicit, our insight into the semantic aspects of sentential derivations is still very fragmentary. At the same time it is obvious that an adequate description of the semantic structures specific both for sentences in literary texts and for whole literary texts presupposes at least an elaborated theory about semantic representations and about their relations with syntactic structures in general. As we noticed in the first part of this book, various proposals have been made, of which no single one provides us with such a general theory. Katz and Fodor's (1964) well-known attempt has received serious criticism in recent years and it has become clear that their model does not perform its main task: the description of semantic structures of whole sentences, because of the simplistic character of the projection rules formulated (cf. Weinreich [1966] for extensive criticism). Similarly, the various attempts to reformulate this interpretative theory have shed light above all on some important lexico-semantic aspects, but did not provide explicit rules for the description of semantic representations (cf. e.g. Gruber [1965], [1967]).

Recent developments in generative semantics seem more promising in many respects, but until now explicit derivations and rules mapping generated semantic representations onto syntactic ones have only been very speculative. In many cases – as was pointed out by Chomsky (1970), (1971), Katz (1970), (1971) and Bierwisch (1970) – they may indeed be viewed as mere notational variants of the interpretative conception of the standard grammar and its extended version (Chomsky [1970], [1971]).

In this situation the description of specifically literary semantic structures will remain unsatisfactory as long as no models are proposed which achieve more adequate characterizations of semantic structures. This is true *a fortiori*, as we saw in chaps. 2 and 3, for the description of semantic macro-structures of texts.

It is within these restrictions that we will now proceed to a description of semantic structures normally considered particularly relevant for literary texts, especially those traditionally known as METAPHORS, and the operations closely related to them. In the next chapter we will consider some aspects of textual deep structure operations.

1.2. We must stress, firstly, that metaphorization is not the only semantic process relevant for literary texts. All the other traditional operations of rhetorics, known as 'figures of thought', should be included. However, their description is on the one hand derivable from that of metaphorization or follows from textual semantics in general, and on the other hand must be based on a theory of reference, such as metonymia.

Secondly, metaphorization is not limited to literary texts and their sentences. Indeed, it is a process operating in natural language in general and its description is an important task of any adequate semantic theory. In this respect also, the remarks of this chapter, although applied to literary texts, have more general linguistic implications, because the very productive nature of processes of metaphorization is one of the most decisive creative aspects of the rules of natural language.

However, although the general mechanisms underlying metaphorization are to be accounted for by linguistic grammars, many regular manifestations of the process seem to be restricted to literary texts like those of (modern) poetry. At least the conditions for literary metaphorization are much more complex than the conventional ones of non-literary metaphorization.

1.3. Our remarks about the still very fragmentary character of linguistic theories of semantics do not imply that our insight into metaphorization, acquired with the aid of the still imperfect tools they provide, has not progressed since – say – the remarks of Aristotle about the subject. This fact is by no means trivial, because, until recently, and at least till the end of the last century, we DID not know much more about metaphor than its description given in Aristotle (1965) 1457b and repeated in nearly all treatises of rhetorics. Metaphorization, there, was essentially defined as a process of SUBSTITUTION OF LEXEMES ('words') based on the common properties of these words or of their denotata.[1] This description was mostly linked with that of the figure of COMPARISON of which metaphor was considered an 'abbreviated' form. Finally, traditional remarks include indications about the appropriate USE of metaphors and the types recommendable in given types of texts. These indications, of course, follow from the general PRAGMATIC nature of classical rhetorics.

It is clear that a formal description of the conditions for the process of lexematic substitution defining metaphor had to wait a more explicit knowledge of the lexical structure of the 'word'. It is striking, however, that intuitive and unexplicit definitions of lexical units, as given by the first semantic speculations at the end of the last

---

[1] There is an extensive traditional literature on metaphor which will not be mentioned here. For an historical account, cf. Meier (1963). Cf. Carnoy (1927), as an example of the systematic sophistication of early work. Most generative approaches to metaphor, although the model used is of course more adequate, are observationally poorer than these studies.

century, already provided us with rather precise descriptions of the possible PROCESSES underlying metaphorization. Although the first formulations about abstract theoretical constructs like distinctive semantic features were given only some twenty years ago in kinship-terms analysis, the abstract, quasimathematical treatment of word-properties in much traditional work already has laid the basis for theoretically more adequate descriptions.

1.4. In some modern semantic theories attention has been paid to the description of metaphorization or, in general, to processes of SEMANTIC CHANGE, though the topic is still considered as of marginal interest for grammatical theory by many linguists. The RULES OF METAPHORIZATION proposed in these studies are, however, rather simplistic and contrast with the sophistication of the models in which they were formulated.[2]

In the following sections we will try to reformulate more precisely this type of semantic rule. It will turn out, again, that an adequate description of metaphorization cannot be limited to sentential structures or to properties of (sentential) semantic well-formedness alone. The conditions of metaphorization and the complex inter-pretation processes involved are to be formulated on the basis of a textual grammar. That is, metaphors are often not even perceptible outside their linguistic co-text. A natural description therefore must explicitly take into account the semantic structure of this (con)text, with respect both to micro-structural relations between successive SR's, and with respect to textual macrostructures.

2. THE STRUCTURE OF SEMANTIC REPRESENTATIONS

2.1. In this section we may recall briefly some main properties of recent theories about the nature of semantic structures. Only then are we able to define explicitly the rules and conditions under which metaphorization can take place. Further, it is essential that we know on which level we must describe this process. At first sight a metaphor can be characterized, rather superficially, as a semantically ill-formed string of lexemes. However, it may be asked, firstly, whether any semantic anomaly is a metaphor, and secondly, if this surface ungrammaticalness has regular processes at

---

[2] The first treatments of metaphor within the framework of generative grammar were, after the occasional remarks of Katz and Fodor (1964), those of Weinreich (1966) (see below) and Todorov (1966). For some recent discussions cf., among others, Reddy (1969), and – for literary metaphor – Bickerton (1969), Petöfi (1969a), van Dijk (1970a), (1970e), Matthews (1971), Thomas (1969), Abraham and Braunmüller (1971). Further, in the linguistic approaches, some few remarks about the relevance of metaphor for semantic theory are made by e.g. Bolinger (1965) 566ff., Katz (1966), (1967), Mc-Cawley (1968a), Leech (1969b) 89ff.

A special issue of *Poetics*, edited by Petöfi and van Dijk, about theoretical aspects of metaphoriza-tion is in preparation. The doctoral dissertation of Dorothy Lambert treating metaphor on the basis of a case grammar was not available to us at the moment this chapter was written.

its basis in the generation of semantic deep structure. It is clear from the outset that the general problem of the relation between syntactic and semantic structures is closely related to such a discussion.

2.2. In the classical account of semantic structures, given by Katz and Fodor (1964) and globally adopted by Chomsky (1965) in his standard theory, the semantic component of the grammar is interpretative, i.e. syntactic structures generated by base rules serve as input to the semantic component. This component assigns interpretations to well-formed syntactic strings in which pre-terminal syntactic (sub-)categories or complex symbols are replaced by lexical units from the lexicon. This process of insertion is based on the compatibility of the semantic features and selection restrictions defining the lexemes in the lexicon (together with syntactic features and phonological matrices). We thus obtain well-formed strings of lexemes obviously possessing a structure identical with the underlying syntactic structure as it is specified by the base rules. The global content of a sentence is formed, however, by a process of amalgamation, in which the lexematic feature configurations are progressively combined into larger configurations. During this process different types of rules have to operate, for example redundancy rules which eliminate recurrent identical features and features automatically implied by them.

This is essentially the model adopted by many transformational linguists, although many of its mistakes are recognized. The type of binary sub-classifications of lexemes into features and terminal unsystematic 'distinguishers' in particular proved incorrect because cross-classifications may occur. These drawbacks have been noticed by many now and need not detain us here (cf. Bierwisch [1969], Gruber [1967]).

2.3. Important for our discussion is the fact that Katz and Fodor and the work inspired by them do not provide explicit formation rules for semantic structures *sui generis*. Syntactic structures seem to model them entirely. That such a position leads to unsatisfactory semantic descriptions can be concluded from many arguments. Firstly, selection restrictions mainly exert their influence within FUNCTIONAL RELATIONS like those between subject and predicate (verb), or verb and (in-)direct object, noun and attributive modifiers, etc. The traditional IC-analysis, as it has been formalized in syntactic deep structure (Chomsky [1957]), does not account for such specific relations (cf. the criticisms by Dik [1968], Chafe [1970] and others). Weinreich (1966) rightly remarked that the interpretative theory did not yield structures at all, because the amalgamation rules only result in a 'heap of features'. Thus sentences like (1) and (2) would have the same 'content'

(1)   the cat chased the mouse
(2)   the mouse chased the cat

To generate correct interpretations we therefore need information about the different relations between *cat, mouse* and *to chase*. Katz (1967) and Bierwisch (1969) established these relations with the aid of a notation derived from a predicate calculus, for example in the following simplified way

(3)   (i)   chase (cat, mouse)
           (ii) chase (mouse, cat)

where the relation *to chase* is defined as a two-place predicate with *cat* and *mouse* as arguments of an ordered couple. The predicate *to chase* might of course be further analyzed (see below).

In a more abstract way we may represent (3) with the aid of indexed variables:

(4)   (i)   chase (x_1, x_2). $x_1 = $ cat $x_2 = $ mouse
           (ii) chase (x_2, x_1)

or even as

(5)   (i) $C\,(x_1, x_2)$
           (ii) $C\,(x_2, x_1)$
           $C = $ *to chase* $x_1 = $ *cat* $x_2 = $ *mouse*.

(cf. McCawley [1968a], [1968b]; Rohrer [1971] and other recent semanticists using predicate logic for notations and formalizations; cf. chapter 3 for a simple notation). In these cases the relational representation is initially independent of the syntactic structure of the sentences, although the conventions of predicate logic for the place of arguments rather closely follow the place and function of subject and (in)direct objects in natural language.

We have argued earlier (chapters 2 and 3) that subject and object do not represent terms of SEMANTIC relations. In (1) and (2) the subject of the sentence is at the same time the Agent of the Action denoted by the verb. Consider however the following sentences

(6)   The cat fears the mouse.
(7)   The cat is following the mouse.
(8)   The mouse is preceding the cat.
(9)   Peter received a letter from John.
(10)   John sent a letter to Peter.

In these cases the semantic function of the subject is not necessarily identical with the function of Agent when we analyze the verbs in pre-lexical configurations. These facts have been underlined in several papers on generative semantics (cf. Ross and Lakoff [1968]). In (6) for example we may describe the semantic underlying structure by a formula like CAUSE (to be afraid (Mouse, Cat)) (cf. Gruber [1967], Lakoff [1970b], Fillmore [1969a], [1969b], Brekle [1969]). Similarly, such deep structure analyses of the prelexical structure of the predicate (verb) permit an explicit account of the (equivalence?) relations linking (7) and (8), and (9) and (10). These transformational relationships between semantic converses cannot be described by syntactic structures alone, nor by syntactic functional relations like subject, object, etc.

2.4. It is not our task in this book to adduce extensive arguments against syntactically based semantic descriptions (cf. however chap. 2) and we cannot go into further detail here. We refer to the recent discussions (see above) in and about generative semantics.

We may conclude however that a theory of semantics has to specify semantic relations and theoretical units in their own right in such a way that an adequate insight into semantic structures and interpretations can be gained. The relation with syntactic structures is a problem which can only be solved if these main issues of semantics itself are clarified first.

We therefore adopted, in the first part of this book, a semantic language with its own categories inspired by the case grammar of Fillmore (cf. also Chafe [1970]) and a notation borrowed from a higher predicate calculus with modal categories. This language must specify well-formed semantic representations of sentences which can be considered to be their deep structure or logical form. These representations must be the formal input to the set of syntactic rules of the grammar because they contain the information determining the syntactic subject-object relations and therefore the order of the *NP*'s involved. Furthermore, the SR's specify the different pragmatic and modal (quantifying, temporal, local) aspects necessary for the syntactic structure (article selection, adverbs, pronouns, tense, etc.) and for lexematization.

2.5. Our description of processes of metaphorization is based on the model outlined above and in chaps. 2 and 3, specifying semantic representations as in the following simplified graph

(11)

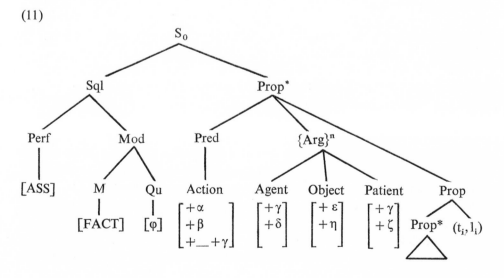

The structured string of semantic terminal categories (which are not complete here) is finally intensionally interpreted by the assignment of LEXICOIDS (the complex units between square brackets; features are indicated by Greek characters; internal structure neglected). Notice that before this assignment the structure is purely formal, i.e. 'syntactic' in the general formal sense.

The assignment of lexicoids is based on their inherent feature specification and the contextual restrictions existing between predicate (Action, State or Event) and the different arguments. Thus Action [+ HUM] requires Agent [+ HUM]. These restrictions do not seem to exist between the different arguments. A sentence like (12) is perfectly well-formed although its Actors (Agent, Patient) have opposite features

(12)   The old man loves the young girl.

which may be represented as follows

$$\left\{\begin{array}{l} + \text{HUM} \\ + \text{MALE} \\ + \text{OLD} \end{array}\right\} + \left\{\begin{array}{l} + \_ + \text{HUM} \\ \rightarrow \text{EMO} \\ \quad + \text{DEGREE} \end{array}\right\} + \left\{\begin{array}{l} + \text{HUM} \\ - \text{MALE} \\ - \text{OLD} \end{array}\right\}$$

This notation is borrowed from Leech (1969b) who rightly stresses the central role of the predicate ('medial') cluster for the selection of lexemes. It does not matter whether predicates are manifested as verbs or as adjectives in this case, and it is therefore misleading to treat adjectives as if they were verbs in syntactic deep structure because of their identical selection restrictions. These restrictions are to be inferred from their identical function – as predicates – in semantic representations, where they specify properties of and relations between arguments.

2.6. It is not quite correct to state simply that there are no selection restrictions between arguments, but only between arguments and predicates. Compare, for instance, the following sentences

(13)   My brother Hannibal has eaten four books this morning.
(14)   The worms have eaten my book.

We would normally specify *book* as [+ OBJ, + LING] or something like that. We could further negatively specify it with [− EDIBLE] in order to be able to recognize (13) as ungrammatical, although it is impossible to state as a feature every property a book has NOT. This combination *eat* and *book* is however perfectly acceptable in (14). Thus, if Agent is specified [− HUM] the object may lose its feature [− EDIBLE].

It is obvious that such indications formalize not our knowledge about semantic structures, but our referential knowledge about the real world (in counterfactuals,

NEG FACT, we may have the acceptable sentence *John dreamt that he ate four books*). For an intensional semantic theory, therefore, (13) is perfectly well-formed because it does not strictly contradict feature specifications or lexical rules (or presuppositions) (cf. Mc Cawley [1968a]).

Consider however the following sentences

(15)   The man has beaten his wife.
(16)   The man has beaten the wife.
(17)   *The man has beaten his husband.
(18)   The man has beaten the husband.

In this case the ungrammatical character of (17) is rather semantically than referentially determined. *To beat* and *husband* (as Patient) do not yield ungrammatical constructions as can be seen in (18). *His husband* however is ungrammatical because it is derived from *He* [+ HUM, + MALE] *has husband* [+ HUM, + MALE, + MARRIED], while *husband* is specified further as a RELATION for example as M (x_1, x_2), where $x_1 = man$, $x_2 = woman$, $M = married$. Thus, because *husband* implies *married* and because *married* (2-place predicate) implies a second argument specified with [+ FEMALE], the Agent (related through *his* with Patient) must have [+ FEMALE]. This fact seems to point to the mutual co-determination of selection restrictions between lexemes/lexicoids manifesting arguments. Nevertheless, these ungrammatical relations do NOT hold between arguments but between arguments and their (n-place) predicates: *husband* is only a surface lexeme covering a complex semantic structure including the relation *to be married with*. At this deep level there is a contradiction between underlying semantic propositions and the meaning postulates of the lexicon (cf. Kuroda [1969b] for such constraints and Kummer [1972b] for the role of meaning postulates for sentential and textual well-formedness).

2.7. The incomplete and brief discussion given above about the formal scope of selection restrictions has made clear that the conditions combining lexicoids into an SR are very complex, but that they are always defined with respect to the predicate. Observe that these restrictions, as we saw in chap. 2, operate also within sequences of sentences. The following text is ungrammatical for the same general reasons

(19)   (i) John does not like fruit at all.
        *(
          (ii) He loves to eat an apple at breakfast.

where *fruit* $\subset$ *apple* and *like* $\subset$ *love* such that NEG [*like* (x_1, y_1)] contradicts *love* (x_1, z_1), where $x_1 = $ John $y_1 = $ fruit $z_1 = $ apple, because NEG [*like* (x_1, y_1)] $\supset$ NEG [*love* (x_1, y_1)] and $(x)[A(x) \supset F(x)]$, that is: for all x, if x is an apple, then x is a fruit.

If an adequate semantic theory formulates axioms and rules of this kind, we may thus formally, i.e. by pure deduction, infer the ungrammaticalness of sentences and sentential sequences.

2.8. Before we can proceed to a description of metaphorization we have to consider briefly a more general semantic problem: LEXICAL CHANGE. Any semantic theory should provide descriptions of mutations in the internal structure of the lexemes in the lexicon, thus giving a formal explanation of a part of linguistic change in general. The socio-cultural and other historical factors of this change do not concern us here, although their importance for the change of the lexicon – and thereby of selection restrictions and rules – is decisive.

In comparison with (13) we may consider such sentences as

(20)   My brother devoured three books this morning.

Let us assume for the moment that we can adequately describe such sentences at the level of intensional semantics alone (cf. however our remarks about (13)). We then have to conclude that (20) is ungrammatical because *books* does not have the feature $[+ \text{FOOD}]$ which is required contextually by *to devour*. Moreover *brother* has $[+ \text{HUM}]$ which prevents the 'normal' possibility of non-human animals eating books.

However, the lexicon does not only specify a verb *to devour*$_1$ as an action of 'eating' but also a verb to *devour*$_2$, defined as an action of 'reading', modally specified with $[+ \text{RAPID}, + \text{INTENSIVE}]$. The meaning of the lexeme is thus perfectly compatible with *books*, because *to read* has $[+ \text{OBJ}, + \text{LING}]$.

We do not wish to debate in detail the thorny traditional problem of whether we are dealing here with two homonyms or with different 'readings' ('paths'; 'sémèmes' in Greimas [1966]' terminology) of the 'same' lexeme (cf. Kooij [1971] for discussion). However, our point is that, if we should distinguish two different homonymous lexemes/morphemes here, we would accept that no systematic relationships exist between to *devour*$_1$ and to *devour*$_2$, following the hypothesis that the lexicon is the 'full set of irregularities of the language' (cf. Botha [1968] for discussion of this well-known viewpoint of transformational grammar).

It is clear, at least in this case, that regular relations actually exist between the 'two' lexemes *to devour* and that they must be considered readings of one lexeme. First of all, in the two senses of *to eat* and *to read* the lexemes share the features $[+ \text{RAPID}]$ and $[+ \text{INTENSIVE}]$. Furthermore, *to eat* and *to read* both have as features $[+ \text{ACTION}]$ and $[+\_\_ + \text{OBJECT}]$ (or $[+ \text{HUM}\_\_]$), whereas the Action itself could probably further be specified with basic common properties: X CAUS (MOVE (Y FROM Z TO X), where X is Agent and Y is interpretable as Object or a part of it, e.g. its visual aspect.

All these common properties seem to admit the selection of *to devour* in a context normally excluding it. The effect or function of this process is mostly to underline exactly those features/properties which permitted the specific selection. In this description there is no substitution of one lexeme, e.g. *to read*, by another, e.g. *to devour*, as was the traditional hypothesis, although our semantic competence may predict a verb like *to read* in a context having *book* as Object. These formal predictions underlie the normal performance process of expectation, which is further determined by conditions of frequency, situation, etc.

The process described is exactly the one denoted by the term METAPHORIZATION, and the trivial example shows that it is quite common in L_N. Characteristic however is the fact that a frequent use of *to devour*, in a context requiring a verb *to read rapidly*, may change the lexeme by extending it with the reading *to read rapidly*. In that conventional case no perception of metaphorization normally occurs, i.e. metaphorical extensions of lexemes are interpreted as regular readings.

These facts are all well-known but had to be mentioned here, firstly, to give an introductory description of the process operating such extensions and, secondly, to stress the differences with non-conventional, non-lexicalized, lexematic extensions. One of these differences lies in the status of the description itself. Metaphorization in normal language may only be described and explained *a posteriori*, whereas in literary texts of a certain type, e.g. modern poetry, they may be predicted by a rule saying that ANY lexematic change is L_L-grammatical under given minimal conditions for deep-structure coherence.

In this perspective we shall try, in the following section, to give a more detailed description of metaphorization and the conditions determining it in literary texts.

3. METAPHORICAL STRUCTURES IN LITERATURE: PRELIMINARY OBSERVATIONS

3.1. We now turn to the description of metaphorical structures *stricto sensu*, i.e. structures not predicted by the specification of lexemes, i.e. derived from the conventions of the lexicon alone, but by transformations of lexemes with general RULES of metaphorization based on feature characteristics of the co-text.

Such transformations, as we have already noticed, are not restricted to L_L and may also occur in L_N, though less frequently and practically always conventionally, i.e. with a certain recurrence in the language or its idiolectal use.

Conversely, literary texts in some cultures or periods may also have fixed or dead metaphors, as in petrarquist and baroque poetry, and also in the Old-Icelandic poetry, where they are known as *kenningar*. In many cases interpretation of these metaphorical lexemes is not predictable by rule, or by rule alone. We can therefore speak of a sort of 'literary lexicon' specifying the irregular, typologically bound, meanings of these lexemes (*eye of the sky* = *sun*, etc.). Such a lexicon may be compared with an idiomatic or 'performance' lexicon as defined by Chafe (1968) and Des Tombes (1970). Similar irregularities have to be accounted for in the description of compound lexemes (cf. Brekle [1969], Botha [1968]).

3.2. A main feature of the process of metaphorization is its RELATIONAL character. Strictly speaking there are no isolated lexemes serving as metaphors, although one may say that the specific selection of an ungrammatical lexeme in a given (co-)textual structure may bring about metaphorization. From the preceding section it is clear that only certain RELATIONS in an SR and/or pragmatic context, e.g. relations between predicates (actions or modifiers) and arguments, can be said to be 'ungrammatical', and the structure of which they are a part 'ill-formed'. This may seem trivial, but it implies that the recognition of metaphors is decidable only with respect to other categories and lexemes of the SR. We will see below that the decision about WHICH of the related terms is metaphorizing has to be drawn from the textual structure of related SR's.

Roughly, then, a metaphor may be defined as an ungrammatical[3] relation between two (or more) lexemes XY, i.e. if X is specified $[+\alpha]$ and Y $[-\alpha]$ and/or if X has a contextual restriction $[+\_\_\_ -\alpha]$ while Y has $[+\alpha]$, and conversely.

Sentences which contain such an ungrammatical relation belong to the class of SEMI-SENTENCES, i.e. they are formally and superficially ill-formed, but they may, under certain conditions, receive an interpretation, *viz.* have well-formed semantic deep structures. If the last condition is not satisfied the sentences will be part of the class of NON-SENSE STRINGS, which form the limit of metaphorization processes.

Thus an adequate theory of metaphor should account formally for the ability of native speakers to perform the following tasks:

(i)   the identification of semantically ungrammatical relations within a sentence or a sequence of sentences.
(ii) the implicit identification of those features of a lexeme which are incompatible with those of the other lexemes of the metaphorical relation.
(iii) the implicit identification of those features which are co-textually non-incompatible.
(iv) the construction of a well-formed SR underlying the ill-formed sentence and based on the co-textually non-incompatible features mentioned in (iii).
(v)   the production of well-formed paraphrases realizing this well-formed SR at the surface level.

The tasks (i) and (ii) are part of general semantic competence while (iii), (iv) and (v) more specifically characterize metaphorical accomplishment. Let us try to make these tasks explicit in the description of some metaphors of modern poetry.

---

[3] Of course, the notions 'grammatical' and 'ungrammatical' are used here and elsewhere in this chapter in a rather restricted sense of semantic well-formedness, *viz.* as defined by the most general rules determining lexematic compatibility (for example as formulated in the standard theory: Katz and Fodor [1964], Chomsky [1965]). As soon as the metaphorization rules are integrated into the grammar, it is, strictly speaking, no longer correct to call ungrammatical the structures derived by such rules. In that case the metaphorization rules specify the general rules, e.g. by providing 'deeper' arguments for the non-applicability of the general rules.

3.3. Our observations will mainly be based on a highly metaphorical poem: *Jour éclatant*, by Reverdy [1964]111. Generalizations and provisional theoretical conclusions will be interspersed with and follow our description. The semantic features postulated, here as elsewhere in this book, are *ad hoc* but will normally be close to those used often in modern semantics. Let us first quote the text in its entirety

3.4.   (i)   Jour Eclatant
(21)

    (ii)   Un mouvement de bras
    (iii)   Comme un battement d'ailes
    (iv)   Le vent qui se déploie
    (v)   Et la voix qui appelle
    (vi)   Dans le silence épais
    (vii)   qu'aucun souffle ne ride
    (viii)   Les larmes du matin et les doigts de la rive
    (ix)   L'eau qui coule au dehors
    (x)   L'ornière suit le pas
    (xi)   Le soleil se déroule
    (xii)   Et le ciel ne tient pas
    (xiii)   L'arbre de carrefour se penche et interroge
    (xiv)   La voiture qui roule enfonce l'horizon
    (xv)   Tous les murs au retour sèchent contre le vent
    (xvi)   Et le chemin perdu se cache sous le pont
    (xvii)   Quand la forêt remue
    (xviii)   Et que la nuit s'envole
    (xix)   Entre les branches mortes où la fumée s'endort
    (xx)   L'oeil fermé au couchant
    (xxi)   La dernière étincelle
    (xxii)   Sur le fil bleu du ciel
    (xxiii)   Le cri d'une hirondelle

3.5.1. It is heuristically interesting to start our (partial) description with lines (ii) and (iii) which actualize an operation often closely associated with metaphor: a COMPARISON. The traditional account of metaphors as abbreviated comparisons (cf. Cohen, 1968) suggests that we actually might consider them to be the DEEP STRUCTURE of a metaphor. The hypothesis harmonizes perfectly with the general conception of deep structures as explicit formulations of all relevant semantic or syntactic structures of a linguistic (surface) structure. In that case metaphorization would simply be described as a series of TRANSFORMATIONAL steps of DELETION.

This transformation would roughly have the following form

(22) X is-similar-to $Y \Rightarrow \emptyset \, \emptyset \, Y$

where X and Y are lexicoids of the deep structure and Y the metaphorical lexeme in surface structure. The reflexive, symmetric and transitive relation of SIMILARITY, which may be represented by the symbol '$\simeq$', may of course be realized directly in surface structure by such lexemes as *like, similar, to resemble, to look like, to be as, to appear, to seem*, etc. In that case we generate a comparison which, itself, is always grammatical, because the perception of similarities, by a speaker, between two or more denotata referred to by the lexemes, expresses an opinion which as such cannot formally be falsified as 'ungrammatical'. Often, however, this perception of similarities is based on common empirical properties which in turn can be related to formal features. Thus *mouvement de bras* and *battement d'ailes* share sufficient properties to be linguistically comparable: [+ MOVEMENT], [+ ANIMATE], [+ LATERAL LIMBS].

3.5.2. Although comparisons in surface structure are not ungrammatical we cannot deny that many comparisons would be rather unusual in L_N both empirically and (therefore?) linguistically.

(23)   ?A book like a tree ...
(24)   ?The sky is like a telephone ...
(25)   ?This stone looks like sincerity ...
(26)   ?The day seems a salad ...

Without further textual specification such structures can be marked ungrammatical if we assume that any comparison presupposes, linguistically as well, that the two lexemes compared share at least a relevant semantic feature (see below). Such a condition may also be considered pragmatic and/or referential, because the details of similarity in the empirical form of abstract or concrete denotata are not necessarily reflected in a direct way in semantic feature specifications. This is a very important point, because it might render any formal theory of metaphor impossible (cf. e.g. the skeptical remark of Chomsky [1968]). We therefore have to adduce strong evidence for the properly linguistic character of metaphorical processes (which does not exclude relations between perceptual categories and semantic features (cf. Bierwisch [1967], [1969a]).
  Similarly, normal language has certain conventionalized comparisons like

(27)   My brother is as strong as a lion.
(28)   My friend is as tall as a tree.

We hardly say however

(29)   My sister is as strong as a lioness.
(30)   My brother is as strong as a thick rope.

The conventionalized character of comparing lexemes like *lion, tree* in these contexts are socio-culturally bound and may differ from language to language (strong as a horse, a bear, an elephant, etc.). This implies, within a given culture, that the comparing lexeme (the *comparant* in structuralist terminology, cf. Cohen [1968]), must be generally known. *This tissue is as blue as the sky* would be acceptable but *This tissue is as blue as the coat of the rightmost figure of the mosaique X in church Y in Ravenna* would be highly unusual. Clearly, this is also a pragmatico-referential condition on well-formedness, or rather on 'appropriate use' of language.

3.5.3. Notice that in (27) and (28) we have comparisons in their first explicit form, whereas (23)-(26) are already abbreviated types. In the full form the common property (*tertium comparationis*) of the lexicoids (or of the denotata) of the two compared lexemes is explicitly realized, often as an attributive predicate. The structure of such comparisons can be represented as follows

(31) $X[+\alpha]$ is as A as $Y[+\alpha]$

where A is a lexematization of the common property $[\alpha]$.

Since such expressions require that the lexeme compared actually has as a feature the property referred to by the tertium comparationis, sentences not satisfying this condition are to be considered ungrammatical or inappropriate. In poetic texts, however, such 'unmotivated' comparisons are admitted as we can see in the well-known line of Eluard

(32)   La terre est bleue comme une orange.

where only the feature $[+ \text{GLOBULAR SHAPE}]$ may link *terre* and *orange* (see below).

3.5.4. There are many different ways to formalize the deep structure of comparisons. We may write (31) simply as a specific relation

(32) $A\ (x_1, y_1)$

where x_1 and y_1 are lexemes and where A can be interpreted as 'has a similarity relation A to'. We are however begging the question since this predicate is obviously complex, and needs further specification.

The full explication of the structure, then, can be informally described as: x is similar to y and this similarity is based on the property a. In that case we might use a higher predicate calculus which assigns properties to relations

(33) $\varphi[S(x_1, y_1)]$

where $S = $ *similar to* and φ the way in which x_1 is similar to y_1 (*strong, tall,* etc.), although the status of φ is not clear.

Notice that a simple notation like $A(x_1) = A(y_1)$ will not do. The relative character of attributive predicates does not ensure that the identical properties have the same degree: a 'strong' mouse is not 'strong' in the absolute sense. A more adequate underlying structure would then be something like: $\varphi(x_1) \wedge \psi(y_1) \wedge \varphi \equiv \psi$. The perception of similarities as expressed by the relative attribute seems to be based on socio-cultural knowledge of norms and 'averages' (cf. Dik [1969], Gruber [1967]).

3.6. We meet similar problems in the description of the metaphorical structures in Reverdy's poem. Their base is often pragmatical or referential and not strictly semantic. Consider such combinations as (underlying)

(34)   Le vent se déploie
(35)   Le silence est épais
(36)   Aucun souffle ne ride le silence

(34) is paradigmatic for many metaphors in the text: the Agent *vent* is characterized as [+ ATMOSPHERICAL PHENOMENON] and the Action *se déployer* pre-supposes [+ [+ OBJECT, + CONCRETE, + PLIABLE]___]. Similarly, *silence* has a feature [+ ABSTR] incompatible with [+ CONCRETE] presupposed by *épais* and *rider*. The violation of the normal selection restrictions of G_N is basic in these cases because it affects elementary features like [+ ABSTR] and [+ CONCR] and secondarily more superficial features as [+ PLIABLE]. This type of contradiction is traditionally considered to form a major type of metaphorization.

3.7. The preceding description is wholly negative, i.e. it gives the formal reason why two lexemes are incompatible, but not the reasons why they actually could be combined in a sentence of a poem. An adequate semantic theory may not fail to explain how and under which formal conditions semantic anomalies may function as metaphorical structures.

In the examples taken from some sentences in L_N it appeared that ungrammatical relations that are interpretable as metaphors may be formed by generating a deviant lexeme instead of a 'normal', (co-)textually grammatical lexeme, if these lexemes share some textually relevant features. It may be asked whether this rough description also applies to the metaphorization processes we are dealing with in literary texts?

Thus, in the collocation *le vent se déploie* we have first the ungrammaticalness caused by [+ CONCR] in the co-textual specification of *se déployer*, while *vent* does not possess such a feature, nor does it have a feature [+ PLIABLE]. However, we may analyze *se déployer* further and arrive at such basic features as [+ MOVEMENT] and [+ OPEN], and possibly [+ GRADUAL] – in order to mark the opposition to *to outburst*, for instance. These features, then, are NOT incompatible with *vent* and we may therefore postulate a set of lexicoids having these features in their specification, like *to blow* or *to rise* (of the wind). Such hypothetic lexemes are to be viewed as surface realizations of a well-formed deep structure. Our semantic competence will force us to select precisely those properties in a metaphorizing lexeme that characterize a lexicoid which is not co-textually incompatible. This seems to point to the fact that in performance we reduce metaphors, taken as semantic surface irregularities, to well-formed deep structures. We will see below to what extent semantic deep structure well-formedness is a necessary condition for meaningful interpretation.

We may informally consider the metaphorization process to be a BLOCKING of the regular derivational process just before the lexematizations take place. For the quoted example of Reverdy, we would have for instance (double arrows indicate transformations)

(37)

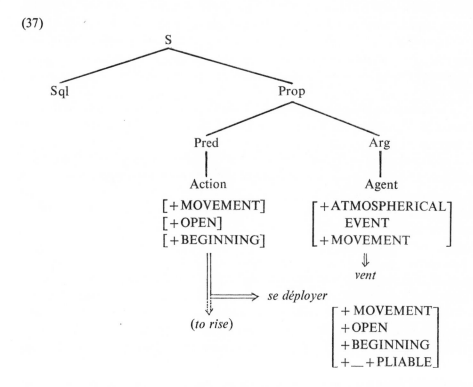

3.8. It is clear from this intuitive description that proper substitution of a lexeme by another does not occur, but the selection of a lexeme instead of another lexeme on the basis of a similar pre-lexical structure. Observe that these pre-lexical elements in deep structure are necessary for a correct, coherent interpretation of the sentence (and the text). In L_L, obviously, this process is quite regular, i.e. further selection restrictions – which are of course lexical and surface aspects –, are irrelevant under given conditions. A sufficient number of shared properties may decide the selection of a lexeme.

The consequences of such a rule are considerable. In the first place the number of possible generatable lexemes increases widely in a given textual position. In performance this extension of selectional possibilities may considerably reduce the 'normal' or 'average' possibilities, which results in an increase of information. This communicative regularity has by now been observed quite often in our description and we will return to its relevance in the last chapter.

At the formal semantic level there is, however, another important consequence. The selection of a preferred but normally incompatible lexeme implies the introduction into the semantic structure of a text of a certain number of selection restrictions and inherent features.

We will assume that, in principle, literary texts like poems will integrate these elements into the semantic coherence (Greimas' *isotopie*) of the text. Thus, the selection of a lexeme is not only LOCALLY described and explained but also GLOBALLY, i.e. with respect to textual structure. We do not yet know whether this hypothesis can be warranted empirically. Perhaps this condition upon literary well-formedness is too strong, although it eliminates random metaphorizing as found in much (allegedly) automatic poetry by the surrealists.

3.9. The description given above, although it does not accept literary metaphorization as a substitution transformation, comes pretty close to classical ideas about the replacement of an 'appropriate word'. Such an approach cannot of course, be ruled out *a priori*, the more while the automatisms of our (semantic) competence will force us to 'correct' ungrammatical strings by reducing them to well-formed ones, i.e. by interpreting a realized lexeme 'as if' another lies at its basis. We have seen earlier that such a process is based on similarity of lexicoidal structure, not on identity of an entire lexematic structure, which would be the case in explicit paraphrasing of metaphors (their 'translation').

This 'correcting' performance of language users is well-known from other phenomena of speech perception and of cognition in general (cf. Hörmann [1967] 110 ff., Neisser [1967] *passim*; and chapter 9). Deviant and/or irregular structures are generally matched – by global and/or componential analysis – with structures and 'schemata' generatable by the well known rules of cognition and competence.

The whole phenomenon of metaphorization rests on this feature abstracting ability of native speakers: the ability to perceive elementary similarities between lexemes and to extrapolate from them to well-formed underlying SR's or parts of SR's.

However, we should also point out that metaphor may not only be considered a stylistic or esthetic surface operation. Its fundamental role in natural language has to be explained also by the fact that it can happen in textual production that a certain lexicoid is used in order to construct a specific SR. It may happen, then, that a given language does not have a specific lexeme – provided with the correct selection restrictions – to realize that lexicoid in surface structure. We then normally have either to revert to description or circumscription or to the selection of a lexeme having the lexicoid at its basis but not the appropriate contextual specification. Metaphorization can in this case be considered a 'normal' process based on semantic 'necessity'. In the lines of Reverdy quoted above we seem to deal with this process. We might want to generate a structure specified with a feature of 'wind' denoting an Action with the following features: $[+ \text{EXPANSION}]$, $[+ \text{OPEN}]$, $[+ \text{BEGIN}]$, $[+ \text{GRADUAL}]$, $[+ \underline{} + \text{CONCRETE}]$ or something similar. A lexeme contextually compatible with the atmospherical phenomenon 'wind' may not be present in the lexicon. In that case a metaphorization rule supplies the necessary semantic material by selecting a lexeme with these features. In L_N this case often occurs when lexemes for new objects, events or other entities have to be defined.

At the same time, as we saw, the selection of a lexeme in a metaphorical process establishes additional relations with textual structures. Further, by its very relational character, metaphorization affects also the interpretation of the other lexemes of the collocation, for example when a metaphorizing lexeme is interpreted literally (see below). In our example, then, 'wind' is represented as a tissue or implicitly compared with a tissue by the fact that its Action is one describable as the 'movement of tissue, paper or of flowers'.

3.10. Finally, we must recall the following very important point. Strictly speaking it is impossible to decide which of two or more terms forming a metaphor are semantically anomalous and which are not, without taking into account the further structure of the sentence and the text. As we will see in the next section, where we will consider in more detail the precise transformational processes involved, we do not know a priori in a collocation such as *le vent se déploie* whether it is *vent* or *se déployer* that is anomalous. First the internal semantic structure of the two lexemes have to be studied (e.g. does *vent* have features in common with another lexeme/lexicoid which is itself compatible with *se déployer*?) and then, if this internal structure permits different interpretations, the structure of the text will decide which term is metaphorizing and which term is a regular manifestation of underlying textual SR's. If the ambiguity is not resolved at that level we may conclude either that it was intentional – which may be a feature of literary communication – or resolvable only at the pragmatic or referential level.

Let us turn now to a more precise treatment of the processes we are dealing with.

4. TRANSFORMATIONAL PROCESSES OF METAPHORIZATION

4.1. It is becoming clear that metaphorization involves at least two concomitant processes. The insertion into a text of an anomalous lexeme entails the introduction of additional features and of a certain number of unsatisfied selection restrictions. This insertion, which we consider to be a transformational process in which a lexicoidal configuration of features is replaced by a lexeme from the lexicon, can also affect the structure of the other lexemes of the sentence. The global condition, mentioned earlier, is probably that we will automatically try to 'regularize' *ad hoc* the ungrammaticalities of a perceived sentence. In that case, for instance, in the example *le vent se déploie*, *vent* may acquire the feature [+ PLIABLE] required by *se déployer*, e.g. by the following EXTENSION RULE

$$(38) \qquad vent \; [+ \; \alpha, \; + \; \beta, \; + \; \gamma]/se \; d\acute{e}ployer \; [...[+ \; [+ \; \delta]\underline{\quad}] \Rightarrow vent \\ [+ \; \alpha, \; + \; \beta, \; + \; \gamma, \; \langle + \; \delta \rangle]$$

where the pointed brackets designate the *ad hoc* character of the addition of feature δ. This process has also been described by Weinreich (1966), Katz (1966), (1967) and others. Weinreich talked about a 'transfer feature' which is automatically assigned, under certain conditions for grammatical relations (which he does not specify), to a lexeme dominated by a lexeme requiring that feature in its co-text. Thus after *during* any noun would be specified *ad hoc* with the feature [+ TEMP] or lexemes would be interpolated having such a feature: *During my pipe I never write*, for example, would then be interpreted as *during the smoking of my pipe*; and this holds for such normal expressions as *during dinner*, *during my walk*, etc. Weinreich (1966) 429 ff. gives the following general rule

$$(39) \qquad A[m_1(n)] \; ... \; B[m_2] \rightarrow A[m_1] \; ... \; B[m_2n]$$

where m_1 and m_2 are the feature specifications of lexemes A and B respectively, and where n is a transfer feature. From this elementary formula it follows that n is simply added to structure m_2 of B. Notice that its origin is no longer detectable because m_1 seems to have 'lost' its n. We here touch upon the well-known problem of RECOVER-ABILITY of transformed structures and the explicitness of transformations in general.

In the process of (semantic) 'linking' described by Weinreich the specific feature fully integrates into the unordered set

$$(40) \qquad A[\alpha, \; \beta, \; (\gamma)] + B[\delta, \; \epsilon] \rightarrow AB[\alpha, \; \beta, \; \gamma, \; \delta, \; \epsilon]$$

The process of transfer implies re-distribution of one (or more?) features along certain derivational paths of related categories.

Weinreich's description, however, is incomplete and not explicit enough, and it has serious theoretical drawbacks

(i)   it is not clear why there should be specific 'transfer-features' in a language, and/or what the conditions are for a feature to become a transfer feature. Any feature may be transferred when the (co-)text requires specification by it.

(ii)   it may be asked further why A transfers a feature n to B, and not conversely.

(iii) the resulting structure is no less ill-formed than the transformed one in (39), because one lexeme has now acquired a feature which the other lexeme has lost; therefore

(iv) there is no reason to postulate that the addition of (transfer) features implies the deletion of that feature from its 'original' lexeme.

The structure of *le vent se déploie*, in isolation, may therefore (cf. ii) also be derived as follows

$$(41) \qquad se\ déployer[+ \ \delta, \ + \ \varepsilon]/vent[+ \ \alpha, \ + \ \beta, \ + \ \gamma] \Rightarrow se\ déployer[+ \ \delta, \ + \ \varepsilon, \\ \langle[+ \ [+ \ \gamma]\underline{\quad}]\rangle]$$

Because there is no formal reason for the fact that metaphorizing lexemes lose that feature when transferring them to their fellow-lexemes, we have to formulate in general

$$(42) \qquad A[+ \ \alpha, \ + \ \beta] + B[+ \ \gamma, \ + \ \delta] \Rightarrow A[+ \ \alpha, \ + \ \beta] + B'[\langle + \ \alpha\rangle, \ + \ \gamma, \ + \ \delta]$$

The output structure, then, is perfectly well-formed because A and B share a feature α.

However, in order to generate well-formed structures we might as well transfer γ from B to A. How, then, do we decide formally which of the two lexemes is anomalous and, once that is known whether the anomalous lexeme transforms the other ones or whether the normal lexemes transform the anomalous ones by 'grammaticalizing' them according to textual coherence. In the process of transfer there are three logical possibilities corresponding to three interpretations of the metaphor

(43)   (i) AB' $[[+ \ \alpha, \ + \ \beta] + [\langle + \ \alpha\rangle, \ + \ \gamma, \ + \ \delta]]$
          (ii) $A'B$ $[[+ \ \alpha, \ + \ \beta, \langle + \ \delta\rangle] + [+ \ \gamma, \ + \ \delta]]$
          (iii) $A'B'[[+ \ \alpha, \ + \ \beta, \langle + \ \delta\rangle] + [\langle + \ \alpha\rangle, \ + \ \gamma, \ + \ \delta]]$

where pointed brackets enclose received features in (42) and (43). We neglected, for reasons of abstractness and generality, the distinction between inherent features and selection restrictions: a feature transferred from A to B, or conversely, becomes a selection restriction, and a selection restriction becomes an *ad hoc* inherent feature. We may interpret these three formulas in the following way for the metaphor of Reverdy

(44)   (i) Le vent se déploie 'atmosphériquement'.
          (ii) Le vent 'pliable' se déploie.
          (iii) Le vent 'pliable' se déploie 'atmosphériquement'.

Further textual SR's will normally select (or rather: cause the generation of) one of these underlying structures. The formal criterion in this case is the coherence relation between one of the lexemes in the metaphor with the rest of the textual structure. *Vent* has a feature [+ NATURE] which is coherent with other lexemes in the text. We therefore conclude that its predicate *se déployer* is the metaphorizing lexeme. In fact it is often the case that predicates (attributes or verbs) are metaphorical, the nouns being a major category for the establishment of textual coherence by their role in identity relations.

4.2. We described above a first hypothetical process underlying metaphorization: the transformational addition of a feature provided by other lexemes of the anomalous construction. This transformation, in fact, 'reduces' the anomalous semantic structure to a well-formed structure. We might also follow the opposite direction and DELETE[4] those features which cause the ill-formedness. Thus, if we eliminate the selection restriction [+ [+ PLIABLE]___] from *se déployer* by transformation we are left with a lexeme with features which are perfectly compatible with *vent*. Suspension of inherent or contextual features is probably the basic characteristic of metaphorization.[5] It is certainly the process underlying metaphorization in L_N: a metaphorizing lexeme is generated ONLY for the feature material needed by the sentential and textual SR's. The other, 'ungrammatical', features are simply placed between parenthesis, i.e. they *ad hoc* stop to exert their regulative function.

In a sentence like *John is as strong as a lion* or *John is a lion* we will only retain as relevant in *lion* such features as [+ STRENGTH] or [+ COURAGE].

The fundamental structural difference with metaphorization in L_N is probably that in literature it is not necessary to delete 'superfluous' features, because these may be needed in the construction of other SR's in the text. In the same way all addition transformations in literature may be normal optional possibilities, independent of the immediate grammaticalness caused by one of them rather than another. Thus all interpretations given in (43) and (44) may be legitimate.

---

[4] We use here the general term 'delete' in order to characterize the type of the transformation involved. It may, however, be argued that such a descriptive term is too strong to characterize the metaphorization process. Although ad hoc deletion is not excluded we may perhaps view this process to have the effect of 'cancelling' or 'neutralizing' the function of the selection restriction. It depends on the logico-semantic possibility for lexemes to have contradictory features (see note 3c).

[5] In fact the problem of (ad hoc) deletion also plays a role in the description by addition/transfer in the preceding paragraph. As soon as we transfer e.g. a feature [+HUMAN] to a lexeme specified with [−HUMAN] the resulting specification is contradictory. (This logical impossibility can be shown easily when we specify semantic features with the aid of meaning postulates). In general we will adopt the hypothesis that the feature received 'cancels' the inherent feature which is contradictory with it. We touch here upon fundamental problems of linguistic and logical semantics in general: it might be the case, for example in literature, that entities referred to by metaphorical lexemes have, in some 'possible world', contradictory features (cf. § 6.6 below). We therefore postulated three (and not one or two) interpretations for a metaphorical combination in literary texts. Metaphorization in L_N, indeed, may then be characterized by the fact that the ad hoc addition of a feature always cancels the contradictory inherent feature. We will return below to some general cognitive implications of our assumptions: what, for example, are the degrees of 'imaginability' related with semantic interpretability in a specific possible world? (cf. Lakoff [1968b]).

The deletion transformation can easily be represented as follows

(45) $A[+\alpha, +\beta], B[[+\underline{\quad}[-\alpha]], +\gamma] \Rightarrow AB'[[+\alpha, +\beta], [\varnothing, +\gamma]]$.

We should notice that our notations neglected the precise semantic structure of the combination of two lexemes or lexicoids. Neither from interpretative nor from generative semantics is it clear what these combinations will actually look like. Our 'linear' notation is roughly comparable with the one suggested by Weinreich (1966), but it is probable that the relations are to be represented in a phrase marker, for example as a labelled directed tree as in (37) where the logico-semantic relations are explicitly indicated (cf. Lakoff [1971a]).

4.3. Let us return briefly to the problem of the textual character of metaphorization and its correct interpretation. We noticed that we can decide about the anomaly of a lexeme in a metaphor if and only if it does not fit regularly into the further semantic structure of the text. In Reverdy's text we know that *vent* is not metaphorical because lexemes like *matin*, *soleil*, *ciel*, *arbre* and a second occurrence of *vent* establish a 'basic line of coherence', which we can call 'isotopy' after Greimas (1966), with respect to which *se déployer* must be the metaphorizing element.

Text, context, or situation therefore decide which element is the TOPIC (cf. chap. 2) and which element is a METAPHORICAL COMMENT. However it is often the case that more than one lexeme or a whole SR should be considered metaphorical with respect to text structure. The recourse to a textual description is even more inevitable here. In a sentence like

(46)   The lion roared ...

we cannot possibly know whether we have to interpret the structure literally or metaphorically as

(47)   The courageous man cried loudly ...

or something like that. In that case we have to know whether the text is further specified with an Argument having [+ HUM] or [+ ANIMAL]. The transformation proposed above will, in the first case be applied to both lexemes of a metaphorical SR. That is, it will retain, especially in L_N, those features relevant for the identification and the modification of textual topic *man* and the textual comments of his Actions. In isolation (46) is therefore basically ambiguous but a text grammar will regularly generate it through a cycle of metaphorization transformations which will automatically assign to it the relevant semantic representation.

Notice that the mere presence of possible disambiguating features in the preceding or following part of the text is not enough. We need precise information about the semantic syntax of surrounding SR's and of the text as a whole. A sentence like *The hunter chased the lion*, preceding (46) implies both [+ HUM] and [+ ANIMAL]. The literal interpretation, in that case, will normally have priority above the metaphorical one. That is, metaphorization takes place if and only if the literal representation of a metaphorical SR does not occur elsewhere in the text and if no other indications (for example the courage of the hunter) can re-introduce ambiguity.

This example of metaphorical SR's brings us to another important issue: the process of linear interpretation/production of the semantic representation of a text. How do we represent formally what can be called *retro-disambiguation* of such ambiguous SR's and in particular of ambiguous or metaphorical lexemes? Apparently, in performance, we must either store directly two relevant possible interpretations (with respect to preceding texts) or we process a structure which is sufficiently abstract to be specified in the following part of the text (cf. Kooij [1971]).

We may conclude that, in general, any SR in a text is HYPOTHETICAL until it has been sufficiently specified by following SR's. This assumption actually suggests that a linear and 'progressive' account of texts as sequences of SR's is unsatisfactory. The global text structure as represented by macro-deep structure has to guide the derivation of the respective sentences in order that coherent semantic representations may be assigned to them. We will return to this problem of macro-semantics below (cf. also chaps. 2 and 3).

4.4. There is a yet stronger form of metaphorization. Not only a whole *SR* but also a whole text (or an embedded text, a textoid) may be metaphorical. Here all SR's must be transformationally derived from a 'literal' deep structure. This type of text is well known from medieval literature: ALLEGORY. Other forms like the parable, pastiche, irony are derived from this type. Characteristic is the fact that the text itself does not specify possible means of disambiguation. We may therefore consider the text to have a coherent SR in its own right, which may receive a literal interpretation. Metaphoricalness then, can be decided only on intertextual, pragmatic or referential grounds, for example with the aid of a 'translation' key provided by the author. The general criterion will in that case be that re-transformation is consequent and coherent: all SR's should be consistently derived from a coherent 'literal' deep structure. Strictly speaking such texts have at least two semantic deep structures, and we can therefore consider them to be proper cases of global TEXTUAL AMBIGUITY. When only local metaphorization or ambiguity occurs the text is partially ambiguous, i.e. at a microstructural level, provided that surrounding sentences do not have disambiguating structures.

5. SOME FURTHER EXAMPLES

5.1. With the aid of the theoretical insight, provisionally built up in the previous sections, into the structures and the processes underlying metaphors in general and metaphors in literary texts in particular, we may now try to give a description of some further examples in Reverdy's text. This description is only partial and informal. We will not provide the precise transformational rules generating the metaphors.

The construction *silence épais* (line vi) is ill-formed because *silence* does not have the features [+ CONCR], [+ OBJECT], [+ VISIBLE] co-textually required by *épais*. Following rule (45) we may delete these selection restrictions and retain only such inherent features as [+ DIMENSION], [+ HIGH DEGREE], indicating the intensity of *silence*, for example. Based on such features would be the normal generation of lexemes like *lourd*. Such a transformation probably models our interpretation of such a metaphorical construction. Conversely, we might, in theory, assign by addition transformation a feature [+ CONCR] to *silence*, which we could also do for *vent*. In practice, however, there are some empirical drawbacks to this possibility. That is, we can not IMAGINE silence as a concrete, visible object. We see that a sound theory of metaphorization obviously must not only be based on a (textual) semantics, but also on different COGNITIVE theories. Textual coherence, as we noticed before, is also based on pragmatical and referential factors: semantic well-formedness is closely related to, but must nevertheless be distinguished from, our knowledge or imagination of actual and possible worlds and the objects and events defining them. The constraints defined at these levels clearly direct our possible interpretations of irregular or metaphorical constructions. We cannot imagine a wind or a silence to be pliable and thick objects respectively and we therefore, in accordance with further textual structure, normally interpret their predicates as metaphorizing. These facts are vague and informal but they are an important part of the theory of metaphor and of a theory of semantics in general, because they co-determine the very notion of semantic well-formedness and its relation to the notion of reference.

5.2. In the following lines of Reverdy's text we observe the construction of a systematic semantic ambiguity, or rather the establishment of two basic isotopies. In *aucun souffle ne ride le silence* which is metaphorical because *rider* requires [+ OBJECT], [+ SOLID] *souffle* is regularly ambiguous because it may contain a feature [+ NATURE] or [+ HUM], referring to wind. The preceding text does not decisively indicate the necessary information because it contains both [+ HUM], in *mouvement de bras* and in *la voix qui appelle*, and [+ NATURE], in *vent*, *silence*, and in the following lexemes of the text. Further the silence might be 'broken' (the interpretative paraphrase of *rider*) both by a human voice and by the sound of the wind.

This systematic metaphorical interference of the features [+ HUM] and [+ NATURE] is very explicit in the following line

(48)   Les larmes du matin et les doigts de la rive.

This compound sentence is ungrammatical (both syntactically and semantically) because the underlying sentoids

(49)   Le matin a des larmes
(50)   La rive a des doigts

are ill-formed, because of the opposition between $[+ \text{HUM}]$ and $[- \text{HUM}]$ which is implied by $[+ \text{NATURE}]$ or by $[+ \text{LANDSCAPE}]$ and by $[+ \text{TEMP}]$ occurring in *matin*.

In both cases we might first, theoretically, transform *matin* and *rive* into structures compatible with the human attributes

$$(51) \quad X[+ \text{CONCRETE}, + \text{NATURE} \ldots]/Y[+ [+ \text{HUM}]\underline{\quad}]$$
$$\Rightarrow X'[+ \text{CONCRETE}, + \text{NATURE}, \langle + \text{HUM} \rangle]$$

This rule is well-known and traditionally classified as PERSONIFICATION, an operation often used in literary texts when objects (or animals) are assigned human properties. We see that the transfer of specific features may be a basis for a further TYPOLOGY of metaphorical structures (cf. Petöfi [1969a] for detail).

Personification or 'humanization' may be explained as a natural consequence of the anthropomorphic tendencies of cognitive processes in general.

Further characteristic examples in Reverdy's text of this humanizing tendency of the metaphorizations are

(52)   L'ornière suit le pas
(53)   L'arbre se penche et interroge
(54)   Le chemin perdu se cache sous le pont
(55)   ?La forêt remue
(56)   La fumée s'endort

The rule underlying these personifications does not imply of course that we imagine these objects as human beings but only that some of their properties might conveniently be actualized by lexemes normally restricted to Arguments having $[+ \text{HUM}]$.

The converse process, in this text, is also possible, if not more likely. Instead of adding a feature $[+ \text{HUM}]$ we may interpret the indication given in the title *jour éclatant* as particularly relevant for the priority of the $[+ \text{NATURE}]$ isotopy in the text. We are then obliged to find lexicoids underlying *larmes* and *doigts* that are compatible with *matin* and *rive*. The selectional restrictions $[+ \text{HUM}]$ will then be deleted first and then the central features, e.g. $[+ \text{OBJECT}, + \text{CONCRETE}, + \text{GLOBULAR}, + \text{LIQUIDITY}, + \text{DISCRETE} \ldots]$ in *larmes* have to provide a hyperonymous lexicoid, *drop* for example. *Matin* does not have these features and we do not seem to be very much advanced. However, temporal lexemes like *day, morning*, etc. may be used normally in L_N to represent – as synecdochical structures (see below) – the events occurring during the time indicated. This implies that we might consider *drop* as a *pars pro toto* for rain, which, in turn, could be the event implied by matin. The interpretative paraphrase would then be something like

(57)   The rain-drops falling in the morning.

A more strict interpretation however is the following: *du matin* can be considered a restrictive predicate of *larmes*: 'the tears characteristic of the morning'. Together with the features [+ NATURE], [+ LANDSCAPE], etc. of the rest of the text we then are obliged to specify *drops* as *dewdrops*, which provides a satisfactory and coherent underlying SR. The process, thus, is double: first we generalize *larmes* to *drops* by deleting [+ HUM], we then specify again under the influence of the [+ NATURE] isotopy and we may interpretatively paraphrase *larmes du matin* with *dewdrops*.

We may schematize this process as follows

(58) $A[+\alpha, +\beta, +\gamma]/B[-\gamma, +\delta] \Rightarrow A'[+\alpha, +\beta, \varnothing] \Rightarrow A''[+\alpha, +\beta, \langle +\delta \rangle]$

where $A' \subset A$ and $A' \subset A''$. The paraphrasing process can be made clear in the following simple way:

(59)   *larmes* $-------------------\rightarrow$ *dewdrops*
         $[+\alpha, +\beta, +\gamma]$ $[+\alpha, +\beta, +\delta]$

                              drops
                              $[+\alpha, +\beta]$

Notice that *dewdrops* is not properly part of the deep structure but only the basic feature configuration on which it is based and which can be lexematized with *drops* for example. The paraphrase interpretation is a superficial process based on semantic contiguities, knowledge of the world and other factors of predicative co-occurrence of elements. This process of ASSOCIATION (as we might call it) is therefore indirect and based on common deep structure properties. The generation of a specific paraphrasing lexeme cannot be formally predicted but is based on semantic probability (expectation) and therefore belongs to performance, if no further indication is provided by the other textual SR's.

5.3. In the previous paragraph we noticed that not only formal features of lexemes may underlie metaphorization. The other main type of semantic operations both in literary and in non-literary texts is METONYMIA, treated also in classical rhetorics as a 'figure of thought'. Here the conditions for generating an anomalous construction are fundamentally different and lie largely outside the domain of formal semantics.

In the substitution conception of these operations we might simply define metonymia (and the specific subtype of SYNECDOCHE) as the substitution of a lexeme X by a lexeme Y based on some EMPIRICAL RELATION between the referents denoted by X and Y. Whereas in metaphorization inherent PROPERTIES (one-place predicates) were involved, which may underlie features of a semantic theory, we are dealing here with referential RELATIONS (n-place predicates).

We postulated above, for example, that the lexicoid *rain* may be manifested as *drops* because rain consists, by definition and empirically, of drops, although we might say that they both share the feature of [+ LIQUIDITY]. A lexeme like *dew* is a similar case. The lexemes metonymically related with it will normally appear in the discursive lexicon definition of it: 'tiny drops of moisture condensed on cool surfaces between evening and morning from water vapour in the air' (from: *The Advanced Learner's Dictionary of Current English*, 2nd edition). We see that many of the lexemes of this description occur in the text and our implicit knowledge of the lexicon therefore enables a native speaker to select *dew* after having generalized *larmes* to *drops*.

It might be asked if and how in such sentences like *He drank two bottles* and other conventional cases metonymia can be accounted for in a formal way. This would be possible if our empirical knowledge (e.g. *a bottle contains liquid*) is 'textually' stored as a set of meaning postulates or presuppositions. The simple rule, then, is as follows

$$(60) \qquad AB \Rightarrow \begin{Bmatrix} A\emptyset \\ \emptyset B \end{Bmatrix}$$

if and only if A is connected with B, i.e. included in B, element of B, a cause of B, a consequence of B, property of B, etc. In accordance with traditional accounts we may say that metaphor is based on the principle of (paradigmatic) similarity and metonymia on the principle of (syntagmatic) contiguity (cf. Jakobson [1960]). If that is true we may have the explicit or 'full' form of a metonymia, as a part of deep structure, as indicated in (60). Metonymia, then, must be based on *deletion transformations* of full lexicoidal elements or even of whole lexemes, for example: *bottle of milk* ⇒ *bottle* ∅.

It is clear that such deletions may occur only under the following conditions
(i) the operation must have been conventionalized in the lexicon or in language use,
(ii) the textual structure specifies the deleted element such that a coherent SR can be re-constructed.

It is once more evident that a formal description requires the explicit co-derivation of the SR's of a whole sequence of sentences, describable only in a T-grammar. We will not go any further into the description of metonymias nor into a possible typology.

Their transformational derivation does not seem to present any difficulties, if of course the empirical contiguities can be formalized.

5.4. Let us take a final example from Reverdy's text and try to indicate how/why a metaphorical lexeme is generated

(61)   Le soleil se déroule

This sentence is probably well-formed from a strict semantic point of view because there is a reading of *se dérouler* having $[+ [+ \text{OBJECT}]\underline{\quad}]$ and $[+ [\text{ROUND}]\underline{\quad}]$ as selection restrictions. This restriction does not contradict the features of *soleil*. However, *se dérouler* seems to be restricted (i) to relatively small objects (ii) to a movement on a solid basis (iii) to longish rollable objects. These constraints are not satisfied by *soleil*. There is another reading of *se dérouler* which has e.g., $[+ [+ \text{LANDSCAPE}]\underline{\quad}]$ as a selection restriction, a restriction nearly compatible with *soleil* which is part of, standing above, the landscape. We notice that of two readings of a lexeme some features $[+ \text{MOVEMENT}]$, $[+ \text{ROUND}]$ of one reading are retained and a selection restriction $[+ [+ \text{NATURE}]\underline{\quad}]$ from the other. Finally *se dérouler* is compatible as a movement with the curvilinear trajectory as a property of the sun. Notice also the parallelism with *se déployer* and *s'envoler*, which also have important features like 'beginning' or 'opening' characteristic of the semantic/ thematic structure of the text as a whole (cf. the remarks at the beginning of the next chapter).

Let us assume that all this partly semantical partly referential information is required in a particular co-text of a poem, and further the topic *soleil*, together with an Action-verb denoting a trajectory movement of a round object in/above the landscape. The formal rule underlying such a 'generative' instruction would then among other lexemes probably produce *se dérouler*

(62) $X[+ \text{MOVEMENT}, [+ [+ \text{ROUND}]\underline{\quad}], [+ [+ \text{CURVILINEAR}]$
          $\underline{\quad}], [+ [\text{LANDSCAPE}]\underline{\quad}] \text{Action}]$

$$/Soleil \left\{ \begin{array}{l} + \text{ OBJECT} \\ + \text{ CONCRETE} \\ + \text{ WARM} \\ + \text{ ROUND} \\ + \text{ CELESTIAL} \end{array} \right\} \Rightarrow \textit{se dérouler } [...]$$

It is very clear that we operate here at the boundaries of formal semantics of and a theory of reference. Instead of on formal features we often base ourselves on referential, empirical properties of denotata. The rule in (62) is one representing normal selection of lexemes in an SR. The formation of metaphorical *se dérouler* is represented directly as if no regular verb exists with these feature constraints. Apparently further transformations were necessary to delete the inappropriate selection restriction of *se dérouler*.

In many cases not only the text itself but other texts of the same author may provide contextual information for the correct assignment of well-formed underlying SR's. Thus we find in Reverdy lines like

(63)   Le soleil tournait encore autour de la maison

$$\text{(Reverdy [1964]69)}$$

where we also find a circular movement, implied in metaphorical *tourner* being combined as an Action with *soleil*.

6. SOME THEORETICAL CONCLUSIONS

6.1. The semantic and textual mechanisms underlying the linguistic and poetic process of metaphorization have been made clear in some detail in the previous sections. This does not mean that all problems involved were actually solved, although some provisional transformations and conditions were formulated.

One of the first points to be stressed is that we must make a strict distinction between formal GENERATION and real PRODUCTION of metaphors, a distinction which was often somewhat blurred in our discussion in order to simulate formally the steps necessary to produce/interpret metaphorical structures. It may be the case, especially in modern poetry, that lexemes are directly selected for their internal feature structure, without the necessary additions or deletions of features. That is, the major condition, that of well-formedness of underlying SR's, is perhaps irrelevant in literary texts.

Furthermore, lexemes may in actual performance be chosen at random in the hope that chance might produce unexpected but acceptable collocations. This random selection may be very conscious, of course, and need not be 'automatic'. In that case we have to rely upon our general linguistic and cognitive ability to establish relations between elements which at first sight – in surface structures – seem totally unrelated. The perception of similarities, when the type of text and the context seem to require it, can be very powerful. This fact is one aspect of the proper indefiniteness of metaphorical structures, and also of their unpredictability. The process is rather general and can be explicitly accounted for, but the final selection of the specific lexeme is almost wholly dependent on pragmatical, referential and other factors of stylistic performance. Actually, this is true for all processes of lexematization.

6.2. Some further discussion about the formal conditions for semantic well-formedness and for interpretability is necessary here, because the problem of metaphorization is directly related to it. Our initial hypothesis was, especially in the preceding chapter, that any linguistically relevant interpretation is based on well-formed semantic deep structures as specified by semantic base-rules. Such an assumption is rather strong and has to be empirically warranted.

Let us observe, first, that this problem is independent of the syntactic well-formed-ness of surface structure. We know that ill-formed syntactic structures may receive perfectly coherent interpretations. This can only be explained if well-formed semantic structures underlie this surface form, and if native speakers have the ability to relate such an irregular surface form to this regular SR.

What, then, can be said about semi-sentences in which major categories are deleted, e.g. such that no verbal predicate is realized? In many regular cases this predicate may be textually supplied, for example when it is the topic of the sentence in which only a new noun phrase need be manifested (cf. chaps 2 and 6). In other cases, which are quite regular in poetry, simple nominal occurrence simply seems to imply the existence of referents, which may produce such interpretative insertions of verbs as *to be*, etc.

In a compound semi-sentence like *les larmes du matin et les doigts de la rive*, for example, there is no further possibility than supplying verbal predicates like *to be* or *to have*. However, are such underlying representations necessary, i.e. is there any formal or empirical evidence that propositions must have a verbal predicate denoting a property or an action? Any static description might in principle be reduced to an enumeration of nouns without such predicates. This is often precisely the case in modern poetry. Moreover, the deletion of verbs or their simple absence leaves the way open for the insertion of the noun in many interpretative (hypothetic) verbal frames: *I see Arg*; *I hear Arg*; etc. Notice also that underlying logical forms do not prescribe at all the selection of verbal elements: this is a pure syntactic surface constraint. A logical formula of predicate calculus is simply well-formed, when it has the following form: $f(x)$, i.e. if an argument variable and a predicate variable are given. Thus *larmes du matin* might simply be noted $(\exists x)[L(x)]$: there is an x such that it is 'tears of the morning'. The basic assertion reduces, then, to the statement that there 'is', textually, at least one individual thing to which the predicate 'tears of the morning' applies, i.e. having the denotation of that predicate as a property, at a time t_i and at a place l_i.

We may concede that this is a minimal and very elementary condition upon logico-semantic well-formedness, but there is no reason to reject it as inadequate for a semantic theory of natural language. Most propositions in natural language assign properties to or establish relations between arguments already having some prop-erties, i.e. not to variables but to constants. We will assume nevertheless that minimal logical *wff*'s are both necessary and sufficient as lower bounds for interpretability in a text. This last requirement is probably necessary because the variable(s) of the formula can only properly be bound when other SR's give it its place in a semantic structure, when no pragmatico-referential operators determine their extension. Of course, our knowledge of the lexicon enables us to 'understand' isolated words. However, this understanding can be considered 'metalinguistic': we know that the word belongs to a given language, and we may assign a co-text to it. As such, however, it refers to a class (of properties, relations) and does not have any pragmatic function with respect to a referential state of affairs. In that case no text in the formal sense can be established. We limit the very notion of interpretability, then, to well-formed propositions of the minimal form defined above – in accordance with the theory of predicate logic.

6.3. Although the issues touched upon in the previous paragraph require extensive discussion both in meta-logic and in a theory of semantics, and although these domains should be clearly distinguished, we may now briefly outline some consequences for a theory of metaphorization.

It was assumed that metaphors are definable only as PROPERTIES OF SEMANTIC RELATIONS. These relations are defined in semantic derivations as specified earlier. Relevant for the theory are those relations upon which semantics formulates specific well-formedness constraints, *viz.* relations between arguments and predicates. These constraints are based on the internal structure of the pre-terminal complex symbols, the lexicoids, of a semantic derivation. Predicates, thus, assign properties to and relations between variables and constants under the general condition that this assignment may not contradict the list of assignments already provided, conventionally, by a lexicon. Thus a proposition underlying the sentence *The table is talking* is ill-formed because

(63)   (i) $(x)[T(x) \supset \text{HUM}(x)]$ $T = talk$
          (ii) $T(a)$
          _____
          (iii) $\therefore \text{HUM}(a)$

contradicts with

(64)   (i) $(y)[Tb(y) \supset \text{OBJ}(y)]$ $Tb = table$
          (ii) $(y)[\text{OBJ}(y) \supset - \text{HUM}(y)]$ (semantic rule)
          (iii) $Tb(a)$
          _____
          (iv) $\therefore - \text{HUM}(a)$

Thus well-formedness is derived from the given lexical rules. In order to generate metaphorical structures, then, these rules have to be changed in certain ways, under specific conditions, and in given co-texts, that is, we suppress either (63i) or (64ii). Because we may assume that predication is not intended to be meaningless, that is at least certain properties/relations are intended to be assigned to the lexematic constants (arguments) of a metaphorical proposition, we may simply delete the basic implications formulated in (63i) and retain the properties of the predicate itself such that their assignment to the arguments becomes meaningful. But how must we imagine this process formally, i.e. in explicit derivations?

6.4. Until now we have conceived of metaphorization as a specific transformation, in which features of lexicoids are added and/or deleted (i.e. 'parenthesized') such that a different class of lexemes may be selected in a given semantic structure. However, if the constraints are already broken so early as to delete fundamental categories like [+ CONCR], [+ ABSTR], etc. we might assume that specific FORMATION RULES may generate ill-formed SR's. However, this solution has serious drawbacks. First of all, we do not have ungrammatical semantic structures, because the normal argument-predicate form is present. Only the pre-lexical structures substituted at the end of the derivation are mutually incompatible. This substitution is already trans-formational. The feature specification is not a sub-categorizing process but the controlled selection of complex symbols. Furthermore, if we assume that all metaphors are generated by ill-formed underlying SR's we would be able to construct only ill-formed interpretations, that is, we could interpret metaphors only literally. But, since one of the conditions upon metaphoricalness is precisely the 'reduction' to meaningful structures, we have to suppose that their ungrammaticalness is a more superficial phenomenon. Similarly, many metaphorical structures, as we saw, may coincide with a whole sentence which in surface structure is perfectly well-formed also. It would be difficult to derive such surface forms from ill-formed deep structures. These sentences are superficially incoherent with surrounding sentences, whereas their deep structures are coherent with them. Ill-formed deep structures can never be coherent with other, well-formed deep structures.

These remarks, it should be stressed, are vague in the sense that we do not yet know exactly how semantic deep structures are formed and how pre-lexical content is assigned to them.

We must conclude, then, that metaphorization is essentially transformational. The process begins after the formation of well-formed SR's and the insertion of 'normal' lexicoids. Transformational rules operate, optionally, on this input, by neutralizing the selection restrictions of the predicates for example, as described above. The desired semantic content may, then, be realized with lexemes the selection of which would normally be blocked by these restrictions.

6.5. It must be observed, finally, that the metaphorical transformations may operate on different levels. Some features/restrictions deleted are quite fundamental, which is often the case and considered typical for metaphorization, e.g. the combination of [+ ABSTR] and [+ CONCR]. Other rules seem to be much more language specific, and occur during the process of feature specification transducing lexicoids into specific lexemes: the equivalent of *le vent se déploie* might have a lexico-semantic structure which is perfectly grammatical in some languages. Accordingly, we might distinguish different DEGREES OF METAPHORICALNESS. A metaphor will have a higher degree of metaphoricalness if the features/restrictions deleted are more basic/general, e.g. [+ ANIMATE] is more basic, according to the redundancy rules of the semantic theory, than $[+ \text{HUM}]$. Thus *le vent se déploie* is less metaphorical than *l'arbre* (...) *interroge* in Reverdy's text.

Similarly, we may on this basis establish a formal TYPOLOGY of metaphorical structures by studying the transformations of lexicoids according to their semantic domains defined by the features added or deleted. Thus in Reverdy's text we clearly have a general transformation type adding $[+ \text{HUM}]$ to lexemes having $[+ \text{NATURE}]$, and thus $[- \text{HUM}]$. Given the close relationships between features and the fundamental components of spatio-temporal perception and cognitive processes in general it is thus possible to describe the 'directions' of the ad hoc lexical changes that are metaphors.

6.6. There is a final question which will, however, not be investigated here: since metaphorization establishes – through rules – ad hoc semantic representations paired with ungrammatical lexematic surface structures, we may describe it also in PRAGMATIC TERMS. That is, we describe it as an expression having meaning x_1 for speaker y_1 and meaning x_2 for hearer y_2 at a given time t, at a given place l and in situational (referential, pragmatic – i.e. locutionary –, historical, etc.) context c (cf. Grice [1969]). Some properties of these pragmatical interpretations of expressions in natural lanusage – considered to be such n-tuples – are treated in chap. 9. We here touch upon the intricate problem of the relations between intensional semantics and logic on the one hand and extensional semantics and logic and the theory of reference on the other hand – questions which are beyond the scope of this book but which will turn out to be of the utmost importance for the formalization of a theory of metaphor (cf. Abraham and Braunmüller [1971]). Thus the grammatical rules for metaphorization in this chapter, which were based on an intensional (linguistic) semantics, may be reformulated as operations on a set of different worlds in a MODAL logical semantics. The basic semantic regularities of a grammar would correspond to those of an arbitrary world w_0 or zero-world. The assignment or deletion of features or selection restrictions would then require an interpretation – have a model – in a different world w_i, where the set of predicates assigned to individuals may be different and hence the set of the possible relations in which they may enter. We will see in the next chapter that one of the basic characteristics of literary texts is this construction of a set of other possible worlds. It is clear, however, that the rather fashionable notion of 'possible world' in this perspective has merely an (important) heuristic value as long as we are unable to provide explicit formal descriptions of such 'worlds'.

8

SEMANTIC MACRO-OPERATIONS.
NARRATIVE STRUCTURES

1. MACRO-STRUCTURES AND LITERARY TEXTS

1.1. One main hypothesis of this book, as it was globally elaborated in chapter 3, has been that any well-formed text must have an abstract deep structure defining its macro-coherence. The structures derivable by the base rules of a semantic text grammar thus serve as the formal input of the different transformational cycles converting this global plan into a linearly coherent set of grammatical or semi-grammatical sentences. The intuitive concept related to the formal notion of textual deep structure is the ability of native speakers to assign a global content to a text or a coherent part of the text. That is, any text of a language is perceived as treating of a given 'subject' or 'topic'. We have tried to demonstrate that this ability could not be properly modelled by a linear S-grammar defining the local transition coherence in a sequence of sentences alone. Memory limitations force the user of natural language to proceed at the same time at a deeper, abstract and global level in order to establish the macro-categories and -relations necessary for production and inter-pretation.

1.2. The notions recalled here are of course valid for LITERARY TEXTS as well. In general literary texts also treat a 'topic', not necessarily more or less complex than in non-literary texts. This is particularly manifest in those literary texts we convention-ally call 'novels'. Here we perceive a global structure which we usually indicate with such terms as 'story' or 'plot' (for the technical differentiation of these terms see below). It is intuitively clear that the notions covered by these terms do not pertain to structures for which the sentential semantic content is particularly relevant. We conceive of a story as a structure in which some 'personages' accomplish certain 'actions', with further specification about the 'characters' of these personages and the motivation, intentions, places and circumstances of their behaviour. We are able, further, to paraphrase the story and to summarize it. In principle any native speaker will recog-nize that it is a story which is summarized and, if he knows the text, which story has been summarized. These abilities, to be sure, are general properties of linguistic (textual) competence and are not confined to literary texts alone. The only point we wish to stress is that at least one class of literary texts have characteristics which they share with any other text of the language.

1.3. We may repeat these remarks for such literary texts traditionally called poems though perhaps in a less clear-cut way. Since such texts are mostly much shorter, macro- and micro-structures often seem to coincide so that 'summarizing' may theoretically be identical with enumerating the sentential SR's of the text. This has actually been done in much traditional 'interpretation' of lyrical texts where we see the translation – sentence by sentence – into deep-structure paraphrases which are more well-formed such that they are 'normally' interpretable.

We have to concede, however, that such lyrical texts do not always 'represent' 'personages' and a series of events or actions in the same intuitively well-known manner as described above for narrative. Especially in modern poetry it is not easy to summarize the 'topic' or 'subject' of the text by a simple paraphrase of the traditional type.

We might ask ourselves, then, whether resumability is a valid indication of the existence of textual deep structures, i.e. for global textual coherence. And, if so, whether the types of structures realized in poems also lend themselves to such a criterion, and, if that should turn out to be the case, what type of paraphrase should then be given.

1.4. If the presence of a deep-structure also defines the literary text, that is, if the criterion of macro-wellformedness is also valid in literature, we must ask ourselves, next,

(i)   whether formal literariness at this level can be defined at all, i.e. whether there are typical 'literary' deep structures of texts,
(ii) if such specific deep structures exist, what are their forms and the rules generating them,
(iii) whether such rules have a formational or a transformational character, that is,
(iv) whether 'normal', well-formed textual deep-structures are transformed into specific transformed macro-structures and these into specific L_L-textual surface structures.

These and related problems are treated in this chapter.

We will focus our attention upon those literary texts where macro-structures are most easily recognizable: NARRATIVE TEXTS. Our discussion about rules separating these texts from non-literary texts (both narrative and non-narrative) and from other literary texts, will draw upon the results of current work in 'structural analysis' of narrative. However, both our theoretical and methodological framework are essentially different. Narrative texts must be formally defined, i.e. by explicit derivations, as a TYPE of text among others for which specific rules must be formulated as part of a future general grammar of texts. Further, our discussion will continue in the direction of thought outlined earlier in this book, based on notions elaborated in generative semantics. Typically literary categories will thus receive their explicit description within linguistic macro-semantics, although their status is obviously literary, as well as the rules manipulating them. This requirement is inevitable when we want to arrive at testable and falsifiable hypotheses in literary theory in general and in narrative theory in particular. Literary (narrative) 'units' and relations can ultimately be recognized only through the linguistic manifestation of a text. We will leave, for the moment, such narrative 'texts' as can be represented by visual means (strips, film, etc.), which give specific problems of testability.

1.5. Our remarks in the previous chapters and in the paragraphs above have tacitly introduced a series of undefined terms such as 'poetry', 'novel', 'narrative text', etc. It is our intuitive, conventional knowledge of the TYPES of texts recovered by these terms which enabled us to formulate some regularities underlying these texts (cf. van Dijk [1971a]). Although we have abstracted in general from type-bound assertions in our definition of literary operations, we have had to stress that many operations are limited to, or dominant in, e.g. poetry or narrative. Similarly, we assumed that surface operations are characteristic above all in lyrical texts. We now suggest that narrative is especially defined at lower and more global levels of description.

At the same time, however, we have to recall that such formal criteria for a future typology of literary texts are not mutually exclusive: metaphor or even alliteration can occur functionally in narrative and a poem may develop an elementary story. In a more abstract manner of textual organization we find in both types structures which we may call 'thematic', a term to be defined below. This remark does not prevent, on the other hand, a formal characterization of textual types by defining the relevant operations which seem DOMINANT in them. That is, we must account for the fact that production and reception of literary texts is also differentiated with respect to their levels: in poetry our attention is focussed on sentential surface structure and, possibly, on thematic text structure, whereas in novels and other narrative our attention is focussed on the macro-units and -relations we enumerated above: personages, events, actions, etc. Surface structures, here, merely have local stylistic function, not unlike similar operations in non-literary texts. Differentiation, of course, is also an aspect of literary performance, but an adequate literary grammar has to provide the formal model accounting for our ability to distinguish and to identify literary texts ALSO on purely structural grounds.

The differentiation of literature into 'genres' is heavily determined by historical and socio-cultural factors, but a high degree of conventionality may normally correspond to the internalization of rule-systems by native speakers/users of literature. It is our task to make these rule-systems explicit in a form corresponding to generative grammars.

Many complex problems, however, remain to be solved especially at the methodo-logical level. For instance, the role of autonomous diachronical development of these types is closely related to our recognition of their underlying structure. Furthermore, even from a synchronic point of view, we are confronted with such texts as *poèmes en prose* and the *nouveau roman*, in which both types may actualize their typical operations. These 'mixtures', of course, may sometimes be due to factors of perfor-mance, but often they lead to independently recognizable and acceptable types of texts for which, then, an independent sub-grammar will be needed. These and similar problems present themselves and they are important in literary theory. However, we need hardly stop to examine them in detail in this book (cf. van Dijk, 1972c). We first want to provide the theoretical language of description for literary texts in general: form of the rules and the grammar and the status of literary (sub-)grammars. Typo-logical, diachronical and contextual implications can only adequately be handled on just such a formal basis of sufficient generality.

1.6. Finally, we must add some observations about a problem raised above: the macro-wellformedness of texts. We postulated that any text by definition has a semantic deep structure as specified by the rules of a T-grammar. However, is this criterion valid without any restriction for literary texts as well?

Intuitively we know that most traditional literary texts, say until the middle of the nineteenth century, are globally interpretable, i.e. they consist of an identifiable coherent set of events, actions or situations. In modern literature, however, it has become increasingly difficult in many texts, especially poetic texts, to identify a 'topic' or global coherence. The central question, then, is whether such texts can be said to have a deep structure and, if not, how they should be defined as texts. A more plausible solution is that textual surface structures of these texts, either micro- or macro-structures, show a lack of linear coherence. In that case the global deep structure exists, determining our perception of the text as a coherent unit, whereas its deviant character, with respect to G_N, is due to transformational rules of different kinds operating on different levels.

To be sure, the presence of a well-formed semantic deep structure in literary texts does not necessarily imply that any speaker is able to paraphrase (or resume) this structure. Its very abstractness, especially in modern poetry, may simply reduce such a paraphrase to the enumeration of certain underlying themes, of which the precise structure can be made explicit only by theoretical description. Deep-structure rules, then, only represent our ability to perceive intuitively the text as a coherent whole.

Thus, as we did for the structure of the sentence, we will assume that any text has a minimal global well-formedness, however elementary in some cases. Texts without such a deep structure will be called NON-SENSE (in the formal sense of that term), i.e. non-interpretable. This does not preclude, we must emphasize, their functioning as literary texts under certain specific conditions. One of these conditions is, for instance, the presence of specific surface characteristics of literary texts, like graphematic structure of a certain kind (cf. dadaist poetry). Furthermore, their very deviance, i.e. their complete irregularity with respect to G_N already partially causes a literary process of perception, because the formal irregularity of written texts with respect to G_N is considered as conventionally 'typical' of literature in our culture.

These extreme cases of literary 'non-sense', which result from a random generator and a lexicon (which in turn may also be reduced to a list of phonemes of the language), are however rather marginal, although their historical function may be important. Most literary texts have global structure of some kind. This does not mean that these are always easily interpretable at the semantic level. We already noted that in many cases they are confined to a thematic taxonomy. Further, in many narrative texts also the macro-structure may be so complex that the perception of global unity is difficult if not impossible for untrained readers. We touch, here, upon the problem of literary 'competence' in general. Is this competence to be defined with respect to literary producers (authors), naive readers or experienced and highly sophisticated readers (for example literary critics) or perhaps with respect to all of them, thus defining the basic and general capacity for reading/interpreting literary texts?

This problem cannot easily be solved, that is to say not on the formal level. It is well-known that the theoretical complexity of sentences and texts may be infinite. The ability of perceiving such structures and of assigning interpretations to them, however, is a problem of a theory of performance, not a grammatical problem. Here we can only suggest possible formal means for differentiating DEGREES OF COMPLEXITY, for instance by measures of repeated self-embedding, measures of metaphoricalness (cf. previous chapter) and measures of semantic coherence (redundancy of semantic recurrence), etc.

Deep structure well-formedness, then, can be defined only with the property of formal derivability, irrespective of the complexity or irregularity of its surface manifestations. We have to see now how these superficial properties are formally reduced to/deduced from abstract underlying structures.

2. THE LINEAR COHERENCE OF LITERARY TEXTS

2.1. Before we proceed to a description of global deep structures of literary texts and their possible transformations, we will consider briefly some aspects of the surface coherence between sentences of literary texts. This problem, therefore, properly belongs to the issue treated in the previous chapter, but its relationship with global coherence demands some treatment here.

In the previous chapter we studied in some detail the different aspects of semantic ill-formedness (with respect to G_N) of isolated sentences in the texts of L_L. We may ask ourselves to what extent we can also find specific operations for the concatenation of sentences in literature.

It was noted that an adequate description of metaphor required a simultaneous description of the surrounding SR's and, ultimately, of the whole text. Similarly, it is possible that intersentential incoherence in L_L can be 'resolved' only with respect to coherence relations in wider (co-)text or at a more abstract level. Many modern poems, for example, can be totally incoherent in their surface structure and may nevertheless be characterized as coherent texts at the level of deep structure. Let us try to make explicit, then, which rules of linear coherence can be violated, or which rules specific of L_L can be formulated at this level.

2.2. For a concrete example we may return briefly to the poem of Reverdy. Its linear coherence is violated in nearly all transitions, and is already indicated by the simple deletion of surface *Agents* (realized as *NP*'s) and *Actions* (through *VP*'s) with respect to which all coherence relations have to be defined in normal texts. Moreover, there are no explicit human actors, which reduces the text to a description of properties and actions of inanimate or non-human objects. Thus *mouvement de bras* cannot be related to *le vent qui se déploie* in a significantly coherent way, that is neither by implication or entailment nor by relations of inclusion, intersection, etc. However, we may relate *battement d'ailes*, implying 'bird', to *vent*, this lexeme being a possible locative or circumstantial for birds and their actions. Similarly, *bras* implies a human being, such that *voix qui appelle* may be related with it by lexical rule defining *voix* (if x has a voice then x is human, and conversely). It is possible also to relate *bras*, through *branches*, to *vent*, as a link with a movement caused by the wind.

Still more indirect are the relations between *silence* and line (viii): *les larmes du matin et les doigts de la rive*. A direct semantic – or syntactic – relationship does not exist between these sentences. Coherence is established more globally: *larmes*, taken literally, presupposes [+HUM] and therefore may be connected with *bras*, *voix*, *souffle*; *larmes*, taken metaphorically for 'dew', may be related with the lexemes denoting different phenomena of inanimate or animate nature. The same remarks can be made for *les doigts de la rive*. These minimal feature relationships underlie our perception of the poem as a description of what could traditionally be called a 'scene' or 'panorama', that is an environment (*Loc* + its specification of properties) and some elementary actions of implicit human individuals and of elementary natural events and phenomena. Linear coherence might thus be based on a type of semantic 'juxtaposition', i.e. the actualization of lexemes from certain semantic domains ([+ NATURE], [+ HUM]), in order to describe different aspects of a given situation. The direct relation between those aspects, then, is not made explicit, as would be the case, probably, in non-literary descriptions, and it is established indirectly over the property defining the whole set.

This type of textual organization characterizes the further structure of the poem, and in fact many modern poems. The only direct relationships are thus coordinative and are realized by the use of *et*. Between (xi) and (xii), however, we find a relation between *sol eil* and *ciel*, empirically (the second as *Loc* of the first) and formally related (by a tentative feature [+ CELESTIAL]). Similarly in (xiii) and (xiv), where *carrefour* and *voiture* may be related by *Loc* of the action *rouler* of *voiture*. The same remarks hold true for these lines and (xvi). Apparently line/sentence (xv) is incoherent with both of them. As for previous lines, we notice that coherence in such texts may be discontinuous, i.e. the semantic relations are not strictly linearly established in consecutive SR's, but SR_i may be related with SR_{i+j} (where $j \geqslant 2$), as is also the case in (xvii) and (xix) where *forêt* and *branches* are related by inclusion. *Nuit*, then, picks up the semantic relation (isotopy) established by the title *jour éclatant* and by *matin* in (viii). Similarly for *hirondelle*, related, indirectly, with *ailes*, and for *couchant*, *étincelle*, *ciel* related to *soleil* and *ciel*.

Although we did not specify the full set of semantic relations, we notice that linear coherence in most cases is indirect, i.e. established 'thematically' over semantic domains. Lexemes are not necessarily intersententially related with each other but form, together, a coherent semantic network, interpretable as a 'panoramic picture of nature'. One of the most characteristic deficiences of linear coherence here is not so much the indirectness of nominal (Agent, Patient, Object) elements, but the absence of a coherent succession of related actions or events which normally define progressive linear coherence. This is partially conditioned by the general type of semantic structure involved here: description of *states*, *processes* or *events*, and not of actions. But even then we would normally have rules directly relating one state/process/event with another, which is not the case here. Semantic coherence is not even respected within compound sentences. In lines (v), (viii), (xvi) the conjunction *et* does not relate semantically compatible propositions, and therefore must be qualified as ungrammatical, or simply as an isolated coordinative element. Such an operation occurs often in modern poetry: conjunction or other intersentential operators, like some adverbials, may be generated independently of deep structure relations.

Our conclusion is therefore that the normal deep and surface constraints for relations between sentences may be violated for directly consecutive sentences. This coherence, however, is recaptured on the level of macro-structures and manifests itself throughout the whole text in discontinuous structures.

2.3. What, then, is the precise character of such MACRO-STRUCTURES in (modern) poetry? In the text of Reverdy we may, first, distinguish, at the most elementary level, the recurrence of some basic features: [+ NATURE], [+HUM] and [+MOVE-MENT]. That is, all Arguments – whatever their functions may be – are representations of the classes defined by the first two features, (whereas their Actions, or rather) the processes which are predicates of them, normally share the last feature. We see that, in addition to a possible, macro-semantic syntax, the lexemes of surface structure are selected according to another global plan: a configuration of some isolated features. We will call such features THEMATIC FEATURES, and the structure defined by them a THEMATIC STRUCTURE (cf. van Dijk, 1969). This structure is not syntactic in the formal sense but paradigmatic or taxonomic and often has antithetic properties (human *vs.* non-human, animate *vs.* inanimate, movement *vs.* immobility, etc.).

It is important to notice that thematic macro-structures have to be defined independently of normal textual deep structure. Similar deep structures may be 'accompanied' by different thematic structures and thus lead to different lexematizations.
We see that the thematic organization of a text directly influences the process of
lexematization in the individual sentences. Here we probably touch upon a crucial formal element of what has traditionally often been referred to as CONNOTATION.

Greimas (1966) and others have shown that such thematic structures may also
underlie narrative: the semantic content of a text may represent a story about certain
concrete personages and have at the same time an antithetic thematic structure 'life
vs. death', or something like that. We will come back to this aspect in the next section,
but it should be emphasized that in many cases, especially in mythic or religious
literature, such 'additional' aspects of semantic structure are in fact themselves
textual deep structures, at different levels, e.g. 'symbolical', 'anagogical', 'axiological',
'ideological', etc. We referred to these structures in the previous chapter, as 'allegorical'.
If they have a full semantico-syntactic structure, they are not thematic. Thematic
'structures' only stand for properties of sets of lexemes, i.e. for individual features
and their abstract mutual relations. They are not related to specific semantic functions
of the lexemes in the sentences (arguments or predicates) unlike the lexicoids of
textual deep structure which define the global content of the textual macro-categories.

Apart from the thematic selection mechanism for lexemes, the poetic text has its
normal semantic deep structure, although this TDS may be very much reduced, which
will normally lead to a decreased paraphrasability. Global textual coherence will be
defined by thematic structure alone, as is often the case in modern poetry.

The micro-structural description given in Reverdy's poem of a *jour éclatant* can
thus be considered highly dominated by the thematic configuration $[[+ \text{NATURE}] +$
$[+ \text{HUM}] + [+ \text{MOVEMENT}]]$. It is not easily describable as a coherent event
or process resumable by some hyperonymic lexemes as is normally the case for stories.
It actually only seems to provide the *Loc* or *Circ* (for circumstance) categories of
a semantic deep structure from which Actants and their Actions are deleted.

Such descriptive literary texts share formal properties with scientific textual
descriptions of objects and their properties, though of course in a less systematic and
less explicit way.

One could consider Reverdy's text PLURI-ISOTOPICAL in the sense that there is not
one central (macro-)argument to which a series of predicates are assigned: $Pred_1$
(ARG), $Pred_2$ (ARG) ... $Pred_n$ (ARG) (mono-isotopy) but rather a set of semantically
interrelated Arguments and a corresponding set of predicates (thematically related
by $[+ \text{MOVEMENT}]$):

(1) $Pred_1$ (Arg_1)
             $Pred_2$ (Arg_2)
             $\vdots$
             $Pred_n$ (Arg_n)

The relations between the Arguments in Reverdy's text are only global in that they are part of a large set of lexemes denoting 'nature'. There is no systematic, linear type of relation between the lexemes themselves. We have to see whether this last formal requirement is typical for texts like poems, by considering a segment from a narrative text.

2.4. The question at issue is: do narrative texts have the normal surface constraints for linear coherence which (at least some) poems do not possess? To answer that question we will briefly examine one concrete example. Of course, more extensive observations are necessary to confirm our hypothesis according to which narrative texts do not, or not systematically, have specific surface operations of the kind found in the modern poem described above. That is, their successive sentences are progressively related by the general semantic and semantico-referential relations which we made explicit in the first part of this book.

Let us take, then, the beginning of a story by Joyce, written in a period comparable – in poetry, and in France – with the one in which Reverdy's poem was written: *Two Gallants* (Joyce [1956] 47). The beginning of this text is even semantically comparable with the structure of Reverdy's poem: the description of a 'scene', which, later, will serve as the *Loc* for the actions of some actors

The grey warm evening of August had descended upon the city, and a mild warm air, a memory of summer, circulated in the streets. The streets, shuttered for the repose of Sunday, swarmed with a gaily coloured crowd. Like illumined pearls the lamps shone from the summits of their tall poles upon the living texture below, which, changing shape and hue unceasingly, sent up into the warm grey evening air an unchanging, unceasing murmur.

Two young men came down the hill of Rutland Square. One of them was just bringing a monologue to a close. The other, who walked on the verge of the path and was at times obliged to step on to the road, owing to his companion's rudeness, wore an amused, listening face. (. . .)

We isolate, from the compound sentences, a set of underlying sentoids, corresponding to the successive SR's of the text, and we see that all SR's have some semantic relation with the previous and the following ones

(3) SR_2/SR_1 *warm* $\equiv$ *warm*

          evening $\cap$ *air*

          August $\in$ *summer*

          streets $\in$ *city*

         SR_2/SR_{1-2} *streets* $\equiv$ *streets*

          warm summer $\leftrightarrow$ (...) $\leftrightarrow$ *dress* $\leftrightarrow$ *gaily coloured*

          (where '$\leftrightarrow$' denotes referential, inductive entailment)

         SR_4/SR_3 *shutter(ed)* $\in$ (house $\in$ *streets*)

SR_3/SR_{1-4} *lamps* $\leftrightarrow$ *evening*

              poles $\in$ *streets*

              living texture $\equiv$ (swarming) *crowd*

SR_6/SR_{1-5} *warm* $\equiv$ *warm*

              grey $\equiv$ *grey*

              evening $\equiv$ *evening*

              air $\equiv$ *air*

SR_7/SR_{1-6} *shape* $\in$ *texture*

SR_8/SR_{1-7} *two young men* $\subset$ *two gallants*

              two young men $\in$ *crowd*

              hill $\in$ *city*

              Rutland Square $\in$ *city*

SR_9/SR_{1-8} *one* man (of them) $\in$ *two young men*

SR_{10}/SR_{1-9} *the other* $\in$ *two young men*

SR_{11}/SR_{1-10} *path* $\in$ *street*

SR_{12}/SR_{1-11} *road* $\in$ *street*

SR_{13}/SR_{1-12} *companion* $\equiv$ *one of them*

etc.

We must further observe the specific surface manifestations of these relations, primarily in the very syntactic structuring as compound sentences. That is: the rules concatenating sentoids into one 'surface' sentence require that these sentoids are semantically related. Similarly, the text has conjunctions and pronouns: *their, which, them, who, he;* quantifiers: *one, the other;* definite articles not motivated by previous mention of the same lexeme: *the streets, the lamps,* etc.

The relations indicated rather roughly in (3) – the precise feature relations of intersection and inclusion are not made explicit but are intuitively accepted as valid – form the topic-comment chain of the text. That is, any sentence introduces a topic, mostly an argument realized as a noun, semantically related (e.g. identical) to a subtree in a previous semantic representation. Notice that the relationship is linear in the sense that any SR_i is connected with one or more representations $SR_1, ..., SR_{i-1}$, NOT with SR_{i-1} alone.

Important for the progressive aspect of sentential concatenation is the predication (comment) of these related arguments. Unlike they do in the poem, these initial predicates do not necessarily share thematic features, although, here, we may isolate connotative features like [+ EUPHORIC], which may be important in defining such vague notions as 'happy atmosphere'.

We may conclude provisionally that our hypothesis is confirmed in this text (and further reading does not provide counter-examples): narrative texts respect the surface structure constraints for texts in general. The typical literary character of this sequence, then, must be inferred on the one hand from such pragmatic indications as the name of the author, the way in which the text is presented and received, etc. and on the other hand from textual indications such as lexematization (non-current in non-literary narrative), the use of comparisons and metaphors, and above all the embedding in a given literary macro-structure (short story).

It is precisely at this point that we touch upon a major difference between the two texts. The poem only realized a semantic representation denoting a 'scene' or 'atmosphere' of a given day *(jour éclatant)*. The narrative text opens with a sequence of sentences having a similar underlying semantic structure. However, this sequence, coinciding with the first paragraph, only serves as one unit in the elaboration of a narrative structure introduced by the second paragraph. It provides the 'scene' for some actions of the actors of the narrative, and thus represents only the *Loc* of the deep-structure organization. This introduction of Place, Time and 'Atmosphere' is rather traditional, and may be deleted in more modern texts, or can be introduced in a discontinuous manner throughout the text. The semantic structure, and its lexico-syntactic surface form, of the first paragraph, then, is not (only) perceived in its own right but as functional in a network of underlying macro-relations defining the text as narrative.

Although there may exist gradual differences, we may therefore conclude that the (short, modern) poem is essentially based on micro-structural surface literariness, whereas micro-structures in narrative have normal constraints (and some optional literary operations) but are inserted in larger structures.

This differentiation of two textual types can only receive further specification when we try to define explicitly of what kind of narrative relations descriptions, like the one by Joyce, have to be functional units. That is, if the literariness of narrative texts is not definable at the sentential surface, at least not at this surface alone, where do the specific literary macro-rules come in, and what are their form and theoretical status within G_L?

3. STRUCTURAL ANALYSIS OF NARRATIVE

3.1. If there is a part of literary theory that received extensive and rather explicit attention in the last few years it is surely the theory of narrative structures. Our observations and the provisional rules which will be set out below will partially be based on the most relevant results of that development, but will at the same time formulate the foundations and the larger theoretical framework for adequate research in this domain.

Our main assumption lies of course in the perspective of this book: narrative can only be adequately described on the basis of a more general theory of texts and, in particular – for its textual structures – upon a generative text grammar (cf. Hendricks [1969b], Wienold [1972], Ihwe [1972b], van Dijk [1970c], [1972d]). It is obvious, further, that the 'de-finition' of the set of texts having the property 'narrative', can only be satisfactory when we have a previous knowledge of the properties of non-narrative texts. Typological insight of this kind can be awaited only within the frame-work of a theory of text grammars in general (cf. van Dijk [1971d]).

3.2. In order to arrive at explicit descriptions of the structure of LITERARY narrative, we should first recall that narrative texts are not restricted to the domain of literature, nor even to linguistic (verbal) texts. Narration is a general linguistic or semiotic human ability (Bremond [1969], van Dijk [1972d]). Our textual competence enables us to account in a 'story' for the events which we observe or in which we were ourselves involved. This is trivial, but only recently the study of narrative structures is recognized as a main task both of linguistics, sociolinguistics (cf. Labov and Waletzky [1967]) and of anthropology. In linguistics, then, we have to formulate those rules of the text grammar, corresponding to this 'narrative competence', which enable us to produce and interpret texts as narratives (Ihwe [1972a], [1972b]).

The two infinite sets of literary texts and of narrative texts intersect: the latter is not included in the former. It is our task, after having outlined some general aspects of narrative, to indicate precisely those properties defining literary narrative. We shall not repeat here the operations at the micro-structural level, characterizing literary texts in general: comparisons, metaphors, etc., as described in the previous chapter. They surely can be one important aspect of the literariness of narrative.

3.3. It is impossible to review here in detail the recent attempts to describe narrative structures; only a few main directions of thought will be recalled.[1]

First of all, most research is essentially inspired by structural linguistics and its methods, especially its European branches as developed by De Saussure, Hjelmslev, Benvéniste and others. The implications of these models have led to all sorts of distinctions made also for texts and narrative: syntagmatic *vs.* paradigmatic ordering, minimal distinctive features, relational functions or 'functors', *signifiant vs. signifié*, etc.

---

[1] General surveys of structural analysis of narrative are rare. An early attempt was made by Barthes (1966). Cf. the same issue (8) of *Communications*, Chatman's (1969) brief account and the critical remarks of Nathhorst (1969). Ihwe (1972a) is most extensive and systematic, especially con-sidering soviet theories. Relations between narrative analysis and discourse analysis are established above all in applied work on the border between linguistics and anthropology, especially after the pioneering studies of Dundes (1964) and Köngäs Maranda & Maranda (1971). Cf. Waterhouse (1963), Powlison (1965), Taber (1966), among other work, for uses of other (tagmemic, stratificational) struc-tural models. Grimes and Glock (1970) work in the same direction but are also inspired by recent work in generative semantics. Schmidt (1971c) relates structural and generative ideas with philo-sophy of language. Generative text grammar as a fundamental basis is used by Ihwe (1972b), (1972a), Petöfi (1972a), van Dijk (1970d), (1972d) and Wienold (1972).

It was against this background that the *analyse structurale du récit* began to develop its descriptions and hypotheses. The main origin of this work, as is now well-known, were the ideas of Propp (1968), especially after his book was translated into English and after the introductory comments by Lévi-Strauss (1960). The further development and correction of these ideas can be localized both within linguistics and poetics and within ethnology and anthropology. The main results have a rather restricted empirical scope: descriptions were based especially on simple narratives like myths, popular stories, etc. Of course, insight into less complex structures will normally be the only possible way of gaining some knowledge of very complicated narrative like most novels of the last three centuries.

Although there are many different 'directions' or 'schools' in what could now be called 'narratology' or 'narrativics', there are some basic ideas retained by most scholars in this field.

A major category, defined by Propp, is the notion of FUNCTION. In its original sense it simply indicated a basic narrative unit at the level of what we called macro-structure. As it was defined for simple fairy-tales, it mainly denoted an ACTION, or a coherent sequence of actions conceivable as 'one' action, by the hero of the story. For certain types of texts (like the corpus chosen by Propp: 100 Russian fairy tales) a fixed number of functions can be distinguished. The functions obey a rather strict 'syntax', defined mostly with respect to (intuitive) (chrono-)logical criteria. For some textual types, their order may be (relatively) fixed, whereas in other types of narrative only sequences of functions have internal fixed order.

3.4. Without entering into more detail here, we may ask, first, which theoretical status can be assigned to these functions, both for narrative theory proper and for their linguistic (or semiotic) manifestations.

They are normally referred to as units denoting 'actions' of a hero, or in general of an actor. Clearly, not any action will have the status of function, for otherwise they would hardly have a fixed number. They must obviously be actions relevant-for-the-narrative-development, e.g. major actions changing a given STATE of the text into another state, as for example DEPARTURE, ARRIVAL, BETRAYAL, etc. Moreover, they should have RECURRENT character within the corpus studied. Occasional actions are not considered functionally relevant, but are thought of either as secondary, derived, minor actions or as stylistic 'variations'. The function, thus roughly defined, acquires the status of a CONSTANT, a sort of macro-lexeme from a primitive narrative lexicon. The grammar operating over this lexicon is extremely simple and has only one category: 'function' and one major rule, enumerating the functions in a fixed order (*N* stands for Narrative)

(2)   (i) $N \rightarrow F_1, F_2, ..., F_n$

and further the rules for the assignment of the macro-lexical 'content'

(ii) $F_i \to$ DEPARTURE
      $F_j \to$ ARRIVAL $(j > i)$
      etc.

This mini-grammar essentially mirrors the theoretical ideas underlying Propp's system. Of course there are some additional conditions upon the rules and a series of selection restrictions for the 'lexical insertion' of narrative units. Further, some functions may be optional.

3.5. The structural analysis of narrative in recent years has taken up these ideas and suggested some further restrictions and regularities, not always without critical remarks with regard to Propp.

One of the main criticisms leveled against Propp's proposals concerned the fixed character of the order of the narrative functions. Bremond (1964) – taking up some ideas of Propp's predecessor Veselovsky – underlined, with other authors, that the order could not be fixed a priori, and that many tales have different syntactic constructions. He therefore stressed the importance of the notion of SEQUENCE. These sequences of actions/functions may appear in a different order, and are defined by an internal 'logic': beginning of the action, action, end of the action. He further recalled that the narrative structure may present EMBEDDED sequences, a fundamental property of any possible generative grammar of narrative texts. Sequences may thus be interrupted by other sequences. They may furthermore undergo deletions and permutations.

All these operations indicate that the 'fixed order' doctrine is inadequate, which is in fact rather trivial, because it would be of hardly any theoretical value to distinguish discrete functional units and affirm that they always occur in the same order. The whole sequence of functions, then, would in fact be one 'immediate constituent'.

3.6. Greimas (1966), (1970) was probably the first who explicitly tried to relate the functional units of narrative with the semantic structure of lexemes and texts. That is, in all previous studies the linguistic manifestation of the functions isolated was only occasionally accorded attention. The descriptions of 'Actions' by the actors of a narrative followed in fact our normal empirical knowledge about actions of real persons. Although it might be possible to study narrative independently of linguistic surface structures of specific languages (cf. Marcus [1971]), it seems inadequate not to relate textual functions to the abstract categories and relations of macro-semantics. Any confirmation of hypotheses concerning underlying narrative structures has to be based ultimately on the linguistic (or semiotic) manifestation of these structures. This is true *a fortiori* when a theory of narrative also wants to study the particular ways in which narrative structures may be realized in structures of a set of sentences.

Greimas' main contribution is twofold. He succeeded first in reducing the number of relevant functions of Propp by describing them with the aid of the elementary semantic features of his system *(sèmes)*, together with some elementary operators for negation and contraries. That is, many functions could thus be further analyzed as complex feature configurations. Note however, that these features are still rather complex from a linguistic point of view. They are elementary only on the level of narrative. This translation of narrative functions into a semantic language of description is of course a first step towards a linguistic/semiotic solution of the problem of interpretation of such narratives.

Perhaps more important still is Greimas' further elaboration of the 'modèle actantiel' of Tesnière (1959) as it was briefly treated in chapter 3 as a possible model for underlying macro-structures in general. The different surface *Acteurs* of a narrative may thus have different underlying (macro-) functions in a text such as *Agent, Patient, Destinateur, Sujet, Objet,* etc.

3.7. It is curious that in this framework Greimas' proposals did not result in further criticism and correction of Propp. In fact, Propp and many others following him, reduced narrative structure to functions denoting ONLY one macro-semantic category of the macro-proposition: ACTIONS. The AGENTS, PATIENTS, ... of these actions were understood implicitly, and/or presumably considered irrelevant for narrative structure as such. This may, partially, be true for corpuses of texts where the Actants are highly conventionalized, for example as a central hero, whose presence is presupposed implicitly. However, for any other type of text, and in general to avoid possible ambiguities, about the precise semantico-syntactic 'roles' of a personage, it is crucial that in a 'schema' of underlying structure (as was given both by Propp and Greimas) the actants of the different actions are indicated as well (cf. van Dijk [1970c], Genot [1972]).

Functions, then, i.e. when the actants accomplishing the actions are also integrated in the syntax, should be described as PROPOSITIONAL structures of some kind and to the grammar of (2) we may thus add the rules

(3)   (i) F_i → Pred (Actant$_1$, Actant$_2$, ..., Actant$_n$) $(n \geqslant 1)$
         (ii) Pred   → Action
         (iii) Actant$_1$ → Agent
         (iv) Actant$_2$ → Patient
         (v) Actant$_3$ → Object
             (...)
             etc.

We thus make explicit (i) that functions are complex propositional structures (ii) that the 'core' of this proposition may be a predicate, (iii) that the predicate must be specified as an action and (iv) that the different actants are specified according to their semantic role (Todorov [1969]).

Let us notice further that Greimas, and many others, were not wholly unaware of this propositional structure. His 'reduction' procedures for discourse description in general retain precisely the categories mentioned above, though without specifying the exact theoretical status. Predicates, in that system, may of course also be 'states', and realized by verbs having a feature [+ STATIC]. Important is his introduction of the modal/aspectual categories of that basic schema, for example as they are represented by such verbs as *pouvoir*, *savoir*, etc.

3.8. We must finally add some remarks about further contributions to these basic syntactic and semantic schemas underlying narrative. Barthes (1966) and Todorov (1967), (1969), (1971) among others, also accorded explicit attention to possible inherent properties of the actants involved. They here renew traditional remarks about the 'psychology of personages'. Clearly, especially in more modern texts, narrative structures may contain elaborate characterizations of the actants, either by explicit attribution or – implicitly – as defined by/inferred from their actions. In some types of novels (e.g. the psychological novel) these attributive predicates may functionally dominate, and the actions and their (chrono-)logical succession may become secondary or even marginal. Traditionally however, they are considered mere paradigmatic 'expansions' of the main functional (actantial) units of the syntax.

A final category isolated was normally that of 'circumstance', which represents place, time, atmosphere of the actions. No systematic account of the narrative relevance of this category has been given.

3.9. After this short treatment of some basic ideas of structural approaches, we now must try – after a few critical remarks – to elaborate a more systematic language of description. It is our task, for example, to define the relevant categories and their relations with the aid of rules. We have already seen that in many ways the categories treated intuitively or more explicitly in extant work correspond to the categories treated in our macro-semantics of texts in general. It is methodologically most adequate, then, to define narrative with respect to that general grammar and to specify the units and rules underlying specifically the subset of narrative texts.

4. ASPECTS OF A GENERATIVE GRAMMAR OF NARRATIVE

4.1. In the current discussions about narrative structures there are several indications about the PRODUCTIVE properties of the schema established by structuralist research (Barthes [1966] Greimas [1970]). This implies that such a general and abstract structure may underlie an infinite number of existing or possible narrative texts. These remarks are important because they can be considered to be a progressive step with respect to strict corpus description. Instead, infinite sub-sets, i.e. TYPES, are described, not collections of TOKENS with recurrent properties.

Moreover, most contributions explicitly stress the possibility of TRANSFORMATIONS of the basic schemata in different texts. Functions may be permuted or deleted, similar functions may appear – on the surface – as different actions or actants, and conversely, etc. The notion of transformation is not clearly defined here, however, and recalls Harris' concept of a mutation of a basic structure into more complex or 'derived' structures.

These ideas, though often still rather intuitive, can serve as initial suggestions for a GENERATIVE approach to narrative structure. It is obvious that we may not identify 'productive', which is a notion of performance ('encoding' etc.), with the formal concept of generative; neither does it refer to notions like 'synthetic' or 'analytic'. As was recalled earlier in this book, a generative description merely denotes explicit algorithmic description, by means of grammatical rules. This algorithm formally enumerates all possible well-formed narrative texts, and assigns a structural description to them. At the same time, it may be conceived as an abstract model for the idealized competence of native speakers to process – i.e. to produce, interpret, etc. – narrative texts. This ability, further, is an instance of necessary testability of our grammar. The derivable narrative texts have to be judged on grammaticalness with respect to the intuitive knowledge of native speakers about the well-formedness of a given/predicted narration (cf. Ihwe [1972b], [1972a]).

4.2. Our narrative grammar, then, will take the form of a text-grammar, of which it is a special subset of rules, conditions and restrictions. This is a theoretical hypothesis because the relevant and systematic description of narrative may use categories and relations very different from those formulated in generative grammars. However, the fact that we restrict ourselves to narrative texts of a linguistic character, naturally forces us to take the underlying narrative system and relate it to textual structures. It is therefore advisable to formulate rules of the same basic form and categories compatible with textual categories (cf. van Dijk, [1972d]).

4.3. One of the first major categories to be considered in our derivation is the TEXT-QUALIFIER *Tql*, especially its PERFORMATIVE component *Perf.* Here we localized the operators (or performative auxiliary sentoids in the manner of Ross (1970)) indicating what may be called the TYPE of text to be derived: Assertion, Question, etc.

We here touch upon a basic problem of linguistics and the philosophy of language in general: can these operators be reduced to a fixed number of basic constants of universal applicability? If this should turn out to be the case, we might hypothetically introduce a pragmatic operator *Narr* to account for the irreducible character of narration as an illocutionary primitive: narratives do not necessarily assert or ask or command something – e.g. about referential truth – (cf. Chap. 9). We shall not decide, e.g. on the philosophical level, whether this hypothesis is correct, we will only introduce *narr* as a provisional category in order to be able to use specific rules and restrictions in further derivation. These are not left entirely to performance description. The performative symbol *Narr* triggers specific operations and is at the same time a formal representation of our ability to distinguish basic types of texts from each other. Pragmatic details will be treated in the next chapter.

4.4. Similarly, the other component of *Tql*, the complex *M* (for 'modal') can receive specific restrictions for the generation of narrative.

It is a traditional view that narrative, and more particularly literary narrative and literature in general, have a FICTIVE character. The precise semantic and referential notions involved here are rather complex and cannot be treated. They belong partially to philosophy as well. Fictionality, sometimes indicated by a feature [+ FICTION] (cf. Ihwe [1972a], Schmidt [1972]) can be defined briefly as the property of statements (made in a discourse) referring to non-existent states of affairs (events, objects) with truth value only in imaginative representation. Fictional statements are thus a subset of all counterfactual statements and may therefore simply be represented by the complex operators *Neg Fact*. However, lies, mistakes, etc. have the same counterfactual property, i.e. that of being contradictory with respect to true assertions about empirical reality. The main difference with these types of texts is pragmatic rather than strictly semantic: the speaker does not intend his utterance to be interpreted by a hearer/reader as empirically true (as in lies), nor does he himself believe that his utterance is empirically true (as in mistakes). Fictional texts are thus modally counterfactual and pragmatically intended as such by a speaker not denying the counterfactualness in the speech-act. We could also characterize them as being dominated by a specific operator for irrealis, *Irr*, which would at the same time underlie the generation of many counterfactual conditionals and their corresponding verb-forms (auxiliaries and verbal morphemes) in natural language. The statements, then, are considered true, under the assumption that their system of reference does not exist in empirical reality, but only as a 'mental picture' (imaginative representation) or in more formal terms: perhaps even as a mere semantic representation.

In general, however, narrative texts do not NECESSARILY have these modal properties: we may state something about real persons, actions and events with the intention of making true empirical assertions. We will see below whether the criterion of fictionality is valid for literature. The presence of *Narr* thus does not eliminate the modal operator *Fact* which will be maintained as a normal optional category in narrative description.

4.5. Rather crucial for the description of narrative are the indicators (arguments or operators) of TIME $(t_0, t_1)^2$ and PLACE (l_0, l_1). In the structural description already

---

[2] Discussions about 'time' in literature, and especially in narrative, characterize nearly all traditional work in poetics. In many cases the distinction time *vs.* (grammatical) tense is not rigorously made, and similarly for semantic (intensional) time and referential (real, physical) time. Cf. Lieb (1970), Wunderlich (1970b). Traditional accounts in poetics are Mendilov (1952), Pouillon (1946) and Hamburger (1968) among others.

In the domains of linguistics and logic work on this topic is abundant. Cf. e.g. Reichenbach's classical description (1947). There is an interesting development within modal logic in this respect. Cf. e.g. Rescher's 'chronological logic' (Rescher, 1968) and recent work in tense logic Prior (1957), (1968), (1971), Rescher & Urquhart (1971), pragmatics and intensional logic (Montague [1968], [1970]). It will be clear that the results of these explorations must ultimately be included in an adequate theory of narrative (cf. chapter 2).

Less attention has been given to the systems underlying PLACE and place operators in linguistics and logic, cf. however Rescher's topological logic (Rescher, 1968).

given, the order of functions was determined wholly by (chrono-)logical aspects of succession, corresponding to our intuitive knowledge of the 'natural order' of events, processes and actions in empirical reality. Any function/proposition in a narrative thus must explicitly receive an indicator (or more specifically a temporal auxiliary) determining the time of the action with respect to the time of preceding and following actions. As a general rule t_{i+k} of S_j will be greater than t_i in S_i if S_j follows S_i (cf. Rescher [1968], cf. chapters 2 and 3 above).

This rule is also valid at the macro-structural level of description: texts (textoids) are normally chronologically ordered as surface sequences in a complex or compound text according to their temporal indices dominated by the semantic time indicator (time-focus). This indicator will further dominate the whole textoid (and surface sequence) and indicate that its actions/processes/events take place at the same time.

As was evident in chaps. 2 and 3 this semantic time can be defined only with respect to the temporal operator of *Perf*, that is with respect to the time of the utterance. If this is true, we are able to derive formally texts which are restricted to only one range of time-points with respect to the utterance. As opposed e.g. to predictions we may assume provisionally that narrative in general has the following restriction

$$(4) \qquad t_0 \geqslant t_i$$

that is, the time of the event described precedes or coincides with the time of the utterance, or more briefly: narrations always refer to past events or – at the limit – to events still going on. At the surface level this fact will result in the selection of one of the categories *Past* underlying the verbs of a narrative text. This surface form, as is well-known, may be a neutral, unmarked *Present*, which will however be inter- preted (under influence of the textual time indicator) as referring to past events. It is clear, further, that the condition given in (4) does not imply that all verbs of all sentences are necessarily past-forms: micro-structural constraints may locally trans- form the verbal tenses, the whole time of the event described being *Past* (for detail cf. Weinrich [1964], Bronzwaer [1970]).

The case in which $t_0 = t_1$ may be reserved for those narrative texts where immediate description of events/actions is intended, as in reportages. If we want to, we may rule out this possibility by definition, but there does not seem to be a valid reason for not considering them to be, formally, narratives.

The last logical possibility, $t_0 < t_i$, is a more serious problem: can we possibly narrate future events? Empirically this is only possible of course under the dominance of such operators as *Irr*, *Neg Fact*, or *Poss*, and we actually find such narration in all types of science fiction, with Orwell's *1984* as a clear paradigmatic example, where $t_0 = 1948$ and $t_i = 1984$. Here we have to deal with the problem to what extent non- real time can be specified as present, past or future, because – as irrealis – it seems rather to constitute a fourth, irreducible temporal category. In this case we must reject (4) as unsatisfactory and add as the only restriction that $t_0 < t_i$ is correct only if the narrative text is *Neg Fact* or *Irr*. Further the 'irreal' temporal specifications must be identical with those for non-fictive narrative. Chronology is assumed to underlie 'well-formed' affirmative representations as well.

We will not treat here the specific surface morphology and the micro-structural constraints in narrative, e.g. as they appear – stylistically – in literature. We will come back, however, to the specific implications of macro-transformations of time-sequences in narrative.

4.6. The next main categories specific for narrative texts must be sought for within the macro-propositions. Let us first consider the PREDICATE part of textual deep structure. We will normally specify predicates either as ACTIONS and EVENTS or as PROCESSES and STATES. (cf. Greimas [1966], Chafe [1970]). It may be asked whether narrative has more restrictive options. This problem, which has been the subject of much recent discussion, is not easily solved. We may intuitively define narrative as a sequence of one or more 'actions' of certain actors, or, more generally as one or more events. We do not normally call narrative the mere description of an animate or inanimate object and its properties alone, as was the case in the poem of Reverdy.

One might make this intuitive knowledge explicit by restricting the specification of narrative predicates to actions and events. However, the theoretical description is not as simple as that.

Let us take, for example, the following underlying textual deep structure

(5)   John is arriving by train.

Although we might imagine a story about John's arrival by train we would hardly consider such a description as typical of narrative. In that case, in order to have a narrative, we probably are obliged to generate some further underlying structures as

(6)   (i)   John was in the train.
          (ii) The train stopped.
          (iii) John got off.
          (iv) John met Mary
                (...)

If such basic macro-propositions are required to generate well-formed narratives, we are obliged to introduce the constraint that in any initial formula of the type

(7) $T \rightarrow T(\& \, T)^n$

n must be $\geqslant 2$. That is mono-propositional texts cannot be narratives.

This constraint can easily be explained. The definition of 'event' – the main category underlying any narrative proposition – can be reduced to a CHANGE OF STATE of a set of (in)animate objects (O) where s denotes 'state':

(8) $s_i(O) \rightarrow s_{i+1}(O)$

Such a description presupposes the presence of an initial state much in the same way as we describe formal machines. That is, even supposing we have only the description of the simple action/event of John's arrival, we have an underlying presupposed proposition denoting John's travelling. This may seem trivial, but its explication seems crucial for an adequate description of any narrative. When we may heuristically define actions/events by questions like *What happened*? we may define narrative propositions as answers to the question *What happened then*?, i.e. under those circumstances (initial state). Actually, in simple unsophisticated narrative, as in stories of children, all narrative propositions will at the surface level be represented by such conjunctions as *and then*.

Here we meet a hypothetical universal trait of narrative structures. In chapter 3 we referred to the five basic functional constituents of all narratives distinguished by Labov and Waletsky (1967) (cf. also Isenberg [1970]), and the main Proppian functions as reduced by Greimas (cf. chap. 3)

(9)   (i)   Orientation   (Initial situation of equilibrium)
             (ii) Complication   (Rupture of this situation)
             (iii) Evaluation   (Arrival/Trial of the hero)
             (iv) Resolution   (Beneficient Action of the hero)
             (v)   Coda   (Re-establishment of initial situation; hero re-compensed).

These five basic functions, which of course may receive other names, essentially represent any well-formed narrative. In actual texts some of these functions may of course be deleted but will generally be implicitly understood and therefore must be present in deep structure. The variable in rule schema (7), then, has to take the value $n = 4$.

A further constraint in this description is perhaps that at least two propositions, e.g. the initial and the final one, are state descriptions in the strict sense, i.e. descriptions of situations, properties, results, etc. of (in)animate objects involved in the action/event/process of the other propositions.

How do we represent the basic universal functions, as distinguished above, in a formal derivation? We have already interpreted them earlier as propositions, or, rather as embedded or coordinate textoids. When we specify the value of the variable in the initial rule schema, we may add in a later rule the condition (for detail see § 4.9. below)

(10) $Pred \rightarrow \left\{ \begin{matrix} \left[\begin{matrix} \text{State} \\ \text{Action} \end{matrix} \right] & \text{for } n = 0 \text{ and } 4 \\ \text{Event} & \text{for } n = 2, 3 \end{matrix} \right\}$

Such a specification is still extremely general and we may therefore, in the final steps of the macro-derivation, replace the terminal categories by assigning to them specific lexicoidal content. It is not easy to give a general rule for this type of semantic constraints upon narrative propositions. Informally, they might represent them as follows

(11)   1. $\left\{\begin{array}{l}\text{State}_i\\\text{Situation}_i\end{array}\right\}$ of $\left\{\begin{array}{l}\text{Actors}\\\text{Environment of Action}\end{array}\right\}$ at t_i

2. External cause changes $\left\{\begin{array}{l}\text{State}_i\\\text{Situation}_i\end{array}\right\}$

   into $\left\{\begin{array}{l}\text{State}_{i+1}\\\text{Situation}_{i+1}\end{array}\right\}$ at t_{i+k}

3. Actors confronted with $\left\{\begin{array}{l}\text{State}_{i+1}\\\text{Situation}_{i+1}\end{array}\right\}$ at $t_{i+k'}$

4. Actor(s) accomplish(es) Action with respect
   to $\left\{\begin{array}{l}\text{State}_{i+1}\\\text{Situation}_{i+1}\end{array}\right\}$ at $t_{i+k''}$

5. $\left\{\begin{array}{l}\text{State}_j\\\text{Situation}_j\end{array}\right\}$ of $\left\{\begin{array}{l}\text{Actors}\\\text{Environment}\end{array}\right\}$ at $t_{i+k'''}$
   (where $\left\{\begin{array}{l}\text{State}_j\\\text{Environment}_j\end{array}\right\}$ may be optionally identical with $\left\{\begin{array}{l}\text{State}_i\\\text{Situation}_i\end{array}\right\}$)

This informal schema of the five basic constitutive propositions (textoids) of a narrative may be represented in a derivation by the internal structure of the lexicoids of the textual SR. The whole schema may be recursive or only some parts of it, e.g. 2 and 4.

Note that this schema, as a global semantic constraint upon narrative text structure, is a very abstract deep structure representation. At the surface level sequences of sentences may actualize transforms of these schema (see below). Further, some parts may receive very extensive surface elaboration – a factor which will change the type of the narrative – while others may be very much reduced or even deleted. Initial state descriptions are rather short in myths, popular narrative, fairy tales, medieval epic, etc. and much longer in modern narrative (novels).

4.7. The other main category of the proposition, the set of ARGUMENTS (or Actants), may also undergo specific constraints in narrative texts.

One of the first conditions that lies at hand is the human, or at least animate, character of Agent and Patient. This condition is both trivial and controversial. On the one hand actions can be accomplished only by animate beings, and since Action was a necessary specification in at least one proposition of a narrative the feature [+ ANIMATE] is required. Similarly, if e.g. natural events occur there has to be a human patient undergoing these events.

Thus, we will assume that a narrative is ill-formed if only inanimate objects serve as actants, although objects may undergo changes of state in the description of processes.

There are some specific conditions under which objects (and also animals) may also function as actants of a narrative and some types of narrative (e.g. the fable) actually realize these structures. In that case, however, semantic transformations take place as described in the previous chapter. A feature $[+ \text{HUM}]$ will be added to these (in)-animate, non-human objects because their behaviour (actions, etc.) is normally described as human behaviour. Metaphorical (personificative) and allegorical narrative of this kind may thus have non-narrative deep-structure (state or process description) but have to undergo some transformations to generate narrative surface forms. We know very little, however, about this type of semantic constraint and the notion of narrative, in this domain, can be empirically blurred by the existence of many transitional types of texts.

The requirement of the presence of human actants can be explained by the implied RATIONAL properties of narrative actants. Since the development of actions in a narrative is directed towards the accomplishment of a task in order to achieve a certain goal, these actions are normally intentional. This property cannot be predicated of inanimate objects and probably not of animals. At least these cannot explicitly account for their motivations for accomplishing certain actions. The exclusive human property of verbal speech and thought seems to be the crucial point here. Therefore probably all narrative will imply embedded sentences or texts referred to as utterances of the actants. At the surface level, of course, these utterances need not to be explicitly presented as such (see below).

We now find ourselves in the field of psycho-social and anthropological speculation about the explanation of certain formal properties of narrative texts, a road which we will not follow further here, but which needs to be explored.

4.8. The constraints indicated informally above are supposed to be UNIVERSALS underlying the generation of narrative texts. They represent, together with the other rules of textual derivation, the abstract definition of narrative texts.

Many additional and specific constraints are possible in given times and cultures. These may be very strict and their non-observance often entails social sanctions.

In classical literature, for example, the dramatic narrative texts had a temporal category specified as 'twenty-four hours', or the time between the rising and the setting of the sun. Similarly, Loc (l_f in chapter 2) had to be replaced by a single constant place of action, other places of action being restricted to embedded texts (narrative of messages). These constraints upon semantic well-formedness can be explained of course by socio-cultural factors (primitive conditions for stage performance, pragmatic properties of the singer/teller and the public of the narrative, etc.).

Similar socio-cultural explanations can be given for other narrative constraints in classical (literary) narrative and in myths, fairy tales, etc.: actants may sometimes be obligatory assigned a special social status, e.g. [+ ROYAL] when they are primary agents or patients, and – connected herewith – their actions/feelings had to have the same property, e.g. [+ NOBLE]. Texts not satisfying these requirements (comedy, farce, *fatrasie*, etc.) acquired specific status by this difference, a problem closely related to the historical notion of 'literature' itself, which we will not treat here.

To give an example from the modern novel: the behaviouristic novel of the thirties restricted its macro-predicates to Actions and to States having the property [+ EXTERNAL], whereas, conversely, in many psychological novels and in the *nouveau roman* we find a dominance of [+ INTERNAL] state descriptions and actions having a feature [+ MENTAL]. We may either try to consider these constraints to be formal conditions of a (sub-)grammar for the TYPE we are describing, or specific 'cultural' performance constraints.

4.9. We may resume our rather brief and rough treatment by stressing that the description of narrative and its different sub-types should proceed along the ways indicated by a textual grammar, i.e. by introducing formal categories, rules, conditions, constraints and selection restrictions in an algorithmic derivation of textual macro-structures.

Let us try to write a part of a short provisional base-grammar for narrative deep structures. For the elaboration of some details, especially those with typical literary implications, see the following section.

(12)   (i) T $\rightarrow T(\& T)^n \mid n \geqslant 4$

(ii) T $\rightarrow Tql\ Prop$

(iii) Tql $\rightarrow Perf\ Mod$

(iv) $Perf$ $\rightarrow Narr(t_0, l_0)$

(v) Mod $\rightarrow M\ Qu\ (t_f, l_f)$

(vi) M $\rightarrow \begin{cases} (Neg)\ Fact & t_f \leqslant t_0 \\ (Neg)\ Prob & t_f > t_0 \end{cases}$

(vii) Qu $\rightarrow \begin{Bmatrix} \exists \\ \iota \\ \lambda \\ \varepsilon \\ \eta \end{Bmatrix}$

(viii) $Prop$ $\rightarrow Pred_k\ (A)^m \mid k \geqslant m$

(ix) $Pred_k \rightarrow \begin{cases} \begin{Bmatrix} St \\ Proc \end{Bmatrix} & n = 1, 4 \\ \begin{Bmatrix} Ac \\ Ev \end{Bmatrix} & n = 2, 3 \end{cases}$

$$(\text{x}) \quad A \quad \rightarrow \quad \begin{cases} Ag \\ Pat \\ Obj \\ Instr \\ Source \\ Goal \end{cases}$$

$$(\text{xi}) \quad Ag \quad \rightarrow \quad x\,[+\,HUM]$$
$$(\text{xii}) \quad Pat \quad \rightarrow \quad y\,[+\,HUM]$$
$$(\text{...})$$

For details of general text grammatical descriptions we may refer to chapter 3. In the derivation proposed here we included time-focus (t_f) and local focus (l_f) in the Modifier category, together with the modal operators and the quantifiers, in order to express that their scope is the entire proposition. Note that t_f of textoid T_i follows t_f of T_{i+j} ($j > 1$). For some subtypes of narrative we may formulate constraints on l_f of the different textoids, e.g. their identity in classical drama. Similar constraints may appear in the specification of the States of the Arguments, especially of Agent and Patient, e.g. [± COURAGEOUS], [± NOBLE] [± GOOD] ,[± BAD], etc. The number of possible Actants is not limited to those used here. We might have specific categories for Beneficiary, Helper, Destinator, etc. as was proposed by Propp, Greimas, Dundes, Maranda, and others.

5. NARRATIVE TRANSFORMATIONS AND LITERARY OPERATIONS

5.1. The tentative rules, or rather the specific constraints upon the rules, formulated above, define well-formed underlying structures of narrative. These structures are the input to various cycles of (MACRO-) TRANSFORMATIONS.

A first series of transformations are those discussed in chapter 3, and these are characteristic for texts in general. They convert macro-structures into semantic deep-structures of a serially ordered set of sentences. They operate, generally, after the macro-transformations we will discuss here.

Our main hypothesis, now, is the following: narrative texts in general are defined by the macro-semantic base rules of the grammar together with the specific constraints formulated above, whereas the subset of LITERARY NARRATIVE TEXTS, is defined by the (transformation) rules and the global constraints operating on general narrative structures, as well as by the micro-structural operations defined in chapter 6. Let us therefore turn to a more detailed discussion of the putative specific macro-trans-formations.

5.1.1. Semantic macro-transformations can be distinguished according to the scope of their input: SINGULARY transformations operate on macro-propositions (textoids) i.e. on their internal structure, and GENERALIZED transformations operate on configurations of macro-propositions. Transformations may be either OBLIGATORY or OPTIONAL. Observe that these transformations change the general underlying structure and not the elementary, transformed structures of other texts, as is often the case in such notions of 'narrative transformations' used in much structuralist work. Transformations in generative grammars are operations upon underlying structures, specified with the following possible properties of structural change: permutation, addition, deletion and substitution.

5.2. The conditions for the operation of transformations are not only formal but also pragmatic and cultural. They often underlie the definition of specific TYPES of literary narrative ('genres') which have varying acceptability conditions at different times. Some transformations which are perfectly grammatical/acceptable in the present day may be ungrammatical/unacceptable in the 17th century. This is quite normal, and we therefore, in our grammar, will restrict ourselves to a type of narrative literary text that was roughly established in the 18th century, a type which was changed only at the beginning of the 20th century with such writers as Joyce (e.g. in *Finnegans Wake*), who nevertheless did not abolish traditional narrative structure. We will indicate the specific operations which this traditional narrative may undergo in the modern period, although we will abstract from concrete historical indications and examples.

5.3. One of the first implications of our transformational treatment of macro-structures in narrative is undoubtedly the elucidation of such well-known notions as STORY and PLOT (*fable* and *sujet* in French) as derived from the original Russian terminology used by Èixenbaum (1965) and Šklovskij (1966).

The intuitive definition of these terminological pairs is roughly as follows: story (fable) was considered a pre-textual abstraction, the global account of the narrative content of a text as it is paraphrasable in an abstract; plot (sujet) is the story as it is told and presented in a coherent text with specific individual (stylistic) alterations to the structure of the story.

It is obvious that these terms correspond, roughly, with our distinction between deep and transformed macro-structures of narrative texts. The historical fact that a story can be told or realized in non-literary texts (conversation, newspaper) and then used as the 'material' for the construction of the plot of a literary narrative (cf. *Madame Bovary* by Flaubert), seems to confirm our hypothesis that the literary character of narrative is due to transformations and not to base rules.

The current French usage in poetics also makes such distinctions as: *récit*, *histoire*, *diégèse*, the definitions of which are however rather vague in many cases (cf. Genette [1969b]). *Discours* normally refers to the micro-structural (sentential) surface manifestation of a narrative text. *Récit* may simply denote any narrative text but also its specific macro-transform (plot, *sujet*), while *histoire* normally corresponds to the underlying structure (story) or the extra-textual material used or referred to. Similar distinctions are made for such terms as *narration, narrant, narré*, etc. referring (presumably) to the act of telling, macro- (or micro-)surface structure and macro-deep-structure of a narrative text. The aristotelian concept of *diégèse* is used to refer to the concatenation of precisely those elements used to produce the characteristic 'progression' in narrative texts (actions changing states, etc.). We will not use such terms because they may confuse the formal treatment of the different relations between surface and deep structure in narrative texts. Their intuitive distinctions, however, have important heuristic value and, if possible, should be made explicit in a grammar.

5.4. *Deletion transformations*

5.4.1. Deletion transformations in any textual derivation will have a very regular character. The abstract and analytic semantic information of deep structure will hardly ever appear directly in surface structure. Presuppositions, implications, etc. will disappear in the concrete text and be left to the interpretative ability of the native speaker. In general, as is well-known, any text can describe only certain aspects, properties, events and actions of a referential or non-referential 'world', but the reader will always supply the absent information and re-construct a full 'picture'. This is trivial and very informal, although cognitive psychology has yet to solve the main problems in this domain. For the interpretation of textual narrative we can merely represent some of these processes in a formal way, by deriving semantic deep structures and deletions.

5.4.2. Thus we must delete, firstly, all the abstract theoretical symbols which only serve to trigger other rules and constraints and modify other categories. The whole *Tql* category is thus deleted after having modified the proposition connected with it. Let us consider, for example, the different consequences of deleting the performative element. When we make the element *Narr* explicit by writing it as a performative proposition: *I tell you*, we should delete this sentence for instance in the following rule

(13) $\begin{bmatrix} _S \ I \ tell \ you \ _S \end{bmatrix}$ *Prop* $\Rightarrow$ $\emptyset$ *Prop*
                              PERF   PERF

This is a regular deletion (cf. Ross [1970]) which can be explained by pragmatic presuppositions: the *I* of any utterance (which is not dominated by an explicit performative sentence without *I*, like *He said*, "I ...", etc.) is interpreted as referring to the same person as the one accomplishing the speech act (cf. next chapter).

   In literary narrative, however, this deletion may have specific effects, when the spatio-temporal properties of the writer-author are known to be different from those predicated in the text of an actor *I*. This divergence from normal pragmatico-referential rules can be decisive for some types of interpretation.

We may simply say, then, that the *I* of a narrative literary text is not necessarily, or even, is never identical with the *I* of the performative sentence, i.e. the producer of the text. This is a traditional observation of the theory of the novel. This difference is one essential formal indication for the assignment of a property [+ FICTION] to a narrative text, or rather: the selection of a modal category *Fict* automatically dissociates the referents, including the *I* of the text, from the 'real' referents of the communication process and the situation, including the author.

In this case the *I* of the text can in fact be considered to be a third person category in deep structure which is realized as *I* in surface structure. Cf. direct expressions of the following type

(14)   He said: "I shall come tomorrow".

where the *I* in the embedded sentence does not refer to the pragmatic *I* of the speaker reporting this sentence, present in deep structure, but to the subject of the explicit clause immediately dominating the embedded sentence: *he*. In the indirect form

(15)   He$_i$ said that he$_i$ would come $\begin{Bmatrix} \text{tomorrow} \\ \text{today} \end{Bmatrix}$

it is impossible to have *I*, because the embedded clause is not immediately dominated by a performative sentence, i.e. the direct object of the verb is not referred to as the product of a speech act, i.e. an utterance, but is only an embedded sentoid.

Analogously we may assume, then, that if the *I* of the performative sentence dominating the whole text, i.e. the author, is not identical with the *I* referred to in the textual proposition, a sentence like *He said* ... is deleted.

Within some narrative texts this deletion may be regular when the agent of an utterance can be inferred from the text.

Let us give the abbreviated graph for describing this underlying structure

(15)

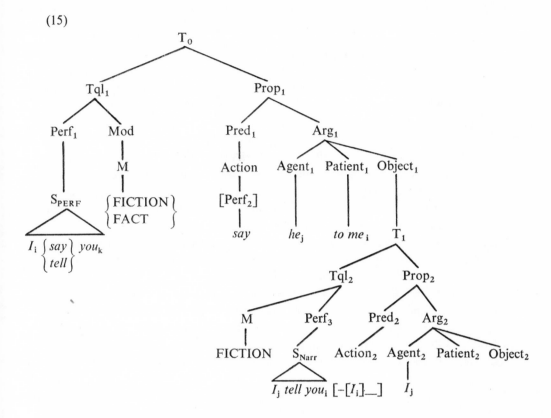

In this derivation tree *Perf$_1$* dominates the performative hypersentence formalizing the utterance as produced by the author *Prop$_1$* is inserted to account for the fact that the *I* of the story told by the narrative text may be different from the pragmatical *I* (the author) as if the author repeats verbatim the story of this narrator (*he$_j$*). *Prop$_1$* is normally deleted. This narrator may, as such, appear in his narrative (*T$_1$*): if *Tql$_2$* is deleted he is only an Agent (*I$_j$*; sometimes, however, other pronouns are admitted, such as *he*, and even *you*) of the story and is called, then, 'implicit narrator', otherwise 'explicit narrator'. If in *Tql$_1$* the modal operator is *Fict* (i.e. *Neg Fact*) than the narrator – and hence his story – is fictive. If the narrator is factual (exists historically) than his story, as reported by the author, may be either fictive or true (as in confessions, stories of personal experience; cf. Labov and Waletzky [1967]). If the whole utterance is intended as an autobiographical report, author (*I$_i$*) and narrator (*he$_j$*) and Agent/Patient (*I$_j$*) coincide. The non-biographicalness of a story, then, is decidable if the predicates of *Prop$_2$* have a selection restriction excluding the author to be an actant of them, for instance when the Agent of the story is stated to live in another age (or other possible world) as the author. For concrete examples we may refer to the traditional literature on the theory of the novel (e.g. as reported in Lämmert [1967]).

These relations have all had extensive treatment in traditional literary theory. We see that their explication in textual phrase markers provides insight into the level of embedding of texts/propositions and therefore into the relations between the different possible narrators: 1. pragmatic narrator (producer of the text), 2. textual narrator (identical with 1 or only semantic representation): either mere narrator/descriptor or narrator-Agent/Patient, either explicit (I_j) or implicit (other pronouns in surface structure).

5.4.3. Within the proposition itself it does not seem to be possible to delete major categories such as predicates or arguments. We argued earlier that deep structures are only well-formed when these categories are present, because the notion of inter-pretability is primarily associated with their combination. Their deletion in sentential derivation always presupposes either (co-)textual or presuppositional presence in deep structure. In macro-derivation this deletion is not possible because without the macro-categories we would not be able to derive a surface structure possessing arguments or predicates throughout the whole text.

It is possible in compound texts, however, to delete lexicoidal specifications of the Agent in the initial textoids, for example in detective stories. Here, only the Action of 'murdering' is realized and the Agent is only manifested as a variable X. The terminal textoid and its surface sequence will then normally reveal the identity of the Agent-murderer and retro-specify X, and the different semantic representations related with it.

5.4.4. Important, however, is the possible deletion of putative presuppositions. Of course, deep structure presuppositions are always deleted, because they are mere implications of, or identical with, other SR's of the text. Their role in the narrative text may be decisive. A macro-structure like

(16)   *A arrives at L at t_i.*

entails *A is at L at t_i, t_{i+k}, ...,* a consequence which need not be realized in surface structure (cf. Bellert [1971]).

Similarly from a proposition like

(17)   *A is shooting at B.*

we may infer the disjunctive *A misses B* ∨ *A hits B,* of which the latter possibility entails inductively *A kills B* ∨ *A wounds B,* which entail *B is dead* and *B is wounded* respectively.

These different steps of semantic and logical inference may all be deleted in the derivation (if they are present in deep structure), which leaves the reader with a certain interpretative task to perform, a task which may be associated with different psychological implications (suspense, uncertainty, esthetic feeling when the task is accomplished, and so on).

5.5. *Addition transformations*

It is not wholly clear what the general role of additions in generative grammars might be. Because deep structure (traditionally, that is, in the standard version) wholly determines the semantic representation, or is identical with it according to generative semantics, the possible additions can only be of a typical 'surface character': formal constraints for surface well-formedness which have no semantic/interpretational value. It is clear that at this abstract level such surface features as intonation, emphasis, contrast, focus, etc. – which according to the extended standard theory (Chomsky [1970], [1971]) have semantic implications – are irrelevant: whole sequences do not have these micro-structural properties.

Furthermore, in any textual derivation, ALL operations on textual macro-structures are EXPANSIVE: in all sentence-formation processes numerous features must be added to generate the specific micro-structural content.

Macro-additions only seem to occur when a part of deep structure, e.g. a textoid is repeated in the whole text. This structure however can be generated by recursive base rules.

5.6. *Permutative transformations*

5.6.1. The operation of permutation is undoubtedly the major transformation type applied to narrative deep structures. The change of order, of course, is irrelevant within the proposition itself: the logico-semantic relationships are not specified by the syntactic order of the categories, and their permutation does not affect the textual SR.

The change of order, then, is characteristic of compound texts, where underlying textoids, ordered by temporal, local and semantic relations of cause and consequence, may undergo permutations.

5.6.2. Although very little is known about the precise conditions determining the ordering of sentoids and textoids we may nevertheless make some elementary observations. Let us take an underlying macro-SR of the following type

(18)   *A* conquered *B*.

This underlying structure of a textoid (see above) has some presuppositions of the type

(19)   *A* is fighting with *B*.

which has to precede (18) in the text, normally both in surface and in deep structure, because *to conquer* presupposes the action of fighting. Similarly (19) will normally be preceded by such textoids as

(20)   *A* hates *B*
(21)   *A* is the enemy of *B*.
(22)   *A* confronts *B*, at time t_i, at place l_i.
             etc.

The relations established are based both on pure logico-semantic (deductive) implications and on semantico-referential (inductive, probabilistic) implications. The order of the textoids is strictly determined by these relations because they determine correct interpretations, i.e. lead to the formation of well-formed SR's.

Now, in principle, in literary texts the grammar for these textual rules is very much weakened by permitting permutations of nearly every kind

$$(23) \qquad \begin{matrix} X & Y & Z \\ 1 & 2 & 3 \end{matrix} \;\Rightarrow\; \begin{Bmatrix} 1 & 3 & 2 \\ 2 & 3 & 1 \\ 3 & 2 & 1 \end{Bmatrix}$$

This type of transformation is known by such terms as 'flash back' and 'prediction' (for a traditional but rather complete account, cf. Lämmert [1967]). Our macro-semantic competence will enable us to interpret surface order of these types according to their 'natural order'. That is, the narration of events explicitly presented as consequences of other, but not realized, events or actions, will cause the expectation of sequences specifying these previous actions. Similarly, future consequences of present actions, situations, etc. may already be pre-figured in the imagination of the actor (embedding) or simply be permuted from a later place.

5.6.3. The literary grammar of narrative thus seems nearly hopelessly powerful because it imposes almost no constraints on the order of surface sequences, i.e. any permuted order is G_L-grammatical. Thus, the burial of an actor may be the initial event narrated in a text in which this actor is an agent (Hendricks [1969b]). Of course, the internal structure of a permuted textoid may not change under this operation. For example, the following text is ungrammatical

(24)   (i) The enemy took the town in January 1750.
             (ii) The enemy besieged the town in February 1750.

There is an interesting exception to this rule of spatio-temporal coherence. Verbs like *to say*, *to present*, *to think*, *to dream*, *to hope*, *to predict*, etc. may have embedded textoids in which temporal indicators and semantic structure are incompatable with related textoids not dominated by those verbs

(25)   (i)   *A* dreamt (t_i): $[B$ is dead $(t_j)]$
            (ii) *B* accomplishes action (t_j)

This contradiction is explained by the operator of (25i) indicating that the embedded textoid is not true (Neg Fact). The performative sentence may be optionally deleted, so that it must be inferred from contradictions in the text like *A is in Amsterdam at time t_j/A is in Tokyo at time t_j*, which imply *A dreams* (imagines) *in Amsterdam at time t_i* (...). Further such inconsistencies are possible of course in texts wholly dominated by such features as $[+ \text{FANTASTIC}]$.

5.7. *Some final remarks*

5.7.1. The different functions of the macro-transformations treated briefly above cannot easily be predicted without an adequate theory of literary performance. Deletions and permutations are infractions upon normal expectations of 'normal' presence and order of sequences. Their interpolation and interpretative re-ordering will produce subjective information and increase the entropy of a narrative text. These variables will take higher values in modern literature. Simple narrative and myths hardly have any permutations of the kind discussed above.

   Additionally, intuitive notions like 'suspense' are associated with permutations of all kinds, especially when uncertain consequences of an action in textoid T_i are given only in textoid T_{i+j} (where $j \geqslant 2$) (cf. Wienold, 1972).

5.7.2. Although the macro-transformations are a major characteristic of literary narrative, they are surely not the only literary rules. Very important also is their realization at the sentential level of the underlying textoids. That is, in literary narrative the macro-transformations may be optional, whereas the surface operations are obligatory as a set, but optional individually. It is not yet clear which typical surface operations are thus required in literary narrative. We should probably locate this problem at the level of stylistic performance, for example in the degree of syntactic complexity (embedding, coordinations) (cf. Hayes [1969], Ohmann [1964]) and the choice of particular lexemes occurring less often in non-literary narrative.

5.7.3. Some important final remarks must be made about scope and status of the theoretical remarks in this chapter. We have assumed that narrative texts are a particular type of text, whereas literary narrative has still further constraints. These constraints have been formulated essentially in linguistic terms, especially at the level of textual (macro-)semantics. This means that a narrative is a type of semantic representation, and a linguistic theory of narrative must thus formulate the required constraints upon all 'possible' semantic representations.

However, as we remarked earlier, narrative is not restricted to texts in natural language, but may also manifest itself in 'texts' of other semiotic 'languages' (systems), such as films, strips, dance, etc. This is trivial, and recent work in different branches of semiotics has often demonstrated this fact. Without analyzing the particular 'expressions' or 'surface forms' of narrative structures in these different systems, we may therefore assume that an adequate theory of narrative must be abstract enough to be related with the more particular forms of narrative in different systems. We may assume further that such an abstract theory be formulated in terms of a 'general semiotic semantics'. Such a semantics, however, does not exist and we therefore are obliged to adopt the reductive hypothesis that such a general semantics may be formulated provisionally in terms of the semantics of natural language. If this semantics is abstract enough it will then provide a model also for the descriptions of narrative in other semiotic systems. This has in fact been the case in much current research. Nevertheless, it is necessary to elaborate at the same time an abstract theory of narrative, of which the features, then, would provide the basis for the constraints upon the semantic representations of texts both in natural language and in other semiotic systems. Such an abstract theory may be conceived as a model for the narrative abilities of humans in general and would therefore belong to anthropological semiotics (cf. the statements by Bremond [1964], [1966], [1970], [1971]).

5.7.4. One of the well-known shortcomings of both traditional and structural descriptions of narrative has been the lack of explicit relations between the specific narrative categories such as 'event', 'action', 'person', 'character', 'plot', 'story', etc. and linguistic categories of textual deep and surface structures. In this chapter we tried to provide some insight into these relations. However, it is possible to elaborate in explicit detail such an 'independent' SYSTEM of narrative, by exact definitions of categories, i.e. the theoretical terms, the formulation of formation and derivation rules and the choice of relevant axioms. We may thus try to arrive at a formal calculus (syntax) with a possible interpretation (semantics) in terms of an abstract narrative theory. We will not here try to axiomatize a theory of narrative, but we will briefly touch upon some of its crucial aspects, such that an idea is formed of how many assumptions made in the previous sections may acquire a formal basis.

Although several systems of formalization are available, it seems most adequate to use a predicate calculus. Since semantic representations may be represented in the same system, it will then also be easy to isolate the specific narrative constraints upon the possible SR's of texts in natural language.

We may take, heuristically, our point of departure in the pre-theoretical conception of narrative as a series of (represented) EVENTS, a conception which goes back to Aristotle (1965). We further know that some COMBINATIONS of events form a narrative, others do not. (Let us stress again that we here consider events at the already rather 'abstract' level of 'events as represented in some semiotic system', i.e. as constructs.)

The restrictions upon possible combinations are of different types and must be elaborated by the theory. At the more general level, then, a theory of narrative is a system $\langle E, R \rangle$ of a set E of events $\{e_1, e_2, ...\}$ and a set R of relations over members of E. We might say that E is a sort of 'vocabulary' of the theory of narrative and R its set of 'grammatical' rules which define the well-formed narrative sequences over E. A NARRATIVE STRUCTURE N is thus defined as an n-tuple of events $\langle e_1, e_2, ..., e_n \rangle$, ordered by one or more relations. One of these relations is the relation $Prec$ (for 'preceding') which will be introduced as an undefined term (see below, however). It is easy to define, then, the notion of 'following' in terms of this relation, $viz.$ as its converse: $Follow\ (x, y) \equiv Prec\ (y, x)$. We may then specify in a set of axioms the properties of this relation of preceding, e.g.: $Prec$ is transitive, asymmetric and irreflexive. The precedence relation may be interpreted as ordering at the same time the TIME points (intervals) which may be assigned to each event or, conversely, it is possible to define to 'precede' as an ordering of time points and derive the ordering of events from it after having assigned to each event a time point t_i: $t_i\ (e_i)$, such that for any e: if $i < j$ then t_i precedes t_j and e_i precedes e_j. Of course we will also need the relations of (full and partial) 'overlapping' of events, which may also be defined in terms of time points and the relations of preceding and following.

Another main type of relation ordering the events in a narrative structure N is undoubtedly the CAUSE (or CONSEQUENCE) relation. We may introduce it as a primitive term, but its interpretation is not without difficulty. The 'causing' of one event by another is a vast philosophical (logical, physical) problem which needs also explication in narrative theory. Firstly, 'causation' is not identical with logical implication as expressed in a conditional like $p \supset q$, because it might very well be the case that 'p and not q' and 'q and not p' when cause (p, q). Nor need the 'consequence'-relation we have in mind be identical with logical consequence, i.e. the conclusion of an operation of deductive inference, e.g. modus ponens. In fact, 'cause' is not a relation between propositions (or sentences) but between events, which may be represented by sentences (see below). What we have in mind is a general type of 'inductive' cause (or consequence) relation, which may be specified as (e.g. physically) necessary, probable or possible with validity for different event-relations in different possible worlds. We will not further go into this intricate matter and adopt a pre-theoretically established primitive relation $cause\ (x, y)$, understood as follows: for at least one x and y, the occurrence of x is a sufficient CONDITION (cf. von Wright [1971b]) for the occurrence of y. Time relations play an important role here. We may therefore formulate the axiom that if x causes y then x temporally precedes y, and derive the theorem that y is the consequence of x, then y temporally follows x.

This is all very general and the important points are to be searched for in further analysis of the notions of 'event' and 'sequence' of events. Although we introduced 'event' as a primitive, it will be necessary to provide a more basic description, e.g. in order to define the cause relation. Thus any event may be defined as an ordered pair $\langle i, f \rangle$ of an initial state and a final state. A change 'modifies' the initial state into a final state. To represent this we will need an appropriate formalism, i.e. a CHANGE or EVENT LOGIC, since change cannot simply be rendered in a standard predicate calculus (cf. von Wright [1963]). The relation of which $\langle i, f \rangle$ is a member may be called the change relation C, such that the expression $C\ (i, f)$ may mean 'the initial state i is changed in a final state f'. At the level of the descriptive language state descriptions are given with the aid of (the logical forms of) sentences, or rather of sequences of sentences. This means in fact that events are not primitives (i.e. individuals in the language) but complex structures consisting of states and a (change) relation over these states. Note that the predicates (verbs) of natural language will normally merely refer to change relations itself (e.g. *to open*, etc.).

Events in narrative structure, however, are, as we saw, 'caused' by other 'events'. Strictly speaking, this would only hold true for natural events bringing about some change in a given (initial) state. We postulate therefore that narrative structure is characterized by ACTIONS rather then by events. 'Action' will be introduced as a next primitive and is intuitively understood as a behavioral unit of human beings. The 'origin' of an action (or 'act') has been called the 'agent', i.e. the human performing the act. We see that, rather trivially perhaps, a theory of narrative partially coincides with a theory of human action in general. This is not strange when we recall that narrative texts themselves somehow 'describe' ('represent', 'construct') worlds of human action. We therefore adopted the axiom that any narrative has at least one act accomplished by a human agent.

Acts have results which may bring about the change of a situation, that is acts may 'cause' certain events, but also acts of (other) humans. Formally, then, we would need also act-descriptions besides state- and change-descriptions, where an act-description may 'contain' a change-description: $A(a, C(i, f))$, where a is agent, and A the Action relation. It is not difficult to elaborate a logical calculus for actions (e.g. specified as *to do* and *to forbear*) in order to specify tautologies and contradictions. Clearly, an act may, at one time point, not lead to the change and to the not-change of a state, etc. (for detail, see von Wright [1963], [1967a], [1967b], [1971]).

The problems in fact lie in the philosophical basis for this calculus. There are many types of acting, related with different types of result, cause and consequence, and with different 'modes' like 'intending', 'trying', 'to be forced', 'to be obliged/permitted' to act, etc. It is problematic, for example, to which extent human agents 'cause' certain events, i.e. bring about certain states of affairs (for detail, see Chisholm, 1969), and how these acts are based on abilities, dispositions, intentions and endeavouring. We may establish different logical (deontic) systems when we take some of these notions as primitives (operators) (cf. Hilpinen, ed. 1971). Thus agents may only accomplish acts for which they have the ability etc. Now, the interesting task for a theory of literary narrative is to determine which rules of such systems are not respected in the 'worlds' described. We see that deontic systems are thus closely related with the modal systems: any state description specifies its 'own' world, and the change relation must define which world can be changed into which other world.

We will here stop these general remarks about the philosophical and logical foundations of a theory of narrative. At the abstract level of semantic representations these logical systems are indispensable for a serious formulation of the 'rules' holding in narrative texts, especially those which do not trivially correspond with the 'empirical' rules of human behaviour in the 'actual' world.

PART III

TOWARDS A THEORY OF TEXTUAL COMMUNICATION

CONTEXT, PERFORMANCE, PRAGMATICS

1. LINGUISTIC THEORY AND THE STATUS OF PRAGMATICS

1.1. There is a persistent tendency in current linguistic theory to consider a grammar as a theory of a language. This view is correct only in a very restricted sense, and probably only applies to grammars of formal languages.

One of the first tasks of this final chapter will be that of providing some arguments for a further extension of the grammar, *viz*. with a PRAGMATIC component. We will argue that a great part of the linguistic phenomena normally left for a so-called theory of performance belong to this component. Finally, we want to show that any theory of verbal performance or communication has to include a generative grammar extended with a set of pragmatic rules and categories. In addition, as was demonstrated earlier, this grammar must be a text grammar. Our very informal text grammar sketched in Part I must therefore be completed, for purely formal reasons also, with a pragmatic component. Only then does it provide a sound basis for psycho- and sociolinguistic theories of verbal performance and interaction, and only then can an adequate theory of literature be based or modelled on it.

The different issues involved here have intricate methodological and meta-theoretical implications. The whole question about the relations between competence and performance is only one aspect of them. In fact, we are dealing here with the problem of the empirical scope of linguistic theories and grammars. It is clear that only some aspects of this issue can be treated, especially with respect to a future completion of text grammars. Furthermore, our discussion will have a very schematic character in order to distinguish different aspects of the various theories involved at this level of linguistic description and explanation.

1.2. Let us briefly recall some tasks and aims of traditional generative S-grammars. Roughly speaking, these only provide a theory about the system underlying linguistic objects, i.e. underlying UTTERANCES and their structures at different levels. At the same time this theory purports to give a formal model for the linguistic abilities of native speakers. We should observe that this competence, for generative grammar, only enables the speaker to produce and to interpret the SENTENCES of his language. In the grammar sketched above this competence was extended in such a way as to be able to process TEXTS. In this hypothesis the theory did not account for such contextual factors as speakers and hearers, their speech acts and intentions, and abstracted from possible conditions, effects and functions of utterances in communication processes.

Recent discussions have underlined the fact that an empirically adequate linguistic theory also has to take into account these various properties conditioning the USE of the grammar/competence in processes of verbal interaction. Since a complete theory of language comprises at least a grammar and a theory of context or performance, we may not consider performance to be a set of untheorizable factors and the waste paper basket of grammatical description. To be sure, any theory of the USE of a language system and its sentences or rather utterances in communication processes presupposes a grammar. On the other hand, however, it turns out that many formal aspects of sentences can be described and explained only when aspects of communicative situations are taken into account.

The point now at issue is: do we have to formalize relevant communicative aspects within the grammar or within one of the possible theories of performance, or perhaps within both of them?

1.3. The solution to these problems must perhaps be sought for, at least partially, in the explicit answer to the following question: if a generative grammar describes how native speakers, ideally, are able to process a potentially infinite set of grammatical sentences or texts, how must we model their no less astonishing ability to use these texts appropriately in given situations? These situations, also, are infinite in number, and a linguistic theory has as one of its main aims the explanation of how, ideally, exactly the appropriate text is produced for a given communicative situation. We must assume, apparently, that the ACCEPTABILITY of utterances is determined by two basic properties of texts: their well-formedness and what could be called their 'well-usedness' or appropriateness. This first property can be called INTERNAL, the second EXTERNAL.

A next step in the argument is the following. We have to assume that native speakers somehow possess the ability to produce appropriate utterances. That is, they have an implicit knowledge of what types of texts can be used in what types of situations. This knowledge can be considered a part of their general linguistic knowledge, viz. as a part of competence. If this is true, a generative grammar must account for this part of the competence by specifying the RULES and CATEGORIES used by native speakers to 'apply' their linguistic products to properties of the extra-linguistic situation.

According to general semiotic theory this part of a linguistic theory can be identified as the PRAGMATICAL component (Stalnaker [1970]) because it specifies the relations between signs or sign combinations and their users. The problem, then, is the purported empirical scope of pragmatics and the possible form of the pragmatic component.[1]

1.4. At this point terminological and methodological confusion lies at hand. Notice, first of all, that linguistic grammars only specify structures of sentences or texts and therefore must be identified with the SYNTACTICAL component of a semiotic theory. Morphophonology, syntax and (intensional) semantics fall within this component. Grammar does not study the relations between signs (with their intensional meanings) and their denotata, a task left for the proper SEMANTIC part of a semiotic theory, normally called THEORY OF REFERENCE in linguistics and philosophy of language (cf. Carnap [1958], Linsky [1967], Strawson [1952], Geach [1962]). Thus, if grammar has to be extended by a pragmatic component we will also be obliged to include a theory of reference or MODEL THEORY, accounting for the ability of native speakers to relate the meaning of texts to, say, mental representations of real or fictive 'reality' (Cohen [1970], Davidson [1970], Lewis [1970]).

Only then are we able to say that the grammar, extended in this way, is a full theory of a language system and/or of a linguistic competence.

1.5. Notice further, however, that this extended grammar is no less a theory of abstract structures, a system of rules accounting for idealized abilities and conventions. Its pragmatic component merely specifies the general, if not universal, RULES describing the relationships between utterances and situations and their elements, e.g. the participants in a set of speech acts.

A theory of language, however, must also account for the actual manifestations of the system or competence. This latter theory necessarily has a probabilistic character, because it studies the use of the syntactic (i.e. syntactic, phonological, morphological and semantic), semantic (i.e. referential) and pragmatical rules of the extended grammar in concrete situations. It will specify for example which conditions underlie this actual use, e.g. by relating extra-linguistic with linguistic (textual) variables.

This theory, which has normally been called the THEORY OF PERFORMANCE, is also

---

¹ It is impossible to provide here a review of traditional and modern work done in philosophical, logical and linguistic pragmatics, which ranges from metaphysical hermeneutics at one side to highly formalised logical theorizing at the other side. For its definition, cf. Peirce (1960), and the studies of his philosophical ideas, and especially Morris (1938), (1946). A Marxist approach, which comments upon the typology of discourse provided by Morris (1946), is given by Klaus (1969). The recent developments within mathematical logic is due above all to Montague (1968, 1970ab). Modern pragmatics within linguistics partly bases itself on these logical theories, cf. Schnelle (1970b). Wunderlich (1970a), partly uses models from sociology and the communication sciences. The progressive integration of theories of reference, of social interaction, grammar and pragmatics can be noticed in a number of recent papers, e.g. Schnelle (1970b), Helmer(1969), (1970). The theory of speech acts, a primary concern of ordinary language philosophy, is an important part of these developments, cf. Rorty, ed. (1967), Searle (1969), Searle, ed. (1971) and Lyas, ed. (1971). The work in textual and literary theory by Schmidt elaborates on these issues (cf. recently, Schmidt [1971c] commenting in an earlier version of this chapter, who provides a summary of current research in pragmatics and who attempts a description of pragmatic structures). Cf., finally, Kummer (1972b) who provides a pragmatic theory of texts based on a theory of action, and especially Harrah (1963), (1969) who provides a logical model of communication, which could not yet be integrated in our sketchy remarks about the pragmatics of communication in this chapter.

concerned, as any theory, with the formulation of regularities and laws, not with the enumeration of ad hoc properties of particular utterances (Fodor and Garrett, 1966). It is important to note further that this theory may not be identified with what was called pragmatics (Wunderlich, 1970a). A system or competence of pragmatic rules has its own (ir)regularities in its actual application: utterances may also be used inappropriately for various reasons. It may be expected, however, that a theory of abstract systems, i.e. grammar, having a pragmatic component can more easily be related to a theory of actual use, i.e. with a theory of performance. If we want to derive predictions from our grammar about the expected (degrees of) acceptability of a given text, we must not only specify its well-formed structure but also the (degrees of) appropriateness in possible situations (Miller [1964], Campbell and Wales [1970]).

1.6. The relationships between grammar and a theory of performance have been clarified above, but their status with respect to general linguistic theory has not yet been made wholly explicit. It is useful, therefore, to distinguish the various levels of description
  - GRAMMARS describe idealized systems of languages i.e. infinite sets of texts and the general conditions for their use,
  - THEORIES OF PERFORMANCE describe the systems underlying the actual use of these systems,
  - GENERAL LINGUISTIC THEORY specifies the possible form of grammars, the possible forms of theories of performance and the character of the relations between these two types of theories.

In a sense, grammars can be considered to be formal abstractions from theories of performance or as central parts of them (Wunderlich [1970a], [1970b]). Formally, these theories, furthermore, have their own syntactic, semantic and pragmatic components (cf. Schnelle [1968], [1970a]). Even within the grammar we may distinguish different sub-theories about the different levels of text structure. Each sub-theory has (i) a syntax specifying the formation rules of the theory, i.e. its well-formed formulas (ii) a semantics for the interpretation of these abstract formula in terms of a specific empirical domain (e.g. phonological, syntactic and semantic categories of natural language), finally (iii) a pragmatics accounting for the assumed role of this theory for the theorist.

1.7. Before we turn our attention to the different components of a theory of textual performance, let us first consider some aspects of the PRAGMATIC COMPONENT OF TEXT GRAMMARS.
  Pragmatics was defined as that component of the grammar which accounts for the system determining the communicative appropriateness of texts, and at the same time, for the ideal knowledge of native speakers of this appropriate use. A theory of pragmatics, then, has to specify

1. the list of primitive symbols of a pragmatic theory/language,
2. the formation rules specifying all *wff*'s of the theory (pragmatic syntax),
3. the rules specifying the equivalence and synonymy of the *wff*'s,
4. the rules relating *wff*'s with pragmatical structures of natural language systems or competences (pragmatic semantics),
5. the rules for the appropriate use of well-formed pragmatic theories (pragmatic pragmatics).

The next task is perhaps still more complicated: pragmatics must be related to the other components of the grammar, especially to the semantic component. We have to know if and how pragmatic structures are mapped onto semantic structures underlying a text. (Searle [1969] 64).

1.8. It is clear that the language of pragmatics we must elaborate along the global lines indicated in the previous paragraph is still in a very primitive state of construction. Actually, before we know HOW to talk about pragmatic structures we must first have to make some distinctions in WHAT we want to describe: the actual domain of pragmatics.

Let us enumerate some of the tentative categories of pragmatics

1. utterance
2. hearer(s)
3. speaker(s)
4. speech act (production)
5. hearing act (perception)
6. time of speech act
7. time of hearing act
8. place of speech act
9. place of hearing act

We have seen that some categories of this list, which should be extended (see below), were already included in what we called the PERFORMATIVE category of semantic deep structure derivations. Actually, the status of that category was noted to be ambiguous: it is not clear whether it is a semantic category, i.e. one which determines the meaning of the text, or a pragmatic category characterizing the speech act in which the text is uttered.

The problems involved here are highly complex and the bulk of traditional and recent discussions in philosophy of language treat this and related issues. Let us try to give a very brief account of the status and properties of pragmatic structures and relate them to structures of the text. Some preliminary remarks should be made. It follows from our discussion of text grammars that only TEXTS can underlie meaningful utterances. Of course, texts may consist of one sentence and this sentence of only one word. Isolated sentences, however, cannot be used in appropriate communicative situations. Any utterance, then, is a token of a text. This may seem a trivial statement, but many traditional problems of the theory of speech acts can be brought closer to a possible solution if we are fully aware of its implications. Furthermore, it is necessary to distinguish between pragmatic categories and referential categories, although there is a very clear relationship between them. Referential categories and rules which have to be defined in a theory of reference (extensional semantics), were formalized in our modal category of textual deep structure. They essentially specify the truth values of the nuclear proposition: true, false, possible, probable. Together with the pragmatic categories they define the appropriateness of the utterance. Notice that both referential and pragmatic appropriateness are thus properties of abstract TOKENS, i.e. of utterances of a text. A text is merely a formal syntactico-semantic construction, and only when we utter it in a concrete situation can we use it to refer to a state of affairs. We will assume that the modal or referential categories are dominated by the pragmatic ones: we can only assign a truth value to an utterance if we know the pragmatic properties of the communicative situation (Stalnaker [1970]).

1.9. A first distinction to be made now is between the 'pragmatic' aspects of an utterance and those of a speech act. The pragmatic aspects of the utterance (which we called 'performative' in earlier chapters) are formal modifications of the modalized nuclear proposition of the text. Because they are a part of their deep structure specification they must be considered a part of their intensional meaning. In texts like

(1)   I believe Peter is ill.
(2)   I know Peter will come.

there is a pragmatic dominating sentence which is part of the meaning of the text. These sentences may also be deleted under certain conditions, e.g. in questions *(I ask you)* and commands *(I order you)*, followed by possible syntactic transformations (inversion, deletion).

These pragmatic aspects of meaning do not necessarily coincide with those of the speech act as a whole.[2] It is well-known that we may make an assertion like *It is cold in here* not primarily to inform a hearer about our opinion about an atmospherical

---

[2] In previous chapters we followed suggestions of Ross (1970), Sadock (1970) and Wunderlich (1970a), (1970b) and integrated some pragmatic aspects into the grammatical derivation of texts. Such a 'provisional' and partial representation of pragmatic categories was necessary to account for some purely formal (textual) structures; e.g. the derivation of tense forms and underlying temporal relations. We will assume that this procedure is, indeed, provisional because the grammar needs a full pragmatic component; the structures of this component are, then, mapped on semantic (and/or syntactic) structures, a mapping which will account, among many other things, for the phenomena studied by those cited above. Only in the case that we want to leave pragmatics outside the grammar it will be necessary to introduce semantic or syntactic categories to do the same formal job. Such a solution, however, seems inadequate to us, and recalls the attempts of early transformational grammar to use obvious semantic notions in syntactic derivations.

property, but in order to elicit some action by the hearer, e.g. to shut the window, to put on the heating, etc. That is, a formal assertion can be used to perform the per-locutionary act of a request. (For the notions 'perlocutionary', 'illocutionary' acts, see Austin [1962], Searle [1969], Todorov, ed. [1970]).

1.10. We may conclude that pragmatic properties of speech acts can be defined in terms of the FUNCTIONS an utterance is intended by the speaker to fulfill. These functions are properties of the relations between the utterance of the speaker and the hearer. Thus, a request is a speech act intended by the speaker to provoke the ac-complishment by the hearer of an action denoted by or implied by the utterance. This action may itself be a illocutionary act, e.g. when we want to have information about a state of affairs, or simply a cognitive act, like 'knowing' as in all assertions. This knowledge may pertain to the attitudes of the speaker with respect to the present, past or future actions of the hearer. An advice, thus, is a speech act by which a speaker wants a hearer to know that a future action of the hearer is considered by the speaker to be of positive interest for the hearer (for detail, cf. Searle [1969]).

All these different speech acts or illocutionary acts have their own complex structure, which we cannot analyze here. The problem is whether we can reduce them to some basic types from which the others can be derived. Attempts in this direction have been frequent, but meet with no success.

1.11. There are further conditions for the appropriateness of utterances besides the internal structure of the speech act in which they are produced and received. We must make a distinction here between general or universal communicative conditions and particular or initial communicative conditions (cf. Schnelle [1970a]).

The first set contains such rather trivial conditions like

1. Speaker can perform a locutionary act.
2. Hearer can perform an auditory act.
3. Speaker and hearer know a common language.
4. The common language is used in the communicative act.
5. Speaker is interested in establishing a communicative relation with the hearer.
6. A communicative relation can be established between speaker and hearer.

These pragmatic universals will be part of the meta-theory of language.

The initial conditions for the different speech acts are of a more specific kind. A command is appropriate only when the speaker knows the hearer can accomplish the commanded action; an assertion only when the speaker has some evidence about a given state of affairs being the case, etc. (cf. Searle [1969], Bellert [1972]).

These universal and particular conditions must be part of the competence of native speakers i.e. they are elements of rules determining the performance of speech acts appropriate to the situation.

The different speech acts, thus, are definable as complex relations between

1. cognitive states of speakers: hope, know, believe, doubt, want, intent, ...
2. cognitive states of hearers: know, believe, want, ...
3. actions of hearers,
4. the truth values of propositions of texts,
5. semantic structures of texts.

The last two terms are relevant here only if we consider the utterance to be a part of the speech act itself.

Let us give as an example the tentative rules that must apply when we produce appropriate questions

A speech act involving an utterance with a proposition *Prop* is a question if
(i)   the speaker does not know *Prop*,
(ii) the speaker believes the hearer to know *Prop*,
(iii) the speaker wants to know *Prop*,
(iv) the speaker wants the hearer to tell him *Prop*.

The utterance, then, will be called appropriate if these pragmatic conditions are satisfied and if the utterance is a token of a text having a well-formed interrogative meaning structure and a well-formed surface structure. Thus a question like *Do I have a headache?* is inappropriate because the pragmatic conditions (i) and (ii) are not satisfied.

1.12. It is still very difficult to say something relevant about the other possible components of pragmatic structure: the implicit knowledge of native speakers comprises at least the notions of time and place of the speech act. As we saw, this knowledge is required for a correct generation of coherent semantic time in texts. Moreover, locutionary verbs like 'to promise' imply that the promised actions occur at a time t_i after t_0 of the utterance. The converse holds for such illocutionary acts as 'to apologize' and 'to thank (for)'. The notion of place is to be included in all sorts of pragmatic rules possessing a deictic character: in order to generate demonstrative pronouns and many local adverbs there must be a rule stating the awareness of the speaker that the hearer, being at the same 'place' of utterance, can actually see denoted referents (Bar Hillel [1954], Wunderlich [1971a]).

Here we touch upon the problems of the theory of reference, which will formulate rules about mutual knowledge of the speaker and hearer about the intended referents denoted by the utterance. An example: an utterance like *Did the doctor tell you you are pregnant?* presupposes that the hearer is female.

1.13. Premature at present are attempts to arrive at satisfactory formalizations of pragmatic structures in natural language with the aid of explicit derivation rules. To be sure, in order to enumerate the infinite set of well-formed pragmatic structures, i.e. structure of communicative acts/situations, we need an algorithm of rules operating on abstract pragmatic categories. Our assumption was that native speakers have an intuitive knowledge of such rules. That is, they are able to recognize which structures are well-formed and which are not. For instance, as soon as one of the categories is lacking, the communicative act is inappropriate: a question is inappropriate if there is no hearer as a participant in the communication act.

Since the formalism is expected to yield structural descriptions, the rules must specify sets of relations between pragmatic categories, for example the relation between speaker and hearer, between utterance and hearer, etc. In that case it is natural to borrow a notation from a relational predicate logic. However, in this stage of research it is more important to arrive at a set of theoretically relevant categories for a future pragmatic component of the grammar. For some attempts towards a formalism, cf. above all Harrah (1963) and further Schnelle (1970b), Wunderlich (1971a), van Dijk (1972a) and Schmidt (1971e) who elaborates in more detail some proposals made in an earlier version of this chapter.[3]

1.14. The analysis of the structure of idealized communicative interaction may begin with general or 'major' categories which are progressively analyzed into smaller constitutive categories.

We will adopt as a basic or 'initial' category a unit which may be called 'communicative act' or 'communicative interaction' and which corresponds roughly to the traditional term 'speech act' (Searle [1969]). The terms used are, however, somewhat misleading because they seem to imply only the actions of the participants and, for example, the conditions for the speech act and factors of situation and/or context. We will therefore use a symbol C, provisionally interpreted as 'unit of communication in natural language'.

C may be defined as a relation between (i) a speech act (ii) a hearing act, and (iii) a communication situation.

The speech act is specified as a production relation between (i) a speaker, (ii) an

---

[3] The form of the rules of such a formalism is still problematic and we here meet with difficulties similar to those of formalizing semantic relational structures. Thus the initial rule of pragmatics might be something like $C \rightarrow SA\ HA\ CS$, that is, establish a relation between speech act (SA), hearing act (HA) and communication situation (CS). Such a rule recalls the traditional rewrite-rule of generative grammars. The fundamental difference, however, is that SA, HA and CS are not immediate constituents in the syntactic sense, that is, there is no linear ordering between them. Nevertheless there must be a relation between them: $SA\ HA\ CS$ does not seem to be an unordered set, but rather an ordered triple, of which the elements, later in the derivation, are also rewritten as ordered n-tuples. The last steps in the derivation will, then, probably replace the terms of the relation by symbols representing sets. These sets can be seen as the lexicon of the pragmatic theory. Of course rewrite-rules are not necessary to make the different relations explicit. A system of definitions in the traditional sense would probably do the same job, e.g. in case we want to axiomatize the theory. Recent proposals from logical pragmatics proceed along this line (cf. Montague [1968], [1970a], [1970b]).

utterance, (iii) a time interval and (iv) a given place. These are essentially the major categories usually introduced – in their syntactic form (I, t_0, l_0) – into recent syntactic derivations.

Similarly, a hearing act is defined as being constituted by a relation of reception between (i) a hearer, (ii) a (perceived) utterance, (iii) a time interval and (iv) a given place.

As a rule we adopt that in ideal communicative acts the produced and the perceived utterances are equivalent, although in actual performance this need not be the case: noise may hinder the phonetic transmission, and misinterpretation may prevent a correct transmission of intents as manifested in the semantic structure of the uttered discourse. The time intervals and the places of speaking and hearing may, but need not be identical. This is the case in telephone calls and especially in written communication. The notions of production and perception, therefore, not only pertain to oral communication (speaking and hearing in the normal sense) but also writing and reading. The implications of the difference between oral and written/printed communication are important to explain differences in structure between written and spoken texts and their sociological status (cf. Lotman and Pjatigorskij [1969], Beneš and Vachek, eds. [1971]).

In a next step we may define both speaker and hearer in an abstract way, that is we do not simply identify these notions with particular human individuals, but conceive of them as sets of pragmatically relevant relations. In sociology and sociolinguistics we could, for example, consider speaker and hearer to be communicative 'roles' (cf. Dittmar [1971]). In the formal sets, then, they may be defined as sets of relations between sets of properties, e.g. (i) a set of physiological properties (ii) a set of psychological properties and (iii) a set of sociological properties, three sets which may exhaustively define any participant in a communicative situation. These three sets are ordered such that elements of one of them are related with elements of the two others. We here find ourselves at the border of psycho- and sociolinguistics, and psychology and sociology, but the difference is that the pragmatic component is restricted to a formulation of the rules, internalized by the native speaker, determining an ideal set of 'expectancies' in communicative situations. Thus, for example, physiological differences between men, women and children may influence the para-linguistic features of the utterance and – in performance – the stylistic form (especially on the lexical level) of the utterance itself.

The three sets introduced here should further be specified each into two subsets, a subset of permanent and a subset of ad hoc or casual properties. Thus sex and age are (relative) permanent properties whereas illness is a casual physiological property. Of course, more relevant are the casual and permanent psychological properties. Thus properties of personality and cognition are relatively permanent. Linguistic competence belongs to the set of cognitive abilities of native speakers. Ad hoc psychological properties, for instance, manifest themselves in knowledge and belief about the other participant, about the communicative situation and about the subject matter ('topic' in the non-technical sense) of the utterance. Similarly, permanent sociological properties are position, status, profession, etc., whereas roles may differ in various situations.

It is obvious that for a pragmatic component to state these properties and relations is relevant only to the extent that they are implicitly known by native speakers as functional components of communicative situations. For the linguist, in the strict sense, they are relevant only when they predict the possible forms of the utterance (discourse) itself. We have seen that knowledge of the speaker about the knowledge of the hearer is a condition to establish the speech act of a question, which in turn is realized in a specific linguistic form. Notice, however, that pragmatic rules regulate the appropriateness of the utterance not necessarily also its form. Thus to give a command is normally restricted to speakers with a position or a role dominating those of the hearer, although the (stylistic) form of the command or request may be determined by the intentions, and role of the speaker and by sociological conventions, e.g. in the case of specific politeness forms of a language (pronouns, auxiliaries, adverbs). In order to generate *tu* or *vous* in French (or *du* and *Sie* in German) we need pragmatic rules determining the status or role of the addressee. This is well-known, but the consequence is that a pragmatic theory – if not integrated into the grammar – must at least be related explicitly with the grammar.

The utterance, which is another component of speech and hearing act, may be defined as a token of a text of language *L* (cf. Carnap [1958] 248ff.). We see that in this category we may establish a link with the semantic and morpho-syntactic levels of the grammar, *viz.* through the notion of text.

The third major component of the communication process *C* is what has been called the communicative situation. Whereas the other components of the communication process are relatively, though intuitively, well-known, we do however have very systematic knowledge of the relevant categories of communicative situations. Tentatively, we may again make a distinction between permanent or general (if not universal) properties and ad hoc properties of such a situation. The general properties are for example the class or culture of the participants. In case class or culture of the participants differ – e.g. together with the language (or code) *L* – it is possible that utterances are inappropriate because of a lack of knowledge of the hearer about the intentions, 'background', etc. of the speaker. This is a well-known fact in linguistic anthropology (cf. Hymes [1962] for references). The same is true for communication between participants from different social classes, because utterances may show class determined differences in grammatical rules, lexicon and their use (style) (cf. e.g. Labov [1970] and below). Universal for oral communication is, for instance, the presence of the participants in one perceptual space, without which gestures – e.g. accompanying linguistic deictics – are impossible.

Ad hoc situational factors are the properties of the place of the utterance and the general or particular events occurring before or during the speech act. At this point the theory of reference must of course be related with the pragmatic theory. Ad hoc also are the visible effects of the utterance on the hearer, which may lead to processes of feed-back.

Instead of the term 'situation' often the term 'context' is used. Here, however, we use situation as defined above and reserve context for the set of all properties and relations of the communication process but without the utterance. For the traditional term 'verbal context' we have used the formal notion of 'text' or 'co-text' (cf. Petöfi, 1971) and the performance notion of 'discourse'.

We will here stop our analysis of the pragmatic structure of the communication process. Many more distinctions might be needed and be made explicit in definitions and/or rules.

2. PSYCHOLOGICAL IMPLICATIONS OF TEXT GRAMMARS

2.1. We will now turn to the non-grammatical aspects of the communication process, i.e. to the various factors determining actual textual performance. We will distinguish two main parts within this theory: a set of statements about the use of the grammatical rules and their conditions by individual speakers and hearers, accounted for by the PSYCHOLOGICAL COMPONENT of the theory, and a set of statements about textual communication in and between groups of individuals, accounted for by the (psycho-) SOCIOLOGICAL COMPONENT of the theory to which we will turn in the next section.

2.2. Since any theory of performance has to include a grammar, we might be able to make some relevant observations about the possible role of text grammars for the study of performance. The well-known difficulties of relating an abstract competence with mental and behavioural abilities requires particular attention in this perspective (Fodor-Garrett [1966]). It has become clear that a postulated competence has at least to be distinguished from the mechanisms processing the linguistic objects and, further, that the assumed 'symmetry' between production and reception models is unwarranted. The general conclusion of recent discussions in psycholinguistics seems to be that the grammar is not a precise model for mental mechanisms determining processes of production and perception, and that psychological phenomena do not directly determine the form of the grammar.[4] Rather poor evidence supports the hypothesis about the 'psychological reality' of syntactic deep structures. The psycholinguistic results obtained could more easily be explained in terms of semantic deep structures (Campbell and Wales [1970]). Recall, comparison, and other mental operations with sentences are based on semantic representations. Syntactic structures

---

[4] The studies arriving at this type of conclusions have been mentioned often in the course of this book: Campbell and Wales (1970), Johnson-Laird (1970), Wunderlich (1970a), Labov (1970).

appeared to be immediately erased from memory, which points at their 'superficial' character (Johnson-Laird [1970]).

2.3. Another possible way to bridge the gap between formal grammars and models of production and perception, was the extension of the grammar with a textual component. Arguments adduced for this extension were partially psychological
– speakers/hearers process sentences differently when occurring at different places of the texts or when being part of different texts,
– speakers/hearers are able to process longer texts as coherent units,
– they are able to recall, summarize and comment on texts without recalling the semantic representations of their individual sentences.
– the memory of humans is not able to store the set of all relevant phonological and semantic relations, constraints and other compatibility conditions holding between any sentence S_i of a text and its preceding and following sentences, therefore
– the production and reception of texts must be based on the construction of macrostructures.

These empirical facts have led to the elaboration of a text grammar. Let us now consider in what respect a text grammar can be considered an underlying model for production and reception of utterances.

2.4. Observe first that models of production and reception are also idealizations, abstractions from particular encoding and decoding processes. The precise verbal strategies used by individual speakers may, of course, vary (Wunderlich [1970a]).

One of the crucial implications of text grammar for psycho-linguistics is presumably the role of macro-units or PLANS in the production and reception of utterances. These plans were used already in early psychological work based on generative-transformational grammar to describe underlying structure (cf. Miller, Galanter, Pribram, [1960], Miller & Chomsky [1963]). The model used, in these studies, was syntactic deep structure. One of the arguments adduced for the existence of these plans was the ability of speakers to postpone the realization of some grammatical elements to a later part of the sentence, although they are grammatically in close relation with earlier elements.

This argument can easily be used for postulating plans for macro-structures. Any production or reception model must include such plans in order to be able to account for such notions as 'global interpretation'.

2.5. The differences between a production and a reception model should be taken into account here. We may assume that, once the pragmatic and referential conditions are satisfied, a speaker in the production process will first construct a very rough global semantic representation for the whole text or for a coherent initial part of it. This global plan may somehow correspond to cognitive structures such as intentions or mental representations. Only then is he able to begin the production of the initial sentences of the text (or rather: of the utterance). The production of any sentence of the uttered text should be regulated by the linear intersentential constraints (as treated in chapter 2) and by the given global plan. This plan, in production, has two main functions: it determines the global order of sequences of sentences in the text and puts further constraints upon the semantic structure of the respective sentences.

The precise nature of this execution of the global plan is still obscure. Probably feedback from the sentence production may change the global plan continuously, which may result in a lower degree of coherence.

In perception an initial global plan does not exist but is progressively constructed. The semantic elements of the successive sentences are generalized and put into the categories of a model of macro-structures. This generalization is a process of hypothesis-formation: further sentences confirm or disconfirm earlier assignments of elements to the global structure. Additional (referential, situational) information will normally influence this process: in many circumstances the global structure of a text can be predicted by the hearer, e.g. in propaganda speeches and in highly stereotyped novels or films.

2.6. In both production and reception the existing or postulated global plan will reduce the subjective information of the text. Any account in terms of transitional probabilities between individual sentences alone will therefore fail to provide a model for the ease of production/reception and for the degree of expectance, etc. (cf. also Miller and Chomsky [1963]). Without such a reduced information rate it would be impossible to process texts cognitively and to store them, as macro-structures, (together with some occasional local stylistic features) in our long-term memory. The general role of patterns or 'Superzeichen' in recognition was discovered earlier (cf. Neisser [1967]), and is important for the description of production and reception of texts (cf. Bense [1969]). Thus, in production, the choice of possible semantic representations for sentences, is restricted by the macro-plan of the text, which reduces the statistical information of the encoding process. Conversely, in perception, the insertion, into global plans, of a great number of various lexemes reduces their total information rate i.e. increases intelligibility (Bruce, 1968).

Clearly, psychological tests are necessary to confirm these and similar hypotheses. A first set of tests will have to compare sequences of sentences without linear (surface) and macro-deep structure coherence respectively. As has been demonstrated at the sentence-level, we may expect that meaningful sequences are more easily (re-)produced and recalled. Similarly, we may expect that texts having a macro-structure but no linear surface coherence, like certain poems, are very difficult to process (cf. Treisman [1968] Marks and Miller [1969]; cf. also the interesting research of Bartlett [1932]).

2.7. We must stress once more at this point that production and perception models are idealizations and generalizations, either as abstract models (e.g. expressed by flow-diagrams) or as formulations in statistical terms. Particular communication acts, and individual speakers, will probably manifest various different strategies of producing or receiving texts. Such habitual performance factors as memory limitations, hesitation, mistakes, etc. interfere with 'normal' production. At the same time reactions of hearers and associations, afterthought, etc. of the speaker himself have feedback on further production of the text. Observe that the different pragmatic aspects of performance (as formalized in grammar) also influence concrete production: beliefs, wants, motivations, knowledge of speaker about hearer, context and expected (re-)actions of hearer. Similarly, for referential aspects: the degree of knowledge of certain states of affairs will also have a decisive influence upon lexical choice. This set of conditions determining textual surface structure, i.e. the STYLE of particular texts, can be extended by many others: personality of the speaker, mental state during production, wish to produce certain rhetorical effects, etc.

2.8. In the search for possible models of performance, *viz.* processes of production and perception, the arguments put forward by Chomsky (1959b), Chomsky and Miller (1963) and others, for sentential performance apply *a fortiori* for textual performance. Thus, the number of possible dependencies in texts can never be accounted for by any stochastic, e.g. Markov, model. If 15-word distances already provide 10^{45} possibilities it is clear that estimates for probabilities in texts having, say, 10,000-word distances, or even 1,000-sentence distances go far beyond the possibilities of mental processes. Inductive knowledge of transition probabilities in texts is therefore impossible: there are hardly any texts of more than one-sentence length which are identical, with the possible exception of formulaic stereotypes.

Similarly, models for selective information may only predict globally that the information of textual production will progressively decrease. When a hearer knows already the macro-structure of a text, its surface elements will be more predictable. However, even at the level of (complex) sentences the relative probabilities of elements like lexemes cannot be statistically calculated: the probability of texts of, say, more than 20 words is practically zero. The total information (entropy) of texts therefore cannot be given. Notice that possible data always pertain to the observable surface structure of utterances (texts): even when we may predict roughly the global semantic structure of a text in specific situations, it is impossible to say the same of the infinitely various possible surface structures of that deep structure. The generation of surface structures was said to be a restricted selection procedure from lexical sets defined by the lexicoids of deep structure. The possible combinations of the elements of these sets are still infinite even when all grammatical, pragmatic, referential, stylistic and contextual constraints apply. Notice finally that these remarks can be made both for selective and for semantic information, although these should be strictly separated. The selective information will decrease because we learn, in reading a longer text, specific characteristic syntactic structures and specific lexical choices viz. the idiolect or style of the text. Similarly, the semantic information will also progressively decrease the more we know about the global meaning of the text. However, in both cases, this redundancy will never reach its maximum value (in first readings). The information remains at a fairly additional rate of increase: if not, further production/perception of texts would be unnecessary.

2.9. A performance theory for texts is not confined to developing sets of models for the description of extra-linguistic and grammatical factors determining the concrete production and perception of well-formed and appropriate texts. Texts, like sentences, may consciously or unconsciously manifest surface structures which are only SEMI-GRAMMATICAL. In order to arrive at valid predictions about the interpretability and acceptability of texts it is necessary to develop possible measures for their deviations. Chomsky and Miller (1963) have provided some data of this type, based on substitutability of lexical elements in certain categories, sets of categories, and so on. This computation, however, simply assumed 'discourses' to be defined as sequences of unrelated sentences, a position which was demonstrated to lead to unsatisfactory linguistic descriptions. Let us give a simple example. Assume some *Adj* like *honest* is generated in connection with an *N*, *carpenter*, in some sentence S_i of a text *T*. In the sentential model of Chomsky and Miller there would be no deviation from grammaticalness if the same *N*, *carpenter*, referring to the same real or fictive person, was connected – e.g. in a novel – with an *Adj* like *treacherous*. In any adequate textual model, such a substitution would probably result in linear or global incoherence. We see that in discourse the high amount of very complex constraints permits a much larger set of possible semigrammatical constructions, both within its sentences and in the relations between its sentences.

From similar examples it is also clear that the chance of possible deviations increases with the length of the text, while heavier semantic constraints lie on combinations of categories (and lexemes) at the end than rather at the beginning. This is true at least for the hearer: a speaker may already know these specific constraints.

There are two opposite forces at play in this domain. On the one hand the complexity of textual rules easily leads to occasional local or global incoherence (together with normal sentential deviations). This is trivial: it is difficult to produce perfectly coherent texts. On the other hand the increasing redundancy in texts will normally guarantee correct interpretation of these semi-grammatical structures: deviations in that case are neutralized by sufficient 'counter-examples'. Note that this is true for all texts, but that in specific types of texts, e.g. in literature, such deviations may have specific stylistic function, or even be governed by a secondary rule system (cf. chaps. 6–8).

2.10. Most familiar in a theory of textual performance is undoubtedly the extensive use of frequency counts for different elements both in isolated texts and in corpuses of texts: phonemes, lexemes, grammatical structures, 'themes', 'topics', etc. These methods are well-known from quantitative linguistics, stylistics, psychology and

content analysis and need no specific comment here. Some remarks in relation with
T-grammar may suffice.

Frequency counts of linguistic units in texts have a surface character. Most data
are based on observable entities. Deviations from mean values are considered in-
dicative, e.g. for personal style or for the style of a particular text, or for some mental
state of the speaker/writer. Only in recent literature on the subject have abstract
operations like transformations also been considered to be relevant units (e.g.
Hayes [1969]).

It is well-known that these statistical approaches to texts have a global nature.
They do not specify local constraints, but general tendencies in the selection of
optional elements of a given language. We may therefore use them to study the global
surface realizations of global deep structures. One of the notorious drawbacks of
textual statistics has been the fact that the calculation of significant deviations or co-
variations is theoretically weak, because lexical selection depends directly on the
'topic' of the text. Comparison of data, therefore, is relevant only for texts having
similar semantic deep structure. This notion, however, is unknown in extant work
in the field, and only intuitive terms like 'same topic' are used. Let us assume, then,
that we are able to establish unambiguously the semantic macro-structure of a given
text. We are able then to study statistically how the macro-categories are lexicalized
in surface structure. At the same time distribution, variation and other properties of
lexical use may be studied on this basis. Important also is a possible statistical study
of the progressive lexical redundancy of thematic structures, i.e. the selection guided
by some specific features or feature combinations with traditional 'connotative'
functions. In both cases, i.e. in normal semantic and in thematic realization, the
knowledge of underlying structure is important because it eliminates one set of
determining conditions from all other possible causes guiding the selection of lexemes.
This means that we may acquire more direct insight into psychological or sociological
parameters of style once all grammatical constraints are made explicit. That is, we
may neglect the general and 'normal' constraints upon processes of selection and
study the real performance aspects of textual production (i.e. specific use of a particular
speaker/writer of the grammatical rules and lexical elements of his language resulting
in significant deviations from the average values of given elements in comparable
texts of the language, etc.) and try to find some explanation for this particular behaviour. Such explanations have some value only when the general causes of specific
choices are known, i.e. when there is significant co-variation between stylistic elements
and non-linguistic properties of speakers/writers. From this perspective the rules of
text grammar provide the necessary basis for the explicit knowledge of the grammatical
constraints in texts: traditional quantitative stylistics could never go beyond sentence-
level rules as formulated in S-grammars. It has become clear that the explanation of
statistical features of language use as it manifests itself in text production can be
relevant only when we base ourselves on an explicit knowledge of these fundamental
text grammatical 'causes' of regularities (cf. van Dijk [1970d]).

3. SOCIOLOGICAL IMPLICATIONS OF TEXT GRAMMARS

3.1. If there is one domain in a general theory of verbal behaviour where text grammars can prove their fundamental relevance it is surely in the sociological component of a theory of performance. The relative poverty in current theorizing in socio-linguistics can partially be explained by this lack of explicit insight into text structures (cf. Wunderlich, [1970a]).

The issue is trivial: verbal interaction between individuals and groups in society is based on production, perception, interpretation, comparison and storage of discourses. Most utterances relevant to this central type of social interaction consist of more than one sentence. Any study of sociolinguistic behaviour restricted to features of sentences in isolation will therefore be inadequate (Labov [1970]). The same remark can be made about those text-based studies in sociology, e.g. frequency and distribution counts, which do not take into account the structural relation between sentences and the nature of textual macro-structures.

3.2. Sociolinguistics has many different domains in which a text grammar may show its theoretical relevance.

First of all, our remarks made about form and scope of text grammars and their fundamental role in the explanation of the individual use of competence in verbal behaviour – production and perception – are also basic for a socio-psychological study of language. People interact linguistically on the basis of their knowledge of text grammars. Notice that this grammar also contains pragmatic rules which are of direct relevance for the study of all general aspects of communication between individuals.

3.3. Observe that our discussion pertains to utterances i.e. to linguistic use, not to linguistic systems such as dialects. The study of social dialects is concerned with the stratified differentiation of phonological, syntactic and semantic rules. In performance studies we may further isolate the specific place of phonetic differentiation both in geographical and social dialects (Labov [1970]). An important feature of social differentiation between systems, or between the different uses of the 'same system', is probably their superficial or stylistic character (Pride [1970]). Most studies in this domain are concerned with phonological variations. Less often a systematic variation of syntactic rules has been reported. Finally, semantic rules seem to be rather uniform within one basic language system. This fact can easily be explained with the assumed general or universal character of semantic base rules. If this is true, it is highly improbable that social dialects would have their specific textual rules: the macro-semantical rules are the least language-specific of all grammatical rules. Dialectal differences can therefore be largely studied within the framework of S-grammars.

However, this view relates to rather uninteresting aspects of social behaviour. That is, it might be much more relevant to study the socially conditioned differences between the use of textual rules. Let us make some tentative observations on this point and leave the confirmation of our hypotheses to the socio-linguist.

Although all members of an assumed ideal speech community (for criticism, cf. Labov [1970]) in principle share the same set of grammatical rules, we may assume that some rules are learned with greater difficulty than others. Their internalization takes place, then, in later stages of development. It is also clear that when no linguistic data provide an empirical base for the acquisition of these more complex rules, these may remain undeveloped. Now, at the level of the sentence there do not seem to be many rules which cannot be thus acquired by all members in all social strata of society (Barth [1971]). Textual rules, i.e. rules for the construction of coherent sequences of sentences, however, seem to be much more difficult. Although all individuals will normally be confronted with elementary texts these may in some social groups be very simple and have a rather high degree of ungrammaticalness, so that macro-rules often remain poorly developed.

Traditional sociolinguistics has often pointed to the fact that differentiation in intelligence, or rather in performing the tasks normally required in school education programmes can be explained by differences in linguistic learning of children. This is true only in some respects. Sentence rules are learned largely independently of social stratification (Labov [1970]). The degree of deviation from grammatical forms shows no significant differences in different social groups, at least in oral utterances.

We claim that the main differences have to be sought at the macro-level of textual production. Children from lower classes do not receive enough training in the production and perception of different types of text. This may be explained by various facts. Their parents will often communicate with one or two sentence-texts, not by long coherent texts. They have less occasion to read or tell stories to their children. Children of lower classes have less occasion (place, money) to read books and will rather be confronted with different types of visual texts (comics, etc.). This lack in their training prevents them from manipulating the complex linguistic structures involved in textual performance.

The consequences of these facts are important. Since school training is mainly based on textual production in the form of narrative, e.g. of personal experience, descriptions, reports, etc., these children will often fail to accomplish the required task. Another consequence might be the following: we assumed that macro-structures are highly abstract and closely related with rules of logic. Both at the superficial level of sentential connection and in deep structure these rules are necessary to construct well-formed texts. A lack in macro-structural training could therefore automatically involve serious shortcomings in the systems of inductive and deductive logic governing (ideally) the thought of humans. This rather speculative assumption would explain the purported differences in intelligence. Only at this textual level, then, may we relate verbal skill to some aspects of intelligence.

There are probably many empirical correlates to this hypothesis. It may be predicted, for example, that children with a lack of textual training will perform normally those tasks not primarily based on macro-structures, e.g. solving of mathematical problems.

A final remark is necessary. It is improbable that macro-rules should be absent altogether. Labov and Waletsky (1967) have demonstrated that people from lower classes at least have the ability to report personal experiences in oral communication. The narrative rules underlying these texts are macro-rules. Deep structure formation rules for texts were assumed to be rather simple and comparable with those for sentences. The problem lies in the highly complex relations of these macro-structures with varying surface structures. The narrative texts recorded by Labov and Waletsky (1967) are superficially very defective in their linear coherence. This coherence is mainly sustained, as in child narrative, by the rules of succession of chronological logic (*then, and then, ...*). The realization of directly observable causes and consequences of the events reported, and the insertions of general conclusions are exceptional. Many similar remarks can be made about the relationships between deep structure and surface structures of text. Future research will be needed to provide exact data for these issues.

3.4. In the previous paragraph we enumerated some conditions which may influence production and reception of texts and the acquisition of their basic rules. These conditions were said to be related to aspects of social stratification. Another set of social conditions is closely related to the FUNCTIONS of different types of texts in society, i.e. their purported effects on hearers and readers. The study of these conditions and functions is not normally considered a part of sociolinguistics, but is practiced in such disciplines as communication research, content analysis, etc. (cf. Jakobson [1960], Hymes [1962]).

The literature on this topic is extensive, and we will limit ourselves to some methodological remarks (cf. Krippendorff [1969], van Dijk [1971e]).

We have often remarked in this book that people express their feelings, opinions, attitudes, observations, thoughts, etc. in discourse. It is in this form that these complex mental structures are encoded and transmitted to other members of society. Our discussion of the pragmatic component of grammar showed that this expression is a function of some intent in the speaker to change the mental or behavioural state of the hearer. He wants to inform, ask, request, command, convince, remember, thank, or greet his hearers by his discourse. Thus our knowledge of the internal states and the actions of others derives from them. Our (re-)actions are therefore highly conditioned by these previous discourses. This is also true for our linguistic responses. Any system of social interaction between humans is thus also based on our knowledge of previous texts. Nearly all historical, mythical, and scientific knowledge derives from it, not from inductive empirical experience. So, too, do all the conventions, values, and norms governing any society.

It is evident that our insight into the structure of these aspects of society can benefit highly from an explicit knowledge of the structures of the texts which have built up this knowledge. It is also clear that superficial grammatical or stylistic features are practically irrelevant here. Essential only is that part of the text which is stored in our memory: semantic deep structure. Any valid approach to content analysis of messages will therefore need this fundamental concept (van Dijk, 1971e), although much research in content analysis is also concerned with stylistic surface structure. Important for our argument is the critique of the traditional account of 'content' of texts in terms of lexical frequencies. Such an approach, which is also made in a more sophisticated form with the aid of computers, is clearly inadequate, because lexical elements are merely stylistic surface aspects of the global content. Since statistical descriptions cannot account for the meanings of sentences, the simple count of their elements has almost no theoretical value (Holsti [1969], Krippendorff [1969]). The global content of a text can be made explicit in the form of its semantic deep structure, therefore all characterizations of lexical choice have to be compared with this structure.

Content analysis, as a technique of the social sciences, is interested in texts only insofar as they reveal some properties of individuals, groups or institutions which have produced the text (cf. Gerbner, *et al.*, [1969]). The aim is based on the well-known hypothesis that many aspects of textual structures are consciously or unconsciously determined by the opinions, attitudes, beliefs and knowledges of their producers. The results of this research can be used for our investigation into the set of non-linguistic performance parameters underlying production and perception. Some of these factors have been discussed earlier in this chapter (§1.14) and will not further be treated in this book.

4. ASPECTS OF A THEORY OF LITERARY PERFORMANCE

4.1. Having outlined some general properties of textual performance and communication, we shall finally briefly enumerate some factors which seem to be specific for literary performance. Nevertheless, a satisfactory description of literary communication can have serious results only when general rules and laws of textual communication have been elaborated. Our remarks therefore will be very tentative (cf. van Dijk [1970g]).

4.2. The relevance of a study of the distinctive features of literary communication is beyond doubt. More than once we have noticed that at the formal level clear-cut differences with other texts could hardly be established: non-literary texts may have metaphors, alliterations, narrative structures, and so on. The very fact that many of these properties seem to have a rather superficial character points to their stylistic status, particularly since most rules are optional. We therefore need, for an adequate definition of literature, an insight into the specific aspects of production, reception, and functions of literary texts in culture. We should also notice however that these properties, taken in isolation, are not always typical. They must rather be jointly realized, together with the specific textual structures.

4.3. Let us first recall some pragmatic aspects of the grammatical description of literary texts, because they are closely related with literary performance.

One of the specific aspects of pragmatic rules in literature is the fact that the *I* of a literary text does not necessarily denote the author of the text. As is well-known, this *I* may realize any type of narrator in a novel or agent/patient in a poem (Romberg [1962]). That this pragmatic rule does not apply in literary communication can be inferred from the knowledge of readers that this *I* need not be interpreted as author-reflexive. We have demonstrated at some length that complex underlying performative sentences may precede this surface agent of a text. Literary texts that apply this rule of author-reflexivity are assigned a special label: autobiographies.

A similar remark may be made about the pragmatic addressee of the text. If there is an explicit *you* to which the *I* (the author or a textual agent) addresses himself, this *you* need not be the reader/hearer, although some types of address (*dear reader*, ...) do occur. *You* in those cases may be either the author-as-manifested-in-the-text, i.e. named as such, or any implicit listener of the narrative. In poetry this *you* will very often be the fictive addressee of the text, e.g. a woman in love poems. Readers knowing this rule will not interpret such texts as being addressed to them.

This type of pragmatic aspect is not without importance for the process of production and reception. In normal communication processes the speaker intends to communicate something to a hearer, in order to change the hearer's mind, attitudes, or opinions, or to provoke actions, etc. This intention in literary production may have specific forms, or even be very weak, as is the case for purely expressive texts, where the utterance is partially or wholly a pathological form of behaviour. Similarly, in many literary processes of production, authors may produce a text solely for reasons of expressive behaviour, like uttering a cry or singing a song. In that case we can say that production serves to satisfy certain creative desires, not unlike the construction of artistic objects. In other cases, e.g. lyrical texts, the author may accomplish an illocutionary act in which the addressee is only a particular named or unnamed individual person. There is no specific communicative intention, then, with respect to the reading public. In fact, to put it in extreme terms, the very first pragmatic rule, establishing a communicative relation between a speech act and an auditory act seems to be suspended: there is hardly any question of communication in the normal sense: a writer may merely intend to produce a text and not necessarily produce any effect in readers. Similarly, readers of literary texts do not necessarily read the text in order to obtain knowledge about the producer or the world. All this is said in a very informal way, but a more specific definition of the weakening or suspension of some basic rules would show that some central properties of literary communication are involved here.

We have in fact already discussed here some properties of the TYPES OF COMMUNI-

CATIVE ACTS on which literature seems to be based. One of the possible features of those types is their expressive character. There is no intent of assertion, question or the like. Nevertheless, the initial rule of communication, of course, cannot properly be suspended, because we can only perceive texts to be literary when we establish a communicative relation. The difference, then, is that no direct information is transmitted, in the current sense of that word. Writers of literary texts normally want their texts to be read and interpreted, and they also intend to change somehow the mental state of the readers. A main property of this change is traditionally referred to as 'emotive'. Readers are expected to like the perceived texts as such. This point is crucial, as a basic feature for the esthetic description of literary processes and has been described in many different terms. Since the communication process is not primarily established in order to convey empirical information, and because the reader knows the text is intended to be evaluated merely as an object, the attention of the reader is directed towards that object itself and to its different structural properties. This phenomenon is known as 'foregrounding' (Havránek, 1964) or 'concretization' (Schmidt [1970a], [1970b], [1971a], [1971b]).

These aspects of literary communication have often been studied in traditional literary research, especially by Russian Formalists and Czech Structuralists, and need no further comment here.[5] Our point is primarily to localize these properties in the pragmatic component of literary grammar and text grammar in general. Notice, finally, that many of these aspects of literature can be derived from its WRITTEN or at least 'fixed' form. In scriptural communication many of the pragmatic factors enumerated above are eliminated, like the equivalence of time and place of producing and receiving the utterance, immediate situation or context, feedback phenomena from reactions of hearers, and often also the knowledge of the interlocutors, etc. These facts will always contribute to an emphasized focus upon the text itself. The difference, however, is that in non-literary written communication only semantic deep structures are objects of this focussed attention and much less their surface realization. This is also the way in which the statements of functional poetics must be interpreted.

Although the central axis of the literary communication act has traditionally been characterized as a relation between creative expression and the elicitation of emotive effect, e.g. resulting in preferential behaviour of one type or another, other 'functions' of the speech act are not absent. A literary text may also be intended as a statement about some real or fictive state of affairs. In that case it may contribute normally to the formation, confirmation or change of opinions and attitudes, etc. Many social novels have this important function and in these cases the differences from a current social report are only those of degree. Here we touch upon the specific REFERENTIAL PROPER-

---

[5] Besides the cited work of Jakobson (1960) and Havránek there are many studies on the functions of language and literature. For a survey, cf. Ihwe (1972a). Further Garvin, ed. (1964), Beneš and Vachek, eds. (1971), especially Havránek (1971) and Lotman and Pjatigorskij (1969) for the implications of the written character of (modern) literature.

TIES of literature. Strictly speaking, some attention of the reader for the text itself is common to all forms of communication, since even the intent to grasp the meaning of the text is a process of (re-)construction of its intended semantic macro-structure. The difference, as we said above, essentially lies in the fact that the reader will also focus upon the surface structure of the text, i.e. the way in which macro-structure ('content') is actually realized. This phenomenon is rare in other types of verbal communication: surface structures are relevant only in so far as they convey semantic information (Johnson-Laird [1970]). There is hardly any conscious focussing on their structure. If this is correct we have isolated a fundamental, although gradual, communicative difference between literary and other types of textual performance. We can now explain why literary rules are dominantly superficial, e.g. based on macro- and micro-transformations of semantic or syntactic structure and on specific additional formation rules on the phonematic and graphematic level.

4.4. Closely related to these pragmatic aspects of literary communication are the specific properties of REFERENCE involved. It is a traditional view that literature does not make statements with a truth value, that is, there is no point in confirming or disconfirming them by empirical observations (Quine [1960]). The well-known label to indicate this property is FICTIONALITY.[6] Literary texts share this lack of truth value with other types of texts such as explanations, questions, orders, dreams, greetings, wishes, thoughts, opinions, and so on (Reichenbach [1947] 274ff.). However these last types nevertheless have some sort of referential relation: they inform the hearer about a state, want or request of an existing speaker about some part of empirical reality or about desired or past actions of the hearer himself. It would be better in that case to say that such texts have reference and an assumed truth value, *viz.* that of being true or being meant to be true expressions of the mental state (for detail cf. Quine, [1960], [1953]).

Further, non-literary texts can also be fictional, i.e. defined as 'having no empirical reference'. All deductive theories fall within this class. Additionally, all dreams, lies, and other counterfactuals, like hypotheses, conditions, etc. can be called fictional. On the other hand, there are literary texts both intended and interpreted to have empirical reference, e.g. historical novels, poems written on occasion of some event, etc. This is partially true for many so-called realistic novels, which may localize fictitious events in a place with empirical denotation (a well-known town) and in which

---

[6] The relevance of the feature of 'fictionality' is suggested by its regular treatment in any literary manual from Aristotle's *Poetics* onwards and has given rise to much, often strongly ideologically biased, discussion. A thorough ontological treatment of the subject is due to Ingarden (1931). Its importance was stressed less by Russian Formalists (cf. Erlich [1955] 163, 208, 210), because they focussed especially upon linguistic surface structures rather than on deep structures and their related truth value status. In recent work the criterion is still considered as basic, cf. e.g. Maatje (1970) and, more theoretically than phenomenologically, Ihwe (1972a). We will not continue to discuss this important problem, which comprises the whole question of 'realism', a central topic in marxist literary theories.

persons are named who have historical existence. Similarly, we may assign historical actions and events to fictive actants. The correlates of this current form of SEMI-FICTIONALITY are important. On the one hand the pragmatic speech act situation assigning a category 'literature' to a text, predisposes a reader to interpret the text not primarily as providing information about historical events or situations. We may say that the referential truth value of the text is conceived of as being potentially IRRELEVANT for literary communication. On the other hand, a reader may at the same time recognize the explicit and implicit intention of an author that he (the reader) should interpret the semi-fictional text as a literary DESCRIPTION of some part of psychological or social reality. In that case he will match the semantic structure of the text with the cognitive structure of his knowledge about reality. If there is a global analogy the text will be said to be 'as real', 'realistic', 'true', 'probable', etc. This correspondence between *vrai* and *vraisemblable* is a well-known semantic well-formedness condition of antique and classical drama, and its validity was also recognized in the novel until the beginning of this century.

There are rather intricate ontological and logical problems connected with the referential status of literary texts. For example, must literary texts having some fictive aspects, e.g. actions of some actants with empirical reference, be considered wholly fictive, i.e. referring only to fictive persons apparently similar to the real historical persons of the same name? The converse is also problematic: can we call 'fictive' a naturalistic novel describing the life of certain real social classes by concrete fictive examples? We may say in that case that the text may globally have reference (a society, a class) and even have truth value, although individual actants do not have reference. We will not pursue here these problems, but we stress only that a knowledge of aspects of the empirical world and the way these are normally described or referred to in different types of texts is essential for the perception of the specific referential character of literary discourses.

4.5. A second set of problems of a theory of literary performance concerns the PSYCHOLOGICAL CONDITIONS determining literary production and perception. We have two sets of models for both processes. More than in normal (oral) communication these models may differ on some essential points. One of the differences in this respect is the status of postulated LITERARY COMPETENCE (Ihwe [1970]). This competence was defined as the internalized ideal ability to produce and interpret the well-formed literary texts of a given language. The recognition by native speakers of regular differences with respect to other types of texts can be explained only by this (sub-)competence. What, then, is the psychological 'reality' of this competence, and how is it put to use in concrete literary communication processes?

4.5.1. All psychological abilities and their conditions which hold for normal textual processing are of course also valid for production and reception of literary texts. However, there are some specific constraints which define literary performance as a special type of communication. The formal pragmatic aspects have already been enumerated above: the intentions of writers with respect to perception by readers are different, the expectancy of readers is different; in both cases there is not primarily a focus on semantic deep structure alone. Furthermore, the text can be processed along the lines of SEVERAL PLANS. Apart from the normal macro-semantic plans, there may be certain transformational plans programming the global surface structure *viz.* the order and connection of sequences. Another type of plan, which has been called THEMATIC, will normally co-determine the selection of lexical elements. Finally, there are PROSODIC PLANS which program the metric macro-structure of the text. In the production model these plans are normally initial or pre-existing. In a perceptual model they are linearly constructed, although some metric plans may be immediately recognized.

The plans, as executed by the writer, may be very abstract and have a very idio-syncratic character. They are therefore not always perceived to be plans as such by the reader. Conversely readers may perceive 'patterns', mostly semantic ones, not consciously intended as such by the writer.

4.5.2. It may be expected that specific focus on textual surface structures both in production and reception may lead to rather marked differences in information (entropy) with respect to non-literary communication.

The well-known 'de-automatization of language' in literary communication (Havrávek [1964]) will in general result in relatively high information values. The number of rules of G_L being larger than those of G_N, the number of possible structures is enlarged accordingly. The result is an increase of subjective selective information. In the process of perception the discovery, establishment or recognition of specific rules/structures will also 'cost' information, the expectancy of a given structure being much smaller. Literary texts, at least in modern literature, will normally deviate from conventional structures both within and outside the literary system.

In particular the coordination of the different plans in well-formed combinations will produce a high amount of information. It is 'difficult' to select lexemes at particular metric positions of a text, the more so when they must also have a particular phono-logical structure.

4.5.3. Not only will additional plans, rules and structures produce extra information but also the frequent lack of well-formed surface structure, e.g. in modern poetry, will cause difficulties of interpretation. A literary perception model will have to predict the selective information necessary to construct well-formed deep structure on the basis of this semi-grammatical input. Semi-grammaticalness further, is not only restricted to sentences but may also affect relations between sentences. It is expected that incoherent literary texts are interpreted with an increased amount of information. In both cases high information values may be related to cognitive and emotive processes of appreciation, surprise, and evaluation. There are important differences in entropy between the types of literary texts. Novels clearly have values rather close to those of normal texts, say of non-literary narrative. Some types of modern literary narrative however may approach high entropy values which are also characteristic of modern poetry.

Finally, all types of stereotyped or conventional structures, also those of plans, will reduce the entropy of the literary texts: in prosodic structures specific phonemes can be predicted, whereas in the production of existing subject matter the semantic macro-structure is largely predictable.[7]

4.5.4. Among the models applicable to the study of literary performance statistical models have already often been used. It is difficult to give general results: frequencies and distributions of textual elements are very different for different authors and different types of texts. As with quantative linguistics, data are significant only when the average values are known.

With the aid of statistical analysis of a more complex type we might try to confirm some of the hypotheses of literary grammar. Thus the optional deletion of verb phrases in modern poetry can easily be detected in the development of the poetic system, by a decrease of verbs and an increase of nouns (Guiraud, 1954). Similar results can be noted for other typical literary syntactic structures in modern literature. Differences between types of literary texts can thus be statistically observed. Poetry will have shorter sentences and shorter words than prose texts, whereas literary prose has longer sentences than non-literary texts, or, of course, spoken texts. Styles of individual authors and groups can be statistically described on the basis of many surface parameters. Conclusions are only valid, however, if we have knowledge of the formal constraints (text grammar) and the average use of rules and lexemes in a given period under given circumstances.[8]

4.5.5. Let us finally make some observations about the SOCIOLOGICAL ASPECTS of a theory of literary performance. The sociology of literature is a branch of theoretical poetics where much research has been carried out, but where very few interesting results have been arrived at. Theory formation in this domain remains rather poor, although sociology itself is now capable of formulating satisfactory models.

We are not particularly interested in the social status of writers, which is a subject belonging to sociology rather than to sociopoetics. Nevertheless, it is clear that the

---

[7] In the last decade, especially in Germany, much work has been done in the domain of literary information theory. Cf. e.g. Bense (1962), (1969), Gunzenhäuser (1962), Moles (1966) and the different contributions in Kreuzer and Gunzenhäuser, eds. (1965), Doležel and Bailey, eds. (1969), e.g. Levý (1969) and Kondratov (1969). For a critical survey, cf. van Dijk (1970b), (1970c).

[8] The statistical study of literary texts will not be discussed here, cf. the two readers cited in note 5 above and the general introduction of Doležel (1969). Nor can we treat here the relevance of other mathematical, e.g. topological and set-theoretical, models. A complete survey of such work and a programme for its use is now provided by Marcus (1970) who explicitly criticizes the often theoretically weak probabilistic studies.

social status of writers may co-determine the structure of literary texts. General data about this determination are too vague to guarantee satisfactory theorizing about correlations. Moreover, the social class in which the writers grow up does not necessarily, through its values, norms and attitudes, determine semantic macro-structures or surface structure of the literary texts produced by its member, as the famous Marxist hypothesis affirms. Many counter-examples can be found, and even normal socio-psychological explanations can be given for this deviation: social achievement will often lead to estrangement from original class values.

We are not interested either in the social group of 'readers of literature', why, how and how often they buy, and what type of literary books they read. More interesting for our discussion is the social reality of LITERARY SYSTEMS, i.e. the global use of idealized literary competence. The acquisition, confirmation and change of such systems in given social structures are some of the most interesting aspects of a study of socio-poetics. We can ask, for example, which conditions must be satisfied before idio-syncratic rules used by an author or group become conventionalized, i.e. accepted as 'typical' by the culture-making group in a society? How are very deviant literary texts received in society and what are the possible sanctions? These specific relations between text structure and cultural response will need extensive explanation, based on the explicit study of the traditions, knowledge, expectations, socio-political climate and cultural system of a group or society. Reception will be different at different times, under different cultural and political conditions (conservative *vs.* progressive) and in different social classes. We expect that lower classes accept changes in the literary system less quickly, if literary texts are accepted at all. Similarly, social stratification will also determine which semantic structure will tend to be most acceptable. Simple narrative of a highly stereotyped form and with strong emotive thematic structure (love, hate, power) will probably dominate in texts accepted by the lower classes. Poetry and experimental prose is read only by a very small group in society, etc.

4.5.6. Whereas the sociology of literature is interested in the topics mentioned above, e.g. the role of literature in socio-cultural systems, socio-poetics will direct its interest toward the role of society in literary texts. To be sure, we are here dealing with the representation of certain aspects of society by means of semantic structures.

First of all, any text which is not fully abstract (e.g. a deductive theory) necessarily realizes some aspects of social structure. The interpretation of any narrative, literary as well, is conditioned by our internal knowledge of laws, norms, institutions, public persons, roles, values, etc. of past or present society. The same is true for our knowledge of psychological behaviour of members of that society, which may be represented as 'personages'. Without that knowledge neither normal interpretation nor the establishment of 'differences' is possible. We only know that science-fiction is futuristic because we know the actions, events and situations are not (yet) realized in present society and technology. Possible correspondence with social reality may serve as important data for our knowledge of past cultures.

It is important to note, as with psychological determination, that the representation of aspects of social structure necessarily and optionally implies a series of transformations. Besides normal selection, which is of course ideologically biased, other deletion, permutation and addition transformations may change the normal empirical description of society. Especially in texts where these transformations are complex, inferences about social structure may often be unwarranted (cf. Holsti [1969]).

5. SOME FINAL REMARKS

5.1. From the discussion in this chapter an impression of dissatisfaction seems to be inevitable. The theory of textual communication, in spite of much research done in this domain, has still to be developed. Many practical studies exist on the psychological and physiological production and reception of texts and speech, but we do not yet know exactly how the rules of a grammar or competence are used in performance. Only a text grammar and its formal account of underlying plans can provide some insight into the cognitive processing of utterances. However, it is still completely obscure how speakers transduce macro-structures into sentential structure, and the reverse. As long as we remain ignorant about these complex processes, i.e. about the rules determining them and the possible strategies used to execute the rules, no conclusive insight can possibly be gained into the relations between mental or social structures on the one hand and textual structures on the other hand.

5.2. Another possible link here is of course pragmatics. However, it remains to be seen whether social conventions as they manifest themselves in communicative situations are rules in the strict sense of grammatical rules. Moreover, what do pragmatic structures look like and how are they related to textual deep structure? The same remarks can be made about a linguistic theory of reference. It is certain that at least some pragmatic and referential parameters have to be formalized in grammar. The performative *I* and *you*, place and time indicators and the deep structure of locutionary acts should probably be integrated in or be related with deep structure descriptions. Similarly, the modal aspects determining the truth value of the textual proposition should be interpreted here also.

5.3. Pragmatics is also the place where linguistic, psychological and sociological parameters interact. All social structures can only influence text structures through individual producers, i.e. their knowledge of that structure and their attitude towards it. It has become clear that insight into the complex socio-cultural communication system of a society is based on the production and perception of all sorts of texts. The different functions of texts in society, both primitive and modern, regulate all human interaction: they codify values and norms and form, establish and transform attitudes, opinions, knowledge and ideas, etc.

This use of texts in interaction can be explained and described only when we have explicit insight into their structures, a task to be fulfilled by a basically different type of grammar, text grammar. The central role of linguistics within the complex of the social sciences will be determined by the results of such an inquiry.

Amsterdam, January–December, 1971

REFERENCES

Linguaggi = Linguaggi nella società e nella technica
(Milano: Edizioni di Comunità, 1970)

Abel, Theodor
  1953 "The Operation called Verstehen", in E. H. Madden, *The Structure of Scientific Thought* (Cambridge, Mass.: The Riverside Press) 158-165.
Abraham, Werner
  1971 "Stil, Pragmatik und Abweichungsgrammatik", in Stechow (1971) 1-13.
Abraham, Werner, and Robert I. Binnick
  1969 "Syntax oder Semantik als erzeugende Komponenten eines Grammatikmodells? Zur Forschungslage der Modelle algorithmischer Sprachbeschreibungen", *Linguistische Berichte*, 4, 1-28.
Abraham, Werner and Kurt Braunmüller
  1971 "Stil, Metapher und Pragmatik", *Lingua*, 28, 1-47.
Adorno, Theodor W.
  1970 *Aufsätze zur Gesellschaftstheorie und Methodologie* (Frankfurt a/M: Suhrkamp).
Agricola, Erhard
  1969 *Semantische Relationen im Text und im System* (Halle, Saale: VEB, Max Niemeyer Verlag).
Akmajian, Adrian and Ray Jackendoff
  1969 "Corefentiality and Stress", *Linguistic Inquiry*, 1, 124-126.
Altham, J. E. J.
  1971 *The Logic of Plurality* (London: Methuen).
Annear Thompson, Sandra
  1971 "The Deep Structure of Relative Clauses", in Fillmore and Langendoen (1971) 78-94.
Apel, Karl-Otto
  1967 *Analytic Philosophy of Language and the Geisteswissenschaften* (Dordrecht: Reidel).
Apostel, Leo
  1960 "Towards the Formal Study of Models in the Non-Formal Sciences", *Synthese*, 12, 125-161.
Aristotle
  1965 *The Poetics*, in W. H. Fyfe (ed.) Aristotle, *The Poetics*; Longinus, *On the Sublime* (London: Heinemann, Ltd.; Loeb Classical Library).
Austin, J. L.
  1962 *How to do things with Words* (Oxford: Oxford U.P.)
Bach, Emmon
  1964 *An Introduction to Transformational Grammars* (New York: Holt, Rinehart and Winston).
  1965 "Structural Linguistics and the Philosophy of Science", *Diogenes*, 51, 111-128.
  1968 "Nouns and Noun Phrases", in Bach and Harms (1968) 90-122.
Bach, Emmon and Robert T. Harms (eds.)
  1968 *Universals in Linguistic Theory* (New York: Holt, Rinehart and Winston).
Badiou, Alain
  1969 *Le concept de modèle. Introduction à une épistémologie matérialiste des mathématiques* (Paris: Maspéro).
Bar-Hillel, Yehoshua
  1954 "Indexical Expressions", *Mind*, 63, 359-379.
  1964 *Language and Information* (Reading, Mass.: Addison Wesley).

1969   "Review of John Lyons, *Introduction to Theoretical Linguistics* (1968)", *Semiotica*, 1, 449-459.
1970   "Communication and Argumentation in Pragmatic Languages", in *Linguaggi*, 269-284.
Barcan Marcus, Ruth
1967   "Modalities and Intensional Languages" (1962), in Copi and Gould (1967) 278-293.
Barker, George
1965   "The True Confession of George Barker" in David Wright (ed.), *The Mid Century: English Poetry 1940-60* (Harmondsworth: Penguin Books) 97-125.
Barth, Erhard
1971   "Überlegungen zur sozialen Differenzierung der Sprache", in Stechow (1971) 14-28.
Barthes, Roland
1957   *Mythologies* (Paris: Seuil).
1966   "Introduction à l'analyse structurale des récits", *Communications*, 8, 1-27.
1970   "L'ancienne rhétorique", *Communications*, 16, 172-229.
Barthes, Roland (ed.)
1968   *Linguistique et littérature, Langages*, 12.
Bartlett, Frederic C.
1932   *Remembering* (Cambridge: Cambridge U.P.)
Baumann, H.-H.
1969   "Review-article of Roland Harweg, *Pronomina and Textkonstitution* (1968)" *Lingua*, 23, 274-300.
Baumgärtner, Klaus
1969   "Der methodische Stand einer linguistischen Poetik", *Jahrbuch für internationale Germanistik*, 1/1, 15-43.
Beaver, Joseph C.
1970   "A Grammar of Prosody", in Freeman (1970) 427-447.
1971   "Current Metrical Issues", *College English*, November, 178-197.
Bellert, Irena
1969   "Arguments and Predicates in the Logico-Semantic Structure of utterances", in Kiefer (1969) 34-54.
1970   "Conditions for the coherence of Texts", *Semiotica*, 2, 335-363.
1971   "On the Use of Linguistic Quantifying Operators", *Poetics*, 2, 71-86.
1972   "Sets of Implications as the Interpretative component of a Grammar", in Manfred Bierwisch and Ferenc Kiefer (eds.) *Generative Grammar in Europe* (Dordrecht: Reidel) (forthcoming).
Belnap, Nuel D., jr.
1969   "Questions: Their Presuppositions, and How They Can Fail to Arise", in Lambert (1969) 23-37.
Beneš, Eduard
1968   "On Two Aspects of Functional Sentence Perspective", *Travaux Linguistiques de Prague*, 3, 267-274.
Beneš, Eduard and Joseph Vachek (eds.)
1971   *Stilistik und Soziolinguistik* (Berlin: List Verlag).
Bense, Max
1962   *Theorie der Texte* (Köln: Kiepenheuer & Witsch).
1969   *Einführung in die informationstheoretische Ästhetik. Grundlegung und Anwendung in der Texttheorie* (Reinbek bei Hamburg: Rowohlt).
Bever, Thomas G. and John R. Ross
1967   "Underlying Structures in Discourse" (MIT, mimeo).
Bezzel, Chris
1969   "Some Problems of a Grammar of Modern German Poetry", *Foundations of Language*, 5, 470-487.
Bickerton, Derek
1969   "Prolegomena to a Linguistic Theory of Metaphor", *Foundations of Language*, 5, 34-52.
Bierwisch, Manfred
1965   "Poetik und Linguistik", in Kreuzer and Gunzenhäuser (1965) 49-66.
1966   "Strukturalismus. Geschichte, Probleme und Methoden", *Kursbuch*, 5, 77-152.

1967 "Some Semantic Universals of German Adjectivals", *Foundations of Language*, 3, 1-36.
1969a "Certain Problems of Semantic Representations", *Foundations of Language*, 5, 153-184.
1969b "Semantics and Placement of Primary Stress", Berlin (D.D.R.) (mimeo).
1970 "Semantics", in Lyons (1970) 166-184.
1971 "On Classifying Semantic Features", in Steinberg and Jakobovits (1971) 410-435.
Bierwisch, Manfred and Ferenc Kiefer
1969 "Remarks on Definitions in Natural Language", in Kiefer (1969) 55-79.
Binnick, Robert I., *et al.* (eds.)
1969 *Papers from the fifth Regional Meeting of the Chicago Linguistic Society* (Department of Linguistics, University of Chicago).
Black, Max
1962 *Models and Metaphors* (Ithaca: Cornell U.P.).
Bolinger, Dwight L.
1965 "The Atomization of Meaning", *Language*, 41, 555-573.
Bonnefoy, Yves
1953 *Du mouvement et de l'immobilité de Douve* (Paris: Mercure de France).
Borko, Harold (ed.)
1967 *Automated Language Processing* (New York: Wiley).
Botha, Rudolf P.
1968 *The Function of the Lexicon in Transformational Generative Grammar* (The Hague: Mouton).
1970 *The Methodological Status of Grammatical Argumentation* (The Hague: Mouton).
Brainerd, Barron
1971 *Introduction to the Mathematics of Language Study* (New York, etc.: Elsevier).
Brekle, Herbert E.
1969 *Generative Satzsemantik und transformationelle Syntax im System der englischen Nominal-komposition* (München: Fink).
Bremond, Claude
1964 "Le message narratif", *Communications*, 4-32.
1966 "La logique des possibles narratifs", *Communications*, 8, 60-76.
1970 "Morphology of the French Folktale", *Semiotica*, 2, 247-276.
1970 "Observations sur la 'Grammaire du Décaméron'", *Poétique*, 6, 200-222.
Brettschneider, Gunter
1971 "Zur Repräsentation koordinierter Nominalphrasen", in Wunderlich (1971) 148-153.
Brinker, Klaus
1971 "Aufgaben und Methoden der Textlinguistik", *Wirkendes Wort*, 21, 217-237.
Bronzwaer, W. J. M.
1970 *Tense in the Novel. An Investigation of Some Potentialities of Linguistic Criticism* (Groningen: Wolters-Noordhoff).
Bruce, D. J.
1968 "Effects of Context upon Intelligibility of Heard Speech" (1956), in Oldfield and Marshall (1968) 123-131.
Bühler, Karl
1934 *Sprachtheorie* (Jena).
Burton, Dolores M. and Richard W. Bailey
1968 *English Stylistics: A Bibliography* (Cambridge, Mass.: MIT Press).
Butters, Ronald R.
1970 "Lexical Selection and Linguistic Deviance", *Papers in Linguistics*, 1, 170-181.
Campbell, Robin and Roger Wales
1970 "The Study of Language Acquisition", in Lyons (1970) 242-260.
Cantrall, William R.
1969 "Pitch, Stress, and Grammatical Relations", in Binnick, *et al.* (1969) 12-24.
Carnap, Rudolf
1957 *Meaning and Necessity. A Study in Semantics and Modal Logic* (1947) (Chicago: University of Chicago Press; enlarged edition, Phoenix Books).
1958 *Introduction to Symbolic Logic and its Applications* (New York: Dover).

Carnoy, A.
   1927 *La Science du Mot. Traité de Sémantique* (Louvain).
Carstensen, Broder
   1970 "Stil und Norm. Zur Situation der linguistischen Stilistik", *Zeitschrift für Dialektologie und Linguistik*, 37, 257-279.
Caton, Charles E. (ed.)
   1963 *Philosophy and Ordinary Language* (Urbana: University of Illinois Press).
Chafe, Wallace L.
   1968 "Idiomaticity as an anomaly in the Chomskyan Paradigm", *Foundations of Language*, 4, 109-127.
   1970 *Meaning and the Structure of Language* (Chicago: University of Chicago Press).
Chao, Yuen Ren
   1962 "Models in Linguistics and Models in General", in E. Nagel, P. Suppes, A. Tarski (eds.), *Logic, Methodology and Philosophy of Science* (Stanford, Cal.: Stanford U.P.) 558-566.
Chatman, Seymour
   1964 *A Theory of Meter* (The Hague: Mouton).
   1969 "New Ways of Analyzing Narrative Structure", *Language and Style*, 2, 3-36.
   1971 *Literary Style* (London: Oxford University Press).
Chatman, Seymour (ed.).
   1972 *Literary Style* (London: Oxford U.P.).
Chatman, Seymour and Samuel R. Levin (eds.)
   1967 *Essays in the Language of Literature* (Boston: Houghton Mifflin Co.).
Chisholm, Roderick M.
   1969 "Some Puzzles about Agency", in Lambert (1969) 199-217.
Chomsky, Noam
   1957 *Syntactic Structures* (The Hague: Mouton).
   1959a "On Certain Formal Properties of Grammars". *Information and Control*, 2, 137–167.
   1959b "Review of B. F. Skinner's Verbal Behavior", *Language*, 35, 26-58 (Reprinted in Fodor and Katz [1964] 547-578).
   1963 "Formal Properties of Grammars", in Luce, Bush and Galanter (1963) 323-418.
   1964 "Degrees of Grammaticalness", in Fodor and Katz (1964) 384-389.
   1965 *Aspects of the Theory of Syntax* (Cambridge, Mass.: MIT Press).
   1968 *Language and Mind* (New York: Harcourt, Brace and World).
   1970 "Some Empirical Issues of the Theory of Transformational Grammar" (Indiana University Linguistics Club, mimeo).
   1971 "Deep Structure, Surface Structure and Semantic Interpretation", in Steinberg and Jakobovits (1971) 183-216.
Chomsky, Noam and Morris Halle
   1968 *The Sound Pattern of English* (New York: Harper and Row).
Chomsky, Noam and George A. Miller
   1963 "Introduction to the Formal Analysis of Natural Languages", in Luce, Bush and Galanter (1963) 269-321.
Christensen, Francis
   1967 "A Generative Rhetoric of the Paragraph", in Steinmann (1967) 108-133.
Cohen, Jean
   1968 "La comparaison poétique: essai de systématique", in Barthes (1968) 43-51.
Cohen, Jonathan L.
   1970 "What is the ability to refer to things, as a constituent of a language-speaker's competence?", in *Linguaggi*, 255-268.
Communications, 16
   1970 *Recherches rhétoriques*.
Copi, Irving M. and James A. Gould (eds.)
   1967 *Contemporary Readings in Logical Theory* (New York-London: Mac Millan).
Corcoran, John P.
   1969 "Discourse Grammars and the Structure of Mathematical Reasoning", in J. Scandura (ed.) *Structural Learning* (Englewood Cliffs, N.Y.: Prentice Hall).

Curtius, Ernst Roberts
  1948 *Europäische Literatur und lateinisches Mittelalter* (1965⁵ Bern-München: Francke).
Dahl, Östen
  1969 *Topic and Comment. A Study in Russian and General Transformational Grammar* (Göteborg-Stockholm: Almqvist and Wiksell).
Daneš, František
  1964 "A Three-Level Approach to Syntax", *Travaux Linguistiques de Prague*, 1, 225-240.
  1970a "Zur linguistischen Analyse der Textstruktur", *Folia Linguistica*, 1, 72-78.
  1970b "Functional Sentence Perspective and the Organization of the Text", Paper contributed to the Symposium on FSP, Marienbad.
Davidson, Donald
  1970 "Semantics for Natural Languages", in *Linguaggi*, 177-188.
Davie, Donald, *et al.* (eds.)
  1961 *Poetics. Poetyka. Poetika.* (The Hague: Mouton).
Deguy, Michel
  1961 *Poèmes de la Presqu'île*, (Paris: Gallimard).
Delbouille, Paul
  1961 *Poésie et sonorités* (Paris: Belles Lettres).
Des Tombes, Louis
  1970 "Competence en het Performance Lexikon" (Doktoraalskriptie Utrecht, mimeo).
Dewees, John
  1969 "Ill-Formed Sentences", *College English*, 31, 289-301.
Dijk, Teun A. van
  1968 "Quelques problèmes d'une théorie du signe poétique" (Paper contributed to the second international symposium on Semiotics, Warsaw) (German translation in van Dijk [1972b]).
  1969 "Sémantique structurale et analyse thématique", *Lingua*, 23, 28-53.
  1970a "Neuere Entwicklungen in der literarischen Semantik", in Schmidt (1970), 106-135.
  1970b "Tekstgenerering en tekstproduktie", *Studia Neerlandica*, 1/4, 1-40 (reprinted in van Dijk [1971b]; German version in van Dijk [1972b]).
  1970c "Informatietheorie en literatuurtheorie", *Forum der Letteren*, 11, 203-233 (reprinted in van Dijk [1971b]).
  1970d "La metateoria del racconto", *Strumenti Critici*, 4, 141-163.
  1970e "Sémantique générative et théorie des textes", *Linguistics*, 62, 66-95.
  1970f "Nogle aspekter af en generativ-transformationell text-teori", *Poetik*, 3, 155-177.
  1970g "Text and context. Towards a Theory of Literary Performance" (Amsterdam, mimeo) in James S. Holmes and F. Miko (eds.) *Text and Context* (forthcoming). (German translation in van Dijk [1972b]).
  1971a *Moderne Literatuurteorie. Een eksperimentele inleiding* (Amsterdam: van Gennep).
  1971b *Taal. Tekst. Teken. Bijdragen tot de literatuurteorie* (Amsterdam: Polak).
  1971c "Some Problems of Generative Poetics", *Poetics*, 2, 5-35.
  1971d "Foundations for Typologies of Texts", Paper contributed to the International Symposium on semiotic poetics, Urbino (Italy), July 19-24, 1971 (to appear in *Semiotica*).
  1971e "Content Analysis en tekstgrammatika", Paper contributed to the Vlaams Filologen-kongres, April 1971, *Handelingen* (Leuven) 228-239.
  1971f "Models for Text Grammars", Paper contributed to the IVth International Congress on Logic, Methodology and Philosophy of Science, Bucharest, August 29 – September 2.
  1972f "Quelques aspects d'une théorie générative du texte poétique", in A. J. Greimas (ed.), *Essais de poétique sémiotique* (Paris: Larousse), 180-206.
  1972a "Een Tekst over Teksten", *Raster*, 5, 542-562.
  1972b *Beiträge zur generativen Poetik* (München: Bayerischer Schulbuch Verlag) (in press).
  1972c "On the Foundations of Poetics", *Poetics*, 5.
  1972d "Grammaires textuelles et structures narratives", in C. Chabrol (ed.) *Structures narratives* (Paris: Larousse) (forthcoming).
  1972e "Aspekten van een tekstgrammatika", in S. C. Dik (ed.) *Taalwetenschap in Nederland 1971* (University of Amsterdam Press) 103-113.
  1973 *Kontekst. Een essay in pragmatiek* (Amsterdam: De Bezige Bij) (forthcoming).

Dijk, Teun A. van, Jens Ihwe, János S. Petöfi, Hannes Rieser
   1971 "Textgrammatische Grundlagen für eine Theorie Narrativer Strukturen", *Linguistische Berichte*, 16, 1-38.
   1972 *Zur Bestimmung narrativer Strukturen auf der Grundlage von Textgrammatiken* (Hamburg: Buske Verlag, Papiere zur Textlinguistik 1).

Dik, Simon C.
   1968a *Coordination* (Amsterdam: North Holland).
   1968b "Referential Identity", *Lingua*, 21, 70-97.
   1969 *Relatieve Termen* (Amsterdam: North Holland).
   1970 "Semantische relaties tussen zinnen in een tekst" (Amsterdam, mimeo).

Dittmar, Norbert
   1971 "Möglichkeiten einer Soziolinguistik: zur Analyse rollenspezifischen Sprachverhaltens", *Sprache im technischen Zeitalter*, 38, 87-105.

Doležel, Lubomír
   1969 "A Framework for the Statistical Analysis of Style", in Doležel and Bailey (1969) 10-28.

Doležel, Lubomír and Richard W. Bailey (eds.)
   1969 *Statistics and Style* (New York: Elsevier).

Donellan, Keith S.
   1970 "Proper Names and Identifying Descriptions", *Synthese*, 21, 335-358.

Dougherty, R. C.
   1969 "An Interpretive Theory of Pronominal Reference", *Foundations of Language* 5, 488-519.
   1970a "The Grammar of Coordinate Conjoined Structures I", *Language*, 46, 850-898.
   1970b "Recent studies on Language Universals. Review of Bach and Harms (eds.), *Universals in Linguistic Theory* (1968)", *Foundations of Language*, 6, 505-561.

Dressler, Wolfgang
   1970a "Textsyntax", *Lingua e Stile*, 2, 191-214.
   1970b "Towards a Semantic Deep Structure of Discourse Grammar", Paper contributed to the Sixth Regional Meeting of the Chicago Linguistic Society.
   1970c "Modelle und Methoden der Textsyntax", *Folia Linguistica*, 4, 64-71.
   1972 "Textgrammatische Invarianz in Übersetzungen?", Paper contributed to the Colloquium "Differenzierungskriterien für Textsorten aus der Sicht der Linguistik und einzelner Textwissenschaften", Rheda (Westfalen, Western Germany) January 20-22.

Drubig, Bernhard
   1967 "Kontextuelle Beziehungen zwischen Sätzen im Englischen" (Kiel, unpublished M. A. Dissertation).

Dubois, Jacques, *et al.*
   1970 *Rhétorique générale* (Paris: Larousse).

Ducrot, Oswald
   1966 "Logique et linguistique", *Langages*, 2, 3-30.

Dundes, Alan
   1964 *The Morphology of the North American Folktale* (Helsinki: FFC).

Eimermacher, Karl
   1969 "Entwicklung, Charakter und Probleme des Sowjetischen Strukturalismus in der Literaturwissenschaft", *Sprache im technischen Zeitalter*, 30, 126-157.

Eixenbaum, Boris
   1965 "La théorie de la 'méthode formelle'" (1925), in Todorov (1965) 31-75.

Eluard, Paul
   1968 *Œuvres complètes* (Paris: Gallimard).

Enzensberger, Hans Magnus
   1967 *Blindenschrift* (Frankfurt a/M: Suhrkamp).

Erlich, Victor
   1955 *Russian Formalism. History. Doctrine* (The Hague: Mouton, 1955^2 revised edition).

Faccani, Remo and Umberto Eco (eds.)
   1969 *I sistemi di segni e lo Strutturalismo Sovietico* (Milan: Bompiani).

Fillmore, Charles J.
   1965 "Entailment Rules in Semantic Theory", ERIC Document Reprint Service.

1968 "The Case for Case", in Bach and Harms (1968) 1-88.
1969a "Types of Lexical Information", in Kiefer (1969) 109-137.
1969b "Toward a Modern Theory of Case" (1966), in Reibel and Schane (1969) 361-378.
1970 "Subjects, Speakers, Roles", *Synthese*, 21, 251-274.
Fillmore, Charles J. and D. Terence Langendoen (eds.)
1971 *Studies in Linguistic Semantics* (New York: Holt, Rinehart & Winston).
Firbas, J.
1964 "On Defining the Theme in Functional Sentence Analysis", *Travaux Linguistiques de Prague*, 1, 267-280.
Fischer, Walther L.
1969 "Texte als simpliziale komplexe", *Beiträge zur Linguistik und Datenverarbeitung*, 17, 27-48.
Flores D'Arcais, G. B. and W. J. M. Levelt (eds.)
1970 *Advances in Psycholinguistics* (Amsterdam: North Holland).
Fodor, Jerry A. and M. Garrett
1966 "Some Reflections on Competence and Performance", in Lyons and Wales (1966) 135-163.
Fodor, Jerry A. and Jerrold J. Katz (eds.)
1964 *The Structure of Language. Readings in the Philosophy of Language* (Englewood Cliffs, N.Y.: Prentice Hall Inc.).
Fodor, Janet Dean
1970 "Formal Linguistics and Formal Logic", in Lyons (1970), 198-214.
Fónagy, Ivan
1965 "Der Ausdruck als Inhalt", in Kreuzer and Gunzenhäuser (1965) 243-274.
1966 "Le langage poétique: Forme et Fonction", in *Problèmes du langage, Diogène*, 51 (Paris: Gallimard) 72-113.
Fowler, Roger
1966 "Linguistic Theory and the Study of Literature", in Fowler (1966) 1-28.
1969 "On the Interpretation of 'nonsense-strings'", *Journal of Linguistics*, 5, 75-83.
Fowler, Roger (ed.)
1966 *Essays on Style and Language* (London: Routledge and Kegan Paul).
Fraassen, Bas van
1971 *Formal Semantics and Logic* (New York).
Freeman, Donald C. (ed.)
1970 *Linguistics and Literary Style* (New York: Holt, Rinehart and Winston).
Gadamer, Hans Georg
1960 *Wahrheit und Methode. Grundzüge einer philosophischen Hermeneutik* (Tübingen: Niemeyer).
Garner, Richard
1971 "'Presupposition' in Philosophy and Linguistics", in Fillmore and Langendoen (1971) 23-42.
Garvin, Paul L. (ed.)
1964 *A Prague School Reader on Esthetics, Literary Structure and Style* (Georgetown: Georgetown U.P.).
Geach, Peter
1962 *Reference and Generality* (Ithaca: Cornell U.P.).
Genette, Gérard
1969a "Rhétorique et enseignement", in Gérard Genette, *Figures* II (Paris: Seuil) 23-42.
1969b "Frontières du récit", in Gérard Genette, *Figures* II (Paris: Seuil) 49-70.
Genot, Gérard
1972 "Foundations of the analyses of literary texts", *Poetics*, 7 (in press).
Gerbner, George, *et al.* (eds.)
1969 *The Analysis of Communication Content* (New York: Wiley).
Greimas, Algirdas Julien
1966 *Sémantique Structurale. Recherche de méthode* (Paris: Larousse).
1970 *Du Sens. Essais sémiotiques* (Paris: Seuil).
Grice, H. P.
1969 "Utterer's Meaning, Sentence-Meaning, and Word-Meaning", *Foundations of Lauguage* 4, 1-18 (Reprinted in Searle [1971] 54-70).

Grimes, Joseph A. and Naomi Glock
  1970 "A Saramaccan Narrative Pattern", *Language*, 46, 408-425.
Grinder, John
  1971 "Chains of Coreference", *Linguistic Inquiry*, 2, 183-202.
Grinder, John and Paul M. Postal
  1971 "Missing Antecedents", *Linguistic Inquiry*, 2, 269-312.
Groot, A. D. de
  1961 *Methodologie. Grondslagen van Onderzoek en Denken in de Gedragswetenschappen* (The Hague: Mouton).
Gross, Maurice and André Lentin
  1967 *Notions sur les grammaires formelles* (Paris: Gauthier-Villars).
Gruber, Jeffrey S.
  1965 *Studies in Lexical Relations* (MIT, Ph.D.Diss., mimeo).
  1967 *Functions of the Lexicon in Formal Descriptive Grammars* (Santa Monica, Cal.: SDC, TM-Series).
  1969 "Topicalization in Child Language", in Reibel and Schane (1969) 422-447.
Gülich, Elisabeth and Wolfgang Raible
  1972 "Linguistische Textmodelle. Stand und Möglichkeiten", Paper Contributed to the Colloquium "Differenzierungskriterien für Textsorten aus der Sicht der Linguistik und einzelner Textwissenschaften", Rheda (Westfalen, Western Germany) January, 20-22.
Guiraud, Pierre
  1954 *Les caractères statistiques du vocabulaire* (Paris: PUF).
Gunzenhäuser, Rul
  1962 *Ästhetisches Mass und ästhetische Information* (Quickborn bei Hamburg: Schnelle).
Habermas, Jürgen
  1970 *Zur Logik der Sozialwissenschaften* (Frankfurt a/M: Suhrkamp).
Hall Partee, Barbara
  1970 "Opacity, Coreference and Pronouns", *Synthese*, 21, 359-385.
Halle, Morris
  1970 "On Meter and Prosody", in Manfred Bierwisch and Karl Erich Heidolph (eds.), *Progress in Linguistics* (The Hague: Mouton) 64-80.
Halle, Morris and Samuel Jay Keyser
  1966 "Chaucer and the Study of Prosody", *College English*, 28, 187-219 (Reprinted in Freeman [1970] 366-426).
  1971 *English Stress. Its Form, its Growth and its Role in Verse* (New York: Harper and Row).
Halliday, M. A. K.
  1961 "Categories of the Theory of Grammar", *Word*, 17, 241-292.
  1967 "Some Aspects of the Thematic Organization of the English Clause" (Santa Monica, Cal.: Rand Memorandum).
  1970 "Language Structure and Language Function", in Lyons (1970), 140-165.
Hamburger, Käte
  1968 *Die Logik der Dichtung* (1957) (Stuttgart: Klett, 2. stark veränderte Auflage).
Hanneborg, Knut
  1967 *The Study of Literature. A Contribution to the Phenomenology of the Humane Sciences.* (Oslo: Universitetsforlaget).
Harrah, David
  1963 *Communication: A Logical Model* (Cambridge, Mass.: MIT Press).
  1969 "Erotetic Logistics", in Lambert (1969) 3-21.
Harré, R.
  1960 *An Introduction to the Logic of the Sciences* (London: MacMillan).
Harris, Zellig S.
  1952 "Discourse Analysis", *Language*, 28, 1-30 (Reprinted in Fodor and Katz, [1964] 355-383).
  1963 *Discourse Analysis Reprints* (The Hague: Mouton).
  1968 *Mathematical Structures of Language* (New York: Wiley).
Hartmann, Peter
  1964 "Text, Texte, Klassen von Texten", *Bogawus*, 2, 15-25.

1968 "Textlinguistik als linguistische Aufgabe", in Siegfried J. Schmidt (ed.) *Konkrete Dichtung. Konkrete Kunst* (Karlsruhe, Privatdruck) 62-77.

1970a "Probleme der semantischen Textanalyse", in Schmidt (1970) 15-42.

1970b "Zur Klassifikation und Abfolge textanalytischer Operationen", Paper contributed to the Colloquium "Zur wissenschaftstheoretischen Fundierung der Literaturwissenschaft", Karlsruhe, October 1970.

1971 "Texte als linguistisches Objekt", in Stempel (1971) 9-30.

Hartmann, Peter and Hannes Rieser

forth- *Einführung in die Textlinguistik* (Braunschweig: Vieweg).
coming

Harweg, Roland

1968 *Pronomina und Textkonstitution* (Munich: Fink).

1971 "Die textologische Rolle der Betonung", in Stempel (1971) 123-159.

Hausenblas, Karel

1964 "On the Characterization and Classification of Discourses", *Travaux linguistiques de Prague*, 1, 67-83.

Havránek, Bohuslav

1964 "The Functional Differentiation of the Standard Language", in Garvin (1964) 3-16.

1971 "Die Theorie der Schriftsprache", in Beneš and Vachek (1971) 19-37.

Hayes, Curtis W.

1969 "A Study in Prose Styles: Edward Gibbon and Ernest Hemingway", in Doležel and Bailey (1969) 80-94.

Heidolph, K. E.

1966 "Kontextbeziehungen zwischen Sätzen in einer generativen Grammatik", *Kybernetika Čislo*, 3, 273-281.

Helmer, John

1969 "The sociology of language", (Harvard, mimeo).

1970 "Saying and Meaning: Reference in sociolinguistic Theory", Contribution to the Seventh World Congress on Sociology, September, 1970.

Hempel, Carl G.

1966 *Philosophy of Natural Science* (Englewood Cliffs, N.Y.: Prentice Hall Inc.).

Hendricks, William O.

1967 "On the Notion 'Beyond the Sentence'", *Linguistics*, 37, 12-51.

1969a "Three Models for the Description of Poetry", *Journal of Linguistics*, 5, 1-22.

1969b *Linguistics and the Structural Analysis of Literary Texts* (Lincoln, Nebr., mimeo).

Hilpinen, Risto

1971 *Deontic Logic: Introductory and Systematic Readings* (Dordrecht: Reidel).

Hintikka, Jaakko

1970a "The Semantics of Modal Notions and the Indeterminacy of Ontology", *Synthese*, 21, 408-424.

1970b "Existential Presuppositions and Uniqueness Presuppositions", in Lambert (1970) 20-55.

Hiż, Henry

1969 "Referentials", *Semiotica*, 1, 136-166.

Hjelmslev, Louis

1943 *Omkring Sprogteoriens Grundlæggelse* (Copenhagen: Munksgaard).

Hjelmslev, Louis and H. J. Uldall

1957 *Outline of Glossematics. A Study in the Methodology of the Humanities with Special Reference to Linguistics*, Travaux Linguistiques du Cercle Linguistique de Copenhague (Copenhagen: Munksgaard).

Hörmann, Hans

1967 *Psychologie der Sprache* (Berlin-Heidelberg-New York: Springer).

Holsti, Ole R.

1969 *Content Analysis for the Social Sciences and the Humanities* (Reading, Mass.: Addison-Wesley).

Holk, A. G. F. van
  1968 "A Semantic Discourse Analysis of the Coffin Maker", in Jan van der Eng, A. G. F. van
         Holk and Jan M. Meyer, *The Tales of Belkin by A. S. Puškin* (The Hague: Mouton) 86-109.
Hughes, G. E. and M. J. Cresswell
  1968 *An Introduction to Modal Logic* (London: Methuen).
Hymes, Dell H.
  1962 "The Ethnography of Speaking", in Joshua A. Fishman (ed.) *Readings in the Sociology of
         Language* (The Hague: Mouton, 1968) 99-138.
Ihwe, Jens
  1970 "Kompetenz und Performanz in der Literaturtheorie", in Schmidt (1970) 136-152.
  1972a *Linguistik in der Literaturwissenschaft. Zur Entwicklung einer modernen Theorie der Literatur-
         wissenschaft* (Munich: Bayerischer Schulbuch Verlag).
  1972b "On the Foundations of a General Theory of Narrative Structure", *Poetics*, 3.
Ihwe, Jens (ed.)
  1971 *Linguistik und Literaturwissenschaft. Ergebnisse und Perspektiven*, 3 vols. (Frankfurt a/M:
         Athenäum).
Ihwe, Jens, Hannes Rieser, Wolfram Köck, Martin Rüttenauer
  1971 "Informationen über das Konstanzer Projekt 'Textlinguistik'", *Linguistische Berichte*, 13,
         105-106 (also in *Poetics*, 3 and *Foundations of Language*).
Ingarden, Roman
  1931 *Das literarische Kunstwerk* (Tübingen: Max Niemeyer).
Isenberg, Horst
  1968 "Überlegungen zur Texttheorie" (Berlin: Arbeitsstelle für strukturelle Grammatik, mimeo),
         also in Ihwe (1971) 150-172.
  1970 "Der Begriff 'Text' in der Sprachtheorie" (Berlin: Arbeitsstelle für strukturelle Grammatik,
         mimeo).
Jacobs, Roderick A. and Peter S. Rosenbaum
  1968 *English Transformational Grammar* (Waltham, Mass.: Blaisdell).
Jacobs, Roderick A. and Peter S. Rosenbaum (eds.)
  1970 *Readings in English Transformational Grammar* (Waltham, Mass.: Ginn).
Jaeggi, Urs
  1968 *Ordnung und Chaos* (Frankfurt a/M: Suhrkamp).
Jakobovits, Leon A. and M. S. Miron (eds.)
  1967 *Readings in the Psychology of Language* (Englewood Cliffs, N.Y.: Prentice Hall, Inc.).
Jakobson, Roman
  1960 "Linguistics and Poetics", in Sebeok (1960) 350-377.
  1965 "Poesie der Grammatik. Grammatik der Poesie", in Kreuzer and Gunzenhäuser (1965)
         21-32.
Johnson-Laird, P. N.
  1970 "The Perception and Memory of Sentences", in Lyons (1970) 261-270.
Joyce, James
  1956 *Dubliners* (1914) (Harmondsworth: Penguin Books).
Kamp, Hans
  1968 "On Tense Logic and the Theory of Order" (Ph. D. Thesis, University of California).
Kaneko, Tuhro
  1971 "Zur Problem der spezifischen NP", in Stechow (1971) 93-99.
Karttunen, Lauri
  1968a "What do Referential Indices Refer to?" (MIT, mimeo).
  1968b "Co-reference and Discourse", Paper delivered at the 43 rd. Annual Meeting of the LSA,
         New York.
  1969a "Discourse Referents", Paper Delivered at the International Conference on Computational
         Linguistics, Sånga-Säby (Sweden).
  1969b "Pronouns and Variables", in Binnick, et al. (1969) 108-116.
  1971 "Definite Description with Crossing Reference", *Foundations of Language*, 7, 157-182.
Katz, Jerrold J.
  1964a "Semi-Sentences", in Fodor and Katz (1964) 400-416.

1964b "Analyticity and Contradiction in Natural Language", in Fodor and Katz (1964) 519-543.
1964c "Mentalism in Linguistics", *Language*, 40, 124-237.
1966 *The Philosophy of Language* (New York: Harper and Row).
1967 "Recent Issues in Semantic theory", *Foundations of Language*, 3, 124-194.
1970 "Interpretative Semantics vs. Generative Semantics", *Foundations of Language*, 6, 220-259.
1971 "Generative Semantics is Interpretive Semantics", *Linguistic Inquiry*, 2, 313-330.
Katz, Jerrold J. and Jerry A. Fodor
1964 "The Structure of a Semantic theory" (1963), in Fodor and Katz (1964) 479-518.
Katz, Jerrold J. and Paul M. Postal
1964 *An Integrated Theory of Linguistic Descriptions* (Cambridge, Mass.: MIT Press).
Keenan, Edward L.
1970 "A Logical Base for a Transformational Grammar of English" (Ph. D. Thesis, University of Pennsylvania).
1971a "Two Kinds of Presupposition in Natural Language", in Fillmore and Langendoen (1971) 44-52.
1971b "Quantifier Structures in English", *Foundation of Language*, 7, 255-284.
Keyser, S. Jay
1969 "The Linguistic Basis of English Prosody" (1966) in Reibel and Schane (1969) 379-394.
Kibédi Varga, A.
1970 *Rhétorique et littérature* (Paris: Didier).
Kiefer, Ferenc (ed.)
1969 *Studies in Syntax and Semantics* (Dordrecht: Reidel).
Kiparsky, Paul
1970 "Metrics and Morphophonemics in the Kalevala", in Freeman (1970) 165-181.
Kiparsky, Paul and Carol Kiparsky
1971 "Fact", in Steinberg and Jakobovits (1971) 345-369.
Klaus, Georg
1969 *Die Macht des Wortes. Ein erkenntnis-theoretisch-pragmatisches Traktat* (Berlin: VEB Deutscher Verlag der Wissenschaften, 5. überarbeitete und erweiterte Auflage).
Klein, Wolfgang and Dieter Wunderlich (eds.)
1971 *Aspekte der Soziolinguistik* (Frankfurt: Athenäum).
Klevansky, Lorraine
1967 "Some Comments on Regularization of Texts" (University of Pennsylvania, Transformation and Discourse Analysis Paper, no 66).
Klima, Edward
1969 "Relatedness Between Grammatical Systems", in Reibel and Schane (1969) 227-246.
Kloepfer, Rolf and Ursula Oomen
1970 *Sprachliche Konstituenten moderner Dichtung* (Bad Homburg: Athenäum).
Koch, Walther A.
1966 *Recurrence and a Three-Modal Approach to Poetry* (The Hague: Mouton).
1970 *Vom Morphem zum Textem. From Morpheme to Texteme* (Hildesheim: Olms).
Köngäs Maranda, Elli and Pierre Maranda
1971 *Structural Models in Folklore and Transformational Essays* (The Hague: Mouton).
Kondratov, A. M.
1969 "Information Theory and Poetics: The Entropy of Russian Speech Rhythm" (1963) in Doležel and Bailey (1969) 113-121.
Kooij, J. G.
1971 *Ambiguity in Natural Language* (Amsterdam: North Holland).
Kraak, Albert
1970 "Zinsaccent en syntaxis", *Studia Neerlandica*, 1/4, 41-62.
Krenn, Herwig and Klaus Müllner
1970 "Generative Semantik", *Linguistische Berichte*, 5, 85-106.
Kreuzer, Helmut and Rul Gunzenhäuser (eds.)
1965 *Mathematik und Dichtung. Versuche zur Frage einer exakten Literaturwissenschaft* (Munich: Nymphenburger).

Krippendorff, Klaus
  1969 "Models of Messages: Three Prototypes", in Gerbner, *et al.* (1969) 69-106.
Kristeva, Julia
  1969a *Sèméiotikè. Recherches pour une Sémanalyse* (Paris: Seuil).
  1969b "Narration et transformation", *Semiotica*, 4, 422-448.
Kummer, Werner
  1971a "Referenz, Pragmatik und zwei mögliche Textmodelle", in Wunderlich (1971) 175-188.
  1971b "Quantifikation und Identität in Texten", in Stechow (1971) 122-141.
  1972a "Outlines of a Model of Discourse Grammar", *Poetics*, 3.
  1972b "Aspects of a Theory of Communication", Paper contributed to the Colloquium "Differen-
          zierungskriterien für Textsorten aus der Sicht der Linguistik und einzelner Textwissen-
          schaften", Rheda (Westfalen, Western Germany), January 20-22.
  forth- *Textgrammatik des Deutschen.*
  coming
Kuroda, S. Y.
  1969a "Remarques sur les présuppositions et les contraintes de sélection" in N. Ruwet (ed.)
          Tendances nouvelles en syntaxe générative, Langages, 14, 52-80.
  1969b "English Relativization and Certain Related Problems", in Reibel and Schane (1969)
          264-287.
  1971   "Two Remarks on Pronominalization", *Foundations of Language*, 7, 183-188.
Labov, William
  1970   "The Study of Language in its Social Context", *Studium Generale*, 23, 30-87.
Labov, William and Joshua Waletzky
  1967   "Narrative Analysis: Oral Versions of Personal Experience", in June Helm (ed.), *Essays
          on the verbal and Visual Arts* (Seattle and Condon), 12-44.
Lämmert, Eberhard
  1967   *Bauformen des Erzählens* (1955) (Stuttgart: Metzler, 2. durchgesehene Auflage).
Lakatos, Imre
  1970   "Falsification and the Methodology of Scientific Research Programmes", in I. Lakatos
          and A. Musgrave (eds.), *Criticism and the Growth of Knowledge* (Cambridge: Cambridge
          U.P.) 91-196.
Lakoff, George
  1968a "Pronouns and Reference" (mimeo: Indiana Linguistics Club).
  1968b "Counterparts, or the Problem of Reference in Transformational Grammar", paper
          presented to the LSA-meeting, July 27, (mimeo).
  1970a "Global Rules", *Language*, 46, 627-639.
  1970b "Linguistics and Natural Logic", *Synthese*, 22, 151-271.
  1971a "On Generative Semantics" in Steinberg and Jakobovits (1971) 232-296.
  1971b "Presupposition and Relative Well-Formedness", in Steinberg and Jakobovits (1971)
          341-344.
Lakoff, George and Stanley Peters
  1969   "Phrasal Conjunction and Symmetric Predicates" (1966) in Reibel and Schane (1969)
          113-142.
Lakoff, George and John Robert Ross
  1968   "Is Deep Structure Necessary?" (mimeo).
Lakoff, Robin
  1971   "If's, And's and But's about Conjunction", in Fillmore and Langendoen (1971) 115-150.
Lamb, Sidney M.
  1966   *Outline of Stratificational Grammar* (Washington, D.C.: Georgetown U.P.).
Lambert, Karel (ed.)
  1969   *The Logical Way of Doing Things* (New Haven and London: Yale U.P.).
  1970   *Philosophical Problems in Logic. Some Recent Developments* (Dordrecht: Reidel).
Lang, Ewald
  1967   "'Jointness' und Koordination" (Eric/Pegs paper, no 70, 1969).
  1971   "Über einige Schwierigkeiten beim Postulieren einer Textgrammatik" (Berlin: mimeo).

forth- *Koordination und Textstruktur.*
coming
Langacker, Ronald W.
 1969 "On Pronominalization and the Chain of Command", in Reibel and Schane (1969) 160-186.
Larin, A. G.
 1971 *Issledovanie processa "Tekst-Grammatika"* (Moskva: Izdatel'stvo "Nauka").
Lausberg, Heinrich
 1960 *Handbuch der literarischen Rhetorik. Eine Grundlegung der Literaturwissenschaft,* 2 vols. (Munich: Hueber).
Leech, Geoffrey N.
 1968 "Some Assumptions in the Metatheory of Linguistics", *Linguistics,* 39, 87-102.
 1969a *A Linguistic Guide to English Poetry* (London: Longmans).
 1969b *A Semantic Description of English* (London: Longmans).
Lees, R. B. and Edward S. Klima
 1969 "Rules for English Pronominalization", in Reibel and Schane (1969) 145-159.
Leroy Baker, C.
 1966 *Definiteness and Indefiniteness in English* (University of Illinois: unpublished Master's Thesis).
Lévi-Strauss, Claude
 1960 "L'analyse morphologique des contes populaires russes", *International Journal of Slavic Linguistics and Poetics,* 122-249.
Levin, Samuel R.
 1962 *Linguistic Structures in Poetry* (The Hague: Mouton).
 1963 "Deviation – Statistical and Determinate – in Poetic Language", *Lingua,* 12, 276-290.
 1964 "Poetry and Grammaticalness", in H. G. Lunt (ed.) *Proceedings of the IXth International Congress of Linguists* (The Hague: Mouton) 308-314.
 1965 "Internal and external Deviation in Poetry", *Word,* 21, 225-237.
Levý, Jiři
 1969 "Mathematical Aspects of the theory of Verse", in Doležel and Bailey (1969), 95-112.
Levý, Jiři (ed.)
 1966 *The Theory of Verse. Teorie Verše. Teoria Stikha,* I (Brno).
Lewis, David
 1970 "General Semantics", *Synthese,* 22, 18-67
Lieb, Hans-Heinrich
 1970 *Sprachstadium und Sprachsystem* (Stuttgart: Kohlhammer).
Linguistique et littérature
 1968 Numéro Spécial *La Nouvelle Critique.* Actes du Colloque de Cluny.
Linsky, Leonard
 1967 *Referring* (London: Routledge and Kegan Paul).
Linsky, Leonard (ed.)
 1971 *Reference and Modality* (London: Oxford U.P.).
Lockwood, David
 1970 "Pronoun Concord Domains in English", *Linguistics,* 54, 70-85.
Lotman, Jurij M. and A. M. Pjatigorskij
 1969 "Le texte et sa fonction", *Semiotica,* 1, 205-217.
Lotz, John
 1960 "Metric Typology", in Sebeok (1960) 135-148.
Love, Glen A. and Michael Payne (eds.)
 1969 *Contemporary Essays on Style, Rhetoric, Linguistics, and Criticism* (Glenview, Ill.: Scott, Foreman and Company).
Lowe, Ivan
 1969 "An Algabraic Theory of English Pronominal Reference (I)" *Semiotica,* 1, 397-421.
Luce, R. D., R. R. Bush and E. Galanter (eds.)
 1963 *Handbook of Mathematical Psychology,* vol. 2. (New York: Wiley).
Lyas, Colin (ed.)
 1971 *Philosophy and Linguistics* (London: MacMillan).

Lyons, John
  1963   *Structural Semantics* (Oxford: Blackwell).
  1968   *Introduction to Theoretical Linguistics* (Cambridge: Cambridge U.P.).
  1970   "Generative Syntax", in Lyons (1970) 115-139.
Lyons, John (ed.)
  1970   *New Horizons in Linguistics* (Harmondsworth: Penguin Books).
Lyons, John and R. J. Wales (eds.)
  1966   *Psycholinguistic Papers* (Edinburgh: Edinburgh U.P.)
Maatje, Frank C.
  1970   *Literatuurwetenschap* (Utrecht: Oosthoek).
Marcus, Salomon
  1970   *Poetica Matematica* (Bucharest: Editura Academiei).
Marks, L. E. and G. A. Miller
  1969   "The Role of Semantic and Syntactic Constraints in the Memorization of English Sentences"
         (1964), in L. Postman and G. Keppel (eds.) *Verbal Learning and Verbal Memory* (Harmonds-
         worth: Penguin Books) 254-262.
Martin, Richard M.
  1963   *Intension and Decision* (Englewood Cliffs, N.Y.: Prentice Hall Inc.).
Matthews, Robert J.
  1971   "Concerning a 'Linguistic Theory' of Metaphor", *Foundations of Language*, 7, 413-425.
McCawley, James D.
  1968a "The Role of Semantics in a Grammar", in Bach and Harms (1968) 124-169.
  1968b "Concerning the Base-Component of a Transformational Grammar, *Foundations of
         Language*, 4, 243-269.
  1970   "Where Do Noun Phrases Come From?", in Jacobs and Rosenbaum (1970) 166-183.
  1971   "Interpretative Semantics Meets Frankenstein", *Foundations of Language*, 7, 285-296.
Meier, Hugo
  1963   *Die Metapher. Versuch einer zusammenfassenden Betrachtung ihrer linguistischen Merkmale*
         (Winterthur: Keller).
Mel'čuk, I. A. and A. K. Žolkovskij
  1970   "Towards a Functioning 'Meaning-Text' Model of Language", *Linguistics*, 57, 10-47.
Mendilov, A. A.
  1952   *Time and the Novel* (London).
Miko, František
  1970   *Text a Štýl* (Bratislava: Smena).
Milic, Louis T.
  1967   *Style and Stylistics. An Analytical Bibliography* (New York: Free Press).
Miller, George A.
  1964   "Language and psychology" in Erich Lenneberg (ed.) *New Directions in the Study of
         Language* (Cambridge, Mass.: MIT Press) 89-108.
Miller, George A., and Noam Chomsky
  1963   "Finitary Models of Language Users", in Luce, Bush and Galanter (1963) 419-492.
Miller, George A., Eugene Galanter and Karl H. Pribram
  1960   *Plans and the Structure of Behavior* (New York: Holt, Rinehart and Winston).
Mönnich, Uwe
  1971   "Pronomina als Variablen?", in Wunderlich (1971) 154-158.
Moles, Abraham A.
  1966   *Information Theory and Esthetic Perception* (1958), Translated from the French by Joel
         E. Cohen (Urbana: University of Illinois Press).
Montague, Richard
  1968   "Pragmatics", in R. Klibansky (ed.) *Contemporary Philosophy* (Florence: La Nuova Italia).
  1970a "Pragmatics and Intensional Logic", *Dialectica*, 24, 277-302.
  1970b "English as a Formal Language", *Linguaggi*, 189-224.
Mooij, J. J. A.
  1963   "Over het interpreteren van literaire werken", *Forum der Letteren*, 5, 148-163.

Morgan, Jerry L.
  1969 "On the Treatment of Presupposition in Transformational Grammar", in Binnick, et al. (1969), 167-177.
Morris, Charles W.
  1938 *Foundations of the Theory of Signs* (Chicago: International Encyclopedia of Unified Science).
  1946 *Signs, Language and Behavior* (New York: Prentice Hall).
Nagel, Ernst
  1961 *The Structure of Science, Problems in the Logic of Scientific Explanation* (London: Routledge and Kegan Paul).
Nathhorst, Bertel
  1969 *Formal or Structural Studies of Traditional Tales* (Stockholm: Stockholm Studies in Comparative Religion, 9).
Nauta, Doede
  1970 *Logica en Model* (Bussum: De Haan).
Nebeský, Ladislav
  1971 "On the Potentially Poetic Aspects of Artificial Languages", *Poetics*, 2, 87-90.
Neisser, Ulric
  1967 *Cognitive Psychology* (New York: Appleton-Century-Crofts).
Nolan, Rita
  1970 *Foundations for an adequate criterion of paraphrase* (The Hague: Mouton).
Ohmann, Richard
  1964 "Generative Grammar and the concept of Literary Style", *Word*, 20, 423-439.
  1967 "Literature as Sentences", in Chatman and Levin (1967) 231-238.
Oldfield, R. C. and J. C. Marshall (eds.)
  1968 *Language. Selected Readings* (Harmondsworth: Penguin Books).
Opp, Karl-Dieter
  1970 *Methodologie der Sozialwissenschaften* (Reinbek bei Hamburg: Rowohlt).
Pak, Ty
  1971 "Fallacy of Formal Discourse Analysis", *Lingua*, 28, 70-81.
Palek, Bohumil
  1968 *Cross-Reference. A Study from Hyper-Syntax* (Prague: Universita Karlova).
Patton, Thomas A.
  1968 "Syntactic Deviance", *Foundations of Language*, 4, 138-153.
Pêcheux, Michel
  1969 *Analyse automatique du discours* (Paris: Dunod).
Peirce, Charles Sanders
  1960 *Collected Papers*, vol. 2. (Cambridge, Mass.: Harvard U.P.).
Perse, Saint-John
  1960 *Œuvre poétique*, I (Paris: Gallimard).
Petöfi, János S.
  1969a "On the Structural Analysis and Typology of Poetic Images", in Kiefer (1969), 187-230.
  1969b "On the Problems of Co-textual Analysis of Texts", paper delivered at the International Conference on Computational Linguistics, Sånga-Säby (Sweden). (German translation in Ihwe [1971]).
  1969c "On the Linear Patterning of Verbal Works of Art", *Computational Linguistics* (Budapest) 38-63.
  1970 "Von der 'Explikation des Begriffes Satz' zu der 'Explikation der Texte'. Zur Frage einer generellen Texttheorie" (Göteborg, mimeo).
  1971 *Transformationsgrammatiken und eine ko-textuelle Texttheorie. Grundfragen und Konzeptionen* (Frankfurt: Athenäum).
  1972a "The Syntactico-semantic Organization of Text Structures", *Poetics*, 3.
  1972b "Towards a Grammatical Theory of Verbal Texts", *Zeitschrift für Literaturwissenschaft und Linguistik* (in press).
Pickett, Velma B.
  1960 "The Grammatical Hierarchy of Isthmus Zapotec", *Language Dissertation*, 56, 80-89.

Pike, Kenneth L.
   1967   *Language in Relation to a Unified Theory of Human Behavior* (The Hague: Mouton).
Pike, Kenneth L. and Ivan Lowe
   1969   "Pronominal Reference in English Conversation and Discourse – A Group Theoretical
          Treatment", *Folia Linguistica* 3 (1/2) 68-106.
Pleynet, Marcelin
   1963   *Paysages en deux* suivi de *Les lignes de la prose* (Paris: Seuil).
Poetics, Poetyka, Poètika, 2
   1966   (The Hague-Warsaw: Mouton).
Popper, Karl A.
   1959   *The Logic of Scientific Discovery* (New York: Harper and Row, 1968²).
Postal, Paul M.
   1969a "On So-Called 'Pronouns' in English", in Reibel and Schane (1969) 201-224.
   1969b "Anaphoric Islands", in Binnick, et al. (1969).
   1970   "On Coreferential Complement Subject Deletion", *Linguistic Inquiry*, 1, 439-500.
   1971   *Cross-over Phenomena* (New York: Holt).
Pouillon, Jean
   1946   *Temps et Roman* (Paris: Gallimard).
Powlison, Paul S.
   1965   "A Paragraph Analysis of a Yagua Folktale", *International Journal of American Linguistics*,
          31, 109-118.
Pride, J. B.
   1970   *The Social Meaning of Language* (London: Oxford U.P.).
Prior, Arthur N.
   1957   *Time and Modality* (London: Oxford U.P., 1968).
   1968   *Papers on Time and Tense* (London: Oxford U.P.).
   1971   *Objects of Thought*. Edited by P. T. Geach and A. J. P. Kenny (London: Oxford U.P.).
Propp, Vladimir
   1968   *Morphology of the Folktale* (1928) (Austin: Texas U.P.) (First edition, Indiana, 1958).
Quine, Willard van Orman
   1953   *From a Logical Point of View* (New York: Harper and Row, 1961).
   1960   *Word and Object* (Cambridge, Mass.: MIT Press).
   1970   "Methodological Reflections on Current Linguistic Theory", *Synthese*, 21, 386-398.
Quirk, Randolph and Jan Svartvik
   1966   *Investigating Linguistic Acceptability* (The Hague: Mouton).
Reddy, Michael J.
   1969   "A Semantic Approach to Metaphor", in Binnick, et al. (1969) 240-251.
Reibel, David A. and Sanford A. Schane (eds.)
   1969   *Modern Studies in English. Readings in Transformational Grammar* (Englewood Cliffs,
          N.Y.: Prentice Hall, Inc.).
Reichenbach, Hans
   1947   *Elements of Symbolic Logic* (London: MacMillan) (New York: Free Press, 1966).
Rescher, Nicholas
   1964   *Introduction to Logic* (New York: St. Martin's Press).
   1968   *Topics in Philosophical Logic* (Dordrecht: Reidel).
Reverdy, Pierre
   1945   *Plupart du temps* (Paris: Gallimard).
   1964   *Main d'œuvre* (1949) (Paris: Mercure de France).
Rescher, Nicholas and Alasdair Urquhart
   1971   *Temporal Logic* (Wien-New York: Springer).
Rieser, Hannes
   1971   "Allgemeine Textlinguistische Ansätze zur Erklärung performativer Strukturen", *Poetics*, 2,
          91-118.
Robbins, Beverly L.
   1968   *The Definite Article in English Transformations* (The Hague: Mouton).

Rohrer, Christian
  1971 *Funktionelle Sprachwissenschaft und Transformationelle Grammatik* (Munich: Fink).
Romberg, Bertil
  1962 *Studies in the Narrative Technique of the First-Person Novel* (Stockholm: Almqvist and Wiksell).
Rorty, Richard (ed.)
  1967 *The Linguistic Turn. Recent Essays in Philosophical Method* (Chicago: Chicago U.P.).
Ross, John Robert
  1969 "On the Cyclic Nature of English Pronominalization", in Reibel and Schane (1969), 187-200.
  1970 "On Declarative Sentences", in Jacobs and Rosenbaum (1970) 222-272.
Roubaud, Jacques
  1971 "Mètre et Vers", *Poétique*, 7, 366-388.
Rudner, Richard S.
  1966 *Philosophy of Social Science* (Englewood Cliffs, N.Y.: Prentice Hall, Inc.).
Russell, Bertrand and Alfred N. Whitehead
  1962 *Principia Mathematica* (to *56) (1927) (Cambridge: Cambridge U.P.).
Ruwet, Nicolas
  1968 *Introduction à la grammaire générative* (Paris: Plon).
Sadock, Jerrold M.
  1970 "Super-hypersentences", *Papers in Linguistics*, 1, 1-15.
Safran Ganz, Joan
  1971 *Rules. A Systematic Study* (The Hague: Mouton).
Sampson, G.
  1969 "Noun-phrase indexing, pronouns and the 'definite article'" (Yale, Linguistic Automation Project, mimeo).
Sanders, Gerald A.
  1969 "On the Natural Domain of Grammar" (Indiana Linguistics Club, mimeo).
Schermer-Vermeer, E. C.
  1971 "De begrippen 'topic' en 'geïdentificeerde referenten'", *Blad* 1, 6-27 (University of Amsterdam, Instituut voor Neerlandistiek, mimeo).
Schmidt, Siegfried J.
  1969 *Bedeutung und Begriff. Zur Fundierung einer Sprachphilosophischen Semantik* (Braunschweig: Vieweg).
  1970a "Text und Bedeutung. Sprachphilosophische Prolegomena zu einer textsemantischen Literaturwissenschaft", in Schmidt (1970), 43-79 (reprinted in Poetics, 1, 83-112).
  1970b "Literaturwissenschaft als Forschungsprogramm", I, *Linguistik und Didaktik*, 1, 269-282.
  1970c "Bemerkungen zur Wissenschaftstheorie einer Literaturwissenschaft", Paper contributed to the Colloquium "Zur wissenschaftstheoretischen Fundierung der Literaturwissenschaft", Karlsruhe, October, 1970.
  1971a "Allgemeine Textwissenschaft. Ein Programm zur Erforschung ästhetischer Texte", *Linguistische Berichte*, 12, 10-21.
  1971b "'Text' und 'Geschichte' als Fundierungskategorien", in Stempel (1971) 32-52.
  1971c *Ästhetizität* (Munich: Bayerischer Schulbuch Verlag).
  1971d "Theorie und Praxis einer literaturwissenschaftlicher Narrativik", Paper contributed to the Symposium on semiotic poetics, Urbino (Italy), July, 1971.
  1971e "Pragmatik" (University of Bielefeld, mimeo).
  1972 "Ist 'fiktionalität' eine linguistische oder eine texttheoretische Kategorie?", paper contributed to the colloquium "Differenzierungskriterien für Textsorten aus der Sicht der Linguistik und einzelner Textwissenschaften", Rheda (Westfalen, Western Germany), January, 20-22.
Schmidt, Siegfried J. (ed.)
  1970 *Text, Bedeutung, Ästhetik* (Munich: Bayerischer Schulbuch Verlag).
Schnelle, Helmut
  1968 "Methoden mathematischer Linguistik", in *Enzyklopädie der Geisteswissenschaftlichen Arbeitsmethoden*, 4, *Methoden der Sprachwissenschaft* (Munich: Oldenbourg) 135-160.
  1970a "Zur Entwicklung der theoretischen Linguistik", *Studium Generale*, 23, 1-29.
  1970b "Linguistics and Automata Theory", *Linguaggi*, 325-340.

360 REFERENCES

Schnitzer, Marc L.
  1971 "A Note on Tagmemic Discourse Analysis: Philosophical Argument", *Linguistics*, 67,
        72-82.
Scott, Dana
  1970 "Advice on Modal Logic", in Lambert (1970) 143-173.
Searle, John R.
  1969 *Speech Acts* (Cambridge: Cambridge U.P.).
Searle, John R. (ed.)
  1971 *The Philosophy of Language* (London: Oxford U.P.).
Sebeok, T. A. (ed.)
  1960 *Style in Language* (Cambridge, Mass.: MIT Press).
Seiffert, Helmut
  1969 *Einführung in die Wissenschaftstheorie*, I, (Munich: Beck).
  1970 id, II.
Seuren, Pieter A. M.
  1969 *Operators and Nucleus* (Cambridge: Cambridge U.P.).
Sgall, Peter
  1967 "Functional Sentence Perspective in Generative Description", *Prague Studies in Mathe-
        matical Linguistics*, 2, 203-225.
Siertsema, Bertha
  1965 *A Study of Glossematics* (The Hague: Nijhoff, 2nd edition).
Šklovskij, Viktor
  1966 *Theorie der Prosa* (1925) (Frankfurt: Fischer Verlag).
Smith, Carlota S.
  1969 "Determiners and Relative Clauses in a Generative Grammar of English", in Reibel and
        Schane (1969) 247-263.
  1971 "Sentences in Discourse; an Analysis of a Discourse by Bertrand Russell", *Journal of
        Linguistics*, 7, 213-235.
Sparck Jones, Karen
  1967 "Notes on Semantic Discourse Structure" (mimeo).
Spencer, John (ed.)
  1964 *Linguistics and Style* (London: Oxford U.P.).
Staal, J. F.
  1967 "Some Semantic Relations between Sentoids", *Foundations of Language*, 3, 66-88.
Stalnaker, Robert C.
  1970 "Pragmatics", *Synthese*, 22, 272-289.
Stechow, Arnim von (ed.)
  1971 *Beiträge zur Generativen Grammatik* (Braunschweig: Vieweg).
Stegmüller, Wolfgang
  1969 *Probleme und Resultate der Wissenschaftstheorie und Analytischen Philosophie*, I. (New
        York-Heidelberg-Berlin: Springer).
  1970 id., II.
Steinberg, Danny D. and Leon A. Jakobovits (eds.)
  1971 *Semantics. An Interdisciplinary Reader in Philosophy, Linguistics and Psychology* (Cambridge:
        Cambridge U.P.).
Steinmann, Martin (ed.)
  1967 *New Rhetorics* (New York: Scribner's).
Strawson, P. F.
  1952 *Introduction to Logical Theory* (London: Methuen).
Suppes, Patrick
  1957 *Introduction to Logic* (New York: Van Nostrand Reinhold).
Stempel, Wolf-Dieter (ed.)
  1971 *Beiträge zur Textlinguistik* (Munich: Fink).
Taber, Charles R.
  1966 *The Structure of Sango Narrative* (Hartford, Conn.: The Hartford Seminary Foundation).

Tesnière, Lucien
  1959 *Éléments de syntaxe structurale* (Paris: Klincksieck).
Thomas, Dylan
  1952 *Collected Poems* (London: Dent).
Thomas, Owen
  1969 *Metaphor and Related Subjects* (New York: Random House).
Thorne, James Peter
  1965 "Stylistics and Generative Grammars", *Journal of Linguistics*, 1, 49-59.
  1969 "Poetry, stylistics and imaginary grammars", *Journal of Linguistics*, 5, 147-150.
  1970 "Generative Grammar and Stylistic Analysis", in Lyons (1970) 185-197.
Todorov, Tzvetan
  1966 "Les anomalies sémantiques", in T. Todorov (ed.) *Recherches sémantiques, Langages*, 1, 100-123.
  1967 *Littérature et signification* (Paris: Larousse).
  1969 *Grammaire du Décaméron* (The Hague: Mouton).
  1971 *Poétique de la prose* (Paris: Seuil).
Todorov, Tzvetan (ed.)
  1965 *Théorie de la littérature. Textes des Formalistes russes.* (Paris: Seuil).
  1970 *L'énonciation, Langages*, 17.
Topitsch, Ernst (ed.)
  1965 *Logik der Sozialwissenschaften* (Köln: Kiepenheuer und Witsch).
Trabant, Jürgen
  1970 *Zur Semiologie des literarischen Kunstwerks* (Munich: Fink).
Treismann, A. M.
  1968 "Verbal Responses and Contextual Constraints in Language" (1965), in R. C. Oldfield and J. C. Marshall (1968) 276-292.
Uitti, Karl D.
  1969 *Linguistics and Literary Theory* (Englewood Cliffs, N.Y.: Prentice Hall).
Ungeheuer, Gerold
  1969 "Paraphrase und syntaktische Tiefenstruktur", *Folia Linguistica*, 3, 178-227.
Vachek, Joseph
  1966 *The Linguistic School of Prague* (Bloomington: Indiana U.P.).
Valesio, Paolo
  1968 *Strutture dell' alliterazione* (Bologna).
  1971 "On Poetics and Metrical Theory", *Poetics*, 2, 36-70.
Vendler, Zeno
  1967 *Linguistics in Philosophy* (New York: Cornell U.P.).
Verkuyl, Henk J.
  1970 "De relevantie van logische operatoren voor de analyse van temporele bepalingen", *Studia Neerlandica*, 1(2), 7-33.
  1971 *On the Compositional Nature of the Aspects* (Ph. D. Thesis, University of Utrecht; to appear with Reidel, Dordrecht).
Wales, R. J. and J. C. Marshall
  1966 "The Organization of Linguistic Performance", in Lyons and Wales (1966) 29-80.
Wallace, John
  1970 "On the Frame of Reference", *Synthese*, 22, 117-150.
Wang, Jün-Tin
  1971a "Zur Beziehung zwischen generativen und axiomatischen Methoden in linguistischen Untersuchungen", in Stechow (1971) 273-282.
  1971b "On the Representation of Generative Grammars as First Order Theories", paper contributed to the IVth International Congress on Logic, Methodology and Philosophy of Science, Bucharest, August 29 – September 4, 1971.
Waterhouse, Viola
  1963 "Independent and Dependent Sentences", *International Journal of American Linguistics*, 29, 45-54.

Weinreich, Uriel
  1963 *Languages in Contact* (The Hague: Mouton).
  1966 "Explorations in Semantic Theory", in T. A. Sebeok (ed.) *Current Trends in Linguistics*, vol. III (The Hague: Mouton) 395-477.
Weinrich, Harald
  1964 *Tempus* (Stuttgart: Kohlhammer).
Wellek, René
  1955 *A History of Literary Criticism* (New Haven: Yale U.P.).
Wheeler, Alva
  1963 "Grammatical Structure in Siona Discourse", *Lingua*, 19, 60-77.
Wienold, Götz
  1971 "Textverarbeitung. Überlegungen zur Kategorienbildung in einer strukturalen Literaturgeschichte", *Zeitschrift für Literaturwissenschaft und Linguistik (LiLi)*, 1, 1/2, 59-90.
  1972 "On Deriving Models of Narrative Analysis from Models of Discourse Analysis", *Poetics*, 3.
Winburne, John Newton
  1964 "Sentence Sequence in Discourse", in H. Lunt (ed.) *Proceedings of the IXth International Congress of Linguists* (The Hague: Mouton) 1094-1099.
Wright, Georg Henrik von
  1963 *Norm and Action. A Logical Enquiry* (London: Routledge and Kegan Paul).
  1967a "Deontic Logic" (1951), in Copi and Gould (1967) 303-315.
  1967b "A Note on Deontic Logic and Derived Obligation" (1956), in Copi and Gould (1967) 316-318.
  1971a "A New System of Deontic Logic", in Hilpinen (1971) 105-120.
  1971b "Deontic Logic and the Theory of Conditions", in Hilpinen (1971) 159-17.
Wunderlich, Dieter
  1970a "Die Rolle der Pragmatik in der Linguistik", *Der Deutschunterricht*, 4, 5-41.
  1970b *Tempus und Zeitreferenz im Deutschen* (Munich: Hueber).
  1971a "Pragmatik, Sprechsituation, Deixis", *Zeitschrift für Literaturwissenschaft und Linguistik* 1, 1-2, 153-190.
  1971b "Terminologie des Strukturbegriffs", in Ihwe (1971), I, 91-140.
Wunderlich, Dieter (ed.)
  1971 *Probleme und Fortschritte der Transformationsgrammatik* (Munich: Hueber).
Wyllys, Ronald E.
  1967 "Extracting and Abstracting by computer", in Harold Borko (1967), 127-180.
Žirmunskij, Viktor
  1966 *Introduction to Metrics* (1925) (The Hague: Mouton).
Žolkovskij, A. K. and Ju. K. Ščeglov
  1971 "Die strukturelle Poetik ist eine generative Poetik!" (1967) in Ihwe (1971).
Žolkovskij, A. K. and I. A. Melčuk
  1970 "Towards a functioning 'Text-Meaning'-Model of Language", *Linguistics*, 57, 10-47.
Zumthor, Paul
  1971 "Rhétorique médiévale et poétique", *Poetics*, 1, 46-82.

INDEX OF NAMES

SUBJECT INDEX

Abstract, 6, 138
Acceptability, 5, 226, 314
  idealized, 180
Actant, 142ff, 147, 287ff, 294ff
Acteur, 287
Action, 146f, 285ff, 292, 308
Addition, 235f, 303
Adequacy, 176
Adjuvant, 142
Adverb
  local, 88
  temporal, 85, 87
Adverbial clause, 70f
Agent, 77f, 147, 287, 294
Agentive, 143
Alethic operators, 152
Alexandrine, 219, 222
Allegory, 262
Alliteration, 216
Ambiguity, 4
  textual, 262
Amphibrachus, 222
Analysis vs. synthesis, 34
Anapaest, 222
Anaphora, Identity of Sense, 60
Appropriateness, 23, 99, 154, 314ff
  and presupposition, 99, 101
Argument, 20, 37, 146ff
  constants and variables, 145ff
  status of, 146ff
Argumentatio, 136
Article, 8, 42ff
Aspect, 9, 85
Association, 265
Assonance, 216
Auxiliary, 82
Axiom, 97
Axiomatization, 181

Beneficiary, 297

Blocking, 255
Boundary marker/symbol, 8, 13
  in literary text grammar, 198f
  metric, 222
  of sequences, 126

Cancelling, 260n
Case, 37
  grammar, 37, 143, 245
Cause, 63, 87, 108f, 307
Change, 178f
  description, 308
  lexical, 248
  of states, 292
Character, 273
Chronological logic, 86, 290n
Classème, 93
Coda, 137
Code, 190
  lexical, 190
Cognitive processes/stategies, 7, 160f, 263, 264
Coherence, 3, 10, 96
  linear, 277ff
  modal, 56
Commanding, 61, 71
Comment, 109ff, 261
  topic and, 8, 9, 73f, 109ff
Communication, 2, 4, 311ff
Communicative situation, 321f
Comparative literature, 170
Comparison, 241ff, 251ff
Competence, 2ff
  communicative, 2n, 313ff
  derived/secondary, 196
  literary, 170, 207
  narrative, 284
  psychological status of, 2n, 324ff
  sub-, 196
  textual, 3ff
Completeness, 181

relations between sentoids, 108
Transfer feature, 258ff
Transformation, 9, 17, 27, 36, 38f, 156ff
  conditions on literary, 235
  generalized, 12, 298
  macro-, 156, 297ff
  narrative, 297ff
  literary, 187, 197, 212, 226ff
  obligatory vs. optional, 298
  singulary, 297
Transition rules, 175
Translating, 6
Truth value, 63, 98ff
  in literature, 336
Types, 195
  of text, 5, 195, 274ff
  of literary text, 211f
Typology of texts, 5

Unique
  individual, 46, 47
  class of individuals, 47
Uniqueness of literary texts, 178
Uniqueness condition, 48, 52, 61
Universals, 295
  literary, 180, 186
  narrative, 295

Universe of discourse/text, 54, 55n, 96, 150
Utterance, 3, 154
  vs. sentence/text, 3, 313f
  function of, 319

Variables, 20
  argument, 20, 37
  event, 20
  predicate, 20, 37
  sentential, 20
Variation, 330
Verb(s), 81ff
  locutionary, 81, 105f
  phrases, 81ff
  world creating, 81
Verbal context (see 'Co-text')
Verse, 220
Versification, 213ff
Vrai vs. vraisemblable, 337

Weak generative capacity, 11
Whole, text as a, 5f
World, 83, 100, 260n, 272, 299, 308
  and metaphor, 272
  and presupposition, 100
  and tense, 83, 86
  possible, 60n, 101, 260n, 272